The Poetry of the Early T'ang

The Poetry
of the Early T'ang

Stephen Owen

New Haven and London
Yale University Press   1977

Printed in the United States of America by Vail-Ballou Press, Binghamton, New York.

Published in Great Britain, Europe, Africa, and Asia (except Japan) by Yale University Press, Ltd., London. Distributed in Latin America by Kaiman & Polon, Inc., New York City; in Australia and New Zealand by Book & Film Services, Artarmon, N.S.W., Australia; and in Japan by Harper & Row, Publishers, Tokyo Office.

Library of Congress Cataloging in Publication Data

Owen, Stephen.
   The poetry of the early T'ang.

   Includes bibliographical references and index.
   1. Chinese poetry — T'ang dynasty, 618-907 — History and criticism. I. Title.
PL2321.O95   895.1'1'209   77-3884
ISBN 0-300-02103-8

To the memory of a friend and teacher
Arthur Wright

CONTENTS

ACKNOWLEDGMENTS

There are cases in which the gratitudes expressed at the
beginning of a book are no more than an enumeration of
the author's friends and family. Here, however, I must
be more precisely grateful to colleagues who devoted
much time and energy to correcting both the infelicities
and gross errors of my manuscript. There were enough of
both to make the experience a chastening one.

First of all, my thanks to Hans Frankel for comments
as wide-ranging as his learning, to Hugh Stimson both
for his editing and for his generous help in explaining
to me the arcana of tonal balance, to Arthur Wright for
his help with Early T'ang historical problems, and to
Frank Westbrook for his discussions of pre-T'ang poetry.
My special thanks to Robert Somers who not only carefully read and edited the manuscript, but also spent
many hours discussing both literary and historical problems with me. Whatever ideas I have developed on the
social background of poetry are derivative of his ideas
on T'ang history and society. Special thanks also to
Maureen Robertson, who never failed to catch me up when
my critical thinking was getting fuzzy and who brought
to my attention numerous points of poetic diction which
I had ignored. Finally, my special thanks to a scholar
who went over the manuscript so thoroughly as to deserve
to be called a collaborator—David Knechtges. The care,
precision, and clarity of his comments have strengthened
this volume immeasurably, and those errors that remain
are the occasions when I stubbornly refused to take his
advice.

Finally, I would like to thank my wife Phyllis for
her support through the preparation of this volume and

Hiroko Somers, who has shown the remarkable fortitude to
type the manuscript twice with the care and patience of
a friend. It is her calligraphy that fills these pages.

INTRODUCTION

The period in the history of Chinese poetry known as the
Early T'ang extends from the foundation of the dynasty
in 618 until roughly 713, when Hsüan-tsung took the
throne. The Early T'ang does not represent a unified
style in its own right: rather it saw the close of a
long era of court poetry and the slow transition to the
new style of the High T'ang. The tradition of court
poetry stands at the center of the changes that were
taking place in the seventh century. "Court poetry"
here refers specifically to the poetry of the later
Southern Dynasties, Sui, and Early T'ang courts. Although poetry was written in the Chinese courts both
before and after this period, it was during the late
fifth, sixth, and seventh centuries that the court was
the real center of poetic activity in China. Not only
was a substantial proportion of the surviving corpus
written for court occasions, the distinctive "courtly
style" also dominated poetry written outside the court.
     During the first half of the seventh century the
courtly style became increasingly mannered and rigid;
strong counter-trends developed which sought either to
modify the courtly style or develop an alternative to
it. The thematic scope of poetry began to broaden as
poets went beyond the strictly limited range of topics
and occasions found in court poetry. Furthermore, the
rigid techniques of rhetorical amplification in court
poetry came to exert a less mechanical control over the
process of composition. In these and other ways, poets
of the late seventh and early eighth centuries moved
toward a new freedom, while retaining much that was good
in the older style.

Literary freedom must be defined negatively: there
must be a background of norm and convention that poets
transgress. Beginning in the late seventh century, the
conventions of court poetry came to serve exactly this
function: they formed a body of poetic expectations
which articulated the freedom of better poets. The
poetry of the mid-eighth century, the High T'ang, is
frequently described as "direct" and "natural"; such
qualities are never inherent in literature. In the case
of the High T'ang, they appear by measuring poems against
the background of poetry of the seventh century.

This book is a study of those normative conventions
and how Early T'ang poets broke free of them, how they
learned to use such conventions for their own ends.
Although this study is limited to Early T'ang poetry,
these same normative conventions form the silent background of eighth- and ninth-century poetry. Poets of
the eighth and ninth centuries had attained an even
greater mastery over the conventions and tradition than
the last of the Early T'ang poets, and they were not
fond of Early T'ang poetry. Instead they admired what
was written before the age of court poetry because it
was in the "ancient manner." Yet in actual practice
they depended on the norms of treatment evolved during
the seventh century.

The eighth-century prejudice against the poetry of
the Early T'ang has lasted more than a millennium. Even
in Chinese and Japanese there have been very few studies
of Early T'ang poetry. Those that exist are primarily
concerned with individual poets or the development of
tonal regulations. Larger literary histories generally
confine themselves to identifying the major poets of the
period and noting the relationship of the Early T'ang
poetic style to that of the Southern Dynasties. There
has been no attempt to treat the period extensively
as a whole or to trace the important changes then

occurring in poetry.

This study must omit two of the most interesting collections of poems, at least part of which date from the
Early T'ang, the poems of Han-shan and Wang Fan-chih.
The omission is unfortunate but necessary: their poems
stand so far outside the mainstream of the poetic tradition and present so many problems of dating and attribution that consideration of them would only distract from
the real literary historical problems of the period.
There is no evidence that their works were even known to
poets of the capital at that time. Another poet, Wang
Chi, whose work superficially resembles that of Han-shan
and Wang Fan-chih, is included because his work represents a self-conscious rejection of the tradition of
court poetry. I have also omitted consideration of Liu
Hsi-yi and Chang Jo-hsü, whose work belongs properly to
the early eighth century. They are often mistakenly
considered Early T'ang poets. [1]

I should mention a few conventions of the text and
translations here. Since measures were rarely used with
any exactitude in poetry, I have felt free to replace
Chinese measure with inexact English equivalents: thus
a Chinese li is translated as a "mile," and so forth.
I have kept the Chinese system of calculating a person's
age, so that a child is one year old at birth. I have
also transposed Chinese lunar years into their approximate western counterparts, so that the twelfth month
of the third year of the Ching-lung reign will be called
709, even though the twelfth month should properly be
710.

As in any work that tries to cover a great deal of
material, I have had to keep the notes to a minimum,
explaining allusions and references in a poem only when
they contribute to the discussion or are necessary to
follow the surface argument of a poem. The texts of
the Chinese poems are often eclectic. Where critical

texts are available, as in the case of Ch'en Tzu-ang's
poetry, I have usually followed them. Very often the
earliest text and the only surviving primary text is
that of the Wen-yüan ying-hua 文苑英華, which is noto-
riously poor. Where no other early texts are available,
I will take the Wen-yüan ying-hua reading over a Ch'üan
T'ang shih 全唐詩 reading, except where the Ch'üan T'ang
shih has corrected an obvious error. Frequently the
text I give is made up of a number of sources. Except
where special problems occur, I will not discuss textual
variants. For the convenience of readers who want to
look up the various early texts and to refer to other
poems not translated I give the numbers assigned to the
corpus of the Ch'üan T'ang shih in the Tōdai no shihen
by Hiraoka Takeo et al.

CHRONOLOGY OF EARLY T'ANG RULERS

618-626   Kao-tsu 高祖
627-649   T'ai-tsung 太宗
650-684   Kao-tsung 高宗 (Wu made empress in 655)
684   Chung-tsung 中宗 (ruled for one month; then deposed by his mother Empress Wu)
684-690   Jui-tsung 睿宗 (ruled for about two months, then banished by Empress Wu, who continued to rule as regent in his name)
690-705   Empress Wu 武后, 武則天 (in 690 Jui-tsung was formally deposed and the name of the dynasty changed to Chou 周)
705-710   Chung-tsung (second reign) (empress sequestered; dynasty called T'ang again; power soon in hands of Empress Wei 韋 and family, who poison Chung-tsung in 710)
710-712   Jui-tsung (second reign) (placed on throne by Prince of Lin-tzu, later Hsüan-tsung, in favor of whom Jui-tsung abdicated in 712)
712-756   Hsüan-tsung 玄宗 (in 756 began joint rule with Su-tsung, but retired from active service)

PART ONE

COURT POETRY AND ITS OPPOSITION

THE AGE OF COURT POETRY

During the period of the Northern and Southern Dynasties,
from the conquest of North China by non-Chinese in 317
until the Sui reunified China in 589, Chinese poetry was
forced to adapt to unprecedented circumstances. In
North China, where political power was in the hands of
the "barbarian" military aristocracy, poets were little
more than gracious adornments of their courts. The
courts of South China, increasingly impotent as political entities, came to devote more time to poetry and
the arts of gracious living than they did to governing.
It was an age of aristocracy, and Chinese poetry was ill
at ease in it.

   To Han Confucians the public function of literature
had been to assign praise and blame to those who gov-
erned, to encourage virtue and criticize corruption;
its private function was to express personal sentiments,
but such sentiments were seen primarily as reactions to
prevailing political and social mores. The value of the
expression of such sentiments was that through them the
condition of society and the moral nature of the poet
would be made manifest. These attitudes were certainly
not a fertile ground for a great imaginative literature,
but they were immensely compelling in that they provided
a legitimate position for literature in the Confucian
state. In the Northern and Southern Dynasties these
ties with Confucian values and the literary and cultural
past were almost broken.

   Disillusionment with Confucian literary values and
the ideal of the scholar-official had appeared strongly
as early as the early third century. At first the dissociation of poetry from the state and its consuming

ethical standards proved to be liberating: poetry found
a wealth of new themes in the act of rejection itself.
Eremitic poetry, landscape poetry, Taoist philosophical
and imaginative poetry flourished. However, the cost of
this liberation was great: the comforting Confucian
assumption that poetry and one's personal experience
might have some lasting significance to the state and
Chinese civilization disappeared. It had been a tenuous
assumption at best, but it was a necessary one.

By the late fifth century poetry was becoming increasingly the possession of the southern Chinese courts. The
dominant concerns of eremitic and landscape poetry during
the preceding two centuries had been reduced to bloodless
clichés. Poetry was in the hands of highly literate and
cultured emperors and the great aristocratic families,
who were the ultimate arbiters of poetic excellence. As
much as poetry had evolved away from traditional Confucian values during the preceding centuries, the great
southern families clung to it as an evidence of their
cultural heritage and their superiority over the North,
whose literature they despised.

The poetic stagnation of the South coincided with its
political decay. The amazing continuity of court poetry
can be largely attributed to the conservatism of the
aristocratic patrons of literature and the highly
stratified social structure: an outsider's entrance into
their poetic world was possible only through absolute
conformity to the canons of poetic taste, decorum, and
grace. Poetry had become an elegant diversion, and the
intrusion of Confucian moralizing or the fierce independ-
ence of the recluse was considered unforgivably boorish.

In the following poem by T'ao Hung-ching 陶弘景 (452-
536), the characteristic defiance of the hermit is less
surprising than the emperor's condescending question.

POEM WRITTEN IN ANSWER TO HIS MAJESTY'S QUESTION: 詔問山中何所有
   "WHAT IS THERE IN THE MOUNTAINS?"[1]   賦詩以答

"What is there in the mountains?" you ask—   山中何所有
Many a white cloud on mountain peaks.   嶺上多白雲
But these are pleasures for me alone,   只可自怡悅
I can't take and send them to my Prince.   不堪持寄君

   Political concerns were likewise felt to be out of
place in the world of poetry and in the amusements of
the court. From the point of view of orthodox Confucian
morality, a person in power should be ever vigilant in
the search for men of talent to assist him in governing;
public matters should always have precedence over private
amusements. But when a certain Yü Kao sought an office
from the Liang aristocrat Hsü Mien at a party, Hsü replied,
"Tonight we chat only of the wind and moon—it's not
proper to touch on public matters."[2] Such a response is
understandable and surely occurred with even the most
grimly serious public officials of the Han, yet the
attitude expressed here by Hsü Mien (that there was a
time when "public matters" were inappropriate) was later
to provoke Confucian reformers to bitter attacks on the
lack of public concern manifested in the literature of
the Southern Dynasties. Perhaps alluding to the above
incident, the Sui Confucian Li O wrote: "Poem after poem
...never got beyond images of the moon and dew; tables
were heaped and chests filled with nothing more than the
descriptions of the wind and clouds."[3]
   Two styles dominated court poetry.[4] First, there
were poems written in a stylized imitation of folk
lyrics, yüeh-fu 樂府; among such literary yüeh-fu love
lyrics were particularly popular, though these were
refined far beyond their simple antecedents. Second,
there were formal occasional poems, celebrating with grace
and wit some object or event in the daily life of the
courtier. The Chinese personal lyric had earlier found

expression not only in the Confucian political context
but also in eremitic and landscape poetry. During the
period of court poetry, however, more often than not the
poet's inner life was submerged in the persona of the
folk lyric or in the role of the courtier.

North China, violent and politically unstable, was a
worse environment for poetry. Some northern folk songs
of the period have real artistic merit, but in general
northern poets either imitated the southern style poorly
or wrote doggerel. Northern rulers, however, desiring
to add poetic adornment to their courts, often solved
the problem with characteristic directness; when southern
poets were sent north on diplomatic missions, northern
rulers would detain them under house arrest. Three of
the finest poets of the sixth century Yü Hsin 庾信 , Wang
Pao 王褒 , and Hsü Ling 徐陵, thus satisfied the northerners' yearning for southern culture.

Sixth-century authors could look back on more than a
millennium of a continuous literary tradition. Even the
dominant poetic genre, the pentasyllabic shih, was more
than five hundred years old, the approximate span of all
English literature since Malory. It is not surprising
that the court poets of the sixth century acutely felt
the burden of their rich and varied literary past. The
Liang Emperor Yüan-ti 梁元帝 writes of this in an almost
despairing tone:

Philosophers flourished during the Warring States, while collections of poems and belles lettres filled the two Hans. It reached
the point where every family had written something, every individual had his own collected works. Among these the finest may
express well their emotions and ambitions, honoring custom, but
the lesser serve only to clutter up the books and wear out those
of us born later. So much has accumulated from those now dead,
and yet future generations continue without end. Though one may
anxiously set one's mind to study, one's hair may turn white

without having read them all.[5]

The court poets of the late fifth through seventh
century practiced a kind of "creative imitation" similar
in many ways to that found in lyric poets of the European
Renaissance. Once the basic themes and forms of court
poetry were set in the late fifth century, poets accepted
their inheritance as the absolute limits of poetry; within
this inheritance poets sought novelty of expression rather
than true originality. What they lost in freedom and
depth, the court poets tried to compensate for in craft,
style, and cleverness. Even when real stylistic and
structural individuation appeared toward the end of the
seventh century, there was still very little innovation
in the cognitive aspects of the themes themselves. For
their limitations the court poets suffered the damnation
of succeeding ages: Li O wrote, "They banished reason
and preserved what was unusual, sought emptiness and
exiled the profound. They competed over the originality
of a single rhyme and contested the cleverness of a single
word."[6]

The development of the court poetry of the Southern
Dynasties into that of the Early T'ang is a gradual
process involving no major or abrupt changes. The fixed
conventions which we will describe here are primarily
true of the Early T'ang, but all had their origins in
the court poetry of the Southern Dynasties. In this
chapter we will give only a brief overview of those
aspects of poetic convention that are generally true for
the entire period of court poetry. In a later chapter
we will examine in greater detail the conventions in
their final form, during the first decade of the eighth
century. What began in the fifth century as an unusually
homogeneous period style was gradually transformed into
a restrictive set of rules that defined poetic good
taste.[7]

   Increasingly in the sixth and seventh centuries court
poetry came to be dominated by those rules of rhetoric
and decorum. They served to make poetry an acquired
skill, a learnable art. Aesthetic judgement was not
based on the degree of originality or complexity and
seriousness of meaning, but rather on how well the poet
operated within those rules. It was an art of subtle
variation in which a premium was placed on a graceful
performance. There was no room here for the untutored
genius. In court poetic compositions, where a premium
was placed on speed of composition, these rules and
conventions facilitated extempore versifying without
awkwardness. In their refinement they set a virtually
insurmountable barrier between the outsider whose
knowledge of poetry came from earlier collections and
anthologies and the young man raised in the milieu of
the court. These aesthetic rules were the possession
of the court, and they produced a poetry aristocratic
both in occasion and in conception. They restrained the
daring and aided the uninspired, leveled genius and
raised mediocrity; they permitted the ordinary courtier
to write a poem that could stand without too much embarrassment beside the work of the greatest court poets.
   First among these unwritten rules was a sense of
topical and lexical decorum. One of the things that
defines a court poem proper is that it is written to a
prearranged topic (sometimes indicated by phrases such
as fu-te 賦得), often to imperial command (ying-chih
應制). In the larger realm in which we are using the
term court poetry (that is, the courtly style), one finds
very little personal poetry. As we have said earlier,
political claims and pleas for preferment were out of
place; eremitic aloofness was gauche. Of course, such
poems were written, but they tend to be by outsiders to
the court, either by young poets who have not yet been
accepted into courtly circles or by older poets exiled

from court or renouncing it. Private poetry occurs most
often in exile or retirement, while social poetry between
colleagues and friends is somewhat less common than in
the eighth century.

The area of lexical decorum is quite complicated.
Words describing objects of everyday life were considered
out of place. One seldom finds the rich, expressive
vocabulary which in earlier literature described intense
emotional states. This is largely due to the avoidance
of emotional extremes in court poetry; feigned distress,
polite awe, and wonder are far more common. Particles
do occur, but sparingly, and they tend to occur primarily
at the beginning or the end of a poem. This tendency
continues through the eighth and ninth centuries. Col-
loquialisms and archaisms are avoided. The basic vocabulary is relatively small and is marked by recurring
elegant terms; for example, lin 臨, "to look down on"
(used instead of the earlier poetic location formula X
有 Y, "at X there is Y"), pi 碧, "jade green" (in preference to ch'ing 青, a more natural green), lung 籠,
"veil" or, literally, "encage."

The normative diction of court poetry is based on
certain kinds of formalized divergences from what we
presume was the norm of the classical language. Here we
find a preference for periphrasis, distorted syntax,
semantic warping, and for figured language in general.
Ornament is always preferable to direct statement, though
this is rarely carried to the extremes that we find in
parallel prose. The excessive ornamentation used by a
poet like Lo Pin-wang is as alien to the norm of court
poetry as the self-conscious simplicity of the hermit-
poet Wang Chi.

Structural conventions played an important role in the
making of a court poem. The basic pattern we will call
the "tripartite form," consisting of topic, descriptive
amplification, and response. As we shall discuss in a

later chapter, this form had its origins in the poetry
of the second and third centuries; late in the seventh
century it was generically codified in regulated verse
and continued to dominate the majority of "old style"
poems, ku-shih 古詩 . The poet begins by stating his
theme as gracefully as possible; Shang-kuan Yi, visiting
a mountain villa, begins:

The highroad arrived at a P'ing-chin Lodge,   上 路 抵 平 津
The rear hall has arrayed a great banquet.   後 堂 羅 薦 陳
                              [02708]

In the middle of the poem, the courtier amplifies the
topic with two or more descriptive parallel couplets,
and then closes with a personal reaction to the scene,
often a witty compliment or an intrusion of personal
opinion or emotion. Closure varies from subgenre to
subgenre: banquet poems, for example, often close with
a version of the theme, "it is evening now and we must
return, though we have enjoyed ourselves so much and
don't want to go." Li Pai-yao:

As the sun slants down homeward riders move,   日 斜 歸 騎 動
But our lingering pleasure fills the mountains   餘 興 滿 山 川
  and streams.
                              [02847]

The formalization of structure greatly facilitated quick
composition on court occasions.
   Parallelism was virtually demanded in the middle
couplets of the poem, and the exigencies of court composition exerted an important influence on the development
of parallelism in poetry. The subtle juxtapositions
which one finds in parallel couplets of the eighth and
ninth centuries are rare in the sixth and seventh centuries; in court poetry, once the mechanics of the
technique were mastered, the hurried courtier had the

answer to the pressing question of what to say next.   In
court poetry there is usually little sense of a necessary
relation between the descriptive couplets of a poem, and
poetic argument is weak, if present at all.

Poetic closure, as a response or comment on the preceding part of the poem, was an important factor in the
strengthening of poetic argument.   The older forms of
emotional response—exclamations, streaming tears, rhetorical questions such as "who understands...," and the
Hsieh Ling-yün closure of regret at the absence of a
friend to share an experience—still occur in certain
subgenres such as parting poems and travel poems.   More
often in formal occasional poetry closure appears as a
clever deduction from the scene accompanied by an expression of surprise, ching 驚, or regret, hsi 惜.   To intro-
duce conclusions drawn from the middle couplets there
were set formulae such as nai chih 乃知 and fang chih
方知, "now/then I understand..."   The sense of twist in
closure often appears in rhetorical question formulae
that dismiss objections or truisms, such as shui wei
誰謂, "who claims...?"

Each subgenre had its own conventions.   In some
subgenres such as yung-wu 詠物, "poems on things," the
conventions were so strong that a virtually independent
tradition of development was created with very little
borrowing from other subgenres.   In other subgenres, the
descriptive middle couplets might be interchangeable
between subgenres, but the conventions of poetic closure
were distinctive.   The conventions and norms of the
various subgenres had begun to take shape in the second
to fourth centuries; by the seventh century they had
grown particularly strong.   Not only did the range of
subgenres delimit what might be treated in poetry, their
own internal laws determined how that topic or occasion
should be treated.

There were numerous other minor characteristics.   The

conventional identification between the court and the
world of the immortals not only provided a readily
available metaphor complex for the purposes of ornamentation, but it also supplied innumerable witty closings
concerning the appearance of the world of the immortals
here on earth. Han place names and personal names
provided another set of elegant substitutions. Finally,
there was a tendency to remove human beings from the
scene, to substitute their gestures, actions, implements,
and clothes for their human presence. Many of these
characteristics can be seen in the following opening
couplet of a poem (02707) by Shang-kuan Yi. The topic
is set: the emperor and the court went to K'uei-lin Hall
for a party. This becomes:

The pacing palanquin emerges from P'i-hsiang Palace,   步輦出披香
Clear singing looks down on T'ai-yeh Pool.   清歌臨太液

T'ang palace names are replaced by Han palace names.
The emperor disappears into his palanquin; the singers
disappear into an impersonal "singing." These songs are
not "at" T'ai-yeh Pool, but instead decorously "look down
on" (lin, with overtones of an imperial "visit") the site.
    Despite its limitations, the acute attention to craft
in court poetry contributed considerably to the development of Chinese poetry. During this period the poetic
language was refined into the condensed and flexible
medium used by the great poets of the eighth and ninth
centuries. From their search for novelty of expression
evolved the syntactic freedom and ability to shift word
classes found in later Chinese poetry. Out of their
sense of structural and tonal decorum evolved the
regulated verse and regulated quatrain. And from their
attention to the surprising use of individual words in
lines evolved a particular concentration on style and
diction which characterizes later poets from Tu Fu to

Wang Shih-chen. Yet their contributions were collective
rather than individual, and, with the partial exception
of Yü Hsin, it would be difficult to point out a single
poet who towers above the rest.

The strength and influence of court poetry was such
that it weathered the violent attacks made against it
for two hundred years. Although a certain amount of
poetry was written outside its scope, its aesthetic
appeal was so great that even those who bitterly attacked
it in theory could not escape from it in practice. In
the eighth century, the center of literary activity
shifted away from the court, but in the court the old
style remained dominant. It was institutionalized in
the examination poem, and it continued to be the appropriate style for poetry addressed to high officials
throughout the T'ang.

2

AN OPPOSITION POETICS AND THE SUI

The rise of court poetry in the late fifth century pro-
voked an immediate reaction; however, this opposition
was a poetics without a poetry, without an aesthetically
appealing alternative. The opposition poetics was
ultimately to develop into the fu-ku 復古, "return to
antiquity," theories which played an important role in
one of the greatest ages of Chinese poetry, from the
early eighth through the early ninth centuries.

Definition of the fu-ku sentiment is difficult because
it meant different things to different people. In some
cases it meant specifically moralistic opposition to
"palace poetry," kung-t'i shih 宮體詩 (a mildly erotic
subgenre initially associated with court poetry), which
describes the emotions and ambiance of a fair lady. In
other cases the fu-ku sentiment meant opposition to
stylistic ornateness in favor of greater directness and
concision. In still other cases it indicated opposition
to poetry without political import. In short, it involved
opposition to any of the various characteristics of court
poetry and the grounds for its opposition were primarily
ethical rather than aesthetic. Thus in these early
stages before the eighth century we shall call it the
"opposition poetics," since it defined itself in negative
relation to court poetry, sometimes implying "return to
antiquity" and sometimes not.

With characteristically Confucian polemical rhetoric,
the opposition poetics were firmly opposed to "decadence,"
"lasciviousness," and pointless "ornateness"—qualities
which no one, even in the sixth and seventh centuries,
could reasonably support. Exactly what works in court
poetry embodied these pernicious qualities was a matter

of debate. The poetic alternatives were equally vague,
though the consensus of opposition critics seemed to
favor either a poetry expressing deep personal feeling
or a poetry that served some didactic and political
purpose.

The first strong statements of the opposition poetics
are found in one of the greatest works of Chinese literary
theory, the Wen-hsin tiao-lung 文心雕龍 , written during
the last decades of the fifth century by Liu Hsieh 劉勰
(465-522). The following passage represents true fu-ku,
containing both opposition to courtly decadence and the
alternative of the classical model. The concept of
literature which it advocates is based on Confucian
statements about literature from the pre-Ch'in and Han.
These same ideas, expressed in innumerable reformulations,
were later to build into a monotonous roar.

> The efficacy of literature is contingent upon its being a true
> offshoot of the Classics: it is the substance through which the
> Rites are performed and the means by which Government Functions
> are carried out. Through it the relationship between army and
> state is elucidated. If you trace the sources of such writings,
> you will find they are always in the Classics. However, as
> times grew remote from those of Confucius, literary forms
> decayed. Rhetoricians loved the unusual and valued the friv-
> olous and bizarre; they decorated feathers merely for the love
> of painting and embroidered patterns on leather bags. They
> have gone too far from what is fundamental in pursuit of the
> false and superfluous.[8]

In this passage Liu emphasizes the function of literature
in the context of the Confucian state and society; in
other places in the Wen-hsin tiao-lung he places emphasis
on literature as self-expression. Distaste for super-
fluous ornament comes through clearly in this passage,
but such ornamentation characterizes not only court

poetry but also the parallel prose style in which the
passage itself is written.

　　By the Liang dynasty (502-56) we find such denuncia-
tions aimed specifically against poetry in P'ei Tzu-yeh's
裴子野 "Essay on Insect Carving" 雕蟲論 .[9] "Insect
carving," like "dragon carving" (tiao-lung) in the title
of Liu Hsieh's work, refers to attention to craft and
ornament; in the form "insect carving" the idea is
pejorative. The force of these polemics soon made itself
felt among court circles: the classical pedigree of the
opposition's arguments made them difficult to oppose.
A few defensive arguments in favor of contemporary
literature appeared; even the great court poet Hsü Ling
(507-82) felt obliged to apologize for the poetry he
had collected in his anthology, the Yü-t'ai hsin-yung
玉臺新詠: "I have put together ten chapters of love
poetry here—of course, not the peer of the Odes or
Hymns, nor an outgrowth of the Airs [the three divisions
of the Shih-ching]—there remains a distinction between
the turbid Ching River and the clear Wei."[10] Hsü is
arguing here that the lascivious, "turbid" poetry he has
collected can exist side by side with the "clear" poetry
of antiquity; like the two rivers alluded to, these two
kinds of poetry will never mix, and the purity of the
classical tradition will not be threatened. Clearly the
court poets felt vulnerable to the attacks of the opposition poetics; the real confrontation was yet to come.

　　When Yang Chien 楊堅, scion of a northern military
clan, completed the creation of a unified empire, he
brought opposition to the courtly style into state policy:
"When Kao-tsu [Sui Wen-ti, Yang Chien] first unified the
government, he gave constant thought to hacking away the
ornate in favor of the simple. He sent forth orders to
get rid of all flowery frills. However, the fashion of
the age was elegant diction, and there remained much
decadent attention to beauty."[11] This was in 584, five

years before the Sui's conquest of the Ch'en dynasty and
the final reunification of the empire. Wen-ti's motives
probably lay in his puritanical dislike for ostentation
and were not those of a Confucian moralist. There is no
mention of a "return to antiquity," no harkening back to
first principles.

However, in his concern for simplicity and directness,
Wen-ti's attitude was close enough to that of the Confucian
exponents of the opposition poetics that his ministers
chose to consider it as a validation of those poetics.
Thus the censor, Li O 李諤 , responded to Wen-ti's commands
with Confucian polemics against the courtly style. I will
quote almost all of Li O's "Letter Requesting the Rectifi-
cation of Literary Style" so that the reader can get the
flavor of such polemics and see the essentials of the
argument.

> I have heard how the wise kings of antiquity civilized the
> people: they had to change the way people saw and heard things,
> curbing their sensual desires and blocking their impulses to
> abandon themselves to evil—they showed the people the path of
> simplicity and harmony. The Five Teachings and the Six Actions
> were the basis for instructing the people; the Book of Songs,
> the Book of Documents, the Book of Rites, and the Book of Changes
> were the gateways to Righteousness and the Way. Consequently,
> nothing was of more importance than being able to bring the family
> back to parental love and filial respect, bringing men to under-
> stand rites and courtesy, rectifying customs and setting manners
> straight. When they presented memorials, offered rhapsodies,
> composed elegies, or engraved inscriptions, it was always for
> the purpose of praising virtue and placing men of integrity in
> their proper place for illuminating merit and verifying the rule
> of Reason. And even if it were not a matter of warning or en-
> couragement, for the sake of the Right, they would not compose
> pointless pieces.
>
> Descending down to later ages, customs and instruction gradually

declined. One after another the three rulers of the Wei were
devoted to literature: indifferent to the Great Way of the
ruler and his people, they took pleasure in the minor art of
"insect carving." Those below follow those above, much as an
echo or a shadow. They competed in driving on this trend to
literary floweriness, and in consequence, it became the custom.
In the southeast during the Ch'i and Liang dynasties, this abuse
reached an extreme: noble and base, sage and fool, all devoted
themselves exclusively to verse. Thus they cast off Reason and
held to what was unusual, sought emptiness and pursued the
trivial. They competed over the originality of a single rhyme
and contested the cleverness of a single word. Poem after poem
and document after document never got beyond describing the moon
and dew; tables were heaped and chests filled with nothing more
than the appearance of the wind and clouds. From such as these
the age derived its standards of excellence, and in such a way
did the court select scholars. Since the road to profitable
employment had been opened, hearts which had already been partial
to such things attached even greater importance to them.

The result was that the ignorant youth of the villages and
the children of the nobles didn't even glance at the basics of
numeration, but instead learned to write poems in pentasyllabic
lines. And when it came to the Book of Changes, to the Book of
Documents, to the discourses of Yi Yin, Fu Yüeh, the Duke of
Chou, and Confucius, they didn't care anymore—they hadn't even
heard of them! They thought that their boastful extravagances
were "pure and selfless"; they thought that expression of their
emotions was a public merit. They pointed to Confucian simplicity
as ancient clumsiness and used rhapsodies [fu] to determine who
was a superior man. Thus belles lettres and utilitarian prose
flourished more each day, while the government became more and
more disorderly. In truth, this arose from the abandonment of
the Pattern of the Great Sages, from fabricating the useless and
thinking it useful. Such destruction of the fundamental and
pursuit of the nonessential has inundated the heartland. They
took each other as their masters, and after a while the flames

were fanned even higher.[12]

Li O goes on to praise the Sui's orders for a rectifica-
tion of literary style; most have honored the edict, but
he fears that pockets of pernicious ornamentation are
still to be found in remote regions. He closes with a
request that reports of corrupt style be sent to him so
that severe punishment may be meted out. The antisouthern
direction of the letter is only thinly veiled.

   Unlike much later fu-ku writing, Li O has made no
attempt to compromise the aesthetic considerations of
literature with its public functions. It is perhaps
difficult to see how this essentially antiartistic
attitude could have such an ultimately salutary effect
on the development of Chinese poetry; however, once the
poet did make a compromise between his art and the values
of the Confucian state, he could feel that his poetry had
lasting significance, and if he wished to reject traditional Confucian values, he had a worthy opponent on whom
to sharpen his argument.

   From Li O's damnation, "they thought that expression
of their emotions was a public merit," the poet was
driven to make his emotions fit the larger context of
the world around him. The protest ballad, the meditation
on history, the commentary on contemporary politics—many
of the great subgenres and themes of eighth- and ninth-
century poetry—were grounded in just this need to speak
in a public context and thus be relevant to the course
of history.

   However, all this lay far in the future; the immediate
results of Wen-ti's proclamation and Li O's letter were
hardly so grand. Outside of the court, as Li O complained,
the southern style lingered on. Within the Sui court
attempts to write moral, instructive poetry were pathetic.
Wen-ti's Confucian minister Li Te-lin 李德林 writes:

Gentleness perfected, His Cultural Instruction
  stretches far,
Yea, our Sage, His military accomplishments
  manifest.
A Great Lord observes the Six Principles
  (of literature),
As the Nobility congratulate His Longevity...[13]

至 仁 文 教 遠
惟 聖 武 功 宣
太 師 觀 六 義
諸 侯 問 百 年

and the infamous Yang Su 楊素:

Of old Heaven and Earth were blocked up,
All things were in Early Difficulty and Folly.
Peace ceased with the Royal Way,
Bitterness and lament knotted men's style...[14]

在 昔 天 地 開
品 物 屬 屯 蒙
和 平 替 王 道
哀 怨 結 人 風

Early Difficulty and Folly are two hexagrams from the
Book of Changes. "Bitterness and lament" are associated
with poetry written in states that are going to ruin
(see p. 34).   These examples are clearly not the sort
of thing to lure people away from the charms of court
poetry.

    The ill-fated Sui Yang-ti 隋煬帝 , the second and
last true emperor of the Sui, was the most considerable
poet of that short-lived dynasty. His work shows the
conflicting pulls of the opposition poetics, adopted by
his father as appropriate for the unified empire, and
the rich, alluring poetry of the South. A man of deep
aesthetic sensibilities, Yang-ti could hardly have been
satisfied with the poetic productions of men such as Li
Te-lin and Yang Su. On the other hand, Yang-ti was no
Ch'en Shu-pao 陳叔寶 , the last and genuinely decadent
poet-emperor of the Ch'en dynasty; many of Yang-ti's
poems reveal a man with dreams of military glory, a man
who takes pleasure in seeing himself as emperor of all
China. It was this latter aspect of Yang-ti's poetry
that the seventh-century historian Wei Cheng seized upon
as though it were a manifestation of Confucian political
concern.

Yang-ti's only statement of the opposition poetics
was made when he first became crown prince; he complained
of some ceremonial songs that their diction was too
"frivolously lush and incapable of manifesting imperial
accomplishment and might."[15] This closely echoes his
father's dislike of ostentatious southern elegance, but
Yang-ti's motives are suspect in that at this time he
was trying to curry his father's favor.[16]

One of Yang-ti's poems selected by Wei Cheng as
exemplary of the proper imperial style is his "Watering
My Horse by the Great Wall: To the Courtiers Accompanying
Me on Campaign" 飲馬長城窟行示從羣臣. The event
referred to is Yang-ti's reconstruction of the Great Wall
and his aggressive policy on the northern frontiers,
which was later to have disastrous results in his campaigns against Korea.

The autumn wind rises moaning,	蕭蕭秋風起
As we march far away for thousands of miles.	悠悠行萬里
Marching thousands of miles away to what end?—	萬里何所行
Across the desert we rebuild the Great Wall.	橫漠築長城
But this was no idea of Our own,	豈台小子智
It was built by wise past emperors:	先聖之所營
They planted here a policy to last thousands of ages,	樹茲萬世策
To secure the lives of their millions of subjects.	安此億兆生
How then could We shrink from such concerns,	詎敢憚焦思
And rest in calm unconcern in the capital?	高枕於上京
Our legions' standards held high by the river's northern reaches,	北河秉武節
For a thousand miles the battle-flags unfurl.	千里捲戎旌
An endless succession of rivers and mountains appear before us, sink away,	山川互出沒
Then plains and steppes stretching to infinity.	原野窮超忽
The gongs are struck to halt the files and columns,	撞金止行陣
And drums are beaten to stir the troops:	鳴鼓興士卒

A thousand chariots, ten thousand horsemen move
And water their horses beside the Great Wall.
Autumn dims clouds from beyond the frontier,
Fog darkens the moon over mountain passes.
Post horses climb up along the steep cliffs,
And beacon fires appear, suspended in the sky.
"What news from the posts at the Great Wall?"—
"The Khan is coming to court; he submits."
Evil's turbid aura clears from Heaven Mountain,
And morning light shines on the palace gates.
The troops are discharged and return peacefully,
Our work on the frontiers now is done.
Drink the cup of victory, tell that We have
    returned!
Our ancestors will learn Our deeds before
    the Temple.[17]

千乘萬騎動，飲馬長城窟。
秋昏塞外雲，霧暗關山月。
緣巖驛馬上，乘空烽火長。
借問長城候，單于入朝謁。
濁氣靜天山，晨光照高闕。
釋兵仍振旅，要荒事方舉。
飲至告言旋，功歸清廟前。

Although Yang-ti speaks of his concern for his people,
what we see here is less an expression of Confucian
morality than an evidence of Yang-ti's consciousness of
being emperor. A fascination with his power and glory
pervades the poem. Whatever the motives, Yang-ti's poem
is still a world apart from Ch'en Shu-pao's effete version
of the same ballad:

A battle steed enters a strange land;
On mountain flowers this night, radiance.
Apart from its herd, it neighs to its shadow;
A fragrance often stirs with the wind.
The moon's color swallows the Wall's darkness;
Autumn sounds are jumbled in the length of
    the passes.
How shall it repay the Son of Heaven?—
By its horsehide it will announce those dead
    on the frontier.[18]

征馬入他鄉，山花此夜光。
離羣嘶向影，因風屢動香。
月色含城暗，秋聲雜塞長。
何以酬天子，馬革報疆殤。

The last line here refers to the practice of wrapping
the dead in horsehide. The delicate sensibilities of

this flower-sniffing steed seem out of place beside its
grisly vows of self-sacrifice to the state, but the Ch'en
emperor's experience of the frontier was purely literary.
The sense of imperial responsibility in Yang-ti's poem is
altogether absent here.

However bloodless and impersonal Ch'en Shu-pao's
vision of the border may be, the superior artistry of
the southerner is also visible in the contrast between
the two poems. The idea of the horse neighing to its
shadow because it lacks companions combines a cleverness
and sensitivity characteristic of court poetry. Nor
could Yang-ti produce anything to match the delicate
stylistic craftsmanship in the middle couplets of Ch'en
Shu-pao's ballad. A less obvious but more fundamental
aspect of southern poetic craft is the tight rhetorical
amplification in Ch'en's ballad that contrasts sharply
with Yang-ti's rambling manner. There were many patterns
of amplification, but most involved splitting up, re-
combining, and expanding elements from earlier lines or
couplets. Furthermore, the repeated elements had to be
expressed in different terms or implied indirectly, for
example, radiance, shadow, and the primary term moonlight.

The first couplet of Ch'en Shu-pao's poem sets the
primary terms: horse and strange land, flowers and moonlight. The second couplet should split and recombine
them: thus in the third line we have horse and moonlight.
The fourth line has the expected flowers but adds a new
term, wind. The third couplet then picks up this secondary antithesis of moonlight and wind and amplifies
it in terms of the "strange land," the frontier. The
irregularity of the fourth line makes the poem less
perfectly symmetrical than many courtly poems, but the
mechanics of the technique are clear:

1st couplet	horse	strange land
	flowers	radiance (moonlight)

2nd couplet	horse	shadow (moonlight)
	flowers	wind
3rd couplet	moonlight	Great Wall (strange land)
	jumbled	passes (strange land)
	sounds (wind)	

Finally, following the rules of the tripartite form,
Ch'en Shu-pao interjects a direct emotional response,
reversing the melancholy tone in the horse's vow of
self-sacrifice. Yüeh-fu tended to use set personae who
voice the formalized response in the closure. With a
horse as the only possible responding figure in the poem,
Ch'en is compelled to place the conventional gesture of
heroic resolve in its mind.

This refined southern sensibility could not help but
attract Yang-ti. Yang-ti never mastered the southern
occasional poem, the courtly style at its most ornate,
but there is no evidence he ever tried to do so. For
poetry bearing directly on the life of the court, he
found the imperial dignity and aesthetic poverty of the
opposition poetics quite appropriate. On the other hand,
the languid folk poetry of the South, the celebration of
the "good life," appears frequently in his work.

THE JOY OF MY PALACE IN CHIANG-TU   江都宮樂歌

Oh, to linger in my old haunts in Yang-   揚州舊處可淹留
  chou

Terraced kiosks, high and bright, where   臺榭高明復好遊
  I love to stroll.

To meet early summer in breeze-blown   風亭芳樹迎早夏
  pavilions, under blossoming trees,

And say good-bye to autumn's end on tracts   長皋麥隴送餘秋
  of marsh and grain-covered slopes.

Cassia oars on clear pools, fishhawk   渌潭桂檝浮青雀
  prows bobbing;

A fruit falls on my golden saddle, the   果下金鞍躍紫騮
  dark steed startles.

Amber wine and pale lees, we drink the
  drifting clouds,

綠醽素蟻流霞飲

Of long sleeves and clear song, a land
  of pleasure and delight.[19]

長袖清歌樂戲州

Like his imperial poetry, much of Yang-ti's poetry in
the southern style betrays a self-conscious love of a
role. In this poem and in others we see a consciousness
of the South as a separate entity, quite different than
the court poet's assumption that the South was the world.
Yang-ti is on the outside looking in.

      At other times, however, Yang-ti is not so self-
conscious and often succeeds in capturing the sensuality
of southern poetry. Since he lacked the rhetorical
panoply of the southern court poet, the result could
have a haunting freshness and beauty.

SPRING RIVER, FLOWERS, MOON, NIGHT

春江花月夜

The evening river, level, unmoving;

暮江平不動

Spring flowers full, just blossomed.

春花滿正開

The rolling waves carry the moon away,

流波將月去

While tide waters come, bearing the
  stars onward.[20]

潮水帶星來

It might be added that the prototype of this song was
composed by none other than Ch'en Shu-pao.[21]

      Although we do find other poems of the style and
quality of Yang-ti's "Watering My Horse by the Great
Wall," the Sui generally failed to produce an aesthetically pleasing alternative to court poetry. Meanwhile,
court poetry flourished as ever. The Sui left this
literary legacy to the T'ang, just as it left the T'ang
its legacy of institutions and military ambitions. The
T'ang inherited the opposition poetics of the Confucian
moralists along with the lingering allure of southern
court poetry. The history of seventh-century poetry
was largely a history of the interaction between these

two contending forces, and it was from the brushes of
former Sui officials that the T'ang found its first,
uneasy compromise of the two values.

3

THE SUI LEGACY: WEI CHENG AND LI PAI-YAO

The two poets who carried the new poetry inspired by the
opposition poetics into the Sui were northerners; in the
South court poetry was still strongly entrenched. The
poetry written by Wei Cheng and Li Pai-yao during the
internecine wars at the end of the Sui and in the earliest
years of the T'ang represented the potential for a vigorous poetry engagé. However, their subsequent development during the T'ang marks the decline of the opposition
poetics: Wei Cheng moved into sterile didacticism, while
Li Pai-yao conformed to T'ai-tsung's proclivity toward
court poetry.

Wei Cheng 魏徵(580-643) was from Wei-chou in the
modern province of Shantung, one of the strongholds of
Chinese culture in the North. Orphaned at an early age,
Wei dabbled in Taoism as a youth, then joined the rebel
Li Mi in his struggle first against the Sui and later
against the T'ang. After Li Mi's collapse, Wei transferred his loyalty to the T'ang. There he rose rapidly,
becoming one of the compilers of the Sui History and an
eminent intellectual in T'ai-tsung's court.

Apart from some ceremonial songs, Wei Cheng's poetic
output was minuscule: only four poems survive. One would
hardly think of him as a poet at all were it not for the
fact that "Expressing My Feelings" was taken by Ming
neoclassicists as the first characteristic production
of T'ang poetry.[22] It is unclear at precisely what
point in Wei Cheng's career "Expressing My Feelings"
was written. It was either soon after Wei, along with
the warlord Li Mi whom he served, submitted to the new
dynasty or shortly after T'ai-tsung took the throne.
In either case the poem is from the early years of the

dynasty and is closer in spirit to much Sui poetry than to the poetry of the first decades of the T'ang.

"Expressing My Feelings" represents a kind of poetry which might have successfully fulfilled the goals of the opposition poetics. Apt parallels have been drawn between it and Yang-ti's "Watering My Horse by the Great Wall": not only does Wei Cheng express admiration for Yang-ti's poem, both poems are products of the same era and the same poetics.[23]

EXPRESSING MY FEELINGS   述懷

When they began scrambling for the crown
  on the central plain
I cast down my pen to serve in a chariot.
My plots and my plans all came to nothing,
But determination and my ardor endure.
I whipped on my horse, swore fealty to the
  Son of Heaven,
Then galloped swiftly out from the passes,
Begged reins to halter Nan-Yüeh's king,
Leaned on my carriage rail, talked Ch'i to
  surrender,
Strode over high mountains on tortuous paths,
Gazed on the plain, coming into view,
  disappearing.
In ancient trees the birds of winter sing,
On deserted mountains the gibbons cry by night.
The eye gazes far, the heart is wounded,
The dreaming soul flies home, startles awake
  again and again.
How can I help but cower at such danger?—
Yet I feel deeply the honor His Majesty
  shows me.
I'm a Chi Pu who need not say yes twice,
I'm a Hou Ying who honors his word.
Human life is impelled by noble spirit—
Who cares for mere glory and fame?

中原初逐鹿
投筆事戎軒
縱橫計不就
慷慨志猶存
杖策謁天子
驅馬出關門
請纓繫南越
憑軾下東藩
鬱紆陟高岫
出沒望平原
古木鳴寒鳥
空山啼夜猿
既傷千里目
還驚九逝魂
豈不憚艱險
深懷國士恩
季布無二諾
侯嬴重一言
人生感意氣
功名誰復論

[02442]

Historical allusions fill this poem; I will confine
myself to those which are absolutely necessary to make
the piece intelligible. The "reins" of line seven refer
to a story told of the Han official Chung Chün, who was
sent as an envoy to the king of Nan-Yüeh to convince the
king to submit to Han suzerainty. On his departure,
Chung Chün is supposed to have expressed his readiness
to serve the state by asking the emperor for long reins
to "halter" the king of Nan-Yüeh and bring him back to
the capital. Like Chung Chün, Wei intends to exert his
persuasive powers to the utmost in the service of his
ruler. The following line refers to the orator Li Yi-chi,
who, working on behalf of the founder of the Han dynasty,
managed to talk a resurgent Kingdom of Ch'i into surrender.
Both Chung and Li met their deaths as a result of their
efforts. Hou Ying and Chi Pu, mentioned toward the end
of the poem, were both known for the strength of their
word and their loyalty.

Even if "Expressing My Feelings" does not possess the
stature that Li P'an-lung and Shen Te-ch'ien claimed for
it, and even if it is, as the modern scholar Wen I-to
聞一多 says, an "ordinary poem," still it possesses a
simplicity of diction, a directness of feeling, and an
expression of political concern that lie further outside
the scope of court poetry than even Yang-ti's ballad.[24]
Wei draws most of his references from history rather
than from earlier poetry, and in the one case where he
clearly borrows from an earlier poem, his choice is
significant. The last couplet of "Expressing My Feelings"
is lifted almost verbatim from one of the rare pieces of
Confucian poetry in the Southern Dynasties.[25] The poem
was written by Hsün Chi 荀濟, a man who fled the Liang
to the Northern Wei because he had stirred the Liang
emperor's wrath by his opposition to Buddhism.

The model for the title, "Expressing My Feelings,"
shu-huai 述懷, is "Singing My Feelings," yung-huai 詠懷,

by Juan Chi 阮籍 (210-63). We know that by the fifth
century Juan Chi's poem series was read as a personal
commentary on the dissolution of the Wei dynasty and
the rise of the Ssu-ma clan, which was to establish the
Chin.[26] By 658 when Li Shan 李善 presented his commentary
on the <u>Wen-hsüan</u> 文選 to the throne, individual poems of
"Singing My Feelings" were being read as topical allegory.
By associating his poem with those of Juan Chi in title
and style, Wei not only points to the larger realm of
social and political concerns, he also suggests an
identification with the qualities of sincerity, boldness,
spontaneity, and intense emotionalism. These qualities
were closely associated with the poetry of the Chien-an
and Wei by T'ang readers; they represented a compelling
primitivism which was felt to have been lost during the
period of court poetry. As we shall see later, the model
of Chien-an and Wei poetry was to be one of the principal
means by which T'ang poetry escaped from the confines of
court poetry.

　　There were also some Southern Dynasties poets interested in the primitivism of Chien-an and Wei poetry, but
their treatment of it is quite different than Wei Cheng's:
to them it was not a means of self-expression, but rather
a quaint artifact to be imitated as a literary exercise.[27]
The first poet to use the model of "Singing My Feelings"
for serious personal ends was Yü Hsin, a southern poet
who wrote much of his poetry during his captivity in the
North. In his work there is a strong sense of regional
style and manner, a feeling that a "northern" poetry
should be different from a "southern" poetry. Yü Hsin
has twenty-seven "Imitations of the <u>Yung-huai</u>"擬詠懷 ;
it is believed that all date from Yü's captivity. Technically these poems are still "imitations," like other
imitations of third- and fourth-century poetry written
by Southern Dynasties poets; however, many of Yü Hsin's
"Imitations of the <u>Yung-huai</u>" are intensely personal,

either directly so or in their analogical implications.
Yü Hsin's series has a range of themes similar to the
original Yung-huai: autumn laments, historical poems,
philosophical pieces, and personal narratives. Later
during the T'ang, fu-ku poetry also spans a wide range
of themes associated with Chien-an and Wei poetry. The
"Imitations of the Yung-huai" are important antecedents
for the poetry that the opposition poetics ultimately
did develop, but they contain a certain amount of heavy-
handed parallelism, virtually inescapable in a poet
raised in the tradition of southern court poetry. The
influence of the "Imitations of the Yung-huai" was not
direct; in the Early T'ang an "imitation of Yü Hsin" did
not refer to the style of the opposition poetics at all,
but to the most precious kind of court poetry. However,
they were probably very much in Wei Cheng's mind when he
wrote "Expressing My Feelings."

Unlike court poetry, which is essentially a poetry of
celebration, Yü Hsin's "Imitations of the Yung-huai" and
Wei Cheng's "Expressing My Feelings" both represent a
poetry of self-expression, harkening back to a principle
stated in the "Great Preface" to the Shih-ching, that
"poetry state intention [chih 志 , 'ambition,' or whatever
one's mind is set on, with strong political connotations]."
The poem is to be centered on the poet and his inner life;
if description of the external world is present, as it is
in lines nine to twelve of "Expressing My Feelings," it
is subordinate to the poet's reaction to it. There is
no attempt at objectivity (Li O's "pure and selfless")
nor the restrained and formalized emotional response of
the court poet. If we compare Wei Cheng's landscape
description with the description in Ch'en Shu-pao's
"Watering My Horse by the Great Wall," we see no interest
in the scene for its own sake as in Ch'en's poem, no
clever arrangement of the elements of the landscape;
rather we see a simply constructed scene each of whose

elements is designed to reveal what stirs the poet's
emotions. Finally, "Expressing My Feelings" is not
didactic: the poet affirms certain principles, but these
are personalized, directly connected with his circumstances.

The threat of didacticism was a greater danger to
this kind of poetry than the lure of court poetry. The
theorists of the opposition poetics saw such poems as
exemplary of proper moral attitudes rather than as a
personal art with ethical dimensions. If the primary
function of poetry was to teach, then would it not be
more proper to teach directly with overtly didactic
poetry? After he rose to high position during the T'ang,
Wei Cheng succumbed to this danger, prodding the great
T'ai-tsung with an audacity highly prized in Confucian
ministers. In the following anecdote T'ai-tsung writes
a poem on imperial ethics, but his ethics have a slightly
Buddhist flavor, Wei Cheng "corrects" the imperial error
in emphasis by an exemplary poem on the Western Han,
concluding with the proper Confucian emphasis on rites.
Such a preference for imperial power and propriety over
common ethics may indeed have represented Wei Cheng's
personal feelings, but the function of the poem is to
teach and not to express.

> When T'ai-tsung was at the Lo-yang Palace, he made an excursion
> to the Pool of Deep Azure. They held a drinking party where
> everyone composed a poem on a given topic.
>
> His Majesty's poem went:
>
> . . .

Many were the benighted rulers who gave free reign to their emotions,	恣情昏主多
Enlightened lords who overcame themselves are few	克己明君鮮
Self-ruin depends upon a string of evils,	滅身資累惡
Lasting fame arises from accumulated good.	成名由積善

Then Wei Cheng wrote a poem on the Western Han that went:

[Wei first describes the military and convivial splendors of the Han]

. . .

In the end His Majesty made use of
   Shu-sun T'ung's Rites,

Only then did one know how exalted
   the emperor was

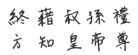

T'ai-tsung then said, "Wei Cheng never fails to bind me up with Rites."[28]

Shu-sun T'ung was one of the men responsible for the state sponsorship of Confucianism during the Han. T'ai-tsung did not miss the point. The opposition poetics was unable to distinguish adequately between poetry that embodied moral principles and poetry that merely stated them, didactic poetry. If "Expressing My Feelings" was a successful example of the former, this later poem by Wei Cheng is clearly didactic. Such didactic poetry could never compete aesthetically with court poetry, and the promise which Wei Cheng's earlier poem showed was lost.

Wei Cheng's importance as a poet is minimal in comparison to his importance as an historian. His "Preface to the Biographies of the Men of Letters" in the Sui History is one of the best reasoned and most generous statements of Chinese literary history as conceived by the opposition poetics. Wei begins by reaffirming the conventional didactic theory of literature, which we saw in Liu Hsieh and Li O. He continues, however, with the theory of self-expression in a political context:

Sometimes there is a banished courtier who has met with slander; sometimes there is a homeless scholar at the end of his road—the way is tortuous and his prince not yet found, his will repressed within and not yet brought forth. In such a state of depression his misery stirs, and he sends some winged writing to the palace—

he springs swiftly from the mud and mire and reaches the Blue
Clouds.[29]

Wei proceeds to describe the literature of the preceding two centuries as a process of the fragmentation of
the ideal unity of wen (文, "pattern," "ornamentation,"
the aesthetic qualities of literature) and chih (質,
"substance"). The wen of southern literature was excessive, while too much chih made northern literature
unpalatable. In the period immediately preceding the
Sui, southern aestheticism was imported to the North.

Such an interest on the part of the moralist and
historian in the process of literary change arises from
an early tenet in Chinese literary thought, that literature reveals the political and spiritual state of the
nation. Thus when Wei Cheng describes the poetry of
Hsü Ling and Yü Hsin as having emotions that are mournful
and full of longing," he is evaluating the political
conditions of the later Northern and Southern Dynasties:
in the "Great Preface" to the Shih-ching we find:

> The Sounds of an age of order are peaceful and happy—its govern-
> ment is in harmony. The sounds of a world in disorder are bitter
> and full of rancor—its government is perverse. The sounds of a
> fallen kingdom are mournful and full of longing—its people are
> in dire straits. Consequently, to understand how things have
> succeeded and how they have failed, to move Heaven and Earth, and
> to stir supernatural beings, there is nothing more appropriate
> than poetry.

In large measure this theory accounts for the moralists'
serious concerns with the propriety of literary style.

Wei Cheng goes on to praise the poetry of Yang-ti,
mentioning specifically the ballad "Watering My Horse by
the Great Wall." This, Wei says, "has the proper style
and represents a return to classical regulation."[30]
Since historians universally condemned Yang-ti's character

and capabilities as a ruler, Wei's evaluation of Yang-ti's
poetry directly contradicts the theory stated above, that
poetry reflects the age. Wei Cheng, quite capable of
quoting scripture for his own purposes, avoids the difficulty by referring the reader to a less popular critical
adage, Analects, XV. 22: "The Good Man does not put aside
the words because of the man"; that is, the moral value
of a work cannot be judged from the author's character.

Thus it seems that to Wei Cheng, who can be said to
represent to some extent the literary historical opinion
of the first decades of T'ai-tsung's reign, the literature
of the Sui constituted a rejection of the courtly style
and a return to classical principles. What is puzzling
is that Wei seems to have deliberately ignored Yang-ti's
more effete, southern-style poetry, which would have been
more consistent with the historian's evaluation of the
man. If we were to speculate as to Wei's motives in
this, it may be that Wei was holding these poems of Yang-
ti up to T'ai-tsung as a prescriptive example in order to
counter the new poetic stars of the 630s and 640s, Shang-
kuan Yi and Hsü Ching-tsung. The work of Shang-kuan and
Hsü represented a resurgence of court poetry without even
a facade of moral concern.

The decline in the effectiveness of the opposition
poetics and the resurgence of court poetry during T'ai-
tsung's reign can be seen also in the changes that took
place in the poetry of Li Pai-yao 李百藥 (565-648), one
of the most popular poets of the day. Li Pai-yao was the
son of Li Te-lin, Sui Wen-ti's leading Confucian minister,
whose unsuccessful attempts at a Confucian poetry we have
mentioned earlier. Yang-ti had had an aversion to Li Pai-
yao and gave the poet a post in the far South. Li par-
ticipated in one of the rebellions at the end of the Sui
and came to incur the wrath of T'ang Kao-tsu. Banished
to Ching-chou because of his unpopularity, Li eventually
met T'ai-tsung. T'ai-tsung, who generally liked those

whom his father disliked, befriended the old poet. When T'ai-tsung took the throne, Li Pai-yao was summoned to court and was one of the principal literary figures of the first part of T'ai-tsung's reign.

The poetry that Li Pai-yao wrote in the South during the latter part of the Sui is close in tone and style to Wei Cheng's "Expressing My Feelings" and Yang-ti's "Watering My Horse by the Great Wall."

ON THE ROAD: EXPRESSING MY FEELINGS

途中述懷

Ts'ai Yung was sent north of the passes,　　伯喈遷北塞
Ts'ui Yin went to Liao Peninsula.　　亭伯之遼東
And I—how have I became a wanderer,　　伊余何為客
All alone, clinging to Cloud Terrace Mountain?　　獨守雲臺中
The road stretches far, the sun has set,　　途遙日已暮
The way of an age of peace is here at its end.　　時泰道斯窮
Roots pulled up, the grass on the shore laments,　　拔心悲岸草
Half-dead, leaves fall from the wu-t'ung
  on the cliffs.　　半死落巖桐
My eyes watch the geese go off to Heng-yang,　　目送衡陽雁
My heart is pained by the maples over the
  river.　　情傷江上楓
Indeed trouble was lurking behind good fortune,　　福兮良所伏
Now in truth it is hard to find success.　　今也信難通
But a man does have his determination and
  his spirit,　　丈夫自有志
So how can he grieve that he won't be ennobled?　　寧傷官不公

[02833]

Contrary to all rules of courtly composition, Li Pai-yao rushes into his poem with two historical precedents for his own condition, the exile of Ts'ai Yung and Tou Hsien's allotment of a miserable post in the northeast for Ts'ui Yin. Both Ts'ai and Ts'ui were Eastern Han scholars. Heng-yang is said to be the point at which the geese migrating southward stop their journey. This poem was written in about 605, when Li was in exile in the South,

thus more than a decade earlier than Wei Cheng's "Expressing My Feelings." Both poems close with affirmations
of principles and moral resolution:

But a man does have his determination and
  his spirit,
So how can he grieve that he won't be ennobled?

丈夫自有志
寧傷官不公

and

Human life is impelled by noble spirit—
Who cares for mere glory and fame?

人生感意氣
功名誰復論

The two poems are also similar in their use of historical
exemplars and in their use of landscape description.

    We will pass over the other poetry written by Li Pai-
yao in the last years of the Sui for the moment and look
at some poems that he wrote during the T'ang. His poetry
written to imperial command is virtually indistinguishable
from that written by T'ai-tsung and his other courtiers.
The poet disappears into the celebration of the outings
of the court:

ANSWERING "EARLY SPRING EXCURSION": TO
  COMMAND

奉和初春出遊應令

Singing fifes emerge from Gazing Garden;

鳴笳出望苑

Carriage canopies in flight descend to
  Mushroom Fields.

飛蓋下芝田

Light beams on water drift in the
  evening sunshine,

水光浮落照

Bright-colored clouds paled by thin mists.

霞彩淡輕煙

The color of willows will last three
  months;

柳色臨三月

Plum blossoms divide two years.

梅花隔二年

As the sun slants down, homeward
  riders move,

日斜歸騎動

Their lingering pleasure filling
  the mountains and streams.

餘興滿山川

[02847]

This shift from a poetry of self-expression to a poetry
of celebration occurs not only in his poetry to imperial
command but also in poetry to his friends. The fragmentation of the world into a pastiche of interrelated scenes,
characteristic of court poetry, stands in sharp contrast
to Li Pai-yao's earlier poem in which he tried to develop
an idea, to understand his circumstances by historical
and natural analogies and to overcome his despair by
moral resolution.

To some extent the stylistic differences between
these two poems are based on a subgeneric difference;
practical circumstances play a large role in stylistic
variation. Li Pai-yao cannot be expected to write the
kind of poetry he wrote in exile and adversity when he
was attending one of T'ai-tsung's banquets. However, a
court poet like Yü Hsin did manage to write personal
poetry in the fragmented, impersonal courtly style, while
moralists such as Wei Cheng managed to avoid it even on
occasions that seemed to call for it. At the court
gathering cited earlier Wei Cheng carefully avoided
writing of the sensual grandeur with which the Western
Han was conventionally associated. The models of a
courtly personal poetry and an anticourtly public poetry
were available to Li Pai-yao and he avoided both. The
crux of the matter lies in the fact that Li Pai-yao and
Wei Cheng did write poetry of self-expression during times
of stress, poetry which did not use the style and conventions of court poetry. For most court poets, on the other
hand, poetry's primary purpose was the tasteful celebration of aristocratic society.

During the Southern Dynasties we do find some huai-ku
懷古 , meditations on the past usually occasioned by a
visit to an ancient site. These, however, are relatively
few; the Southern Dynasties was one of the least historically minded periods in Chinese history. The Sui
unification brought with it a renewed interest in the

past, particularly in the Han dynasty as a model for
the unified empire. One of the most potent influences
on the T'ang <u>huai-ku</u> was Pao Chao's 鮑照 (412-66?)
"Weed-covered City" 蕪城賦, a meditation on the past
splendor and present ruins of a great city.

Li Pai-yao wrote many meditations on ancient sites,
usually following the pattern established by "Weed-
covered City," describing first the glory of the city
at its height, then the desolation of its ruins, and
closing with a meditation on the changes of fortune.
We will see this theme appearing again strongly in the
capital poetry of the 670s. Such <u>huai-ku</u> appear frequently in the first three decades of the seventh century,
and it was during this time that the subgenre took on
the characteristics it was to retain throughout the rest
of the T'ang.

Li Pai-yao's "Meditation on the Past at Ying" (02834)
is perhaps his finest poem. Ying was the capital of the
Warring States Kingdom of Ch'u. Unfortunately the poem
is so laden with historical allusions that it makes
cumbersome reading in translation. Li follows closely
the outline of Pao Chao's <u>fu</u>, but while Pan Chao associates their fall with the arrogance of their age of
glory, Li Pai-yao is more concerned with the inevitable
patterns of rise and fall:

Their cycle ran out—they were set amid   運厄屬馳驅
  galloping horses;

The age was Difficulty, when the whips   時屯恣敲朴
  were unleashed.

This is a powerful combination of abstraction, allusion,
and vision of Armageddon. In the second line of the
couplet, the fall of Ying is interpreted in terms of
the hexagram <u>ch'un</u> 屯, Initial Difficulty, from the <u>Book</u>
<u>of Changes</u>. Ch'u was defeated by the state of Ch'in,
and "the whips" is a phrase from a famous essay by Chia

Yi on the tyranny of Ch'in.

The following undatable poem (02832) is a more personal and generalized treatment of the theme of ruins. The melancholy which pervades the poem will become character-istic of T'ang huai-ku.

CLIMBING AN ANCIENT WALL ON AN AUTUMN EVENING   秋 晚 登 古 城

Sunset, the road I travel stretches far,   日 落 征 途 遠

In depression I look down from this
  ancient wall.   悵 然 臨 古 城

On its tumbled ramparts wrens of winter
  gather,   頹 墉 寒 雀 集

From weedy parapets evening crows fly up
  in surprise.   荒 堞 晚 烏 驚

Impenetrable and gloomy, dense forests rise,   蕭 森 灌 木 上

Far in the distance a lone column of smoke
  appears.   迢 遞 孤 煙 生

Vision of red clouds, gleaming in last
  sunlight,   霞 景 煥 餘 照

Dew-filled air clears the evening cool.   露 氣 澄 晚 清

An autumn wind whirls the falling leaves—   秋 風 轉 搖 落

How can I set my mind at rest?   此 志 安 可 平

Here we can begin to see a shift from the relatively objective treatment of nature found in court poetry to the conflation of mood and scene characteristic of T'ang poetry. The ruins serve here as only one element in a scene of autumnal melancholy.

Li Pai-yao's work shows a versatility unusual in the poetry of the first half of the seventh century. He wrote a few excellent "palace poems" of uncertain date and was equally adept at the courtly skill of writing a clever couplet:

Wave-flowers, blossoming, folding in;   浪 花 開 已 合

Wind-blown patterns, straight and then
  joined.   風 文 直 且 連

[02840]

The changing forms of the water, moving from one extreme
to the other, suggest the notion of plasticity and change,
but the visual scene is ingenious: the rising and sinking
of the waves appear to be like flowers blossoming and
folding up. It is also possible that the "flowers" are
sparkles of light appearing on the waves, their flashing
compared to the blossoming and folding of flowers.

Unlike Wei Cheng, whose poems were at most peripheral
to his other activities, Li Pai-yao was as well-known
as a poet as a historian. Perhaps being the son of Li
Te-lin kept him from court poetry in his youth. In his
youthful poetry written during the Sui the force of the
opposition poetics can be felt, but later, required to
participate in the poetic celebrations of T'ai-tsung's
court, he abandoned his stronger, more personal style.
During T'ai-tsung's reign the new poetry of opposition
poetics began to fade into the background, and with the
defection of Li Pai-yao to the courtly style, the opposition poetics lost its best hope to produce a viable
alternative to the courtly style.

4

POETS OF T'AI-TSUNG'S COURT

In 621, before he took the throne, Li Shih-min 李世民 (T'ai-tsung 太宗) gathered eighteen of the leading literary men and scholars of the day to found the College of Literature (Wen-hsüeh kuan 文學館). These men formed the nucleus of T'ai-tsung's cultural establishment and included such famous figures as K'ung Ying-ta 孔穎達 (574-648), a commentator on the classics, and the historian Yao Ssu-lien 姚思廉 . Only three of the eighteen have more than one poem extant today: Yü Shih-nan 虞世南 , Ch'u Liang 褚亮, and Hsü Ching-tsung 許敬宗.

All three of these poets were from the southeast: Ch'u Liang and Hsü Ching-tsung were from Hang-chou, while Yü Shih-nan was from nearby Yüeh-chou. This was the heartland of Southern Dynasties culture and of court poetry. Hsü Ching-tsung was only thirty years old when the College was founded, but both Yü Shih-nan and Ch'u Liang were protégés of the great court poet Hsü Ling. Thus despite the infusion of moralizing Confucian poetics during the Sui, the direct tradition of Southern Dynasties court poetry continued into the T'ang and into T'ai-tsung's court.

Yü Shih-nan (558-638) was one of the leading intellectuals of this time and by far the ablest poet of the three men mentioned above. Yü grew up under the feeble Ch'en dynasty where his youthful poetic endeavors received the attention not only of Hsü Ling but also of Chiang Tsung 江總 (518-90), another master of court poetry. Yü Shih-nan was a multifaceted Southern Dynasties intellectual: he dabbled in Buddhism and as secretary in the Sui Imperial Library, he compiled the Pei-t'ang shu-ch'ao 北堂書鈔, a famous encyclopedia. He served in and

wrote poetry for the court of Yang-ti, where his elder
brother Yü Shih-chi 虞世基, was one of Yang-ti's most
trusted counsellors. Thus, by the time Yü Shih-nan came
to serve T'ai-tsung, he was already one of the grand old
men of literature. Like many of the ministers of the
early part of T'ai-tsung's reign, Yü Shih-nan had a close
and informal relationship with the sovereign. T'ai-tsung
was genuinely fond of him, and when Yü Shih-nan died,
T'ai-tsung was said to have remarked, "Shih-nan was like
my very self."[31] Such terse imperial comments are part
of biographical convention, but they probably do represent genuine feeling.

In Yü Shih-nan's poetry we find an uneasy grafting of
the opposition poetics onto the base of court poetry.
Though a court poet by training and nature, Yü could not
escape the influence of the opposition poetics during
its heyday in the first decades of the seventh century.
The following anecdote reveals an at least pro forma
sense of the moral responsibilities of the court poet:

> His Majesty [T'ai-tsung] wrote a poem in the palace style and
> ordered Yü Shih-nan to write another using the same rhymes. Yü
> Shih-nan responded, "Your Majesty's composition is well wrought,
> certainly—but the style is not seemly. When a ruler likes
> something, those beneath him like it in the extreme. I fear
> that if this poem is handed around, the customs of the empire
> will become decadent. Thus I dare not accept your command."
> His Majesty said, "I'll try your suggestion," and then wrote a
> poem describing the process of dynastic rise and fall.[32]

To the opposition poetics the "palace poem" was the most
irritating of court poetry's subgenres. We should note
here that Yü Shih-nan, more courtier than moralist,
prefaces his remonstrance with a compliment to the
aesthetic qualities of T'ai-tsung's poem. Furthermore,
his argument is flatteringly predicated on the emperor's

power and influence. The ethically acceptable alternative is the poem on history, closely related to the
theme of the huai-ku, the rise and fall of a great city
or state.

   "Palace poetry" did decrease sharply during the Sui
and Early T'ang, though it did not disappear. This is
probably because it was the one form that the opposition
poetics agreed constituted literary decadence: it was
considered morally reprehensible to write poetry about
beautiful women. One of the popular literary historical
misconceptions about Early T'ang poetry is that it is
made up largely of "palace poetry." Most Early T'ang
poets do have a few "palace poems," but these constitute
a far smaller percentage of their works than in poets of
the Southern Dynasties or in many poets of the High and
Mid-T'ang. Yü Shih-nan, for example, has more surviving
border poems (poems about frontier warfare and the life
of frontier troops) than "palace poems."

   Yü Shih-nan's poetic exchanges with T'ai-tsung reveal
a condescending pedagogic tone which must have sorely
tried the imperial patience and embarrassed the imperial
ego. Yü appears as the learned encyclopedist, the
culturally smug southerner, and the Confucian moralist
all conjoined. T'ai-tsung writes:

ON THE BAMBOO LOOKING DOWN ON THE POOL   賦得臨池竹

Their pure stalks screen off the twisting   貞條障曲砌
    stairs,
Azure leaves that bear the winter's frosts.   翠葉負寒霜

They brush the window—you discern dragon   拂牖分龍影
    shadows.
Look down on the pool—await the phoenix   臨池待鳳翔
    in flight.

                          [00091]

The third line, echoing numerous traditional associations
between bamboo and dragons, suggests the similarity of

the shadows of the bamboo on the window to dragons; the
fourth line refers to the legend that phoenixes nest
only in bamboo. But in the second line T'ai-tsung has
made a poetic "error," a violation of decorum, by introducing the theme of the bamboo's endurance of winter in
a spring or summer scene. T'ai-tsung asked for a
response from Yü Shih-nan, and this is what he got:

ON THE BAMBOO LOOKING DOWN ON THE POOL:
  TO IMPERIAL COMMAND

Pale azure and substance of highest
  clouds,

Their bright colors fall, shine back
  in the clear pool.

Waves float their reflection full of
  wind,

And current shakes branches that
  fend off the dew.

Dragon scales drifting in Hsieh Valley,

Phoenix wings brushing the ripples.

But if you want to see their nature
  that lasts the winter,

It can only be known in the cold of
  the year.

[02573]

The fifth line refers to the legend of Li Ling, musician
of the Yellow Emperor, who was ordered to go to Hsieh
Valley, where a special variety of bamboo grew, in order
to cut some for a set of panpipes.

Yü's poem is both an implicit and an explicit "correc-
tion" of T'ai-tsung's quatrain. T'ai-tsung did not keep
to the topic, which should demand a description of the
bamboo in relation to the pool. In the first couplet
Yü Shih-nan contrasts the "height" of the bamboo—their
physical height, their color, their lightness, and their
spiritual "loftiness," all like clouds—with the "lowness"
of their reflections on the pool. The second couplet is

a brilliant amplification of the theme of disparity: the
waves, stirred by wind, capture in reflection the form
of the bamboo stirred by wind (or the shaking of the
bamboo's reflections in the waves make them seem windblown when in fact they are stationary), and a large
amount of water ironically traps the form of things
which fend off small amounts of water, the dew. In the
third couplet, Yü shows T'ai-tsung how to bring in the
dragon and phoenix associations while keeping to the
theme of the bamboo in reflection: the pool becomes the
stream of Hsieh Valley in which their "dragon forms" are
reflected; the arrival of the phoenix in the reflection
seems to "brush the ripples."

    After demonstrating to T'ai-tsung the "proper" treat-
ment of the topic, Yü Shih-nan points out the explicit
error in the quatrain: one must wait until winter to
speak of the bamboo's endurance of the cold. This
quality of the bamboo has strong ethical associations:
like the evergreen, the bamboo is a symbol of integrity,
of resolute endurance of hardship. Thus Yü Shih-nan is
implying that one may praise such qualities only when
they are tested.

    When we speak of the "proper" treatment of a topic,
we are referring not only to the structural conventions
of amplification and keeping to the subject, we also
mean the use of the body of lore, of literary references
and stories, which grew up around each of the common
poetic topics. This lore, along with examples of the
proper literary treatment, came to be codified in the
literary encyclopedias. For the poetry of the Southern
Dynasties and the Early T'ang the two relevant encyclopedias are the Yi-wen lei-chü 藝文類聚 compiled by Ou-
yang Hsün 歐陽詢 (557-641) et al. under imperial auspices,
and the Ch'u-hsüeh chi 初學記 , compiled by Hsü Chien
徐堅 (659-729) et al., also under imperial auspices.
These encyclopedias formed a concise "burden of the past"

which set the limits of elegant variation of a topic.
Though the encyclopedias were directed at students and
poets of less than encyclopedic learning, they give us
a good idea of how more learned poets conceptualized the
material that went into making a poem. To a poet like
Yü Shih-nan the literary past and its conventions were
immediately present, but an encyclopedia can show us
how that past was used. If we wanted to write a court
poem on a cicada, we would look up the entry "cicada" in
an encyclopedia. Here we would find the traditional
"facts" about the insect, (if we used the Ch'u-hsüeh chi),
the references and anecdotes we might allude to, and
finally a number of literary examples. From the latter
we could borrow phrases and get an idea of what aspects
of the topic should be treated in our poem.

   The following quatrain (02582) is characteristic of
Yü Shih-nan:

THE CICADA

蟬

Dipping its proboscis, it drinks clear dew;
Its floating echoes emerge from the sparse
    wu-t'ung.
It dwells high, its voice naturally goes far,
And it need not depend on the autumn wind.

垂緌飲清露
流響出疏桐
居高聲自遠
非是藉秋風

A brief survey of cicada lore and literature in the
Ch'u-hsüeh chi can fill in much of the background here.
In the first of the "anecdotal parallels," shih-tui
事對, we are told that "unless it can drink the dew,
it will not eat."[33] The "parallel" to this is the fact
that it "listens for the wind"; this is substantiated by
a line from the "Cicada Fu" of Fu Hsüan 傅玄 (217-78):
"It listens for the shang [autumn] wind and sings along
with it" 聆商風而知鳴 .[34] Yü Shih-nan has followed
this parallel closely, matching the singing with the
dew-drinking.

The "dwelling high" first appears in the section on
literary examples in an earlier "Cicada Fu" by Ts'ao
Chih 曹植 (192-232), in the couplet: "It roosts in the
lofty branches and raises its head,/Rinses its mouth
with the pure streams of morning dew 棲喬枝而仰首兮,
嗽朝露之清流 .[35] Most of the elements of Yü Shih-nan's
quatrain appear together in the following passage from
Ch'u Kuei's 褚玠 (529-80) "Fu on the Cicada in the Wind":

There is an <u>autumn</u> <u>wind</u> coming into my courtyard,	有秋風之來庭
On the <u>high</u> willow, a singing cicada.	於高柳之鳴蟬
At times its lonely chanting breaks off for a moment,	或孤吟而暫斷
Then suddenly the jumbled <u>echoes</u> return continuous.	乍亂響而還連
It <u>dips its</u> black <u>proboscis</u> and its moaning stills, . . .	垂玄緌而嘶足...
Then again <u>drinks</u> the glittering dew.[36]	方復欽露兮光葉

We find the wu-t'ung tree, the distance of the voice,
and the idea of something being carried afar by the
autumn wind in the following passage from a poem by
Chang Cheng-chien 張正見 (?-575):

The cold cicada cries out in the willow;	寒蟬噪楊柳
The north wind attacks a wu-t'ung tree.	朔吹犯梧桐
Its leaves go far, fly, and can't be stopped;	葉迥飛難住
The branches remain, their shadows all bare.	枝殘影苯空
Its voice remote, after it drinks the dew.[37]	聲踈欽露後

Chang Cheng-chien here plays on the word <u>su</u> 踈, used to
describe the "remoteness" of the cicada's voice, but
also meaning the "sparseness" of a tree after its leaves
have been stripped by the wind. Thus the cicada's voice
is "like" the leafless tree. Yü Shih-nan also uses <u>su</u>,
but he uses it to describe the "sparseness" of wu-t'ung,
conventionally associated with autumn.

It should be emphasized that Yü Shih-nan's use of
these commonplaces is not an allusion to individual
literary works, such as we find in poetry of the eighth
century and afterward (though the use of commonplaces
occurs then too). The lore of the cicada grows up through
the additions of individual works, but for the most part
it is independent of them. If an author uses a particularly clever idea or makes a bold innovation, then
that idea or innovation may come to be associated with
a specific work, but this is not the case in any of the
sources quoted above.

The above examples should suffice to show that almost
every element in Yü Shih-nan's poem is a convention. Yü
varies those conventions and comments on them. Yü places
his cicada in the autumnal wu-t'ung rather than in the
conventional willow; by doing so he stresses the unity
of the autumn world, willows not being traditionally
associated with that season. Then Yü gracefully reverses
the convention that the cicada sings along with the
autumn wind: it is rather because the cicada dwells
"high" (associated with a pure and noble nature) that
its voice is carried far, and not because it needs the
autumn wind. Yü's poem is a work of gracious craftsmanship, not truly original but possessing a certain novelty
when set against the tradition of cicada lore.

Most poetry is created from a fusion of literary
tradition and personal, extraliterary experience. Of
the two, the latter is the expendable element. For court
poets, the literary tradition, "literary experience," is
primary, and there is a tendency to write poems purely
as an exercise on topics the poet knows nothing about.[38]
The frontier, one of the most popular of yüeh-fu topics,
could be credibly evoked by poets who would have fainted
at the sight of a hostile Tartar in the flesh. Border
poetry was very much a literary experience, but it taught
later poets who went on campaigns or into exile how to

"see" that stark world.   In Yü Shih-nan's version of the
popular ballad "Watering My Horse by the Great Wall"
(02561), we read: "The moon is out, the passes still
dark" 有月關猶暗. Ominously dark fortifications in
the moonlight are part of the border scene.   In Ch'en
Shu-pao's version: "The moon's color swallows the Wall's
darkness" 月色含城暗 ; and in Yang-ti's: "Fog darkens
the moon over mountain passes" 霧暗關山月 . We do not
read of the Great Wall or the fortified passes in the
light of noon; we do not read of their color, their
height, or their majestic solidity.   The darkness of
walls in the moonlight is an essential literary unit in
building a border scene.

     Yü Shih-nan is not a great poet, but his work has an
undeniable charm.   He has the ability, rare among court
poets, to combine conventional elements to produce a
fresh effect.   In the restricted aesthetics of court
poetry, this may be the highest form of praise.

SPRING NIGHT   春夜

In the springtime garden the moon tarries;   春苑月裴回
A bamboo hall opens at nightfall.   竹堂侵夜開
A startled bird cleaves the forest in passage, 驚鳥排林度
As windblown petals come from across the water. 風花隔水來
                                    [02579]

This shows the court poet's attention to the incidental,
to a moment of beauty in the world.   In the all-important
craft of the couplet, Yü surpasses most of his contemporaries.   Of a pair of cranes he writes:

Shining on the sea they seem floating snow,   映海疑浮雪
Brushing a torrent they pour out a flying   披澗寫飛泉
    stream.

                  [02567]

The second line, in which the pair becomes a white

frothing waterfall leaping from the stream, shows an
almost Marinistic ingenuity. Sometimes the urge toward
a novel treatment of conventional elements can produce
brilliant couplets which must be based on sensitive
observation of nature:

Soaked, the grain on the slope grows still
  more azure;   隴麥霑逾翠
Wet, the flowers on the mountain flame still   山花溼更然,
  brighter.

[02572]

Here the wetness brings out the special brilliance of
the colors; later Tu Fu was to echo this intensification
of colors in a famous couplet:

From the green of the river the birds are
  still whiter;   江碧鳥逾白
From the blue of the mountains, the flowers   山青花欲然,
  are about to burst into flame.

[11355]

In this case the intensification of color is brought out
by comparison with another color. Tu Fu's couplet has a
long tradition of invention and improvement. Certainly
Yü Shih-nan contributed the most with his idea of the
intensification of color, but he borrowed the metaphor of
red flowers seeming to burn from earlier poets—from Liang
Yüan-ti: "In the woods the flowers seem about to burst
into flame"林間花欲然, ;[39] and from Yü Hsin: "Mountain
flowers, flames blazing" 山花焰火然, .[40] The material
Tu Fu used for his couplet was a collective accomplishment, but not only does his revision of it show brilliant
craftsmanship equal to any court poet, he integrates its
complex symbolic overtones into the poem as a whole.
This the court poet, Yü Shih-nan, cannot do, and it sets
the major poet, Tu Fu, apart from the craftsman, Yü.
    Yü Shih-nan can be taken as representative of scores

of other competent court poets of T'ai-tsung's reign:
for example, Ch'u Liang, Hsü Ching-tsung, Ch'en Shu-ta
陳叔達, Yang Shih-tao 楊師道, and Yüan Lang 袁朗.
Some excelled in particular aspects of court poetry—Yang
Shih-tao, a northerner, in the description of nature;
Ch'en Shu-ta, a descendent of the Ch'en royal house, in
stylistic grace.   At the center of these poets was T'ai-
tsung.

     T'ai-tsung, who ruled from 627 to 649, was neither as
complex an individual nor as talented a poet as Yang-ti.
He was, however, a more successful ruler.   The surviving
corpus of his poetry is one of the largest of the period,
and despite his limitations as a poet, it is clear that
he devoted much attention to the craft.   During the first
part of his reign he seems to have encouraged Confucian
moralizing and the elegance of court poetry equally,
admitting both as appropriate to his royal dignity.   The
result was the uneasy union of the two opposing currents
that can be seen in Yü Shih-nan's poetry.

     T'ai-tsung's poetic experience was not unlike that of
Yang-ti and Li Pai-yao: he was an outsider to the highly
cultured circle of court poets that surrounded him.   He
lacked both their erudition and their education in the
court poet's craft, but still he tried to force his
poetry into their mold.   Unfortunately T'ai-tsung lacked
the poetic sensitivity of Yang-ti and Li Pai-yao, and in
his poetry the contrast between the strong personality
of the man and the impersonal grace of the court poet
is striking.   In the following poem (00017), the emperor
is first the court poet, describing a visit to his former
home with balance and objectivity; in the final couplet
his true self emerges, blunt and proud of his own rise
in the world.

PASSING MY FORMER HOUSE   過舊宅

I halt my purple carriage here at Hsin-feng,   新豐停翠輦

Stay the singing fifes in the town of Ch'iao.　　譙 邑 駐 鳴 笳

My garden is grown with weeds, its one path
  lost;　　　　　　　　　　　　　　　　　　園 荒 一 徑 斷

The terrace has aged—half its stairs are
  aslant;　　　　　　　　　　　　　　　　　臺 古 半 階 斜

And from my pools the old water has seeped
  away,　　　　　　　　　　　　　　　前 池 消 舊 水

Yet my former trees put forth new flowers.　昔 樹 發 今 花

One morning I took leave of this land　　　一 朝 辭 此 地

And the entire earth became my home.　　四 海 遂 為 家

Another couplet in a similar vein runs:

Long ago I went off riding a single horse,　昔 乘 匹 馬 去

Now return, driving thousands of chariots.[41]　今 驅 萬 乘 來

Had T'ai-tsung seen the merit in such straightforwardness,
he might have become a much better poet. But like so
many northerners, T'ai-tsung felt the aesthetic superiority and smugness of court poetry. Though he did write
a number of moral pieces and tried in several cases to
emulate the sturdy, personal style of the late Sui, the
majority of his poems show a man working hard to write
in the courtly style, particularly in the latter part
of his reign. He had the most elegant of courtly
stylists, Shang-kuan Yi, revise all his drafts, and
with imperial license he was even freer than most court
poets about borrowing good lines and clever ideas from
others. Ch'u Liang, for example, wrote of a candle,
punning on the work hua 花 , "flowers," referring both
to real flowers and to "sparks."

Don't say that spring is getting late—　莫 言 春 梢 晚

Here the candle constantly blossoms—
  spark-flowers.　　　　　　　　　　　　自 有 頌 開 花

T'ai-tsung writes:

ON A CANDLE [first of two]   詠燭

The flame stirs—it senses the coming wind;   燄聽風來動

Its flower-sparks blossom, not waiting for   花開不待春
  spring.

In a thousand constant streams its tears roll   鎮下千行淚
  down,

But not because it longs for anyone   非是為思人

                    [00086]

In the idea of the candle's sparks/flowers substituting
for the flowers of spring, we have a new, almost baroque
twist on the pun, which was already well-worn by earlier
poets. We cannot tell whether T'ai-tsung or Ch'u Liang
had the idea first, but judging from T'ai-tsung's other
borrowings and the almost mechanical ingenuity of his
poem, we may guess that Ch'u Liang was the willing donor.

   T'ai-tsung did not reject the opposition poetics
entirely. He has a version of the popular "Watering My
Horse by the Great Wall" (00011) which is so close to
Yang-ti's version in structure that it must be an imitation of it. T'ai-tsung's sensitivity to the demands of
the opposition poetics is particularly evident in the
preface which he wrote to the ten poems entitled "Imperial
Capital." This is an important document in the development of the opposition poetics into fu-ku, and in part
probably accounts for the reason most later T'ang
literary historians associate the literary return to
antiquity with the founding of the T'ang. T'ai-tsung
is satisfied neither with the simple opposition to court
poetry of Sui Kao-tsu nor with the gradual process of
literary decline described by Wei Cheng:

   I am the last to follow in the footsteps of the hundred kings,
   but I send my heart a thousand years into the past. Deeply
   stirred I meditate on antiquity and imagine the men of wisdom
   then. I hope to wipe away the vileness of Ch'in and Han [their
   literary style and everything since] by the style of Yao and Shun,

to use the Hsien and Shao melodies to change the lewd, indecent
tunes [of the present].

[00001]

Music is here a metaphor for poetry, which in turn is
important primarily as a manifestation of moral government. Such hyperclassicism is characteristic of T'ang
fu-ku: present "decadence," the burden of the real poetic
past, if thrown off by a resolution to recapture the
poetry of "high antiquity," a poetry that was no longer
extant.

The ten poems that follow the preface by no means live
up to the high ideals T'ai-tsung had set for them. They
are conventional court poems, praising the splendor of
the capital and of imperial outings. Here and there the
poems affirm his fu-ku poetics, but there is nothing else
in the style or the content of the poems to separate them
from the work of other court poets. The first poem begins
grandly:

In the streams of Ch'in, a powerful emperor's   秦川雄帝宅
  residence,
In Han Pass, mighty royal dwelling.   函谷壯皇居

and continues lamely:

Filagree halls rise a thousand yards,   綺殿千尋起
Detached palaces, more than a hundred feet up.   離宮百雉餘
Tiers of tiled roofs reach the Milky War afar,   連甍遙接漢
Soaring pavilions pass remote into the void.   飛觀迥凌虛
Sun and moon are shaded by the layered gate-   日月隱層闕
  towers,
Wind and mist emerge from the filagree ornament.   風煙出綺疏

[00001]

As grandly as T'ai-tsung's first poem begins, it is
basically a composite of clichés on the capital of
Ch'ang-an drawn from capital fu. The opening and other

parts of the poem are particularly close to a problematic
poem on the capital ascribed to the Liang and Ch'en poet
Chang Cheng-chien, "Where the Emperor Dwells" 帝王所居篇
(CCS, 2.14b, WYYH, 192.1b). This begins:

In Yao and Han passes, a powerful emperor's
    residence,   峭函雄帝宅
At Wan and Lo a mighty royal dwelling.   宛洛壯皇居

What makes the poem problematic is that these are specifically northern capitals, while Chang was a southern
poet who died before the reconquest. The fourth poem
illustrates T'ai-tsung's difficulty in finding a poetry
for his poetics:

Singing fifes approach the pleasure pavilion,   鳴笳臨樂館
In this season of fragrance eye and ear
    rejoice.   眺聽歡芳節
Shrill flutes in tune with vermilion strings,   急管韻朱絃
And clear song that freezes the white snow.   清歌凝白雪
In dazzling color the stately phoenix
    descends,   彩鳳蕭來儀
While black cranes from ranks in multitudes.   玄鶴紛成列
Here we are rid of Cheng and Wei's degraded
    song   去茲鄭衛聲
And now can delight in the proper tones.   雅音方可悅

                          [00004]

No one, least of all T'ai-tsung, was exactly sure what
the alternative to literary decadence might be. In this
poem it seems that simple affirmation of the opposition
poetics made the poem morally "proper." Or it may be
that because T'ai-tsung felt his court was exemplary of
Confucian morality, poetry celebrating that court was
therefore moral. The first four lines are so typical of
courtly banquet poem that they are virtually anonymous.
The third couplet modulates into a glittering, metaphorical
Confucian mode, quite acceptable in court poetry: the

phoenix and the two-thousand-year-old "black cranes"
come in response to the virtuous music of antiquity.
In the last couplet T'ai-tsung tacks on his affirmation
of the opposition poetics. It is a strange, uneasy
compromise and is typical of T'ai-tsung's work.

Whatever their shortcomings, these poems are landmarks
in their own way: they are the first examples of poetry
written with the stated purpose of fulfilling the aims
of fu-ku poetics. Though they may be the worst, they
were certainly not the last. A second and equally
important effect of these poems was to stimulate a
number of poems in praise of Ch'ang-an. In a later
chapter we shall discuss how this topic merged with
poetry on ruined cities to produce some of the finest
poems of the Early T'ang.

Great cities were easily seen as metaphors for states.
The most visible reminders of the Period of Disunion
between the fall of the Han and the founding of the Sui
were the ruins of capitals and great cities. The splendid
city of Ch'ang-an was equally the most visible evidence of
the power and wealth of the united empire. With the resurgence of Confucian and historical studies in T'ai-
tsung's reign, poets were not only impressed with the
splendor of the present, but developed a romantic fascination with the past and were deeply moved by the contrast
between splendor and fall. To mention just a few of the
examples of both themes in this period, Li Pai-yao wrote
a no longer extant series on the "Imperial Capital" in
response to T'ai-tsung's.[42] Yüan Lang has a poem on the
splendor of Ch'ang-an (02398); Lu Ching 陸敬, a poem on
the decay of the Sui eastern capital at Lo-yang (02496);
Yang Shih-tao, a poem on Han Lo-yang, meant as a metaphor
for the T'ang capital (02505); Yü Shih-nan, a haunting
short poem on the ruins of the capital of the Three
Kingdoms state of Wu (02569); and Wang Chi, a poem on
the rise and fall of an unspecified Han city (02641).

As we shall discuss later, the conventions of these poems derive both from the capital _fu_ of the Han and Pao Chao's "Weed-covered City." Wang Chi's poem may be taken as a characteristic treatment of the theme of rise and fall; I quote a passage from it:

Kingfishers on bright pearled curtains,
Mandarin ducks in halls of white jade.
On cool mornings they ate from precious
    vessels,
On calm nights the scent of aloes wafted.
The finest steeds came on the road
    eastward,
The fairest ladies poured down from the
    north.
In the might and majesty of their glory,
They said they would hold its magic
    forever.

翡 翠 明 珠 帳
鴛 鴦 白 玉 堂
清 晨 寶 鼎 食
閒 夜 鬱 金 香
天 馬 來 東 道
佳 人 傾 北 方
何 其 赫 隆 盛
自 謂 保 靈 長

The last line quoted is a variation on Pao Chao's "They planned to make their generations eternal and make heaven's mandate stay with them."[43] This time-conquering arrogance on the part of the people of the city is one of the most durable conventions of the theme and inevitably begins the description of the decline of the city. The balancing half of Wang Chi's vision is even more convincing:

Phantoms and spirits hoot on the altars of
    the state;
Jackals and tigers fight on the high
    balconies.

. . .

Fox and hare startled up lurking demons,
Amid the crazed screeching of vultures and
    owls.
Over deserted walls the winter sun sets,
Across the plain evening clouds yellow.

魂 神 吁 社 稷
豺 虎 鬥 巖 廊

狐 兔 驚 魍 魎
鴟 鴞 嚇 備 狂
空 城 寒 日 晚
平 野 暮 雲 黃

Green thorns burn in a wild blaze,
The wind blows mournfully through the
   poplars. . . .

[02641]

烈烈焚青棘
蕭蕭吹白楊

5

WANG CHI

During the age of court poetry the eremitic themes that
dominated the poetry of the late Wei and Chin dynasties
had all but disappeared: there was little room in the
elegant world of the court poet for the eccentric drinker,
the cantankerous hermit, and the self-sufficient farmer.
The confrontation between the independent hermit and the
refined aristocrat has been seen earlier in the poem by
T'ao Hung-ching.

The powerful but plain poetry of T'ao Ch'ien 陶潛
(365-427), now generally considered the finest poetry
before the T'ang, was not popular during the age of
court poetry. Yang Hsiu-chih 陽休之 (509-82) in his
"Preface to the Works of T'ao Ch'ien," wrote: "I have
looked over the writings of T'ao Ch'ien, and though
there is nothing outstanding in the elegance of his
diction, still there are surprises and marvellous phrases
throughout."[44] Yang apologizes for the lack of courtly
elegance and directs the reader to look out not for moving
simplicity and conviction of values but for "surprises
and marvellous phrases." Whatever his own opinion of
T'ao's work, Yang Hsiu-chih knew the aesthetic taste of
the readers of his own age.

In the early seventh century T'ao Ch'ien had a kindred
spirit in Wang Chi 王績 (585?-644). Wang turned away
from both the effete style of the court and the soporific
poetry of the opposition poetics to assume the role of
the drunken and eccentric poet-farmer, the role of T'ao
Ch'ien. Wang began state service as a "corrector of
characters" in Yang-ti's famous library, where he perhaps
met Yü Shih-nan. He soon quit this post, supposedly
because he found it boring. His biography in the official

histories says that he then took a minor county post,
whose duties he shamelessly neglected because of his
drinking. Up to this point his biography is relatively
consistent, but as is the case with so many poets of the
period, fact, legend, and role all obscure one another.
The Old T'ang History says that during the chaotic conditions at the end of the Sui, Wang Chi returned to his
farm and remained there some thirty years, living by his
own toil, without wife or children. It then goes on to
say that at the beginning of the T'ang he took a minor
post in the Chancellory, and following that, an even
lower post in the "Office of Sublime Music," supposedly
because of the wine-brewing talents of its director.
This second version of his life says that he quit office
and retired at the beginning of T'ai-tsung's reign (627).
Even in the unlikely event that Wang Chi went through
two offices in the preceding year (626), this thirty-year
retirement would have Wang quitting his post in Yang-ti's
library at the age of eleven, nine years before Yang-ti
ascended to the throne.

     As to Wang Chi's having no wife and children, we read
in the poem "Early Spring": "I called to my concubine by
the stove,/And told the news to my wife at her weaving"
(02606); and in "Sitting Alone":

My three sons have married into fine families,　三 男 婚 令 族
My five daughters have taken worthy husbands.　五 女 嫁 賢 夫
                              [02615]

It is best to assume that Wang Chi is being neither
overwhelmed by the model of T'ao Ch'ien nor deliberately
mendacious. He is certainly not simply iterating a
poetic convention: in court poetry mention of the family
was virtually taboo. Not only did Wang have a family,
he also served during the T'ang. This latter point can
be deduced from the fact that he has prose pieces to the

court poet Ch'en Shu-ta, given as his superior in the
Chancellory.[45]   Thus the version of his biography that
has him retiring for thirty years at the end of the Sui
is certainly pure fabrication, an attempt to fit the man
into the conventionalized role of the hermit.

Wang Chi's poetry is a unique phenomenon in his age
(if we discount the problematic collections of Han-shan
and Wang Fan-chih).   He possesses a simplicity of diction,
a directness of syntax, and a lack of ornament which are
like a fresh breeze in the rarified atmosphere of contemporary court poetry.   Wang Chi's peculiar manner, his
revision of T'ao Ch'ien, was to develop into one of the
most successful styles available to the poets of the
eighth century.   Only a few of his poems, such as
"Passing an Ancient City of the Han," fall into easily
recognizable contemporary poetic "types."

Wang Chi's poetry is filled with references to and
echoes of Juan Chi and T'ao Ch'ien.   Wang Chi saw a very
different Juan Chi than did Wei Cheng: to Wang, Juan
Chi was the eccentric who disdained public life, not the
historically minded moralist who lamented the decline of
the Wei Dynasty.   Both elements exist in Juan Chi's
poetry, and both versions were to be significant in later
T'ang poetry.   As Wang Chi admires Juan Chi and T'ao
Ch'ien, so those two poets wrote at length of their
admiration for the hermits of antiquity.   Yet there are
significant differences in the stance assumed by the
T'ang poet and those of the two older poets.   Juan Chi
and T'ao Ch'ien both assumed the role of the recluse,
but each had his individual version of that role; each
had his own specific concerns.   In their writings, Juan
and T'ao are anything but intellectually consistent, yet
they show a strong focal personality which united their
variations on the role of the recluse.   In Wang Chi we
find a fascination with the ethos of the late Wei and
Chin as much as with the role of the hermit.   Wang Chi

accepted the multiplicity of Wei and Chin eremitic themes
without qualification, without the least concern for the
contradictions between them. While Juan and T'ao sought
personal, ethical models, Wang Chi seems primarily
interested in capturing the mood or manner of a historical period and making it live in the present. In
this he shares his contemporaries' almost romantic
fascination with the past; this treatment of the past
was to grow through the seventh century and become one
of the dominant characteristics of T'ang poetry.

In his poems Wang Chi runs blithely through the gamut
of possible eremitic responses. In "Leaning on My Staff,
Seeking the Hermit" (02620), he compares himself (or
possibly the hermit in question) to Lü Shang, the minister
of Chou Wen-wang, who first met his prince while fishing;
the implication is that he lives a reclusive life, refusing to serve, because he is awaiting recognition by a
virtuous ruler. This was a popular excuse for not serving,
but on the other hand, Wang Chi evokes the Wei and Chin
scorn for Confucianism:

Music and Rites imprisoned the Duke of Chou, 禮樂囚姬旦
The Songs and Documents tied up Confucius. 詩書縛孔丘
[02613]

Wang can be the impassioned seeker after the secrets of
eternal life: "My wild nature lusts for the elixir pill"
(02607). He can just as easily reject the idea of
immortality in favor of the pleasures of the simple life:

I ask you, what more do I need 問君樽酒外
Than a flagon of wine, sitting alone . . . 獨坐更何須
My life will end as it is fated 百年隨分了
With no desire to mount the immortal isles. 未羨陟方壺
[02615]

Wang Chi is equally varied in his reasons for drinking.

On the one hand, he can use the venerable theme of true
sanity lying behind seeming insanity, an opposition to
the true insanity which lies behind the seeming sanity
of the world:

DROPPING BY THE TAVERN II 　　　　　　　過 酒 家 五 首 之 二

I spent the whole day in the muddle of drink,　此 日 長 昏 飲
And it wasn't to care for my "divine spark"—　非 關 養 性 靈
My own eyes saw everyone else was drunk,　　眼 看 人 盡 醉
So how could I bear to be sober alone.　　　何 忍 獨 爲 醒

                              [02625]

In the second line Wang rejects the notion that he affirms
elsewhere, that the spontaneous behavior achieved by
drinking was good for the soul. In other cases, drinking
can be a way to avoid awareness of impermanence:

DRUNK　　　　　　　　　　　　　　　　醉 後

Juan Chi was seldom sober,　　　　　　阮 籍 醒 時 少
Most days T'ao Ch'ien was drunk.　　　陶 潛 醉 日 多
How else can we pass the years of our lives　百 年 何 足 度
But by following our whims and long songs?　乘 興 且 長 歌

                              [02632]

Intellectual consistency was never the hallmark of the
Chinese poet. The literary tradition offered a variety
of roles and responses from which the poet could select;
he could use them and put them off again as suited his
fancy and his personal needs. In court poetry the
variety of roles and responses was severely limited,
and the potential for originality within them was greatly
depleted. Poetry was no longer performing the creative
and psychological functions it was supposed to perform.
Wang Chi's solution of searching in the poetry of the
past for new roles and responses was essentially the
same as Wei Cheng's and Li Pai-yao's; Wang's personality

simply directed him to a different kind of past poetry.
To see Wang Chi's poetry as merely "natural" is to
misunderstand him: his spontaneity is articulated through
the model of T'ao Ch'ien and against the backdrop of
court poetry.

   Wang Chi is not an "imitator" even in the sense of
some eighth- and ninth-century poets who tried to rewrite
some of T'ao Ch'ien's poems. Rather the model of T'ao
Ch'ien was a means for renewal; it was an open model.
Throughout Wang Chi's poetry we sense a genuine delight
in the physical world, as though its beauty had just
been revealed to him. The arrival of spring, a hackneyed
theme in court poetry, can seem like a total surprise to
Wang Chi.

EARLY SPRING   初春

The last morning I went out to walk in the
   garden
There wasn't a flower in the whole grove,
But today at dawn when I came down from the
   hall and looked,
The pond ice had been broken up for quite
   some time.
Snow fled from the plum trees by the south
   porch,
Winds hurried the willows in the north yard.
I called to my concubine by the stove
And told the news to my wife at her weaving:
The season has come just at the right time—
Let's get busy on the spring wine that fills
   the jugs.

前旦出園遊
林華都未有
今朝下堂望
池冰開已久
雪避南軒梅
風催北庭柳
遲呼竈前妾
卻報機中婦
年光恰恰來
滿甕營春酒

                    [02606]

Framed in the middle of this relaxed, unconventional poem
is the third couplet—parallel, descriptive, and using
cleverly metaphorical verbs in the second position. Though
it would have fitted comfortably in a court banquet poem,
it does not seem out of place here.

The eremitic poet was always in danger of being confused with the Neo-Taoist poet and the quest for immortality. At times Wang Chi is careful to dissociate the two, choosing the lazy, physical life of this world instead of the quest for immortality.

FARMERS I

All his life Juan Chi was lazy,
And Hsi K'ang was a carefree spirit.
When they met, they drank their fill,
Sat alone, wrote a few lines,
Tried raising cranes by a tiny pool,
Pastured piglets in tranquil fields.
Grass grew over T'ao Ch'ien's path,
Flowering trees hid Yang Hsiung's
  cottage.
Lie on your bed, watch your wife
  weave,
Up a hill and urge your son to hoe—
Then turn your head and the quests for
  the immortals
Become all one great emptiness.

[02598]

田家三首之一
阮籍生涯懶疏
嵇康意氣飽書
相逢一醉行養鶴
獨坐池聊且牧豬
閒田生元亮徑居
草花暗林雲婦織
倚壠課兒鋤
登頭尋仙事
迴是一空虛

Elsewhere in Wang Chi's work, he can evoke a strong sense of Taoist nihilism, as in the following tantalizing fragment, which has an abstract strength rare in Chinese poetry:

I sent my body a thousand years into the
  past
To stroll for a while at the beginning of
  of all things.
I was about to command that Nothing turn
  into Being,
But then realized how substance becomes
  Nothingness.[46]

寄身千載下
聊遊萬物初
欲令無作有
翻覺實成虛

If it seems paradoxical that a man who could delight so

much in the arrival of spring would also threaten to stop
the very force of creation, we should remember that the
thread which unifies Wang Chi's poetry is essentially
negative. Like the opposition poetics, Wang Chi's poetry
is a counterstatement to the aristocratic and worldly
glory of court poetry. If their poetry is formalized,
he seeks spontaneity; if they react blandly to spring's
arrival, he reacts to it with boisterous enthusiasm; if
they delight in physical beauty, he calmly declines to
set the process of creation into motion. His counter-
statements to court poetry may be drunkenness, pastoralism,
or Taoist nihilism, but all these responses may be defined
in negative relation to court poetry and the aristocratic
society that produced it.

    Wang Chi does seem to have been something of an
alcoholic, and his obsession with wine surpasses even
that of T'ao Ch'ien. Chinese poets were usually less
interested in the wine itself than in their vision of
themselves drunk. Wang Chi is no exception, but in
addition to the conventional self-image of drunken freedom
Wang Chi enjoys contemplating himself in a helpless stupor:

Only when propped against the tavern can I get   倚鑪便得睡
　　some rest,
Or lying across a jug can I get some sleep.   橫甕足堪眠

                        [02627]

Wang is at his best in poems on drinking:

DROPPING BY THE TAVERN I   過酒家五首之一

I've got no mansion in Lo-yang   洛陽無大宅
And lack a patron in Ch'ang-an,   長安乏主人
So if my gold isn't all spent yet,   黃金銷未盡
It's because this tavern is so cheap.   祇為酒家貧
                        [02624]

DROPPING BY THE TAVERN V   過 酒 家 五 首 之 五

If I have a guest, I make him drink;   有 客 須 教 飲
If I've got no money, I get it another   無 錢 可 別 沽
   way.
I come in, say "Put in on my bill!"   來 時 長 道 賒
Embarrassing the Turk who runs the   慚 愧 酒 家 胡
   tavern.

                 [02628]

WRITTEN ON THE TAVERN WALL   題 酒 店 壁

Last night a jar was emptied,   昨 夜 瓶 始 盡
This morning a new jug opened.   今 朝 甕 即 開
In dream I foresaw that the dream would end, 夢 中 占 夢 罷
And I would come back to the tavern.   還 向 酒 家 來

                 [02633]

DRINKING ALONE   獨 酌

How long can this floating life last?   浮 生 知 幾 日
A formless creature chasing empty glory.   無 狀 逐 空 名
Better to brew a lot of wine,   不 如 多 釀 酒
To tip your cup often in a bamboo grove.   時 向 竹 林 傾

                 [02636]

All of these poems show a sequential, almost narrative
unity which is rare in court poetry. One line is a cause
or an antecedent condition for the next. The structure
of a well-written court poem is quite different, amplifying its theme almost synchronically.

    In the six poems entitled "Ancient Theme," ku-yi 古意,
Wang Chi assumes quite a different stance than he does
in his wine poems. These are philosophical and moral
pieces, thematically and stylistically close to some of
Juan Chi's Yung-huai, "Singing My Feelings." Wang Chi's
"Ancient Themes" are even closer to Ch'en Tzu-ang's
Kan-yü 感遇, "Stirred by My Experiences," written some
fifty or more years later. These poems of Ch'en Tzu-ang

are often taken as the beginning of the High T'ang style,
as a rejection of court poetry, and as an expression of
that poet's fu-ku sentiments. The predominant philosophical orientation in all three series—"Singing My Feelings,"
"Ancient Themes," and "Stirred by My Experiences"—is
Taoist. But Ch'en Tzu-ang's series, read in the context
of his fu-ku polemics, was to be remembered and have a
lasting influence on T'ang poetry. Wang Chi's series was
forgotten as were most of the poems written in response
to the opposition poetics of the Sui. Perhaps "Ancient
Themes" was not as aesthetically satisfying as "Stirred
by My Experiences," but probably the real reason for
their failure is that they were written in isolation at
the wrong moment in the history of Chinese poetry.

I will quote the fifth poem of the series; its style
is consciously simple and graceless, and its philosophical
message is explicit.

This cassia tree, so rich and green,
Flowers still more fragrantly as autumn comes.
It's claimed that its nature, enduring the
  cold,
Knows nothing of the dew and frosts.
The recluse honors this power it has,
And plants them before his hall.
Eight or nine trees, sinuously bending,
Two or three rows, thrusting skyward.
Branch twines itself around branch,
Every leaf stays face to face.
There a pair of geese come and go,
Two mandarin ducks also roosting:
It's not because the flowering shade is
  dense,
But because no axe will ever harm it.
When, with loyal heart, I promise to serve
  my lord,
How can I forget the lesson given by these?
[02595]

桂樹何蒼蒼
秋來花更芳
自言歲寒性
不知露與霜
幽人重其德
待植臨前堂
連蜷八九樹
偃蹇二三行
枝枝自相斜
葉葉自相當
去來雙鴻鵾
栖息兩鴛鷟
蕊蔭誠不厚
斤斧亦勿傷
丹心許君時
此意那可忘

The cassia tree is a traditional symbol of moral rectitude
and endurance of hardship, flowering and nurturing itself
in seclusion. Though the "lesson" is not to be forgotten,
it is not at all clear whether the lesson is perfect
loyalty or avoiding the "axe" by remaining in seclusion.
If we compare this poem to the poems on bamboo by T'ai-
tsung and Yü Shih-nan, we can see how artless the descriptive style is here.

   One of Wang Chi's most famous poems is a strange and
beautiful regulated verse with a restrained dignity
entirely uncharacteristic of Wang Chi's other poetry.
"Plucking bracken" in the last line refers to the story
of the hermits Po Yi and Shu Ch'i, who refused to serve
the newly founded Chou dynasty and instead retired to the
hills, eating bracken until they starved to death.   In
this case, the allusion suggests eremitic purity rather
than political criticism.

VIEW OF THE WILDS   野望

Toward evening on East Hill gazing,   東皋薄暮望
Hesitant, uncertain, nothing to depend on. 徙倚欲何依
On tree after tree, the colors of autumn, 樹樹皆秋色
On mountain after mountain, radiance of   山山唯落暉
  setting sun.
The herdsman turns back, driving his calves, 牧人驅犢返
The hunter's horse returns, bearing a bird. 獵馬帶禽歸
I look at them; I do not know them.   相顧無相識
A long song and a yearning to "pluck the   長歌懷采薇
  bracken."

                    [02612]

The subtle and enigmatic juxtapositions here put this
poem well ahead of its time. The poet climbs a high place
and faces a world of autumn, of old age and decline. The
tranquil, pastoral figures in the third couplet, beginning
their symbolic "return," are entirely in harmony with the
peaceful scene, but even here the poet does not belong.

The seventh line powerfully expresses the poet's aliena-
tion from the scene, the isolation of someone who is
out of place in human society, of someone who has no
place to which to "return."

6

SHANG-KUAN YI

As the generation of poets who had reached their maturity
during the Sui gradually died away, there seems to have
been a resurgence of court poetry. For a few decades in
the mid-seventh century we find no <u>fu-ku</u> declarations
and no poetic endeavors to realize the opposition poetics.
This period of court poetry is represented by the work of
Shang-kuan Yi 上官儀(608-64). Judging from his twenty
surviving poems, Shang-kuan Yi is entirely within the
courtly tradition, but his wit and refinement earned him
the honor of being the first T'ang poet to have a style
named after him, the <u>Shang-kuan t'i</u> 上官體 , the "Shang-
kuan style."[47] His poetry was widely imitated, and it
is said that T'ai-tsung depended on him to polish up
imperial infelicities.

In Shang-kuan Yi's poetry we see the reassertion of
court poetry's primary function, that of celebration.
The moral tone that appears in many of the poets of the
preceding generation is altogether absent in Shang-kuan
Yi; he does not even affect the compromise between the
opposition poetics and court poetry that we saw in Yü
Shih-nan. The reasons for this are uncertain: for one
thing, Shang-kuan Yi reached his maturity in the T'ang,
and the opposition poetics was associated primarily with
the Sui; yet another reason may be that in his later
years T'ai-tsung grew increasingly autocratic and less
receptive to criticism.

Shang-kuan Yi first served in the government as an
auxiliary scholar in the College for the Development of
Literature (formerly the College for Literature). Because
of his age, his entry could not have been earlier than the
630s. It was probably there that Shang-kuan Yi was

initiated into the subtleties of court poetry. His style
closely resembles that of one of the older, regular
scholars, Hsü Ching-tsung, whom we have mentioned earlier.
Hsü's poetry is equally ornate and devoid of ethical
concerns, but he lacked Shang-kuan Yi's talent; what is
celebration in Shang-kuan Yi's poetry is in Hsü Ching-
tsung's work mere obsequiousness. Ironically, these two
poets whose styles are so similar were members of opposing court factions during Kao-tsung's reign. Hsü's name
is held in infamy by traditional historians for his
support of Empress Wu and his machinations to bring down
the statesman Chang-sun Wu-chi. Shang-kuan Yi, as we
shall see, lost his life by being on the other side.

   Transferred to a post in the Imperial Library during
T'ai-tsung's reign, Shang-kuan Yi rose to be under-director
in the reign of Kao-tsung. Once, Kao-tsung took it in
mind to depose the powerful Empress Wu and summoned
Shang-kuan Yi to draft the edict. The empress, however,
got wind of the affair and confronted Kao-tsung. Kao-
tsung characteristically backed down and blamed everything
on Shang-kuan Yi. He and most of his family were executed.
For his part in this incident Shang-kuan Yi has received
favorable notices in the official histories, but this
should not obscure the fact that he was no moralist,
having yielded to the autocratic tendencies of the age
that sense of moral responsibility to the state which a
poet was supposed to feel.

   The following piece (02707) is characteristic not
only of Shang-kuan Yi's work but also of the courtly
banquet poem at its most gracious.

EARLY SPRING IN K'UEI-LIN HALL: TO COMMAND 　早春桂林殿應詔

The pacing palanquin emerges from Pi-hsiang
    Palace;　步輦出披香
Clear singing looks down on T'ai-yeh Pool.　清歌臨太液
Morning trees with warbling orioles filled,　曉樹流鶯滿

Spring slopes with fragrant plants swelling.   春 堤 芳 草 積
Scene's radiance spread out on dew's traceries,   風 光 翻 露 文
Blossom-flakes of snow rise on the sky's emerald.   雪 華 上 空 碧
Flowers and butterflies had not stopped coming,   花 蝶 來 未 已
When the mountain light darkened toward evening.   山 光 曖 將 夕

We have mentioned the first couplet of this poem earlier
when discussing the general conventions of court poetry.
The tripartite form is followed perfectly, with the
conventional banquet poem closing which suggests the
possibility of continued pleasure prevented by the
necessity of returning home in the evening.

Shang-kuan Yi's talents appear most clearly in his
handling of parallel couplet. Indeed, traditionally he
is credited with a sixfold and an eightfold classification of parallelism.[48] The third couplet of the poem
above is an excellent example of his overripe courtly
wit. The poet sees the radiance of spring, its traditional attribute, or perhaps the spring scene itself as
a flashing reflection on the drops of dew. The snowflakes
(literally "snow flowers") are blown upward, as though
falling back to the emerald green sky that gave them
birth, much as a real flower falls to earth. It is the
court poet's special art to pick out the unique "wonders,"
ch'i 奇, of the natural scene.

Shang-kuan Yi's poetry at times shows a sensitivity
to the minutiae of nature and the subtle relations between
elements of the visual scene. The master craftsman can
observe and describe them, but he cannot give them depth
in the context of the poem as a whole as the greatest
High T'ang poets could. Even in the pitifully few poems
that survive we can see the artfulness for which he was
admired in couplets like:

Falling leaves flutter cicada shadows   落 葉 飄 蟬 影
The level stream sketches the lines of geese.   平 流 寫 雁 行
                        [02722]

A sense of the fragility of autumn things is captured
here with consumate artistry. Two symbols of autumn,
cicadas and falling leaves, are mingled and each is
potentially a metaphor for the other. We do not know
whether the falling leaves (or their shadows) flutter
like the shadows of cicadas, whether the cicadas (or
their shadows) flutter like falling leaves, or whether
the real leaves flutter past the shadows of cicadas.
The potential for mutual metaphor as well as for direct
description stresses the unity between the two things,
as well as a sense of the tininess, helplessness, and
insecurity which are part of the vision of autumn. The
second line of the couplet echoes the theme of impermanence in the flowing stream and the southward passage
of the geese. Since the two lines must be read in parallel,
the second line should suggest that the nonmetaphorical
description is the dominant interpretation, though
both metaphorical interpretations are possible.

Another line of particular beauty (ironically preserved to illustrate a stylistic fault) is: "Green
mountains cage the snow-flowers (flakes)" 青山籠雪花 .[49]
The scene is early spring, and the immense, solid vitality
of the mountains seeming to imprison the fragile snowflakes.

Though Shang-kuan Yi is best known as a court poet,
it is not surprising that his finest lines were not
written to imperial command. The following fragment
(02723) was written during Kao-tsung's reign and shows
some of the vitality that characterizes the poets of
the 660s and 670s.[50] It draws from court poetry the
unwillingness of the poet to intrude his emotions into
the scene, but looks forward to later poetry in its
ability to create a whole scene, a panorama, rather
than a fragmented world of minutae.

Shang-kuan Yi

Silent I gaze, the broad stream flows,

I gallop my horse past the long sandbars.

Magpies fly past the mountain moon in
    dawnlight,

And cicadas chirp in the autumn wind of
    the wilds.

脈脈廣川流
驅馬歷長洲
鵲飛山月曙
蟬噪野風秋

PART TWO

AWAY FROM COURT POETRY: THE 660S AND 670S

7

THE FOUR TALENTS OF THE EARLY T'ANG

It was in the first year of the Lung-shuo Reign [661] that there
was a change in style in the world of letters. Then they were
competing to construct the delicate and subtle, vying to make
the ornamented and the crafted, confounding the gold and the
jade, the dragon and phoenix, confusing vermilion and purple,
yellow and green, copying each other in their greed for great
merit, artificing parallelisms to proclaim the loveliness of
their craft. Informing point and spirit were utterly gone;
strength and subtleness unheard of.

Yet yearning to excise these faults that they might bring
glory to the deeds of their ambition were Hsüeh Yüan-chao of
the Secretariat, the elder man of letters in court, who formed
friendships with his juniors and urged this total change, and
Lu Chao-lin, a genius in the ordinary world, who observed the
true pattern and brought a halt to those activities man should
strive against.

Those who understood literature joined them; those who understood the men themselves followed them. Thereupon, they set
their minds drumming and dancing, put forth their usefulness,
so that all within the eight points of the compass gathered
headlong through their thoughts, while myriad ages appeared and
disappeared under the tips of their brushes. . . . And in these
mighty mirrors men found the hegemons of letters, powerful but
not empty, strong yet able to enrich, ornamented but not precious,
stable and growing ever sturdier. . . . And as when, shaken by
the constant wind, the multitude of fine sprouts bend to it
naturally, so they moved the hosts of shallow artists, who came
to lack even the security of a hedge, and the profusion of lesser
talents, who came to lose their fastnesses of metal walls and
moats of boiling water. In but a single morning the filagree
preciousness of many years was swept clear and open, spacious

79

was the garden of brushes, and the forest of fine phrases grew
ever more imposing.

Yang Chiung, "Preface to the Collected Works of Wang Po"[1]

Yang, Wang, Lu, and Lo—the style of that
age—   楊王盧駱當時體

"Not serious in their writing"—the sneering   輕薄為文哂未休
never stops.

But you who sneer, your bodies and names will   爾曹身與名俱滅
fade away altogether,

Without stopping the great river that flows   不廢江河萬古流
on forever.

Tu Fu, second "Playful Quatrain" [11229]

Like many others before and after him during the Sui
and Early T'ang, Yang Chiung proudly proclaimed the great
literary reformation, dating it precisely in the year
661.   Even so, by the mid-eighth century the only voice
raised in defense of the Early T'ang was that of Tu Fu,
a long time admirer of court poetry.   Although Tu Fu's
quatrain is polemical rather than a balanced evaluation
of their merits, to him the "Four Talents of the Early
T'ang" are the great river and as such will outlast
their detractors.   But even though he maintains insistently that the "Four Talents" are superior to his
contemporaries, in the third of his "Playful Quatrains"
(11230) Tu Fu bows to the conventions of fu-ku literary
history, that the "Four Talents" are inferior to the
poetry of the Han and Wei, which is closer to the ancient
poetry of the Shih-ching and the Ch'u-tz'u.   Tu Fu under-
estimated the influence of his contemporaries: to this
day the quatrain of Tu Fu's that is quoted above is more
famous than any poem by the "Four Talents of the Early
T'ang."

Yang, Wang, Lu, and Lo—Yang Chiung 楊烱, Wang Po ·
王勃, Lu Chao-lin 盧照鄰, and Lo Pin-wang 駱賓王 —
were grouped together as the "Four Talents of the Early

T'ang" 初唐四傑 by the first decade of the eighth century,
though the source claims that the name is earlier.[2] The
real bond among the four writers is their parallel prose
style rather than their poetry, but because of the traditional grouping, their poetry is usually represented
as a homogeneous style. Although there were contacts
between individuals of the four at various times, they
never seem to have been all together at any one place at
any one time. Furthermore, as the modern scholar Wen
I-to points out, they belong to two distinct generations,
Lu Chao-lin and Lo Pin-wang being older than Wang Po and
Yang Chiung. Three met tragic deaths; one, Yang Chiung,
led a relatively stable life as a court poet of Empress
Wu. Two, Wang Po and Lu Chao-lin, moved toward a simplification of the courtly style in their poetry. At
the other extreme, Lo Pin-wang's poetry moved toward
ornamental periphrasis and learned allusion; this excess
of figuration was as alien to the realm of court poetry
as the more personal poetry of Lu and Wang. Though he
wrote a number of excellent poems, Yang Chiung never
really found his own poetic voice, and because much of
his work is indistinguishable from that of his fellow
courtiers, we will not consider it here. All but Yang
Chiung did most of their work in the 660s and 670s when
Empress Wu was wresting power from the weak and uxorious
Kao-tsung.

   Although Lu Chao-lin, Lo Pin-wang, and Wang Po all
were connected with the court at some period in their
lives, it is no accident that they did their most characteristic work when separated from the court. With
the exception of Wang Chi they were the first major
literary figures in many centuries to achieve widespread
poetic fame through essentially private compositions.
Even Yang Chiung, in the preface quoted above, speaks
of Lu Chao-lin's fame as "a genius in the ordinary world"
（人間才傑）, in contrast to Hsüeh Yüan-chao, the courtier.

Wang Chi's renown was less widespread and more due to his eccentric character than to his literary oeuvre. Because of the tremendous conservatism of court poetry, dissociation from the court seems to have been necessary for poetry to find a new direction.

8

LU CHAO-LIN: THE FAILURE OF COURT POETRY

Among the poets who moved away from the decorous world
of court poetry in the 660s and 670s, Lu Chao-lin's
transformation was the most dramatic. In his public
occasional poetry he was a competent practitioner of
the graceful Shang-kuan style, but by the end of his
life he was writing bitter, exclamatory lyrics of a man
unbalanced by disease. Like his junior, Wang Po, Lu's
departure from the courtly style did not occur through
any general change of taste; judging from his treatment
of the highly conventional Southern Dynasties' yüeh-fu
themes, he seems to have had an inherent urge to complicate the traditional responses. However, the primary
impetus to his revision of the courtly style were
experiences whose pain and complexity could find no
place in the stately conventions of aristocratic verse.

Lu Chao-lin was from Fan-yang in the far northeast,
a region which was later to be the base of the rebel An
Lu-shan and the home of the Mid-T'ang poet Chia Tao.
Though his family was not as nationally prominent as that
of Wang Po, it was one of the great elite families of the
northeast. In his youth Lu studied with two eminent
scholars who had retired from the court of T'ai-tsung
and later became a favorite in the entourage of a T'ang
prince. For reasons that are not altogether clear in
669 he was transferred to the low post of "subprefectural
manager" in Hsin-tu, Ch'eng-tu, the cultural center of
the Szechwan region.

In 673 we find him again in Ch'ang-an, sick. After
moving from place to place, eventually both feet and one
hand were paralyzed. It was probably at this point that
he bought a small estate in Ho-nan where he lived out

his remaining years. It is said that finally, unable to
bear the pain of his disease any longer, he committed
suicide by drowning himself in the Ying River. His dates
are uncertain, but we may set them tentatively at 634-84.[3]
As with the other "Four Talents" his collected works
survive independently of the anthologies. There remain
just over a hundred poems, including ritual songs, heptasyllabic ballads, formal occasional poems, travel
poems, Ch'u songs, and yüeh-fu. These represent the
full topical range of Early T'ang poetry, with the
notable exception of court poems proper.

It is impossible to date any of Lu Chao-lin's poems
before his demotion to Szechwan. If, as Yang Chiung
claims, he was a central figure in a literary reformation
of 661, it is not apparent in his works. Lu's formal
occasional poetry after his return from Szechwan shows
him an able, but undistinguished follower of Shang-kuan
Yi, a master of the elder poet's powers of description
if not his ingenuity. In this case it is the subgenre
rather than the date that makes the style, and it would
be difficult to imagine Lu writing formal occasional
poetry in any other style before his exile. In fact, it
was probably Yang Chiung's affiliation with Empress Wu
that caused him to set the great literary reformation
in 661; Lu himself set the reformation at the beginning
of the T'ang, consonant with his political associations.[4]
There was a strong tendency to·use literary history and
the dating of the great literary reformation as an
affirmation of dynastic loyalties rather than as an
independent literary historical judgment. However,
these purely political motives could rebound on poets,
who might feel that some change should be manifest.

There is a charm in Lu's formal occasional poetry,
but it is the charm of court poetry, which admits no
individual personality. Lu's "Third Month Banquet by
the Meandering River: to the set rhyme tsun" (02747)

closes:

Over stretches of sand the white terns fly,　　連 沙 飛 白 鷺
And on lonely isles black gibbons shrill.　　孤 嶼 嘯 玄 猿
Sun-cast shadows fall before peaks,　　日 影 巖 前 落
Cloud flowers roll upon the river.　　雲 花 江 上 翻
Then, our pleasure over, horses and carriages scatter,　　興 闌 車 馬 散
As evening birds babble by forest pools.　　林 塘 夕 鳥 喧

One should not be surprised to find earlier in this poem
the line: "The way of the Odes survives again today"
雅 道 今 復 存 . Like similar lines in T'ai-tsung's "The
Imperial Capital," this bow to the opposition poetics
is not a serious comment on the style of the poem, and
in this case is assimilated as an additional compliment
to one's host and fellow poets. In the passage above Lu
follows the conventions of the banquet poem, building up
the evening scene before announcing the close of the
banquet: birds return to their roosts for the night, and
the peaks cast long shadows. The closing couplet re-
arranges elements that appear time and again in the last
couplets of banquet poems. To cite just two examples,
Shang-kuan Yi has:

Now I regret that our flowing goblets are full—　　方 惜 流 觴 滿
Evening birds have left the city gates.　　夕 鳥 去 城 闈
[02708]

and Li Pai-yao has:

As the sun slants down homeward riders move,　　日 斜 歸 騎 動
But our lingering pleasure fills the mountains and streams.　　餘 興 滿 山 川
[02847]

It is appropriate to mention the evening birds, the
pleasure (hsing 興) of the guests, and the departure of

the horses and carriages.

Lu Chao-lin was quite capable of writing sparse and convincing eremitic poetry; however, under the influence of the courtly style demanded in formal occasional poems, even this theme can become incongruously bejeweled.

TO THE RHYMES OF "A SUMMER DAY IN MY MOUNTAIN VILLA"[5]

和 夏 日 山 莊

On those idle days in the Orchid Office

蘭 署 棃 閒 日

You are wont to hide away behind your rustic gate.

蓬 扉 狎 遁 棲

There dragonlike boughs grow bare over the jade well

龍 柯 疏 玉 井

And phoenix leaves descend upon the gold-fast bastion.

鳳 葉 下 金 堤

Light on the stream shakes arrows through the water,

川 光 搖 水 箭

Mountain mists raise ladders into the clouds.

山 氣 上 雲 梯

When the pavilion is secluded, hear the cry of the crane;

亭 幽 聞 唳 鶴

Dawn breaks through the window, listen to the rooster's crow.

窗 曉 聽 鳴 雞

Jade carriages advance into the winds,

玉 軿 臨 風 奏

Marble broths are carried, reflecting moonlight,

瓊 漿 映 月 攜

Farmers indeed have their own private joys—

田 家 自 有 樂

Who would willingly leave this blue creek?

誰 肯 謝 青 溪

[02800]

When Lu wishes to compliment this unknown official of the Imperial Library as an exemplary recluse-farmer, the "jade carriages" and "marble broths" which he summons up rest uneasily beside the closing affirmation of his simple pleasures. The last line is probably an echo of Kuo P'u's 郭璞 second "Poem on the Wandering Immortals" 遊仙詩 : "The valley of blue creek, a thousand yards deep and more, / Therein is a single Taoist" 青谿千餘仞, 中有一道士 .[6] Our protean farmer-recluse-immortal-courtier of Lu Chao-lin's poem lives in a different poetic world from that of T'ao Ch'ien or Wang Chi.

    Such ornate graciousness faded quickly as Lu Chao-lin set off for exile in Szechwan. The narrative of personal experience was already a subgenre with its own conventions, and the real hardships of the journey to Shu (Szechwan) was a yüeh-fu theme; even so, in poems like the following there is a credible starkness and power that rises above the conventions of the subgenre. Such exile-travel poems were later to play an important role in the breakup of the Early T'ang style during the first decade of the eighth century.

MORNING: CROSSING THE WATERSHED

早度分水嶺

In the years of my prime I wander the roads
  to Shu,

丁年遊蜀道

Hair streaked with white, I face toward
  Ch'ang-an.

班鬢向長安

I have wasted the rice of the King of Chou,

徒賣周王粟

Aimlessly dusted the cap of the servant of
  Han.

空彈漢臣冠

My horse's hooves, almost gouged away,

馬蹄穿欲盡

Sable cape turned to tatters and ever colder.

貂裘敝轉寒

Layers of ice stretch across the coiling roads,

層冰橫九折

Heaps of stone rise over the twists and turns.

積石凌七蟠

I have gone down to drink from stream after
  stream,

重溪既下漱

And have crossed up over the jutting peaks.

峻峯亦上干

Then I've heard the drums from the Lung-t'ou
  forts,

隴頭聞戍鼓

And the moaning cascades from southern ranges.

嶺外咽飛湍

Rustling now, the wind grows faster in the
  pines,

瑟瑟松風急

Then the mountain moon, round in the dark,
  dark sky.

蒼蒼山月團

I send these words back to those who shall
  follow—

傳語後來者

These roads are hard indeed, like no others.

斯路誠獨難

[02746]

To "waste" the King of Chou's rice is polite self-depreca-
tion: the poet has received a salary without being competent enough to perform his duties. To "dust the cap"
is a cliché meaning to retire from office; from what we
know about Lu Chao-lin's life—admittedly not much—he
did not retire from office at this point. Either he is
treating his humiliating transfer-exile as a "retirement,"
or he actually did retire and took the minor post of
"subprefectural manager" only later, perhaps as a means
of subsistence.

Though the differences between this poem and the
preceding one should be apparent, there remain some
fundamental similarities between the technique of this
poem and that of court poetry. The tripartite form of
introduction, description, and emotional response remains
constant. The opening couplet of a poem on an imperial
outing will often oppose starting point to destination;
for example, Shang-kuan Yi's "Early Spring in K'uei-lin
Palace: to command" (02707):

The pacing palanquin emerges from P'i-hsiang   步輦出祇香
  Palace.
Clear singing looks down on T'ai-yeh Pool.   清歌臨太液

Lu Chao-lin properly mentions his starting point and
destination in the opening couplet, but wanting to focus
attention on the starting point, Ch'ang-an, he inverts
the order. The closing response of Lu's poems borrows
conventions from the yüeh-fu "Hard Roads to Shu" 蜀道難 .
A contemporary of Lu's, Chang Wen-tsung 張文琮, , closed
his version of the ballad:

Alone I clasp my bridle, heave a long sigh,   攬轡獨長息
Now knowing these roads are hard indeed!   方知斯路難
                    [02701]

Li Po 李白 was to use the same convention in his famous

version of "Hard Roads to Shu":

The hardships of the roads to Shu are
   harder than scaling the blue skies,　　蜀道之難難於上青天

I lean my body, gaze westward, and　　　側身西望長咨嗟
   heave a long sigh.

[07926]

One need only compare Lu Chao-lin's poem and Li Po's
ballad to see how much more energetic a High T'ang
treatment of the theme could be.[7]

   Framed between the opening, which sets the limits of
the journey and its ostensible motives, and the closing
emotional response are the parallel descriptive couplets.
These couplets are the new wine in old jars—stark,
personal situations treated with the perfect, almost
monotonous symmetry of the court poet's craft. The
uneasy intrusion of ugly reality into this highly controlled artistry finds an emblem in the sable cape, mark
of wealth and power, turning to tatters from the hardships of travel. Such juxtaposition of extremes is part
of a larger fascination with ironic twists which characterizes Lu Chao-lin's poetry as a whole. This goes against
a primary requirement of court poetry, harmonious decorum.
Even as he obeys the unwritten rule to set the limits of
his journey in his opening couplet, he notes the incon-
gruities of his situation: he is "in his prime," yet his
hair is already "streaked with white."

   The bulk of Lu Chao-lin's poetry dates from his
residence in Szechwan. The following huai-ku is a
regulated verse in all but tone pattern: it has the
length and structure of a regulated verse, and the
parallel couplets are in the correct places. It is
surely a mistake to see regulated verse as a fixed form
in the seventh century; rather, it is an unconscious
ideal toward which a large number of "imperfect" versions
tend. The "imperfect" as well as the perfect regulated

verse had been very much associated with formal court
poetry. Lu, like his fellow exile Wang Po, was one of
the first to use it for genuinely personal ends. The
style becomes more straightforward, the argument more
unified, and the themes different.

SSU-MA HSIANG-JU'S LUTE TERRACE

I have heard of a soft and gentle land,

For a thousand years none dwell nearby.

In its groves and gardens, windblown mists of
the past,

By pool and terrace the pines and shrubs turn
spring.

Clouds seem the poet composing his _fu_,

The moon like his lady, listening to the lute.

Silent now where the orioles are singing—

A helpless pain to the wanderer's soul.

[02781]

相如琴臺
聞有雍容地
千年無四鄰
園院風煙古
池臺松槚春
雲疑作賦客
月似聽琴人
寂寂啼鶯處
空傷遊子神

Ssu-ma Hsiang-ju 司馬相如 , a native of Szechwan and the
most famous _fu_ poet of the Han dynasty, eloped with Cho
Wen-chün, the daughter of a wealthy merchant. Lu Chao-
lin, visiting a site associated with these famous lovers,
here indulges in a meditation on the continuity of nature
set against the impermanence of man. The mists, the
evergreen trees and shrubs (which are associated with
tombs), and the songs of the birds are the same as ever;
indeed Nature seems to mimic the forms of the ancient
lovers, and the present songs of the orioles remind the
poet of the silence of Ssu-ma Hsiang-ju's lute. The
total effect of the poem up to the last line is character-
ristically T'ang—understated, unornamented, and evocative
—but the closure reverts to the direct statement of
emotion of earlier meditative poetry.

   Living in Szechwan a hundred years later, Tu Fu
visited the Lute Terrace and, like Lu Chao-lin, composed
the following huai-ku to commemorate the occasion. Note

that the last two couplets of Tu Fu's poem closely echo
the corresponding couplets of Lu Chao-lin's version, but
that Tu Fu has gotten rid of the primitive "it makes me
sad" closing response.

THE LUTE TERRACE

琴臺

After his great sickness at Mao-ling
And still in love with Cho Wen-chün,
There was his wineshop in the world of men
And the lute terrace among the sunset clouds.
Her beauty marks are kept on in the wildflowers,
And in the vines can be seen her skirts of
    gauze.
But the theme of phoenix seeking his mate
Is no longer heard in the vast, empty expanse.

茂陵多病後
尚愛卓文君
酒肆人間世
琴臺日暮雲
野花留寶靨
蔓草見羅裙
歸鳳求皇意
寥寥不復聞

                [11159]

The last couplet refers to an allegorical love poem then
attributed to Ssu-ma Hsiang-ju.

    During the last years of his life, Lu Chao-lin seems
to have written very little poetry. Among the most
interesting of his last poems are three songs in the
Ch'u style appended to parts of a remarkable piece of
poetic prose, "Release from Sickness" 釋疾文 . Songs
in the Ch'u style were strongly associated with an
exclamatory emotionalism that stood diametrically
opposed to the restraint of court poetry. In Lu Chao-
lin's short lyrics this generic mode is heightened by a
sense of madness, real or feigned, which makes them
extraordinary productions for their age. The following
is the third of the set.

There is bracken on Tz'u Mountain, there
    are ripples in the Ying,
Po Yi is the cypress that bears its
    cones in autumn,
Shu Ch'i is the willow that flies in
    the spring rain.

茨山有薇兮穎水有漪
夷為柏兮秋有實
叔為柳兮春雨飛

Suddenly laughter—float off at Ts'ang-lang and never return. 倏爾而笑 汎滄浪兮不歸

[02769]

Po Yi and Shu Ch'i were the two exemplary recluses of antiquity mentioned earlier. When the Chou dynasty conquered the Shang, Po and Shu retired to the mountain as an act of political protest, "refusing to eat the rice of Chou." Instead they ate bracken and eventually starved to death. It is quite possible that Lu's reference to these two figures was intended as a slur against Empress Wu, who had total control of the government during the last years of Lu's life. It might further suggest that Lu was contemplating suicide as an act of political protest rather than as an escape from the pain of his disease; however, there is no way to verify this.

The Ts'ang-lang of line four is associated with the famous song of antiquity:

When the waters of Ts'ang-lang are clear, 滄浪之水清兮
I can wash my hat ribbons; 可以濯吾纓
When the waters of Ts'ang-lang are dirty, 滄浪之水濁兮
I can wash my feet. 可以濯吾足

Though the song appears elsewhere in early literature, Lu Chao-lin is here referring to the context of its use in "The Fisherman" 漁父, a narrative poem in the Ch'u-tz'u. In the older poem Ch'ü Yüan encounters an old fisherman and bemoans how he has been unjustly slandered and how he refuses to be corrupted by the evil in the world. The fisherman responds that it is better to ride with the time and stay alive, but Ch'ü Yüan will hear none of it. Finally the fisherman laughs and goes off, singing the song quoted above, the allegorical point of which is that one should adapt one's behavior to political realities. Soon afterward Ch'ü Yüan committed suicide.

In Lu Chao-lin's short poem it is not clear whose part he is taking, that of the fisherman on Ch'ü Yüan;

the latter would seem more reasonable from the context.
The poem is haunted by righteous suicide, old legends
emerging from the natural world in fragments of sight
and sound. The courtly trope of resemblances in nature—
Ssu-ma Hsiang-ju in the clouds and Cho Wen-chün in the
moon—has been transformed into a demonic reality as the
noble suicides of antiquity appear in the forms of trees
and the fisherman's laughter breaks in from nowhere, mocking his resolve.

   As we said earlier, Lu Chao-lin's poetry covers almost
the entire spectrum of subgenres and topics in seventh-
century verse. As one example, we may look closely at
some of Lu's border poetry to see what new elements he
brought to this highly conventional subgenre.

THE BLACK-MANED BAY   紫騮馬

The bay steed, its golden saddle shining,   騮馬照金鞍
After battle's shifting tactics, enters Fort   轉戰入皐蘭
  Kao-lan.
At the barrier gates the wind grows sharper,   塞門風稍急
By the Great Wall the rivers at their coldest.   長城水正寒
Its clinking harness weighs heavily under   雪暗鳴珂重
  snow-darkened skies,
The mountain stretch long—it suffers jade   山長噴玉難
  ice streams.
Yet it won't balk at crossing the whole Gobi—   不辭橫絕漠
When will its flowing blood ever dry?   流血幾時乾
                                    [02737]

Like earlier border ballads, Lu Chao-lin builds the poem
out of fragments of scenes, arranged more or less chronologically. In contrast to earlier versions of this
ballad, however, here there is a greater sense of violence
and dramatization.[7] The sense of increasing hardships
serves to intensify the courageous resolution of the
horse expressed in the seventh line. Lu cannot resist
the closing twist which undercuts the value of the horse's

courage by suggesting the futility of it all: the blood
will never dry because the region will never be conquered,
and one brave horse has turned into whole generations of
brave battle steeds which, like the soldiers they stand
for, have ridden out into the Gobi to die.

Although border poetry has been commonly associated
with the High T'ang, it was in fact one of the most
conservative of the poetic subgenres. High T'ang poets
often continued the seventh-century practice of juxtaposing fragments of scenes; however, their greatest successes
in this mode came from vivid dramatization in the fragments
and stark contrasts in the juxtapositions. From these
crucial fragments the reader was to extrapolate a whole
scene, then string those scenes together to form something
like a narrative. The following poem (05782) by Wang Wei
uses a technique identical to that of Lu Chao-lin's poem,
but Wang Wei uses it with High T'ang sophistication.

ARMY BALLAD   從軍行

The bugle blows, setting the marchers moving,   吹角動行人
A grumbling hubbub as the soldiers rise.   喧喧行人起
Fifes screech, a tumult of neighing horses   笳悲馬嘶亂
As they struggle to ford the Golden River.   爭渡金河水
Sunset at the edge of a great desert,   日暮沙漠陲
Sounds of battle within the dust and mist.   戰聲煙塵裏
Having bound up the necks of all the famous   盡繫名王頸
   chieftains,
They return to report to the emperor.   歸來報天子

For all the effectiveness of Wang Wei's juxtaposition of
the violence of battle with the placid border scene, his
is a much smugger poem than Lu Chao-lin's. Along with a
fascination for border warfare went an interest in the
bravo, the yu-hsia 遊俠, who appears variously as a hot-
headed young tough, as a courageous righter of wrongs,
and as a war hero. The ballad "Pacts with Friends on the

Sporting Fields of Youth" 結客少年場行 had once tended
to stress the failure of young men who went off to the
frontiers to achieve fame and honor.[8] Under the influence
of court poetry's aversion to all forms of unpleasantness,
sixth- and seventh-century versions of the ballad tended
to emphasize the heroism and gallantry and mute the theme
of failure.[9] As in the "Black-maned Bay" Lu plays along
with the conventional treatment up to the last line.

Ch'ang-an honors its bravos,	俠雄騎 遊富財 長安洛陽
Lo-yang is rich in wealth and courage.	
Jade swords, riders like floating clouds,	玉劍浮雲 弓
Golden riding whips, bows bent like the bright moon. . . .	金鞭明月
Beacon fires like the moon by night,	烽火夜似月
Then at dawn the aura of the troops forms rainbows.	兵氣曉成虹
They march abreast along with their comrades,	橫行知從朝胡 已戎
Arrows slung on their backs on a far campaign.	負羽遠
Their dragon banners darken the northern fog,	龍旌捲 霧風
Their battle ranks roll up the Tartar dust.	鳥陣 海山 咽空
When they rush in pursuit, the Gobi moans,	追奔瀚
Then the battle over Yin Mountain left bare.	戰罷陰
Back they go to thank His Majesty,	歸來謝天子
Old men on horseback.	何如馬上翁

                              [02740]

All of a sudden the gallant young warriors appear as old
men, and our admiration for their lives spent in service
to the emperor falls prey to the tragedy of their age.
Lu seems to be unconsciously using the traditional
technique of the Han _fu_, praising something at length,
then attacking it at the very close of the poem. The
application of this technique in this _shih_ is more
effective than in the _fu_, because rather than simply
raising a moral objection, it becomes a genuine devalua-
tion of the theme previously treated with admiration.

The link between the appearance of this technique in the
shih and fu probably occurs through the capital poems,
which we shall treat in chapter 9.

Lu Chao-lin's delight in juxtaposing contrary values
is matched by his sense of paradox, which likewise runs
counter to the need for harmony in court poetry. This
sense of paradox is left unresolved in the following
poem (02739), one of Lu's most famous.

PLUM BLOSSOMS FALL

梅花落

When the blossoms first emerge on plum ridges,
The snow has not yet opened up on Heaven
  Mountain.
Those snowy spots seem filled with flowers,
Where flowers are, snow seems to swirl.
Windblown they enter the dancers' sleeves,
Mixed with powder, fall in ladies' chambers.
Tens of thousands of miles away, the Hsiung-nu
Don't even know that spring has come.

梅嶺花初發
天山雪未開
雪處疑花滿
花邊似雪迴
因風入舞袖
雜粉向妝臺
匈奴幾萬里
春至不知來

As in some earlier versions of this yüeh-fu, Lu Chao-lin
plays on the visual similarity of plum blossoms and
snowflakes, a similarity strengthened by the fact that
a "flake" of snow is in Chinese a "flower" of snow (see
line 4). But Lu plays this simple metaphor into a strange
confusion of "white worlds." Despite the confusion, the
two worlds are opposites: in the barbarous, male northland
it is still winter, while in the delicate, feminine South
it is already spring. In ordinary court poetry the snow
world should be a metaphor for the plum world or vice
versa; the impulse on the part of the reader to make
these traditional metaphors strengthens the identities
and points up the distinctions. Puns also bind the two
worlds: in the North the snow has not yet "opened up"
k'ai 開 , a word also meaning "to blossom." Another
association of k'ai which might operate here is "opening

up" the frontiers, the spreading of imperial civilization.
Lu avoids the temptation to round the poem off by making
some clever point about the relation of the two worlds;
rather, he leaves the reader with the strange image of
the barbarian Hsiung-nu amid the snow and two worlds
which are both the same and the opposite.

   All the above elements of dramatization, paradox, and
the fusion of contrary worlds can be seen in the following border poem (02775).

SONG OF THE FALLING SNOW

At autumn's end nomad horsemen come down,
Clouds over the passes, flat for thousands
   of miles.
The snow seems dark as the Tartar sands,
The ice as bright as the Chinese moon.
At Tallgate Pass the gates are made of silver,
And the wall of the Great Wall turns to jade.
The standards and banners have all fallen
   away,
And the Son of Heaven knows not their glory.

The ice and snow turn the Great Wall into a palace of
silver and jade, a palace for immortals, yet ironically
this is where the Chinese troops met their deaths. The
proper "ellipsis of battle" is maintained, but the
implied violence of their deaths lies behind the stately
and tranquil scene of the Great Wall, where the clouds
are "flat" (p'ing 平 , also meaning "pacified").[10] The
word used for "fallen away," ling-lo 零落, of the banners
is ironically most commonly associated with the trees
losing their leaves in autumn. Unknown to their lord
and unperceived by us, who see only the "even calm,"
p'ing, of the scene and the jewel fortresses, the soldiers have all perished, their banners falling to earth
as gently as autumn leaves. Their "glory," ming 名 , is
literally their "names": no humans are left in the scene

except for the anonymous dead. A new interest in pre-
sixth-century yüeh-fu was one means by which to escape
the sterility of court poetry without going off into
uncharted territory. Songs of heptasyllabic and irregular
line lengths had long been associated with direct emotion
and popular poetry. Lu Chao-lin, like many of his contemporaries, turned to these and the model of Pao Chao
鮑照 (412?-66), author of a series of poems entitled
"Hard Travelling," Hsing-lu nan 行路難. These poems,
primarily on the themes of impermanence and personal
failure, seem to have captured the imaginations of the
poets of the 660s and 670s.

     Lu Chao-lin's "Hard Travelling" uses a dead tree as
its "stimulus" (hsing 興, a natural object that evokes
a specific emotion). In doing so he lyricizes an object
which had been used allegorically earlier in a fu by Yü
Hsin and also allegorically in a fu of his own.[11]

HARD TRAVELLING   行路難

Can't you see, there north of Ch'ang-an's   君不見長安城北渭橋邊
    walls, by the Wei River bridge,

That bare, withered tree, chopped across,   枯木橫槎臥古田
    lying in an ancient field?

In days of old it filled with red,   昔日含紅復含紫
    then filled with purple,

And always there lingered the fog,   常時留霧亦留煙
    and also lingered the mist.

In spring light and spring wind   春景春風花似雪
    its flowers seemed like snow,

A constant rumble, scented-wood carriages   香車玉輿恒闐咽
    and coaches fitted with jade.

Was there ever any traveller   若箇遊人不競攀
    who failed to break a spray?

Was there ever any singing girl   若箇娼家不來折
    who failed to snap a sprig?

Singing girls with jeweled breastbands,   娼家寶襪蛟龍帔
    dragon-broidered robes,

Young nobles on silver saddles,   公子銀鞍千萬騎
    riding past in thousands.

Lu Chao-lin

One by one the orioles
  were coy among its flowers, 黃鸝一一囘花嬌

And, pair by pair, bluebirds
  played there with their young. 青鳥雙雙將子戲

Its thousand-foot boughs,
  its hundred-foot branches, 千尺長條百尺枝

Blotted out moon's cassia
  and the elm of the stars. 月桂星榆相蔽虧

Upon its leaves of coral
  there were mandarin ducks, 珊瑚葉上鴛鴦鳥

And in the nests of phoenixes
  were the phoenix brood. 鳳皇巢裏雛鸞兒

The nests fell, the branches broke,
  the phoenixes went away, 巢傾枝折鳳歸去

Boughs withered, leaves fell,
  bearing the blasts of the wind. 條枯葉落任風吹

In one morning it was stripped bare,
  and no one came any more, 一朝零落無人問

Then an eternity of ruin—
  how can you understand? 萬古摧殘君詎知

In human life glory and want
  never cease to change, 人生貴賤無終始

Goes in a flash, goes in an instant,
  cannot trust to it long. 倏忽須臾難久恃

Who is there can halt the sun
  over the western mountains? 誰家能駐西山日

Who is there can dam and stop
  the eastward flowing stream? 誰家能堰東流水

Trees on the tombs of the House of Han
  fill the land of Ch'in, 漢家陵樹滿秦川

All coming hither or going hence,
  all to be lamented. 行來行去盡哀憐

Since ancient days the dukes and lords
  had their ton of rice a year, 自昔公卿二千石

And all made plans that their glory
  last a hundred centuries; 咸擬榮華一萬年

Where now do you see their crimson lips,
  their fair faces? 不見朱脣與白貌

You only hear of pale thorns on the graves
  and the Yellow Springs. 唯聞素棘與黃泉

A time will come when your gold and your sable
  must be sold to buy wine, 金貂有時須換酒

Jade flakes of flowers ever cast
   fluttering countless coins.

I send these words to you who lodge
   in the offices of "the gods,"

When you hang here between life and death,
   you see true friendship.

Come not to the foot of the palace,
   the Gate of the Blue Dragon,

I, at least, will surely go off
   to White Crane Mountain.

No hope to reach Heaven or immortal isles—
   too far, too far—

And when again shall we ever be
   so openheartedly in accord.

I wish only the span of King Yao,
   a mere million years,

To be forever the hermits Ch'ao and Yu,
   never leaving that life.

玉屑恆搖莫計錢

寄言坐客神仙署

一生一死交情處

蒼龍闕下君不來

白鶴山前我應去

雲間海上邈難期

赤心會合在何時

但願堯年一百萬

長作巢由也不辭

[02761]

There are a number of allusions and references in this
poem, but most of them are clear from the context. Ch'ao-
fu and Hsü Yu, who close the poem, were hermits of high
antiquity. Ch'ao-fu, the "nest father," made his dwelling
in a tree, while Hsü Yu washed out his ears when he was
asked to take over rule of the world. Though in his
desire for spontaneity Lu lapses into occasional hysteri-
cal non sequiturs, the poem succeeds in conveying the
urgency of a vision of the bones beneath the skin. The
tree is both a physical presence, a "stimulus" for Lu's
meditation, and also a metaphor for the process of flour-
ishing and decline, companionship and abandonment. The
stock yüeh-fu phrase, "Don't you see," chün pu-chien
君不見, retains some of its original verbal force as
the poet frantically points out this symbol of mortality
and mutability.

    As a relatively straightforward memento mori, this
poem has little intellectual interest, but it does have
a great deal of poetic and literary historical interest.

Like Ch'en Tzu-ang several decades later, Lu Chao-lin
turns back to an older form of poetry to escape from the
confines of court poetry. From Yü Hsin through Lu Chao-
lin the "dead tree" became an important symbol object in
the poetry of the eighth and ninth centuries, a symbol
of greatness brought low and abandoned. Tu Fu, for
example, has a number of poems on dead and dying trees
(see 10676-79), and the symbol plays an important role
in his "Ballad of the Old Cypress" (10768).

Eremitism and the quest for immortality are major
themes in Lu's poetry. In most such poems we do not
find the frenetic intensity of "Hard Travelling" or the
songs from "Release from Sickness"; instead there is a
controlled quietism. In these poems Lu borrows themes
and diction from T'ao Ch'ien and the landscape poet
Hsieh Ling-yün 謝靈運, a contemporary of Pao Chao. At
times he may quote T'ao Ch'ien almost verbatim as in the
second line of the following passage:

In utter silence I have ceased welcoming
   strangers,
At my gate there's no sound of horse and
   carriage.
Lute set before me, I answer the mountain
   and rivers,
Opening a scroll I peruse the lives of great
   men.

寂寂罷將迎
門無車馬聲
橫琴答山水
披卷閱公卿

[02804]

Like his younger contemporary Wang Po, Lu Chao-lin was a
master of the descriptive couplet; both poets show a
movement away from the ornateness and preciousness of
the court couplet. At least one of Lu's couplets was
cited in the Sung dyansty as an exemplar of good couplet
construction, under the category of "shock lines," ching-
ts'e 警策:[12]

The grass impedes, men walk slowly;   草 礙 人 行 緩
The flowers tangled, birds cross leisurely.   花 繁 鳥 度 遲

[02803]

The semantic distinction between English "slowly" and
"leisurely" is sharper than between the Chinese synonyms
huan 緩 and ch'ih 遲. We have two structurally identical
situations—figures moving slowly through a density of
vegetation. But the individual semantic relations of the
other parallel elements—plain grass versus attractive
flowers, the tangle which impedes versus the tangle of
lushness, the walking movement whose goal is hidden
versus of the crossing which can get beyond—all these
ultimately call attention to the difference between earth-
bound man and the freedom of the birds, between a slowness
of constriction and a slowness of choice. In this subtle
juxtaposition of similarities and differences, the shock
is not obvious as in courtly wit, but rather the surface
simplicity draws the reader to look into the couplet more
deeply and find there a more general significance. The
external simplification and internal complication of the
parallel couplet is an important process in the ultimate
development of the High T'ang style.

    Except perhaps in "Ch'ang-an: ku-yi," which we will
discuss in chapter 9, Lu Chao-lin's poetry never rises
to the greatness of the major High T'ang poets. But Lu's
range of style, and of tone is extraordinary for his age,
from courtly grace to unbalanced intensity to an honest
and direct beauty not easily matched in the seventh
century. Shang-kuan Yi might have written a descriptive
couplet with more cleverness, but he could never close a
poem:

If by chance you meet someone loyal and kind,   倘 遇 忠 孝 所
Tell them for me—I remember Ch'ang-an.   為 道 憶 長 安

[02758]

THE CAPITAL POEMS

To the poets of the first half of the seventh century
Ch'ang-an excited only wonder; it was <u>the</u> city, the
marvel of its day, the living proof of T'ang power.
Being employed there meant or held out the hope of success; being an official elsewhere meant failure. Losing
the great city, most responded as Lu Chao-lin did, with
longing—they "remembered Ch'ang-an." But in the 660s
and 670s the T'ang royal house seemed to be stumbling
as Empress Wu assumed more and more of the real authority
of government. It is not surprising that loss of confidence in the stability of the dynastic house and a
feeling that something was deeply wrong in the government
should appear in a critique of the capital. For this
there were solid traditions.

Such capital poems drew on two literary traditions,
one an outgrowth of the other. The earlier of the two
is to be found in the capital <u>fu</u> of the Eastern Han. The
manner in which Ch'ang-an was treated in these <u>fu</u> is of
central importance in understanding the associations
which the seeming praise of the capital in these T'ang
poems held for the contemporary reader. When Kuang-wu-ti
restored the Han dynasty in A.D. 25 he moved the capital
from Ch'ang-an to Lo-yang; this transfer became the
subject of fierce controversy. Tu Tu's 杜篤 "Fu on the
Capital," <u>Lun-tu fu</u> 論都賦, took the part of Ch'ang-an,
praising the former capital in terms of its strategic
and historical significance. Perhaps in response to
this work Pan Ku 班固 wrote "Fu on the Two Capitals,"
<u>Liang-tu fu</u> 兩都賦, in which a partisan of Ch'ang-an
and a partisan of Lo-yang dispute the merits of the two
cities. Ch'ang-an was portrayed as representing the

materialistic and aggressive, the military aspects of
Chinese civilization. The pro-Ch'ang-an interlocutor
was to be utterly confounded by the advocate of Lo-yang,
which represented restraint, frugality, and the Confucian
virtues. Long after the political controversy had died
down, the two capitals continued to be topics for fu,
coming to symbolize two contrary principles of society.
Thus the rich, sensual Ch'ang-an represented in these
capital poems of the mid-seventh century already carried
with it an element of criticism.

The second important tradition, which grew out of the
capital fu, began in Pao Chao's "Weed-covered City" and
developed into the poetry on ruins which we saw earlier
in the seventh century. Lu Chao-lin had turned to Pao
Chao as a model for his songs on impermanence, but the
juxtaposition of the city in its glory versus the city
in ruins, the formula evolved in "Weed-covered City,"
was even more influential. A version of this formula
can be seen in the description of the withered tree in
"Hard Travelling." Combined, these two traditions formed
a warning about the instability of human society and the
need for restraint in order to preserve it.

It is impossible to date precisely these poems on the
capital, but they fall between the 660s and the early
680s. Afterward the theme all but disappears until the
High T'ang, except in a few huai-ku. Though we cannot
arrange the following poems chronologically, we can place
them on a scale of ornateness, ranging from the dense
and allusive "Imperial Capital," Ti-ching p'ien 帝京篇 ,
of Lo Pin-wang to the relatively straightforward "Looking
Down from the High Terrace," Lin kao-t'ai 臨高臺 , of
Wang Po. Somewhere between the two lies the finest of
them all, Lu Chao-lin's "Chang-an: ku-i," 長安古意 .

Ku-yi 古意 , "ancient theme/attitude," is a difficult
term whose significance varies with the age and the
individual writer. Originally it was equivalent to

ni-ku 擬古, "imitation of an old theme," but came to mean
anything from huai-ku, meditation on the past (usually
an occasioned poem written on a visit to an ancient site),
to "ancient morality," to what seems to be the case here,
the use of a historical subject—Ch'ang-an of the Han
dynasty. The use of a historical example as a mirror
for the present was a practice as old as Chinese literature itself:

CH'ANG-AN: KU-YI   長安古意

Ch'ang-an's broad avenues
    link up with narrow lanes,[13]   長安大道連狹斜

There black oxen and white horses,
    coaches of fragrant woods,   青牛白馬七香車

Jade-fit palanquins go left and right
    past the mansions of lords,   玉輦縱橫過主第

Gold riding whips in a long train move
    toward barons' homes.   金鞭絡繹向侯家

Dragons bite jeweled canopies,
    catching the morning sun,   龍銜寶蓋承朝日

The phoenix disgorges dangling fringe,
    draped with evening's red clouds.   鳳吐流蘇帶晚霞

A hundred yards of gossamer strands
    strain to enwrap the trees,   百丈游絲爭繞樹

While a single graceful flock of birds
    join their cries among flowers.   一群嬌鳥共啼花

Cries among flowers, playful butterflies,
    by the palace's thousand gates,   啼花戲蝶千門側

The emerald trees, the silver terraces,
    thousands of different colors.   碧樹銀臺萬種色

Double-decked passageways, intertwined
    windows make the union of lovers.   複道交窗作合歡

Paired tower gates, rising layers of tiles
    which sweep as phoenix wings.   雙闕連甍垂鳳翼

The Liang clan's muraled tower
    rises into the skies,[14]   梁家畫閣天中起

The Emperor of Han's golden columns
    jut straight beyond the clouds.[15]   漢帝金莖雲外直

But those you gaze on before great
    buildings are those you do not know,   樓前相望不相知

And those you meet upon the paths,
  no acquaintances of yours.

Tell me of her who plays the pipes
  off into purple mists—

She has spent her years of beauty
  in the study of the dance.[16]

If we could become the pi-mu fish,
  why should we flee from death?[17]

Could we but be the mandarin ducks,
  no yearnings to be immortals.[18]

The pi-mu, the mandarin ducks,
  are truly worth our yearning—

They go in pairs, they come in pairs—
  can't you see them now?

Most I hate that single phoenix
  woven in the top of the drape,

Most I love the swallow pair
  fixed on the curtained door.[19]

Pairs of swallows fly in their pairs
  around the painted beams,

There, gauze hangings, the kingfisher
  quilt, scent of turmeric.

Then one by one, hairdos like clouds,
  cicada-wing curls hanging,

Eyebrows slender like new moons
  above the tawny oils.[20]

Tawny with oil, white with powder,
  they step from coaches,

Charms within, loveliness within,
  hearts not fixed on one.

Bewitching boys on jeweled horses
  with ironblack spots,

And courtesans, pins of coiling dragons,
  golden legs bent under.[21]

In the office of the Censorate
  the crows cry by night,[22]

By the Constabulary gate
  the sparrows go to roost.[23]

Mightily rising Vermilion Walls
  look down on roads like jade,

In the distance azure carriages
  sink behind gold-fast bastions.

陌上相逢詎相識
借問吹簫向紫煙
曾經學舞度芳年
得成比目何辭死
願作鴛鴦不羨仙
比目鴛鴦真可羨
雙去雙來君不見
生憎帳額繡孤鸞
好取門簾帖雙燕
雙燕雙飛繞畫梁
羅幃翠被鬱金香
片片行雲著蟬鬢
纖纖初月上鴉黃
鴉黃粉白車中出
含嬌含態情非一
妖童寶馬鐵連錢
娼婦盤龍金屈膝
御史府中烏夜啼
廷尉門前雀欲栖
隱隱朱城臨玉道
遙遙翠幰没金堤

Slings are clasped, falcons flown
  north of Tu-ling,

挟弹飞鹰杜陵北

Lots drawn for killing by sworn companions
  west of the Wei.

探丸借客渭桥西

Greeting each other the bravos
  with lotus-hilted swords,

俱邀侠客芙蓉剑

Spend nights together on paths to peach
  and plum, the houses of singing girls.[24]

共宿娼家桃李蹊

At sunset in singing girls' houses
  are skirts of purple gauze,

娼家日暮紫罗裙

And a verse of clear singing
  comes swelling from their mouths.

清歌一啭口氛氲

In the northern halls night after night,
  people move as the moon,[25]

北堂夜夜人如月

On southern paths at every dawn,
  riders move as the clouds.

南陌朝朝骑似云

Southward paths and northern halls
  link through the Northern Quarter,

南陌北堂连北里

Then great crossroads and wide highways
  rein in the Markets.

五剧三条控三市

Pliant willows and green ash
  hang brushing the earth,

弱柳青槐拂地垂

Sweet air and red dust
  rise darkening the skies.

佳气红尘暗天起

Royal heralds of the House of Han come,
  a thousand outriders,

汉代金吾千骑来

Then kingfisher-colored liquors
  in parrot-shaped goblets.

翡翠屠苏鹦鹉杯

Blouses of gauze and jeweled sashes
  are taken off for you,

罗襦宝带为君解

The songs of Yen, the dances of Wu
  for you performed.

燕歌赵舞为君开

But there are others bold and splendid,
  called "minister," "general,"

别有豪华称将相

The day turns, the heavens rolls,
  and neither will yield to the other.

转日回天不相让

Haughty spirits ever willing
  to push aside a Kuan-fu,[26]

意气由来排灌夫

A hold on power which cannot give
  in the least to a Minister Hsiao.[27]

专权判不容萧相

Haughty spirits, hold on power,
  the stuff of ruthless heroes,

专权意气本豪雄

Blue Dragon and Purple Swallow,
  great steeds in the spring wind.

They said themselves their songs and
  dances would last a thousand years,

And claimed a pride and extravagance
  beyond the Great Lords.

But the glory of each thing in its
  season was not to wait on them,

Mulberry fields and green oceans
  interchange in an instant.

Where once were the golden stairs,
  the halls of white marble,

We now see only
  the green pines remaining.

Silent there in the emptiness,
  the dwelling of Yang Hsiung,[28]

Year after year, every year,
  his whole bed covered with books.

Alone are the cassia flowers,
  blooming on South Mountain,

They fly back and forth,
  fly into his sleeves.

[02762]

青虯紫燕坐春風

自言歌舞長千載

自謂驕奢凌五公

節物風光不相待

桑田碧海須臾改

昔時金階白玉堂

即今唯見青松在

寂寂寥寥揚子居

年年歲歲一牀書

獨有南山桂花發

飛來飛去襲人裾

    The poem opens with the reader's eyes somewhere on the great roads of Ch'ang-an, watching the traffic. The aspect which Lu Chao-lin emphasizes about this noble society is that of socializing, travelling and meeting, visiting patrons and lovers. To this is opposed the dwelling of Yang Hsiung at the end of the poem. But in the capital everything is movement and mobility, a flux that mirrors the larger theme of impermanence: the poet focuses on descriptions of coaches, palanquins, passageways, all the means by which people can move and get together.

    The seasonal motif is spring, associated with sexuality and physical prowess in the young bravos, the yu-hsia. Spring is a prodigal season and its lushness finds an echo in the ostentatious extravagance of the wealthy and noble. With this aristocratic society of the court is

associated the yearning for immortality—dragons, phoenixes, buildings (which symbolically "rise into the sky")
painted with murals of the immortals, and the golden
columns with their dewpans from which was to be made the
elixir of eternal life.

At this point Lu Chao-lin weaves in the first dissonant
note. Despite all the hustle and bustle, the visits and
parties:

> But those you gaze on before great
>   buildings are those you do not know,   樓 前 相 望 不 相 知
>
> And those you meet upon the paths,
>   no acquaintances of yours.   陌 上 相 逢 詎 相 識

This is a "big city," and like all big cities, it is full
of strangers. With this in mind, all the travelling and
visiting takes on a new aspect, a quest for companions
in a world of strangers. Like the quest for the immortals
it is a constant striving out of one condition to another,
not a stable, secure world of human relations. As estrange-
ment undercuts the theme of companionship, the treatment
of this splendid world in terms of spring growth undercuts
the quest for immortality. In lines 17 and 18 there is a
question about a lady, first in the guise of the daughter
of the Duke of Ch'in, then as Chao Fei-yen; the answer
tells how she "spent her years of beauty" (literally
"spent her years of fragrance," tu fang-nien 度芳年).
Such images recurring in the poem enforce the identity
between this sensual life in the capital and the vegetative
life of spring, a fragile and impermanent beauty. By the
end of the poem we are left only with the pines of the
tombs and the cassia which endure the cold.

At this early point in the poem, however, the poet
takes a less extreme stand than he does in the end. He
counters the false hope of immortality with an affirmation
of the constant but mortal love of the pi-mu, the mandarin
ducks, and the swallows. He sees through the frantic

search for companions in the aristocratic world to its
essential solitude and fickleness; this he hates. This
hated solitude is unlike the noble solitude of Yang Hsiung
at the end of the poem. The relation of the images of
mortal love to the intense but brief spring life and
affairs with singing girls is analogous to the relation
of the hermit to the figures of political power: both
reject intensity and extravagance for restraint, striving
and activity for contentment.

The idleness of the Censorate and Constabulary, seen
in the behavior of the birds, might be positive at this
point in the poem, suggesting that the peace and order
of the times makes their work unnecessary; it might also
be negative, suggesting that their work is being neglected.
This latter interpretation of the omens becomes more and
more inescapable as we see young bravos choosing lots to
assassinate their enemies. The mood of violence and
aggression, hidden behind the beauty of spring, increases
as the poet moves into the political sphere, to the
struggles for power of the ministers and generals. In
them the heroic spirit, appearing in more attractive
forms earlier in the poem, turns to arrogance, and the
quest for immortality becomes hubris. Here appears the
fixed topos which precedes the description of the city
in ruins in "Weed-covered City" and the poems in that
tradition: "They said themselves their songs and dances
would last a thousand years."

Next the poet brings in the explicit theme of impermanence: men and their empires are cyclical and seasonal,
passing from flowering to ripeness to ruin. But Lu Chao-
lin does not stop there: he offers the enigmatic alternative of Yang Hsiung, appearing as the hermit. His silence
contrasts to the city's bustle; his solitude contrasts to
their gregariousness; his bed of books contrasts to their
sensual concerns. And though he is not granted more than
a mortal span, the phrase "year after year, every year,"

nien-nien sui-sui 年年歲歲 , gives a sense of stability
and continuity, set against the impermanence of the
struggle for glory and the futility of the quest for
immortality in the capital. The cassia, traditional
symbol of purity and virtue, grows on South Mountain,
traditional symbol of eternity. The haunting last line
brings back the world of change in the image of the
falling blossoms, but beside the hermit these seem almost
inconsequential as they are blown back and forth by the
wind and into his sleeve.

The theme of impermanence here is too meekly universal
to be full-fledged topical political protest. On the
other hand, one cannot miss a general disillusionment
with the world of the court. Yang Hsiung, representing
learning and Confucian values, takes the place occupied
by the praise of Lo-yang in the "Fu on the Two Capitals,"
a silent reproof and mockery of the world of Ch'ang-an.[29]

Lo Pin-wang's "Imperial Capital" is a virtuoso performance in seventh-century rhetoric. As in most of his
other poetry, here Lo unfolds a dazzling display of
periphrasis and erudition, to the detriment of the poem
as a whole. In its shifting line lengths the poem is
metrically more innovative than the heptasyllabic "Ch'ang-
an: ku-yi," but rather than the rhythms of yüeh-fu and
popular song which irregular line lengths usually suggest,
here the shifting pentasyllabic and heptasyllabic lines
approximate in poetry the shifting rhythms of parallel
prose with its tetrasyllabic and hexasyllabic lines.
Instead of disillusioned attack as in Lu Chao-lin's poem,
Lo Pin-wang's piece is a persuasion designed to win the
poet recognition. Lest the point be missed, the poem is
provided with a preface in the most abstruse parallel
prose. The theme, however, was hardly an apt one for
Lo's purpose, prophecies of doom being hardly the best
way to win over a prospective patron.

The title Ti-ching p'ien is the same as that of

T'ai-tsung's ten-poem series, and Lo's opening echoes
the conventions of the capital theme which appear in the
first of T'ai-tsung's poems. T'ai-tsung begins:

In the streams of Ch'in, a powerful emperor's
    residence,
In Han-ku Pass, mighty royal dwelling.

秦 川 雄 帝 宅
函 谷 壯 皇 居

[00001]

Lo Pin-wang amplifies:

Mountains and rivers, a thousand-mile domain,
Palace wall towers, the ninefold gates.
Without beholding the might of the royal
    dwelling,
How can you know the majesty of the Son of
    Heaven?
Royal dwelling, Imperial compound in Yao
    and Han-ku Passes.

山 河 千 里 國
城 關 九 重 門
不 覩 皇 居 壯
安 知 天 子 尊
皇 居 帝 里 崤 函 谷

[04148]

From the very beginning "Imperial Capital" has the signs
of panegyric, but for all its shimmering rhetoric, it is
a simpler poem than "Ch'ang-an: ku-yi." Scenes, objects,
and themes are remarkably similar in the two poems, but
in Lo's poem they are strung together in epideictic
enumeration, while in Lu's work they are fused into
significant scenes. When "Double-decked passageways,
intertwined windows make the union of lovers," 複道交窗
作合歡 ("Ch'ang-an: ku-yi," line 11), Lu Chao-lin combines the idea that the passageways enable lovers to meet
("make for the union of lovers") with the clever visual
image that the passageways and windows seem themselves
to be linked in a sexual embrace ("act out the union of
lovers"). The historical dimension is answered in the
Lover-Union Palace of Han, while the sexual implications
are given a discreet botanical veil in the mimosa tree,
the ho-huan 合歡, "lover-union tree." The "double-decked

passageways" reappear in Lo Pin-wang's poem, but instead
of taking on the lusty forms of the activities they
permit, they simply "slant across to Bluejay Pavilion"
複道斜通鳿鵲觀 ("Imperial Capital," line 15).

While Lu Chao-lin weaves disillusionment through his
praises, Lo Pin-wang holds to the traditional technique
of the Western Han fu, clearly separating the closing
censure from the preceding praise. In contrast to Lu
Chao-lin's very skillful use of this technique in his
yüeh-fu, which we saw in chapter 8, Lo Pin-wang's use
of it has all the abrupt incongruity of its use in the
fu. Of "Imperial Capital" one could well make Yang
Hsiung's famous critical comment on the fu: "That's
protest poetry!? I'm afraid it dosen't avoid encouraging
[the kind of behavior it is supposedly protesting]."[30]
The strong fu traditions that lay behind these shih on
the capital always threatened that the poem become no
more than a poorly done fu. Lo succumbed to the danger,
not only in the simple praise-blame technique described
above, but in his use of purely epideictic rhetoric, unsubordinated enumerations of objects and scenes. When
Lu Chao-lin goes into his long description of the traffic
on Ch'ang-an's avenues, it is to prepare us for the
knowledge that everyone is a stranger, that a deeper
isolation underlies the festive gatherings. In Lo Pin-
wang's poem the description exists for its own sake.

Level Terrace, In-laws Compound lined with lofty ramparts,	平臺戚里帶崇墉
The "smoked gold," the jade tidbits await the ringing bells.	炊金饌玉待鳴鐘
Smaller halls with lacework curtains, three thousand doors,	小堂綺帳三千戶
Great roads and blue brothels, twelve layers deep.	大道青樓十二重
Jeweled awnings, carved saddles, horses with golden halters,	寶蓋雕鞍金絡馬

Orchid windows, filagree columns,
  coiling dragons of jade.

蘭 窗 繡 桂 玉 盤 龍

Filagree columns, alabaster capitals,
  stucco walls shining,

繡 桂 璇 題 粉 壁 映

Tinkling gold and ringing jade,
  princes and barons in glory.

鏘 金 鳴 玉 王 侯 盛

[lines 29-36]

If this works in poetry, it works in the peculiar realm
of aesthetic values that belong to the fu.

  From praise of the capital's glory, Lo moves abruptly
into a lament for impermanence:

Since ancient times glory and fame
  were like floating clouds,

古 來 榮 利 若 浮 雲

You cannot split off the highs and
  the lows in human life.

人 生 倚 伏 難 分

First you see the T'ien's and the Tou's
  climb above each other,

始 見 田 竇 相 移 奪

Then suddenly hear of Wei's and Huo's
  achieving great deeds.

俄 聞 衛 霍 有 功 勳

[lines 59-62]

The T'ien's and the Tou's were the two most famous ministerial families of the Han, while Wei and Huo were the
surnames of two of the Han's greatest generals. Lo next
moves to those who achieve high office and then desert
their former friends: his real motives in the poem are
coming to the fore. Instead of a noble hermit, Lo closes
with a series of allusions to historical figures to serve
as analogies for his own condition and desire for advance-
ment. Yang Hsiung appears appropriately, but in a different guise: "Yang Hsiung served the Han, but lacked a good
matchmaker," 楊雄仕漢乏良媒 (line 90). The "matchmaker"
derives from the erotic metaphors of the Ch'u-tzu and
refers to someone who could recommend him to the ruler.
At the very end Lo emerges as Chia Yi, the young Han
statesman and writer, who fell from favor and was banished
to Ch'ang-sha in the South to serve as a tutor to an

imperial prince.

Who pities the tutor of Ch'ang-sha,　　　　誰惜長沙傅
Who alone is confident in the talent of　　獨負洛陽才
  Lo-yang?

                    [lines 95-96]

Chia Yi was indeed a native of Lo-yang, but one can see
here a clear echo of the Han capital argument: Lo Pin-
wang, like Chia Yi, is a representative of the Lo-yang
side, of frugality and Confucian virtues set against the
extravagance of Ch'ang-an.

　　Wang Po's "Looking Down from the High Terrace" is a
yüeh-fu with its own tradition, but Wang's version is
much closer to the poems on the capital than it is to
earlier poems with the same title. Metrically varied
like "Imperial Capital," Wang Po's version of the capital
theme is the simplest and most lyrical of the three. Its
closing memento mori is the most perfunctory of the three
poems, and it is more a simple lament for impermanence
than a social critique of aristocratic society. "Ch'ang-
an: ku-yi" is seen from the street; Wang Po's vision of
the capital is from a "high terrace," echoing the old
theme of a high place giving an "overview" which leads
to understanding.

LOOKING DOWN FROM THE HIGH TERRACE　　　　臨高臺

Look down from the high terrace,　　　　　臨高臺
The high terrace, rising away, out of　　高臺迢遞絕浮埃
  drifting dust.
Its marble railing and carved structures　瑤軒綺構何崔嵬
  stand towering in the sky,
Where song and flute of immortal birds　　鸞歌鳳吹清且哀
  ring still and mournful.
Peer down now on the roads of Ch'ang-an,　俯瞰長安道
And the greenery along the royal moat,　　萋萋御溝草
Then look sideways to Sweetspring Palace　斜對甘泉路
  road,

Where the trees stand dark on the tombs
of Han.   蒼蒼茂陵樹

From the high terrace it's the same all
around—   高臺四望同

A richness in the air, full and sweet,
of the Royal Domain.   帝鄉佳氣鬱蔥蔥

Purple towers and red mansions shine
sparkling everywhere,   紫閣丹樓紛照耀

Jade-plaqued chambers, ornately painted
halls, laid out like latticework.   璧房錦殿相玲瓏

To the east lose sight of Ch'ang-lo
Pavilion,   東迷長樂觀

To the west point straight to Wei-yang
Palace.   西指未央宮

Great walls of vermilion shine in the
morning sun,   赤城映朝日

Green trees sway in the spring wind.   綠樹搖春風

A hundred lanes of bannered shops, the
New Market appears,   旗亭百隧開新市

A thousand tiles of great mansions split
the In-laws Ward.   甲第千甍分戚里

Red wheels and azure canopies cannot
bear the spring,   朱輪翠蓋不勝春

Layers of kiosks, files of columns rise
face to face.   疊榭層楹相對起

And then there are the blue brothels
along the great roads,   復有青樓大道中

Doors, beams, and windows carved to
intricate patterns, turning with color.   繡戶文窗雕綺櫳

Where the brocade coverlets are not
folded up by day,   錦衾晝不襲

And gauze bed-curtains at night not
yet empty.   羅帳夕未空

At dawn they hide in the azure of the
singing screens,   歌屏朝掩翠

And look to their evening rouge in
the make-up mirrors.   妝鏡晚窺紅

It's for you she sets her jeweled
coiffure,   為君安寶髻

Moth eyebrows quitting the clumps
of flowers.   蛾眉罷花叢

In a cloud of dust those narrow lanes
darken toward evening,   塵間狹路黯將暮

Then clouds open to the moon, as white
  as silk.

雲開月色明如素

Over Mandarin Duck Pool they fly
  pair by pair,

鴛鴦池上兩兩飛

Beneath Phoenix Hall they pass
  two by two.

鳳凰樓下雙雙度

The bright beauty of things being
  as it is,

物色正如此

Why should you not hope to meet
  your lady?

佳期那不顧

Silver saddles, embroidered hubs,
  the splendor and the glory,

銀鞍繡轂盛繁華

And wonderful to spend this night
  at the singing girl's home.

可憐今夜宿娼家

Tell the youngest of them there
  she must not frown—

娼家少婦不須嚬

Peach and plum in the eastern garden
  have but a moment of spring.

東園桃李片時春

Just look where the high terraces
  were in days gone by,

君看舊日高臺處

From Po-liang, from Copperbird Terrace
  the yellow dust rises.

柏梁銅雀生黃塵

[03443]

Wang Po's vantage point is from high above the ubiquitous
dust, first stirred by the throngs of carriages making
their way to the gay quarters and later seen rising from
the ruins of ancient terraces in the poet's imagination.
Po-liang Terrace, site of a famous group poem composition
by Han Wu-ti and his ministers, augurs the end of poets;
Copperbird Terrace, in which Ts'ao Ts'ao ordered that
his palace ladies be cloistered after his death, augurs
the end of fair ladies. But up on the high terrace now,
the music, associated with immortal birds, is clear and
sad, suggesting the burden of knowledge gained by gazing
down on the city and seeing the impermanence of its beauty.

   From far vistas the scene gradually focuses in on the
gay quarters, the "blue houses," and the theme turns to
love. Although Wang's description of the city depends
much less on allusion than the two preceding poems, he

is more subtle as his eyes pick out evidence that the
lovers have spent the day and night together:

The brocade coverlets not folded up by day,	錦衾晝不襞
And gauze bed-curtains at night not yet empty.	羅帳夕未空

But Wang Po's resolution to the poem is neither an
eremitic renunciation of the shining world nor a plea
for preferment; his theme is rather carpe diem. He
advises the young ladies to take advantage of the "bright
beauty of things" and not to frown; he recalls how the
dust from the carriages of lovers turns into the dust
rising from ruins where lovely ladies of ancient times
wasted their lives cloistered.

    The shifting valences of the capital theme can move
from an eremitic critique of aristocratic splendor to
carpe diem, but by far the most common use of it was in
the huai-ku. Huai-ku tend to be in pentasyllabic rather
than heptasyllabic meter, and are stylistically quite
distinct from the songs translated above. Such poems
had been written earlier in the seventh century, but
fine ones are to be found in the 660s and 670s.

    One of the most effective variations on the theme of
splendor and ruin is the "Ballad of Fen-yin," 汾陰行 ，
by Li Chiao 李嶠 (644-713), a poet whose work spans five
decades, from the time of the "Four Talents" to the end
of the Early T'ang. It is impossible to date the "Ballad
of Fen-yin," but its style is very much that of the
heptasyllabic songs of the 660s and 670s. The topicality
of the historical incident referred to might suggest
there is some topical, political intent behind the poem.
Fen-yin was a minor county that enjoyed a brief moment
of glory when Han Wu-ti performed the sacrifices to Earth
there.

BALLAD OF FEN-YIN   汾陰行

Haven't you seen in olden days when the
Western Capital was in full glory,   君不見昔日西京全盛時

His Majesty himself made sacrifice to
the Earth at Fen-yin.   汾陰后土親祭祠

In the fasting room he spent the night,
set out the offering,   齋宮宿寢設儲供

Then they rang bells, beat the drums,
planted the feathered banners.   撞鐘鳴鼓樹羽旂

The House of Han's fifth generation,
brilliant and bold,   漢家五葉才且雄

Who banqueted the hosts of spirits, who
brought the barbarians to court.   賓延萬靈朝九戎

And when the great feast and poem
session at Po-liang was over,   柏梁賦詩高宴罷

An edict was made and the Royal Coach
went on tour to Ho-tung.   詔書法駕幸河東

The Governor of Ho-tung himself swept
the region clean,   河東太守親掃除

Humbly welcomed the Most High, led
the belled palanquin.   奉迎至尊導鑾輿

Set out as guards, Imperial Armies
lined all the roads,   五營夾道列容衛

The three River Provinces permitted to
watch, their villages emptied.   三河縱觀空里閭

Banners circled, His Majesty halted on
the field where the spirits come down,   回旌駐蹕降靈場

Incense was burned, libations offered,
to invite a hundred blessings.   焚香奠醑邀百祥

The golden tripod's beauty shone
forth its aureate sheen,   金鼎發色正焜煌

The spirits and Earth God shimmered,
unfurling their radiance.   靈祇煒燁攄景光

Jades were buried, sacrifices spread,
the rites were ended,   埋玉陳牲禮神畢

Then pennons lifted, horses mounted,
and He left on the palanquin.   舉麾上馬乘輿出

The bends of the river Fen were
perfect for excursions,   彼汾之曲嘉可遊

His oars were of magnolia, his boat
of cassia.   木蘭為楫桂為舟

Rowing songs hummed softly, painted
  cormorant prows drifted,

Flutes and drums played mournfully,
  an autumn of white clouds.

Then joyous banquets were provided
  and gifts for great princes,

Home after home sent men to court,
  all given meat and wine.

The sounds and the brilliance stirred
  Heaven, such joy there has never been,

"A thousand autumns, ten thousand years—
  live as long as South Mountain!"

But since the Son of Heaven went back
  toward the passes of Ch'in,

The jade-fitted palanquins, gilded
  coaches never returned again.

The pearled screens and feather fans
  are silent forever,

How can one hold to the dragon's whiskers
  that leap from Tripod Lake?[31]

A thousand years of human deeds can
  vanish in a morning,

The whole world is an emperor's home,
  but not the road there.

Where now are their bold manners, their
  proud spirits?—

Altar fields and palace halls, all
  covered in weeds.

On the road I met an old man and he
  heaved a great sigh:

"The way of the world is a whirling
  ring, not to be fathomed,

Where in the blue brothels long ago
  they faced the songs and the dances,

Today there is yellow dust, clusters
  of brambles and thorns."

Mountains and rivers fill my eyes, tears
  soak my robes,

Riches, glory, and honor—how long can
  they endure?

Don't you see right now, there above
  the river Fen,

棹 歌 微 吟 緤 鷁 浮

簫 鼓 哀 鳴 白 雲 秋

歡 娛 宴 洽 賜 羣 后

家 家 復 除 戶 牛 酒

聲 明 動 天 樂 無 有

千 秋 萬 歲 南 山 壽

自 從 天 子 向 秦 關

玉 輦 金 車 不 復 還

珠 簾 羽 扇 長 寂 寞

鼎 湖 龍 聲 安 可 攀

千 齡 人 事 一 朝 空

四 海 為 家 此 路 窮

豪 雄 意 氣 今 何 在

壇 場 宮 館 盡 蓬 蒿

路 逢 故 老 長 歎 息

世 事 回 環 不 可 測

昔 時 青 樓 對 歌 舞

今 日 黃 埃 聚 荆 棘

山 川 滿 目 淚 沾 衣

富 貴 榮 華 能 幾 時

不 見 祗 今 汾 水 上

Only the autumn geese, flying by year
   after year.   唯有年年秋雁飛

                    [03535]

About half a century later we hear again of Li Chiao's
ballad:

> Toward the end of the T'ien-pao Reign [754-55, just before the
> outbreak of the An Lu-shan Rebellion] Ming-huang climbed the
> second story of Ch'ing-cheng Hall to enjoy springtime, and he
> ordered his court musicians to play him a few stanzas. And when
> they sang:

> Mountains and rivers fill my eyes,   山川滿目淚沾衣
>   tears soak my robes,
> Riches, glory, and honor—how long   富貴榮華能幾時
>   can they endure?

> and the following verse, His Majesty, who was getting on in
> years, asked, "Whose poem is that?" Someone answered, "Li
> Chiao's." Tears streamed down His Majesty's face, then he rose
> abruptly saying, "Chiao was a man of genius." Later that year
> when His Majesty had fled to Szechwan, he climbed Po-wei Ridge
> and gazed into the distance for a long time. Again they sang
> this song, and he responded, "A genius indeed!" And from Kao
> Li-shih on down all were wiping away their tears.[32]

It is rare to find someone in the eighth century paying
tribute to an Early T'ang poem. But the imperial music-
ians seem to have performed High T'ang surgery on the
poem, stripping away the lush description and leaving
only a lyrical quatrain. To those who knew Li Chiao's
entire poem, the first part of the poem served as a
significant background context for the quatrain, contrasting Han Wu-ti's glory to Ming-huang's (Hsüan-tsung) impending
doom. The "Ballad of Fen-yin" was quite popular and was
anthologized not only in the T'ang-shih chi-shih 唐詩記事,
but also in the Sou-yü hsiao-chi 搜玉小集 , the Wen-yüan

ying-hua 文苑英華, and most surprisingly in the sternly
fu-ku T'ang wen-ts'ui 唐文粹.

All four of the poems quoted in this chapter are either
heptasyllabic songs or songs of irregular line length
based on a predominantly heptasyllabic meter. Heptasyllabic songs had been written as early as the Wei and had
found a brief moment of glory in the hands of Pao Chao.
However, it was in the Early T'ang that the heptasyllabic
song attained the characteristic themes, diction, and
syntactic conventions which were handed down to the poets
of the eighth century.

10

WANG PO: A NEW DECORUM

Wang Po's transformation of the courtly style was less
extreme than that of Lu Chao-lin, and perhaps for that
reason its influence on subsequent poetry was more long-
lasting. His regulated verse began the trend toward
simplification and personalizing which ultimately led
into High T'ang regulated verse. Even when the court
was again the center of poetic activity in the later
reign of Empress Wu and Chung-tsung, one no longer finds
the extreme mannerism of a Shang-kuan Yi. Unlike Lu
Chao-lin, Wang Po's best work was in regulated verse
and quatrains. His innovations are not to be found in
the treatment of thematic conventions, but rather in
poetic technique—in the art of the parallel couplet and
in poetic closure. Although Wang's poems lack the form-
arized decorum of court poetry, they have a restraint all
their own, a balance that continues to characterize
regulated verse in later centuries.

Wang Po (ca. 650-76) represents a distinct biographical
"type," the promising young talent who dies tragically
before his time. Wang Po's family was illustrious and
aristocratic, including the bibulous Wang Chi, whose
poetry we have already discussed. His education was
surely the best available, and he is supposed to have
offered a critique of Yen Shih-ku's commentary to the
Han History at the age of nine. Such stories are part
and parcel of biographies of literary men, and while we
need not completely doubt its veracity, it seems likely
that such precocious displays of learning were watched
for carefully and embellished by doting relatives.

At the age of twenty Wang Po passed a special examination and entered the court, taking service with a prince

who was particularly fond of cockfighting. For the prince's delectation, no doubt, Wang wrote a comic piece entitled "Mobilization of the Prince of Ying's Cock," which must have been a parody of imperial military documents. Kao-tsung, however, was not in the least amused, and Wang Po found himself dismissed from office. He then began a series of wanderings which took him first to the southeast and later to Szechwan.

Once in Szechwan Wang managed to find a minor post; however, his ill star had not left him. He gave refuge to an escaped slave, then relented, worrying lest he be caught. Unfortunately his solution was to kill the slave, and whole affair was discovered. For this crime he was sentenced to death, but received a pardon before the sentence was carried out. His father, however, had lost his post because of Wang Po's crime and had been exiled to a magistracy in Vietnam. Wang Po left Szechwan to join his father, but was drowned while crossing the South China Sea.

It would be tempting to believe that Wang Po's move away from the style of court poetry was in some way connected with his own rather dramatic removal from court. This, however, does not seem to be the case. The following poem, Wang's most famous and one of his least courtly, was written while he was still in the capital.

MAGISTRATE TU, ON HIS WAY TO TAKE OFFICE IN SHU-CHOU

杜少府之任蜀州

At the palace gates that support the land of Ch'in,

城闕輔三秦

Gazing into the windblown mist of Five Fords,

風煙望五津

Thoughts of parting shared with you,

與君離別意

Being both men on official journeys.

同是宦遊人

If in this world an understanding friend survives,

海內存知己

Then the ends of the earth seem like
    next door.

So let us not, at this crossroads,

Like a young boy and girl soak our robes
    with tears.

天涯若比鄰
無為在歧路
兒女共霑巾

[03456]

Five Fords stands for Szechwan where Magistrate Tu is
going. Besides being one of Wang Po's least courtly
productions, it is also one of his least characteristic.
From certain stylistic idiosyncracies we can be relatively
certain that the poem is indeed Wang's own, but the
Confucian dignity of the poem belies the real direction
of Wang Po's talent, the descriptive couplet. The poem
begins by setting up the distance which will lie between
the two men: from the palace, the center of the state,
to the hazy distance of Shu-chou where Tu's post lies.
We may notice the variation of the conventional opening
which sets the starting point and destination of a journey.
Against this distance which will divide them, Wang Po
sets up a series of unities—of emotion, of circumstance,
and finally of the Confucian sentiment of the brotherhood
of good men (Analects, XII. 5). Through these unities
the poet opposes the natural sorrow of parting.

This is a remarkable poem for the 670s: it has a tight,
internal unity rare in the poetry of the period; instead
of descriptive middle couplets, it has personal and philosophical affirmations; and in the closure it consciously
inverts the "response of tears," appropriate to parting
poetry. This is a poetry of ideas rather than a poetry
of celebration, as court poetry is. Its straightforwardness contrasts favorably with the mannered style of the
day.

The theme of the unity of the spirit as a counter to
the pain of separation is a favorite of Wang Po's. When
he speaks of it, his usually carefully crafted style tends
to take on a simple dignity.

PARTING FROM HSÜEH SHENG-HUA[33]

別薛升華

The many sending you off have come to the
    end of their journey,

送送多窮路

Now restless, you alone will ask of the
    ford.

遑遑獨問津

Sad and chill, this thousand-mile road,

悲涼千里道

Broken by sorrow, man's hundred-year span.

悽斷百年身

But in heart we shall share your drifting,

心事同漂泊

To life's end, be with you in suffering.

生涯共苦辛

Speak no more of departure and staying—

無論去與住

We are together men in a dream.

俱是夢中人

[03449]

"To ask of the ford" is what Confucius requested of his disciple Tzu-lu (Analects, XVIII. 6). The two plowmen Tzu-lu asked turned out to be "crazy" Taoists who responded dementedly that the world was in flux and flood and that there was no "ford." As in the Analects passage, the phrase here is used ambiguously, "to find one's way," both in a physical and spiritual sense. Although in this case the unity of spirit cannot overcome the grief of parting, as it did in the preceding poem, it offers some consolation to the person leaving. Structurally this poem is quite similar to the preceding poem, particularly in the negative imperative of the last couplet, the rejection of a common response. The particular phrasing of Wang's affirmation of unity in the last line is a pattern he uses repeatedly:

We are together men in a dream,

俱是夢中人

and in "Magistrate Tu," line 4:

Being both men on official journeys,

同是宦遊人

and elsewhere:

We arc together men in the land of Yüeh.

俱是越鄉人

[03488]

We are together men weary of travel.   俱是倦遊人
            [03490]

This pattern is not a convention of court poetry, but
what is interesting is that, having become fond of it,
Wang Po uses it as though it were. It goes into his
mental warehouse of poetic conventions to draw out and
use as building block in a poem whenever it seems appropriate. It is a curiously intermediary stage between
sixth- and seventh-century conventionality and eighth-
century originality.

    We can also see a modification of the courtly style
in many of Wang Po's quatrains. Courtly quatrains used
the same mannered diction as longer court poems, but
depended even more heavily on wit, to the point that the
quatrain was becoming almost an epigram. Of the two
dominant forms of poetic closure, which we shall discuss
later, the quatrain was increasingly dominated by the
witty twist, which has come to sound almost like a "punch
line."[34] Wang Po was one of the first poets to use a
grand understatement, often a single image or descriptive
line, to close the quatrain. Because it left the quatrain
open and suggestive, this technique became one of the
dominant forms of poetic closure in the eighth and ninth
centuries.

PARTING BY MOONLIGHT IN A RIVER   江亭夜月送別其二
   PAVILION II

Wild mists veil the emerald stairs,   亂煙籠碧砌
The moon in flight heads toward the   飛月向南端
   southern horizon.
Silence, the pavilion where we part   寂寂離亭掩
   is closed—
Mountains and rivers cold this night.   江山此夜寒
            [03493]

Characteristic of courtly descriptive techniques are the

"emerald stairs" and the cliché metaphorical verb "veil"
籠 , literally "encage" (cf. Shang-kuan Yi, p. 75).
However, the elegant opening couplet is transformed by
the simplicity of the last line, which besides explaining
why the pavilion is closed, suggests a feeling of ubiquitous chill shared by both the men and the landscape.
Loneliness and chilliness are strongly associated in
the poetic tradition, and on this final night before
parting, the men are locked in together against the
spiritual chill of solitude as well as against the physical cold. The sense of cold seeping in from the outside
and extending over the deserted night landscape is far
more powerful than some clever twist on the part of the
poet.

Epigrammatic quatrains continued to exist alongside
the open-ended, suggestive variety through the subsequent
history of Chinese poetry, but it was in the latter form
that the Chinese quatrain found its true greatness. The
following poem, another example of this new technique,
was among the most popular of Wang Po's poems in later
ages.

IN THE MOUNTAINS

山中

Grief at having lingered by the long river,

長江悲已滯

Longing for future return over thousands of
 miles.

萬里念將歸

Even more, set in this evening when the
 wind is high,

況屬高風晚

And on mountain after mountain the yellow
 leaves are flying.

山山黃葉飛

[03503]

In the first couplet Wang Po sets himself in time, between
an unsatisfying past and a desired future. His wish to
return home is intensified by his awareness of autumn
and the dissolution of the forest scene in the autumn
wind. But most of the interest in the poem lies in the

hidden parallel, of which the reader is unconsciously
aware, between the poet and the leaves. As they are
breaking loose and flying away, he too longs to "break
loose" from his "fixed" position, to be set in motion
also, to fly away to his home (cf. Shen Ch'üan-chi,
"Rejoicing at a Reprieve," lines 7-8, p. 362). But the
fall of the leaves also indicates autumn and impending
destruction, lending a sense of urgency to his return.
The structural relation between the two halves of the
poem is not explicit: the poem is left "open" with an
objective scene, left for the reader to sense or decipher
why it is "even more" urgent on this evening.

In a less personal mood, Wang Po was quite capable of
writing clever, mannered quatrains in the courtly style.
By way of contrast I offer the following pair:

PARTING ON AN AUTUMN RIVER

I

Early I met early autumn in a strange
    land,

By a river pavilion the bright moon was
    carried on by the river's flow.

I had known that the stream's passage
    onward wounds thoughts of parting,

But look now how the ford trees hide
    the boat you leave on.

[03512]

秋江送別二首
其一
早是他鄉值早秋
江亭明月帶江流
已覺逝川傷別念
復看津樹隱離舟

II

Homeward boats, homeward riders, form
    a strict line,

North of the river and south of the
    river, gazing at one another.

Who says that these waves are only
    a strip of water?—

I now understand that mountains and
    rivers are two different lands.

[03513]

其二
歸舟歸騎儼成行
江南江北互相望
誰謂波瀾纔一水
已覺山川是兩鄉

Both poems employ playful word repetitions, something of
a tour de force: the first- and sixth-position words in
each line of the first couplet of the first poem are
identical, as are the first- and third-position words
in the first couplet of the second poem. Wang Po is
playing with one of the most common and enduring antitheses in the parallel couplet, the opposition of land and
water. In the first poem the poet is already distressed
by the river and its actual and symbolic significance to
those parting, but he finds it particularly perverse that
the trees on the land should add to his difficulty by
blocking his friend from sight. In the second poem Wang
uses one of the most common of courtly tropes to set up
a clever comment: "Who says X is true (when X most certainly _is_ true), because Y (clever idea) contradicts it."
Through parting, the river becomes not a tiny area but
a division between two different worlds.

As might be expected from one of China's greatest
parallel prose stylists, Wang Po's real strength lies
in his descriptive powers and his ability to write a
perfect couplet. Although Wang's characteristic couplet
style is quite different, if he so desires he can outdo
any court poet in mannered excess:

On plum swards fall evening blossoms,　　　　梅 郊 潜 晚 英
In willow realms startle up first leaves.　　柳 甸 驚 初 葉
Flowing water draws forth strange fancies,　 流 水 抽 奇 弄
Toppling clouds sprinkle scented tablets.　　崩 雲 灑 芳 牒
                          [03435]

The growth of the leaves is compressed in time to a
"startling up," _ching_ 驚, "to rise up swiftly with surprise"; the waves are "sprouting" into strange forms, or
"drawing forth," _ch'ou_ 抽, the poet's fancies by their
forms. The "toppling clouds" sprinkle the poet's writing
tablets with light rain, the external circumstances of

the composition as well as their topic.   The uncharacteristic ornateness of this passage can be attributed to the
fact that it is a banquet poem, the most tenacious and
rigidly prescribed of the courtly subgenres.

As he worked to simplify the parallel couplet without
letting it get dull and mechanical, Wang learned to frame
his startling images in lines that were otherwise direct.
In this way attention was focused on the image and its
effect heightened by contrast.   For example, the following line: "A hawk-wind withers the evening leaves," 鷹風
凋晚葉 (03454).   "Hawk-wind" is original; Wang Po excelled
in creating compounds in which the relation between the
two elements is suggestive and undefined.   There is a
resemblance between the way in which the destructive
autumn wind strikes the leaves and a hawk strikes its
prey: both are keen, swift, and convey a sense of sharpness and violence.   To an earlier court poet "withers"
would probably have been too direct a verb and "evening"
too simple a modifier for the leaves; such a poet might
have written: "A hawk-wind touches the jade leaves"; the
extraneous ornament would have destroyed both the precision of the line and the power of the phrase "hawk-wind."

In his descriptive lines Wang Po went far beyond the
creative imitation practiced by the court poets to
original observation of Nature.   Instead of the parks
and groves of the court poet's excursions, Wang Po was
fascinated by the grander aspects of Nature:

Lightning whips drive on the dragon light.   電策驅龍光
                    [03439]

or:

Fish-beds—waters invading the banks;   魚牀侵岸水
Bird-roads—mist entering the mountains.   鳥道入山煙
                    [03463]

or:

Compound cliffs delude daylight's bright beauty,　褪嶂迷曙色
Empty crags differentiate streams in darkness.　虛巖辨暗流
                                    [03473]

With this interest in the larger natural world Wang Po
was drawn to scenes of steepness and sheerness, to precarious situations.

Layered gates look down on a huge abyss,　　重門臨巨壑
Linked beams rise on lofty mountain bends.　連棟起崇隈
                                [03448]

Towers and terraces look down on sheer slopes.　樓臺臨絕岸
                                    [03450]

The road to the ford looks down on a huge abyss,　津塗臨巨壑
Village huts framed on precarious cliffs.　　村宇架危岑
                                [03474]

Much can be learned about a poet by studying the kinds
of landscape he sees; the traditional correlation of the
poet's inner state with the external landscape was based
on his ability to structure and select elements from a
real landscape before him which serve as parallels to
his own state. Wang Po's obsession with peril mirrors
the perils of his experience, and the poet who sought
out dangerous forms in the landscape was the poet who
implicated himself in one dangerous situation after
another.

　　The innovations of Wang Po in the poetic closure of
quatrains extend to a lesser degree into his regulated
verse and longer poems. The problems of poetic closure
were complicated because they involved basic concepts of
what constituted a poem, a shih. The evolution and codifi-
cation of the tripartite form in shih was no accident:
the tripartite form was the structural manifestation of

a particular concept of poetry as a description of an
external scene or experience and an internal response
to it. The earliest and simplest form of this concept
of poetic closure was in exclamatory sighs or tears.
This basic "it makes me sad" closure went through periods
of relative disuse, but it never disappeared entirely.
As one may well imagine, it permitted very little verbal
variation and often dangles like a familiar, formulaic
appendage at the end of an otherwise brilliant poem.
During the fourth and fifth centuries other intellectual
and meditative closing forms evolved, each a different
kind of "response" to the main body of the poem. By the
seventh century, however, the only real competitor with
the direct, emotional closing was the witty closure of
court poetry. Though such cleverness may seem less a
"response" than the other forms, it is still usually
internal in comparison to the external scene: it may
involve some new and clever perception or understanding
of the scene, some novel interpretation of the external
world. Often the emotional component of the "response"
will be affirmed as the poet expresses his "surprise" at
the observation.

    Trapped into a choice between supercilious wit and
dull sighs, there appeared a third and very attractive
possibility for poetic closure: the emotional response
was transferred from the poet to the reader by leaving
the closure open, by using a scene or image to generate
a complex mood or emotion, like the ancient "stimulus,"
hsing. The reader is invited to set the closing image
in relation to the scene and mood already established.
This technique for poetic closure antedates Wang Po, and
we saw a contemporary use of it in the closing of "Ch'ang-
an: ku-yi." But Wang Po was one of the first poets to
apply it to the quatrain—with brilliant results. It
appears also in some of his longer poetry, as in the
following regulated verse (03472).

DEPARTING FROM YI-YANG IN THE EARLY MORNING

I packed my bags in dawn moonlight,

Wait on the fading stars to speed up my
riding whip.

From the sheer tower make my way over
cinnabar cliffs,

Off twisting bridges reach to azure screens.

Among clouds I'm lost in the shadows of
trees,

Then in fog can't make out the forms of
the cliffs.

And now again a chill gust comes,

Sets flying night's fireflies in deserted
mountains.

易 陽 早 發
飾 裝 候 曉 月
奔 策 候 殘 星
危 閣 尋 丹 障
回 梁 屬 翠 屏
雲 間 迷 樹 影
霧 裏 失 峯 形
復 此 涼 飆 至
空 山 飛 夜 螢

The "azure screens" are probably cliffs covered with
green foliage. This is a brilliant application of the
court poet's miniature descriptive art on a larger canvas.
The relationship of the cold gust of wind and the flight
of fireflies in the dark expanse to the arduous day's
journey is a complex one: in many ways it resolves the
poet's sense of being confined, fogged in, and hard
pressed. Somehow it works and works far better than if
he had merely stated his dissatisfaction with the journey.
Beneath a mask of impersonality the closing couplet
manages to be deeply personal.

    In the majority of his poems, however, Wang Po suffers
the court poet's inability to weld the diverse elements
of his poems together into a powerful whole. Ironically,
some of his most thematically unified poems are occasional
court poems such as "Banquet at Lo-yu Gardens on a Spring
Day" (03435), in which the pervasive wetness of the scene
symbolizes the kindness and generosity of his companions.
Many of Wang's travel poems are weak precisely because
of his reliance on the older form of poetic closure. The
following poem exemplifies this problem: Wang sets the
perils of travel by water against the perils of travel

by land in a series of superb descriptive couplets;
however, the couplets lead to nothing, and the poet can
say no more in the end than that it disturbs him.

MUD GULCH   泥谿

I rest my oars to pass through a swift ravine,

And put down my whip to pace a steep mountain
   path.

River billows emerge from banks dangerous,

Peak steps enter the clouds perilous.

The current sharp, boat's patterned wake a
   jumble,

Precipices slant, the rider's shadow shifts.

Then mist on the water veils azure isles,

And mountain sunshine falls on rust red slopes.

The wind rises in the leaves of reed shores,

Dew glistens on the branches of bamboo pools.

Trips by water are supposed to be wonderful—

Who can understand the song of my hardships?

                   [03476]

The surprise and beauty of these scenes lies not in the
observation of the quirks and minutiae of Nature, but
rather in a freshness of perception achieved through the
syntactic distortions that were the legacy of court
poetry. In the second couplet we cannot be sure whether
the bank or billows are dangerously high, whether the
steps or clouds hangs perilously above the poet. Instead
of rising in the "reed leaves on the shore," Wang Po's
wind chooses to appear in the "leaves of reed shores"
蘋浦葉. Such syntactic rearrangements of a line
became standard in the diction of regulated verse, the
above poem being an extended regulated verse, a p'ai-lü
排律.

    Though he modified the courtly style, Wang Po was
never far from it; he never made the sharp break with
court poetry which we find in at least some of Lu Chao-

lin's poetry. With the dignified descriptive grace of
his new style, Wang will write:

Pulling at flowers, make my way through the
   purple valley,
Then treading leaves I descend to a clear
   creek.

攀花尋紫澗
步葉下清谿

[03465]

but in the next line he will speak of the stream as a
"nephrite broth" 瓊漿.

    Wang Po's collection contains a number of eremitic
poems and poems on the immortals, but neither of these
types has the power of his parting and travel poems.
There are a few heptasyllabic songs, the best of which
is "Looking Down from the High Terrace," discussed in
chapter 9. One of Wang's most famous poems in his "Tower
of the Prince of T'eng," which follows Wang's best-known
piece of parallel prose, the "preface" on the banquet
there. Certainly much of the poem's fame is due to the
preface. The poem is an eight line, heptasyllabic "old-
style" verse, ku-shih 古詩, more successful than Wang's
other ku-shih because its symmetrical tightness and
regularity bring it closer to regulated verse, in which
he excelled. A sense of generic propriety demanded that
the theme of the impermanence of worldly glory be treated
in heptasyllabic "old-style" verse.

TOWER OF THE PRINCE OF T'ENG

滕王閣

The Prince of T'eng's high tower
   looks down on river isles,

滕王高閣臨江渚

Jade bangles and ringing phoenixes
   have ceased their songs and dances.

珮玉鳴鸞罷歌舞

Morning—its painted beams
   send flying Southbank's clouds,

畫棟朝飛南浦雲

Evening—beaded curtains
   roll up the rain on western mountains.

珠簾暮捲西山雨

Calm clouds, reflected in pools,
   go on and on each day,

閒雲潭影日悠悠.

But things change, constellations move—
   how many autumns gone by?

物換星移幾度秋

And where today is the prince of the tower?—

閣中帝子今何在

Beyond the railing the great river
   flows on and on alone.

檻外長江空自流

[03444]

The tower is a world of singing and dancing, a world of
sensual pleasure that lasts only a short while; against
it is set the great river which is eternal. "Morning
clouds" and "evening rain" are together a euphemism for
sexual intercourse, but with strong associations of the
impermanence of sensual pleasure. They derive from a
story told in the preface to the Kao-t'ang fu 高唐賦,
attributed to Sung Yü 宋玉, of how the King of Ch'u met
the goddess of Wu Mountain in a dream and made love to
her.³⁵ As she left him she recited these verses:

I live on the sunny slope of Wu Mountain,   妾在巫山之陽

On the steep places of the high hill—   高丘之阻

At dawn I am the morning clouds,   旦為朝雲

At evening, the moving rain.   暮為行雨

Afterward the King of Ch'u sought her again, but like the
"morning clouds" with which she had identified herself,
the goddess had moved on. Looking into the physical scene
before him, Wang Po sees these emblems of sexuality: they
are haunting reminders of past joy much like Lu Chao-lin's
version of the lovers Ssu-ma Hsiang-ju and Cho Wen-chün
in the landscape around Lute Terrace.

   The opening of Wang's poem is a closing, the end of
the feast. The unwritten banquet poem celebrating this
feast and the Prince of T'eng's past feasts is over, and
what follows is an expanse of time, a string of mornings
and evenings that contain emblems of Nature's permanence
and human impermanence. This landscape filled with the
hermetic signs of the passage of time undermines the joy
of the feast and transforms celebration into elegy.³⁶

11

LO PIN-WANG: POETRY AND RHETORIC

Among the poets of the seventh century Lo Pin-wang's
work is distinguished both by complexity and size (about
130 poems in all), yet his poetry presents the most
difficult problems of interpretation and evaluation.
Like Lu Chao-lin and Wang Po, Lo Pin-wang was a master
of parallel prose rhetoric, but while Lu and Wang made
a clear distinction between their various poetic styles
and parallel prose, Lo Pin-wang brought the structure
and diction of poetry closer to that of prose rhetoric.
Like Lu and Wang, Lo Pin-wang was moving away from the
decorum of court poetry, not toward a new simplicity and
directness, but rather toward the complexity of rhetorical
exposition.

Ironically, this hermetic style responded in many ways
to the demands of the opposition poetics. The parallel
prose model offered the poet the kind of moral and intellectual seriousness that was felt to be lacking in court
poetry. Parallel prose possessed a structural and intellectual vocabulary for expressing complex ideas, developing a meditative theme, and narrating personal experiences.
Lo made extensive use of these elements from parallel
prose: although he did write a number of courtly occasional lyrics, he has far more meditative poems and
personal narratives than any T'ang poet before him.

Unfortunately what Lo Pin-wang gained in seriousness
of topic he lost in poetry. Lo seems incapable of direct
or moving statement; he preferred any form of circumlocution, metonymy, metaphor, or allusion. Parallel prose
brought him excessive artifice along with seriousness.
More than any poet before Han Yü, Lo was an intellectual
poet: to him a poem seemed to be a highly ornamented idea.

In the classical West, poetry and the art of persuasive
rhetoric were old friends; in China this meeting was late,
and judging from Lo's poetry, we may be grateful that the
two soon parted company. Lo's reputation as a parallel
prose stylist endured, but his poetry fared even more
poorly than Lu's or Wang's. The "Imperial Capital" is
a partial exception. In the ten anthologies which survive
from the T'ang and in the T'ang wen-ts'ui there is only
one poem by Lo Pin-wang, and that is in the Sou-yü hsiao-
chi, an anthology of Early T'ang poets in which many of
Lo's contemporaries figure heavily.

     Unlike Wang Po, Lo Pin-wang (ca. 640-84) was not from
the upper levels of officialdom, though his father was
a county magistrate of some local fame. Like many young
intellectuals of the period, Lo began his career by
entering the service of a T'ang prince, the Prince of Tao.
It was probably after the prince died in 664 that Lo
received a minor post as Secretary of Rites and later
as a textual editor in the Chancellory.

     In 670 Lo was banished to the northwestern frontiers
for an unknown offense or association. There he partici-
pated in the wars against the Tibetans. In the years
following that he travelled southward through Szechwan
to the extreme southwestern corner of the empire, where
he held several minor posts. In 676 was recalled to
Ch'ang-an where he served first as a registrar and later
in 678 as a censor in the court of general affairs. The
censorate was not a particularly safe position to be in
during Empress Wu's regency, and like so many other
officials, Lo found himself on the wrong side of the
struggle for power. Soon after his promotion to the
censorate, Lo was imprisoned for remonstrating with the
empress. In 679 he was released in the amnesty that went
with the adoption of a new reign title and the transfer
of the capital to Lo-yang.

     His release did not change his unpopularity with his

superiors.   In 680 Lo was exiled to a minor post in the
county of Lin-hai in modern Chekiang Province.   Lo was
in no great hurry to reach this post, and when he arrived
there, he found the job so distasteful that he soon quit.
Out of work and out of favor he joined Hsü Ching-yeh's
rebellion against Empress Wu, which broke out when she
assumed absolute authority.   His contribution to the
rebellion was a famous and effective proclamation against
the empress which was said to have excited her admiration
for his style as much as it annoyed her.   When the rebellion was crushed, Lo was captured and presumably executed.
There is an apocryphal legend that he escaped and became
a Buddhist monk, to be discovered many years later by his
old friend Sung Chih-wen.

   Lo Pin-wang's early work is quite securely within the
structural confines of court poetry; however, even then
he shows a tendency to extreme circumlocution and display
of erudition.   Mooring one evening in early autumn at
the Yangtze port of Chiang-chen, Lo saw ships from the
imperial fleet.   The essentials of the situation appear
straightforwardly in the title, "Mooring by Chiang-chen
in the Evening" 晚泊江鎮(04235), plain words in their
proper order.   But as he moves into the poem proper, he
is taken by a seemingly irresistable urge to elegantly
deform, elaborate, and replace:

The fourfold cycle shifts to the Yin pitch-
    pipes,   四 運 移 陰 律
The Three Wings float on Baron Yang.   三 翼 泛 陽 侯

The educated contemporary reader would certainly know
that the "fourfold cycle" was the cycle of the seasons,
that the "Yin pitchpipes" were associated with autumn,
and that Baron Yang, as the god of the waves, represented
the river.   It might have taken a bit more trouble to
remember that the Three Wings were the three classes of
war galleys.   There would probably have been a certain

amount of admiration at Lo's technical prowess in finding
a "three" and "Yang" in the second line to match a "four"
and "Yin" in the first. But the courtier's sharp eye
and clever wit are absent here; no one could miss the
fact that Lo has said something very banal with extreme
elegance.

    Taken as a whole "Mooring by Chiang-chen in the Evening"
is a far better poem than the first couplet promises. The
descriptive section is competent but not brilliant, and in
the expanded response section we can already see tendencies
to complex argumentation.

MOORING BY CHIANG-CHEN IN THE EVENING   晚泊江鎮

The fourfold cycle shifts to the Yin
  pitchpipes,   四 運 移 陰 律

The Three Wings float on Baron Yang.   三 翼 泛 陽 侯

The scent of lotus melts away late summer,   荷 香 銷 晚 夏

As breath from chrysanthemums enters new
  autumn.   菊 氣 入 新 秋

Night crows chatter on whitewashed battlements.   夜 烏 喧 粉 堞

Geese descend for the night on isles of
  reeds.   宿 雁 下 蘆 洲

Ocean fogs veil the frontiers,   海 霧 籠 邊 徼

A wind from the river encircles the fortress
  tower.   江 風 繞 戍 樓

The whirling tumbleweed startles at signs
  of parting,   轉 蓬 驚 別 緒

The shifted orange grieves for departure's
  sorrow.   徙 橘 愴 離 憂

My soul flies to the slopes of the Pa Mounds, 魂 飛 灞 陵 岸

My tears are used up in Lake Tung-t'ing's
  currents.   淚 盡 洞 庭 流

I'll stir my shadow, my thoughts on the
  "swan over the plain,"   振 影 希 鴻 陸

And flee renown, withdrawing from Anthill.   逃 名 謝 蟻 丘

But then I sigh at how far the capital is—   還 嗟 帝 鄉 遠

In vain I gaze on the white clouds drifting.   空 望 白 雲 浮

                [04235]

The last eight lines require a paraphrase:

> I, a wanderer like the whirling tumbleweed, am shaken when I see
> something that reminds me of parting and being away from home;
> in the same way I am like the orange, which grows only in the
> South and changes to a different tree if transplanted in the
> North, thus a symbol of steadfastness and purity. Since my
> body cannot go there, my soul flies off to the Pa Mounds, near
> Ch'ang-an where I long to be; since I cannot go there I use up
> all my tears weeping here in the South. In the Yi-ching we read,
> "The wild swan slowly crosses the plain, but the wanderer does
> not return." The best visual evidence of my motion will be in
> my shadow, so I'll set it moving to emulate that wild swan and
> return home. In avoiding political success and fame I'll be like
> that tavern keeper at "Anthill" in Ch'u who left his tavern to
> avoid meeting Confucius. But even though I would like to return
> home and renounce worldly glory on one level, I cannot help but
> yearn for the distant capital and worldly success on another.
> Thus as I gaze toward the capital, my vision is blocked by white
> clouds, suggesting to me both those who "block" me from Her
> Majesty's/His Majesty's favor and the cloudlike vanity of my
> desires.

Such an argument built up of multiple allusions is characteristic of parallel prose.

Lo Pin-wang was easily capable of using new and recon-
dite allusions, but there is a tendency to use the same
ones over and over again. A little downstream from
Chiang-chen Lo writes in another poem (04226):

The Imperial Walls look down on the shores of the Pa,	帝城臨灞涘
Yü's cave rests on the Yangtze's banks.	禹穴枕江干
Further on, the orange's nature will surely change,	橘性行應化
And the tumbleweed's heart goes off uneasily.	蓬心去不安

At times Lo Pin-wang could outdo even Shang-kuan Yi

in clever and mannered description:

Flowers in her mirror shake the water chestnut
  sun,
Robe's musk enters the lotus-scented wind.

鏡花搖荇日
夜麝入荷風

[04215]

The meaning of the first line of this couplet is open to
various interpretations. The "flowers" are probably
flashes of light shining off of it, rather than real
flowers reflected or the fair lady herself, a "flower."
These reflected flashes may quiver on the water chestnuts
as tiny "suns" or mingle with the sunlight shining on
them. Lo is reworking a couplet of Yü Hsin:

Sunbeams move as flames on her hairpins,
Light through the window shakes flowers
  in her mirror.[37]

日光釵燄動
窻影鏡花搖

However, such visual ingenuity is not usually characteristic of Lo's poetry.

    Lo Pin-wang's strong sense of rhetorical argument and
prose amplification enabled him to write poems much longer
than was common in the seventh century. Besides his
"Imperial Capital," Lo has several other long pieces that
aim at a seventh-century sense of seriousness. The preface to one such poem (04132) begins with Confucian
literary dogma, "What is in the heart as intention is
poetry when it appears in speech. Still, what is written
cannot completely express what is spoken, and what is
spoken cannot completely express what is in the mind,"
and proceeds to apply these principles to the poet's own
experiences. Lo's formulation of Confucian dogma stresses
that serious literature is about oneself, and Lo applies
himself energetically to this, his favorite topic. One
of Lo's most successful poems is thus the mammoth "Long
Ago," Ch'ou-hsi p'ien 疇昔篇 (04149), a highly ornamented
poetic autobiography in two hundred lines.[38] This poem is

one of the earliest examples of long poetic autobiography,
a subgenre which was to become important in the eighth
and ninth centuries. The tendency of the later subgenre
to extreme ornamentation may derive in part from the model
of "Long Ago."

As Lo Pin-wang borrowed the diction, structure, and
themes of parallel prose, only the formal differences and
extended treatment of parallel prose remained to differentiate the two genres. We can see this clearly in the
relationship of the preface and the poem in the following
allegorical piece.

A FLOATING LOG

As my eyes drifted over the stream, they spied a floating log,
tossing aimlessly like that wooden statue riding the current, lost
and not knowing where it was going.

I observed how its roots coiled and how its trunk and branches
spread out all around. In its larger parts there was material for
beams and oars; in its smaller parts it might have served for wheel
axles and rafter eaves.

Were it not endowed with the surging spirit of Heaven and
Earth, did it not possess within itself the pure essences of
the universe, how could it have relied on that outward form which
passed up over the clouds and measured the sun, how could it have
clasped within such a frame on which the snow piled and which the
frost encased?

And while it was able to keep its material to itself in some
hidden marsh, to hide its flowering behind layered cliffs, then
it cut off from its sight the glory of the Temple's porch, where
the plans of state are made, then it banished its form from ruin
by axe and hatchet. Securely it could spread down its shade over
ten thousand acres and hang bright radiance up through the nine
layers of the sky; it could compare its height with the (legendary)
Chien tree and could equal the long life of the mighty Ch'un tree.

But it set down its roots on a perilous cliff, trusted its
substance to dangerous paths; above it was smashed by gales and

sudden gusts, beneath was dashed through by rushing billows and
swift waves. Since its base was enclosed by the soil, its position was rendered precarious by the lay of the land.

The order of its increase and decline was not bound up with
the times, nor were the principles of nurture and husbandry within
its own control. Once it fell into the stream valley, it bobbed
and swirled ten thousand miles, floating then sinking under the
waves, moving off then stopping according to chance.

Though some Yin Chung-wen may sigh that its life is gone (as
he did seeing the withered tree in the courtyard), though Confucius, Eminent Father, may realize how hard it is to work rotten
timber—all the same, if it comes upon a fine craftsman or meets
some immortal, then it can tie up at Ox Jetty after floating over
the vault of Heaven, and the path ahead of the Jade Ornament—found
by T'ai-kung in a fish—will not be long. Then Craftsman Shih
will size it up, and it will not be far from becoming a vessel
for the Emperor, Lord of Ten Thousand Chariots. When I think of
these possibilities, I realize that it is purely chance whether
this material is to be used or not. Alas!

This being true, how can it be that among the myriad things
only those of the same voice and same spirit may respond to one
another? Deeply stirred, I have written this poem to offer to
those who suffer the same sickness.

浮槎幷序

遊目川上。觀一浮槎。汎汎然若木偶之衆
流。迷不知其所適也。觀其根柢盤屈。枝
幹扶疏。大則有棟梁舟楫之材。小則有輪
轅榱桷之用。非夫稟乾坤之秀氣。含宇宙
之淳精。孰能負凌雲槪日之姿。抱積雪封
霜之骨。何使懷材幽藪。藏穎重巖。絶望
於巖廊之梁。遺形於斤斧之患。固可垂蔭
萬畝。懸映九霄。與建木較其短長。將大
椿齊其年壽者。而委根險岸。託質畏途。

上為疾風衝飆所摧殘。下為奔浪迅波所激射。基由壞拮。勢以地危。豈盛衰之理繫乎時。封植之道存乎我。一墜泉谷。萬里飄淪。與波浮沈。隨時逝止。雖殷仲文歎生意已盡。孔宣父知朽質難雕。然而遇良工。逢仙客。牛磯可託。玉璞之路非遙。匠石先誤。萬乘之器何遠。故材用與不用。時也。悲夫。然則萬物之相應感者。亦其同聲同氣而已哉。感而賦詩。貽諸同疾云爾。

Of old it relied on its thousand-foot substance,
And on high, looked down over nine-cubit peaks.
Its pure heart surpassed the cassia late in the
  year,
Its sturdy resolve outdid the winter pine.
Suddenly it met with a gale, was broken,
Then was struck by billows and waves,
To no purpose it rages against its ruin
And has become useless through knottiness.
Three thousand miles into the Sea of Po,
Through how many layers of sand and mud?
It seems a boat, rolling, unstable,
Or like that statue, floating to what end?
To the last it will be hard to find an immortal,
Nor will it be easy to meet a good craftsman.
In vain it harbors a vessel for the emperor,
But who will make measurements for the crafting?

昔負千尋質，高臨九仞峰。
真心凌晚桂，勁節掩寒松。
忽值風飆折，坐為波浪衝。
摧殘空有恨，擁腫遂無庸。
渤海三千里，泥沙幾萬重。
似舟飄不足，如梗泛何從。
仙客終難托，良工豈易逢。
徒懷萬乘器，誰為一先容。

[04236]

Originally a "preface," hsü 序 , was meant to establish a historical or biographical context in which a poem or event could signify fully. This classical form appears in Wang Po's "Tower of the Prince of T'eng": the preface describes the banquet, scene, and history of the event,

and the poem responds to the situation. The distinction
between the poem and the parallel prose preface is clearly
drawn. In "A Floating Log," however, the preface says at
length what the poem says succinctly. The primary variation is that the preface sets up the hope that the log
will be used, that the wanderer will be employed, and the
poem destroys that hope. With the exception of the closing, however, the poem closely follows the argument of
the preface, both in categories of discussion and in
phrasing.

The third paragraph of the preface corresponds to the
first couplet of the poem: its height, "relying on that
outward form which passed up over the clouds and measured
the sun," 負凌雲概日之姿 , is stripped to "Of old it
relied on its thousand-foot substance," 昔負千尋質 .
The fourth paragraph of the preface concerns the tree's
safety in its seclusion and how it flourished there; in
the poem this is rendered in the seclusion and endurance
of the pine and cassia. The poetic version has stronger
ethical associations, punning on "pure heart/trunk," 心 ,
and "sturdy resolve/joints," 節 . The preface presents an
elegant and graceful version of the traditional hyperbolic
trope in which some object is compared favorably to a
mythical exemplar; "it could compare its height with the
(legendary) Chien tree and could equal the long life of
the mighty Ch'un tree," 與建木較其長短, 將大椿齊其
年壽者 . In the poem this elegant phrasing must be
discarded in favor of the concise clichés of the "surpassing" trope: "surpass," 凌 , and "outdo" (literally "cover
over"), 掩 . The legendary trees of the preface are
replaced by the emblematic pine and cassia mentioned
above.

Again in the third couplet, the expressive phrasing
of the preface is stripped to a weak echo by verse's
demands for economy; from "above it was smashed by gales
and sudden gusts, beneath it was dashed through by rushing

billows and swift waves," 上為疾風 衝飆所摧殘；下為奔浪 迅波析激射, to "Suddenly it met with a gale, was broken,/Then was struck by billows and waves," 忽值風飆 析, 坐為波浪衝 . The painful inferiority of the poem to the parallel prose of the preface exemplifies the problem of trying to make poetry work like parallel prose: the stylistic devices of poetry had been evolved to function in the economy of the pentasyllabic line; the ornament of parallel prose required longer periods and looser structure, and when "translated" into verse, it became flat and thin.

Lines seven to twelve of the poem disengage themselves from the meditation on chance and fate which is to be found in the corresponding section of the preface. Instead the poem elaborates on the insecurity and helplessness of the log; no one appreciates it. As the poem breaks free from the argument of the preface, it may turn around and comment on what was said in the preface: it gives a neg- ative answer to the hope expressed in the preface that the log may meet a good craftsman. In this the poem complements the preface, but the difference is partially a function of generic demands: the closing expression of distress is the natural coda of the <u>shih</u> tradition.

Lo's poetry ranges from the sort of versified argument which we see in the preceding poem to a peculiarly dense and allusive lyric style which appears in his formal exercises on set topics and in his famous "On the Cicada: in prison." This poem too has a parallel prose preface, but in this case there is a distinction between the pro- siac and poetic treatment.

ON THE CICADA: IN PRISON

The Western Course: a cicada's voice singing;	西 陸 蟬 聲 唱
A southern cap: longing for home intrudes.	南 冠 客 思 侵
How can I bear those shadows of black locks	那 堪 玄 鬢 影
That come here to face my Song of White Hair?	來 對 白 頭 吟

Dew heavy on it, can fly no farther toward me,　　霧重飛難進

The wind strong, its echoes easily lost.　　　　風多響易沈

No one believes in nobility and purity—　　　　無人信高潔

On my behalf who will explain what's in my
　　heart?　　　　　　　　　　　　　　　誰為表予心

[04190]

This certainly requires a paraphrase:

> When the sun moves through the Western Course of the heavens, a
> sign of autumn, the cicada sings. Its singing causes homesick-
> ness in me, like that once felt by Chung Yi of Ch'u, wearing his
> southern cap as a memento of his homeland when a prisoner in the
> state of Ch'in. Like him I am a southerner imprisoned in the
> North. How can I bear that those wings of the cicada, so often
> used to describe the curls of beautiful ladies, come to listen
> to my "Song of White Hair," like that which Cho Wen-chün sang
> when Ssu-ma Hsiang-ju abandoned her? Those black cicada wings
> like curls remind me of youth and attractive beauty, unbearable
> to one who is growing old and feels rejected by his ruler.
> Futhermore, since the singing of the cicada is a reminder of
> autumn, the season associated with the coming of old age how
> can I bear that it come any closer to me, reminding me of my
> own aging? But perhaps I have misunderstood the cicada: asso-
> ciated with purity and old age, it may be a kindred spirit. If
> my ruler hears it, it may remind him of my purity and old age,
> and thus obtain my release. In this respect its singing is like
> pleading my case to the throne. But it, like me, is caught up
> in the autumn situation which it represents: the dew is so heavy
> on it it can fly no further and thus will not be able to get
> into the palace and reach the ruler's ears; furthermore, though
> I might hope that its singing will be heard from outside, the
> autumn wind is so strong that its voice will be drowned out.
> Even if his singing, or my own in this poem, were to reach near
> the throne, it would do no good, because no one believes any
> more in nobility or purity—neither mine, my innocence of crime,
> nor that of the cicada. Thus there is no one to state my case

    for me.

Expanded by paraphrase, the logic of this poem does come
close to a parallel prose argument; however, the poetic
economy of hint, allusion, and ambiguity reduce it to
something quite different than "A Floating Log." Lo's
looser, more discursive style is more common than the
density of the poem above. By way of comparison there
is another poem of the same imprisonment, "Brief Notes
to My Friends from Prison," 幽繫書情通簡知己 (04251),
the first eight lines of which follow:

In years gone by I met my Yang Te-yi,   昔歲逢楊意
Observing the radiance, they honored Ch'u's   觀光貴楚材
  genius.
It seemed the cinnabar phoenix would rise   穴疑丹鳳起
  from its cave,
It was as if a white colt came from among   場似白駒來
  the willows.
One order sunk some bait for the proud,   一命淪驕餌
A "thrice-sealed" warned of calamity's womb.   三緘慎禍胎
Before speaking I suffered waxing and waning,   不言勞偃伏
Here suddenly encountered twists and turns.   忽此遘邅迴

This continues for twenty-eight more equally turgid lines.
The lines above say only that Lo found someone who appreciated his talents, but that no sooner were his fortunes
on the rise than he fell into disfavor.

    However unsuccessful they were, such attempts to
achieve a poetry that could serve as a vehicle for self-
expression were an important phenomenon of the period.
Two decades later in the work of Ch'en Tzu-ang, a better
vehicle was found.

PART THREE

CH'EN TZU-ANG

INTRODUCTION TO PART THREE

[Wu had once been a state on the lower Yangtze; it later became
an elegant designation for the general region. The Wu region was
the cultural center of the Southern Dynasties. In the Chronicles
of Wu and Yüeh, a romanticized history of the lower Yangtze region
a millennium before the Southern Dynasties, there is a story that
after the wise minister Fan Li had aided Yüeh in conquering the
neighboring state of Wu, he left the service of Yüeh. In memory
of Fan Li's accomplishments, the King of Yüeh had artisans cast
a golden statue of him.]

Shen Ch'üan-ch'i and Sung Chih-wen dashed
  over the field of literature—　　　　　沈宋橫馳翰墨場

Courtly men who at first couldn't abandon
  the Ch'i and Liang,　　　　　　　　風流初不廢齊梁

But if we judge whose is the credit in
  conquering Wu,　　　　　　　　　　論功若準平吳例

They ought to compose the shining gold
  to cast a Ch'en Tzu-ang.　　　　　　合著黃金鑄子昂

    Yüan Hao-wen, "Quatrains on Poetry" VIII[1]

In the eyes of the famous thirteenth-century poet and
critic Yüan Hao-wen 元好問, Sung Chih-wen and Shen Ch'üan-
ch'i, whose poetry had been the glory of the last decades
of the Early T'ang, were in fact mere craftsmen, fit only
to glorify the true talent of the age, Ch'en Tzu-ang
陳子昂 . To Yüan, Ch'en Tzu-ang was the man responsible
for the literary defeat of Wu, the southern courtly style,
just as Fan Li had been responsible for the military
defeat of the ancient state of Wu.

Yüan Hao-wen was a champion of the northern poetry of
his own Chin dynasty against that of the Southern Sung
and thus had his private motives for praising Ch'en Tzu-
ang as the conqueror of the poetic style of the Southern
Dynasties. However, in his admiration he followed an
already long-established tradition that credited Ch'en

153

with changing the stylistic norms of poetry single-
handedly. Tu Fu, usually an admirer of court poetry,
seems to be suggesting Ch'en's role as the first to
restore the greatness of ancient literature in the following lines from a poem on Ch'en's former dwelling in
Szechwan:

It caused you no pain that your office was low,

Sage wisdom and virtue were what you honored.

Talent you had—to continue the Odes and Sao,

"Great craftsmen" fell short of your stature.

Born to the line of Ssu-ma Hsiang-ju, Yang Hsiung,

Your fame hangs in the heavens with sun and moon.

位下曷足傷
所貴者聖賢
有才繼騷雅
哲匠不比肩
公生揚馬後
名與日月懸

[10709]

Ch'en Tzu-ang's contentment with his low office echoes
a strain of Confucian thought which associates virtue
and poverty. Fu-ku sentiments had always been attractive
to those outside court circles, those who never made it
to the top of the official hierarchy. Ch'en possesses
the talent to "continue" ancient poetry after a hiatus
of many centuries. "Great craftsmen" had been a positive
term, but in this passage Tu Fu is clearly using it in a
somewhat pejorative sense, referring to those like Sung
Chih-wen and Shen Ch'üan-ch'i who put the craft of poetry
ahead of its political and moral content. Finally Ch'en
is filiated to Ssu-ma Hsiang-ju and Yang Hsiung, partially
because all three writers were natives of Szechwan, but
primarily because Ch'en is seen as an upholder of Confucian
morality in the court.

   Three decades later, in a poem recommending his friend
Meng Chiao for office, Han Yü 韓愈. recited the standard
fu-ku version of Chinese literary history: before the
T'ang there had been a constant process of literary
decline, but:

In our dynasty literature again flourished.　國朝盛文章
Ch'en Tzu-ang was first to mount to the skies.　子昂始高蹈

[17828]

Like other later T'ang writers, Han Yü was anxious to
forget almost a century of T'ang court poetry. The phrase
"mount to the skies," 高蹈, is usually associated with
attaining immortality; the primary implication here is
that Ch'en was been an "immortal of literature," but Han
Yü may be also commenting ironically on Ch'en's fascination with the cult of immortality. Although fu-ku writers
generally acknowledged Ch'en Tzu-ang as their literary
ancestor, Ch'en's commitment to Confucian social values
was not single-minded.

Following such comments by Tu Fu, Han Yü, and others,
Ch'en Tzu-ang's prestige and place in literary history
was assured. Even today he is considered the first major
figure in T'ang poetry and the forerunner of the High
T'ang.[2] In his own time, however, Ch'en was a peripheral
talent, overshadowed by men such as Li Chiao, Tu Shen-yen,
Sung Chih-wen, and Shen Ch'üan-chi. The last decades of
the seventh century and the first decades of the eighth
century were the last great age of court poetry, its
"Indian summer," and the mutations of the courtly style
that occurred then probably had more lasting significance
for the development of T'ang poetry that did Ch'en's
complete rejection of court poetry. Still, it was Ch'en's
name that was remembered, not Sung's or Shen's; to later
poets Ch'en represented the necessary illusion of a
complete break with the recent literary past.

12

CH'EN TZU-ANG'S POETIC CAREER

Ch'en Tzu-ang was born in 661 to a Szechwan family of
some local importance that was undistinguished by service
to the central government. From our accounts of his
youth it hardly seemed that he would grow into someone
who would deal a mortal blow to court poetry. His biog-
raphers say that he took absolutely no interest in studies
until the age of eighteen, at which time he began to
apply himself diligently. By the time he was twenty-one
he felt qualified to go to the capital at Lo-yang and sit
for the chin-shih examination. Unfortunately, Ch'en's
examiners felt otherwise, and in 682 Ch'en failed in his
first attempt at the chin-shih.

When Ch'en Tzu-ang was a youth, the three greatest
poets of the empire—Wang Po, Lu Chao-lin, and Lo Pin-
wang—were all in Szechwan at one time or another. Ch'en,
however, acknowledges no debt to them, nor does his poetry
show more than a few hints that he was familiar with the
work of the older poets. It seems rather that Ch'en grew
up in relative isolation from contemporary literary
culture. What he knew about poetry was probably learned
from books like the Wen-hsüan, which on the whole presented a very different kind of poetry from what was then
being written in Lo-yang. The art of court poetry was
a social art, developed through intercourse with other,
elder poets and was not to be learned from books. Ch'en's
friendships with local Szechwan poets, such as with the
monk Hui 暉 , seem to be of a later date. Furthermore,
Ch'en's early poems do not show familiarity with the
corpus of poetic lore to be found in encyclopedias such
as the Yi-wen lei-chü, so important to the court poet's
education in the proper techniques of amplifying a topic.

Courtly yung-wu poems, such as those by Li Chiao, are
altogether absent; these represent the kind of exercises
in craft which we expect to find from an aspiring young
court poet. Of course, it is possible that Ch'en excluded
such pieces from those poems which were to be circulated,
but his early poems which do survive show no hint of such
training.

A number of poems survive that probably date from
Ch'en's first trip to Lo-yang to take the examination.
A version of the tripartite form is followed in these
poems, though the descriptive middle couplets are on the
whole quite different from what one finds in court poetry.
When he does try his hand at a courtly descriptive couplet,
his range is limited, as we shall see. Still these poems
possess a directness which is not to be found in poems
written at the court; it is not the artful directness of
great poetry, but rather that of an intelligent young man,
well enough read in the poetic tradition to avoid awkwardness, but who had not submitted himself to the constraints
of court poetry.

MEDITATION ON THE PAST AT WHITE EMPEROR CITY   白帝城懷古

The sun sinks—evening on the blue river   日落滄江晚
I rest my oars to ask of local customs.   停橈問土風
These walls look out on the land of Pa,   城臨巴子國
While into the terraces sink the palaces of   臺沒漢王宮
  the King of Han.
A wild region—still in Chou's domain,   荒服仍周甸
Deep in its mountains remain the deeds of Yü.   深山尚禹功
Peaks hang, their green cliffs broken off,   巖懸青壁斷
Terrain perilous, the emerald stream goes   地險碧流通
  through.
Ancient trees rise at the edge of the clouds,   古木生雲際
Homeward sails emerge in the fog.   歸帆出霧中
My river road goes off without end—   川途去無限
This wanderer's longing now seems endless too.   客思坐何窮

                    [04451]

A unity of structure, diction, interests, and sentiment binds this poem with the following three poems, which can be located at successive stages of Ch'en's voyage down the Yangtze.

CROSSING CHING-MEN, GAZING TOWARD CH'I

I have left the Wu Gorges far behind,
Ever gazing, descend to Chang-hua Terrace.
Gone are the mountains and streams of Pa,
And Ching-men appears amid parting mist and
    fog.
A city wall wedges in beyond the azure plain,
Trees break off in the folds of white clouds.
Today a madly singing wanderer—
Who knows he is coming into Ch'u?

[04417]

楚峽臺盡開外限客來

望巫章川霧野雲歌入

門去下國煙蒼白狂知

荊遙望巴荊城樹今誰

度遠望巴荊城樹今誰

MEDITATION ON THE PAST AT HSIEN MOUNTAIN

I graze my horse above the wild domain,
Climb a high spot to view an ancient
    capital.
Still there is grief for the "monument of
    tears,"
And I can yet imagine the Resting Dragon's
    diagram.
Far away the city demarcates Ch'u territory,
The mountains and rivers are half into Wu.
In vain do burial mounds come out before me—
How many saints and sages have rotted away?
A tree in the wilderness breaks off in the
    blue gray mist,
A building at a ford, alone in the evening
    air.
Who knows of this wanderer from a thousand
    miles away,
Irresolute and faltering now, in meditation
    on things past?

[04452]

Hsiang-yang, the city visible from Hsien Mountain, had
once been the headquarters of the Three Kingdoms warlord
Liu Piao. Ch'en Tzu-ang probably did feel some of the
Early T'ang fascination for the vanished glory of ancient
cities, so strongly associated with the opposition poetics,
and in his eagerness to find a "ruined capital" he probably
chose Hsiang-yang as the nearest at hand. The "monument
of tears" is associated with the Chin dynasty magistrate
Yang Hu 羊祜 , who vowed that if his soul endured after
death, it would reside on Hsien Mountain. Because of
his virtue local residents erected a monument to him on
the mountain, and it became customary for visitors to
Hsiang-yang to climb the mountain and shed tears for
Yang Hu's soul. The "Resting Dragon" is Chu-ko Liang
諸葛亮 , minister of the Three Kingdoms state of Shu-
Han. A group of prehistoric monoliths in the region were
commonly believed to represent a schematized battle plan
devised by Chu-ko Liang for an attack upon the state of
Wu.

STAYING IN LO-HSIANG COUNTY FOR THE EVENING   晚 次 樂 鄉 縣

My homeland is infinitely far—   故 鄉 杳 無 際
Here, setting sun and a solitary journey.   日 暮 且 孤 征
Streams and plains hide my former country,   川 原 迷 舊 國
A road moves out toward frontier walls.   道 路 入 邊 城
A fortress in the wilds, moor mists break   野 戍 荒 烟 斷
   it off,
Deep in the mountains, ancient trees level.   深 山 古 木 平
What is it like, the grief of this moment?—   如 何 此 時 恨
Screeching shrilly, gibbons cry by night.   嗷 嗷 夜 猿 鳴
                        [04418]

These four poems might best be characterized as "tourist
poems," describing the young westerner's first journey
into the Chinese heartland, albeit its southern fringes.
He is constantly looking back to Pa (Szechwan), and is

careful to note "the domain of Chou" (which excluded
Szechwan), the land encompassed by the "deeds of Yü."
He repeats the broadest geographical designations as
though they held some magic interest in themselves. He
is fascinated by the history and antiquity of these
regions. His meditation on the past (huai-ku) at White
Emperor City focuses neither on a historical event nor
on a process of rise and fall, but rather on the antiquity
itself which links it to the heartland of Chinese civilization.

The melancholy which rides along with the huai-ku form
modulates easily into his sentiments of solitude and
homesickness. Unlike the rhetorical exercises of more
proficient poets, these poems are more concerned with
evoking a mood than with craft. Ch'en Tzu-ang is much
closer to the travel poems of Li Pai-yao than to those
of Wang Po, Lu Chao-lin, or Lo Pin-wang. Ch'en's couplets
roll out less mechanically than Wang's or Lu's; Ch'en's
style is even farther from that of Lo Pin-wang, whose
meditative travel poems show that highly mannered diction
can obscure even the most genuine sentiments and completely
deform the mood of a poem.

Ch'en's parallel couplets describing natural scenes
are nothing like Shang-kuan Yi's in complexity, yet when
they appear in these poems, they stick out and disrupt
the poem's flow. In these Ch'en betrays some influence
of court poetry by his metaphorical use of verbs to
describe the visual scene. It is interesting, however,
how few of these he has at his command:

Peaks hang, their green cliffs broken off.　　巖懸青壁斷

Trees break off in the folds of white clouds.　　樹斷白雲隈

A tree in the wilderness breaks off in the
azure mist.　　野樹蒼煙斷

A fortress in the wilds, moor mists break it off.　　野戍荒煙斷

A disruption of a visual continuity is inevitably a
"breaking off" 斷 . If the continuity is resumed after
the interruption, the interruption becomes a "wedging in"
or a "dividing" 分 . This common spatial usage is often,
as below, indistinguishable from the use of <u>fen</u> as a verb
of perception: "to make out."

A city wall <u>wedges in</u> beyond the azure plain.   城分蒼野外

Far away the city <u>demarcates</u> Ch'u territory.   城邑遙分楚

If a visual continuity is unbroken, stretching into the
distance, then it is said to "enter"   that distance:

The mountains and rivers are half into [enter]   山川半入吳
  Wu.

A road moves out toward [enter] frontier walls.   道路入邊城

Neither the metaphorical use of verbs in general nor the
metaphorical use of these verbs in particular are at all
uncommon in seventh-century poetry; however, Ch'en's
marked tendency here to describe spatial relationships
in active terms imparts a certain vigor to his lines.
Though he is less interested in the visual "wonders,"
<u>ch'i</u>, of the landscape than Wang Po, Ch'en Tzu-ang shares
something of the elder poet's preference for vistas over
minutiae. Also like Wang, Ch'en Tzu-ang understands that
in order to concentrate the reader's attention on one or
two well-chosen words in a line, he must keep the rest
of the line plain. But Ch'en clearly lacks Wang Po's
mastery of visual description, and when he finds a scene
or a phrase that pleases him, he does not mind seeing
that scene again in similar words farther down the river.
    In spite of the legend, preserved in various sources,
that Ch'en Tzu-ang's works were immediately acclaimed on
his arrival in the capital, it seems more likely that
poems such as the ones above would have been looked on

with some condescension: as his friend and biographer
Lu Ts'ang-yung 盧藏用) said: "Those of the age did not
understand him."[3]   There is another famous story of Ch'en's
arrival in capital, which is amusing, if almost certainly
apocryphal:

> When Ch'en Tzu-ang first came to the capital he was an unknown.
> There happened to be someone asking a million cash for a Tartar
> lute he was selling, and none of the young nobles and men about
> town who were passing it around to have a look at it knew its
> true worth. Suddenly Ch'en Tzu-ang popped out of the crowd and
> said to the by-standers, "I'll take it for a thousand strings
> of cash." When people asked in surprise why he would pay this
> amount, he answered that he was really good at that kind of music.
> Everyone then asked if they might hear him play for them, and
> Ch'en told them to gather the next day in Hsüan-yang Ward. When
> the appointed time came, everyone went there together, and there
> they found wine and delicacies set out for them with the lute
> placed in front. After eating, Ch'en picked up the lute and
> said, "I, Ch'en Tzu-ang of Shu, had a hundred scrolls of writing.
> When I came riding into the capital, there were droves of common,
> worldly scholars, and I was unknown to anyone. This sort of music
> is for a low artisan and not worth your attention." Thereupon he
> lifted the lute, shattered it, and passed around his writings.
> In one day his fame filled the capital.[4]

Whatever the good qualities of his early poetry might
have been, they were not those of court poetry and therefore not elegant enough to win him the chin-shih. Leaving
Lo-yang in 682 after failing the examination, Ch'en wrote
for the first time in the eremitic vein that characterizes
much of his later work.

RETURNING WEST AFTER FAILING: PARTING FROM　　落第西還別魏四懍
  WEI LIN

The tumbleweed that rolls, not now at rest;　轉蓬方不定
Plummeting wings shudder when the bowstring　落羽自驚弦
  whirs.

Once I leave these mountains and rivers,   山 水 一 為 別

How many years before our joy here returns?   歡 娛 復 幾 年

The parting pavilion, dark with wind and rain,   離 亭 暗 風 雨

The road I must travel leads into clouds and   征 路 入 雲 烟
  mist.

To return I shall follow the footpaths of   還 因 北 山 逕
  North Mountain,

Home to care for the fields of Eastslope.   歸 守 東 陂 田

[04427]

The tumbleweed had been a popular metaphor in Chien-an
and Wei poetry for someone cut off from home on endless
travels.   The same archaizing metaphor appeared earlier
in two of Lo Pin-wang's poems where the deep emotional
associations it was supposed to carry were submerged
under Lo's involute rhetoric.   In the simplicity of his
poem, Ch'en captures something of the metaphor's power.
A failed examination candidate was often referred to as
someone struck by an arrow or a shot-pellet.   North
Mountain probably refers to the famous "Proclamation on
North Mountain," a satire on insincere hermits, which is
preserved in the Wen-hsüan.[5]

    If this poem is any indication of what Ch'en Tzu-ang
did on the examination, it is no wonder that he failed.
The poem clearly sets up a regulated verse pattern of
tonal antithesis, but the serious tonal violations in
line five, seven, and eight cannot be excused even by
looseness of Early T'ang regulated verses.   Only a few
hints of the tripartite form can be seen: the third
couplet is an acceptable descriptive couplet in the right
position, but the hypotactic second couplet is not.   The
metaphors of the first couplet are out of place, while
the last couplet begins an entirely new topic in its
response.   The form is just close enough to the proto-
lü-shih of the Early T'ang to appear as a conscious
violation of the genre.   This generic violation corresponds
to the eremitic rejection of the search for office.   In

another poem written after his failure (04426), Ch'en
shows he can produce a structurally and tonally perfect,
if plain and dull, regulated verse.[6]

In 683 Ch'en Tzu-ang returned to Ch'ang-an to take
the examination a second time. In the spring of 684 he
passed and became a chin-shih. In early spring Chung-
tsung was still the nominal ruler, though Empress Wu held
all power. By autumn, when Ch'en received his first post
as Corrector of Characters in the Secretariat, the Empress
formally assumed the regency in the name of Jui-tsung.
Six years later, in 690, she abolished the T'ang altogether
and set up her own Chou dynasty.

As has been discussed in earlier chapters, the opposition poetics, which we may now call fu-ku, had found the
most support from those who were outsiders to the court
poetic tradition. Although Ch'en Tzu-ang eventually
mastered the courtly style well enough to make a respectable showing of himself, he was not a craftsmen of the
same caliber as a Sung Chih-wen or a Shen Ch'üan-ch'i.[7]
It is doubtful that he ever could have won in the court
poetic competitions, which we will discuss in the next
section. From his early travel poems we can see that
Ch'en was conscious of the distinction between his homeland and the Chinese heartland; even in the apocryphal
anecdote translated above he announces, "I, Ch'en Tzu-ang
of Shu [Szechwan]..." It was not that Szechwan was not
a civilized place in the seventh century—it was just
that it had not produced many poets or cultural figures
for some five hundred years. Szechwan had been the home
of many of the greatest writers of the Han dynasty, and
this may be part of the reason that Ch'en Tzu-ang filiated
himself to the literary past rather than to contemporary
literature: he was "of the line of Ssu-ma Hsiang-ju and
Yang Hsiung." Because of this sense of regional identity
and because of his initial rejection by the literary
arbiters of the capital, it was natural for Ch'en to turn

to the opposition poetics and <u>fu-ku</u>. There he found
justification for the kind of bold simplicity that was
already present in his earlier poetry.

The <u>fu-ku</u> argument certainly found sympathetic ears,
and court poetry still had developed no counter argument
to it. The following poem and its famous preface cannot
be dated precisely, but they are clearly from a time when
Ch'en Tzu-ang was in Lo-yang. In the preface we can see
Ch'en Tzu-ang reiterating the venerable arguments of the
opposition poetics with a new energy and specificity, but
we should remember that this does not represent disinterested theorizing; rather, it was written to flatter and
gain the favor of a high official who shows sympathy for
Ch'en's kind of writing. The poem that accompanies the
preface is justly less famous, but it is of some importance in showing another kind of poetry associated with
<u>fu-ku</u>: it is an ornate moral and political allegory.

THE LONG BAMBOO

To His Excellency Tung-fang Ch'iu:
The Way of Literature has been in a sorry state some five hundred
years now. The strong style of the Han and Wei was not passed
on in the Chin and Liu-Sung: there is ample evidence of this in
the literary productions of that time. In leisure hours I have
carefully examined poems of the Ch'i and Liang, works of flashy
beauty that strove for ornateness, but which were utterly lacking
in deeper significance. Always then I would sigh, brooding on
the ancients, in constant fear lest they become lost in their
distance from us and perish. The Airs and the Odes of the <u>Book
of Songs</u> are not being written, and thereby I am disquieted.

The other day at Mr. Chieh's house I saw Your Excellency's
poem "On a Lone Wu-t'ung Tree." Its style and structure soared
straight upward; its tone and mood were terse and abrupt. It
was both splendid and refined, possessing the sound of imper-
ishable metal and stone. Thereby my heart was washed free of

petty concerns, my vision was enhanced, and all that had been
repressed deep within me was brought forth. I had not expected
to see the tone of the Cheng-shih [Wei reign period, associated
with the poetry of Juan Chi and Hsi K'ang 嵇康] appearing here
once again; it would bring the authors of the Chien-an to look
at one another and smile. Mr. Chieh said that Chang Hua, Ho Shao,
and Your Excellency were all of the same ilk [Chang Hua and Ho
Shao were both poets and high officials of the Western Chin].
I further consider you to be someone who understands the art of
language. Thus, stirred to sighs by your proper and refined
creation, I have myself written a poem entitled "The Long Bamboo."
Assuredly there will be someone who understands both it and myself,
one who will hand it down and show it to others.

The dragon bamboo grows on the Southern peak,	龍種生南嶽
Where it stands azure and alone, tall, dense with leaves;	孤翠鬱亭亭
Peak and precipice tower above it,	峯嶺上崢嶸
While beneath is the murky dark of mist and rain.	烟雨下微冥
At night it hears the screech of flying squirrels,	夜聞鼯鼠叫
By day gives ear to the voice of valley streams.	晝聆泉壑聲
No sooner has spring wind swept and shaken it,	春風正澹蕩
Than it feels the chill of autumn's white dew.	白露已清泠
It resounds mournfully, wind-stirred to tap rhythm,	哀響激金奏
Colors dense, blossoms of marble moist.	密色滋玉英
In the cold of the year when frost and snow are harsh,	歲寒霜雪苦
It alone is green, retaining its splendor.	含彩獨青青
It does indeed hate the biting ice,	豈不厭凝冽
And is shamed beside spring plants in their glory;	羞比春木榮
Yet the glory of spring plants will sometimes fade,	春木有葉歇
While in its steadfastness it is never stripped bare.	此節無凋零

It had only wanted to be strong as metal or
  stone,
Preserving hard purity for all time,
And had not expected the flutemaster Ling Lun
Would blow on it, imitating the phoenix's call.
Then it was paired with a zither from Yün-ho
  Mountain,
An orchestra performing in the courtyard of
  Heaven,
Wondrous tunes in a thousand variations,
The ancient Hsiao-shao played nine times.
Truly it has been made lovely by the carving
And has always wanted to serve the immortals.
The blue dragon carriage went galloping
  onward,
Repressed emotion from the purple phoenix
  sheng.
The maid of Ying's Terrace joined her lover,
And they played on it as they mounted the
  heavens.
Hand in hand they climbed to the bright sun,
Wandered afar, sporting by Red Wall,
High, then low, the black cranes dance,
Stopping, continuing, bright clouds appear.
Forever following the troops of immortals
  away,
On the Three Mountains, to visit the Capital
  of Jade.

始願與金石
終古保堅貞
不意伶倫子
吹之學鳳鳴
遂偶雲和瑟
張樂奏天庭
妙曲方千變
簫韶亦九成
信蒙雕斲美
常願事仙靈
驅馳翠虬駕
伊鬱紫鸞笙
結交嬴臺女
吟弄升天行
攜手登白日
遠遊戲赤城
低昂玄鶴舞
斷續綵雲生
永隨眾仙去
三山遊玉京

[04387]

We have already seen some of the proper bamboo "lore"
used in T'ai-tsung's and Yü Shih-nan's poems on bamboo:
reference is made to the fact that they stay green through
the winter, thus showing their "steadfastness" (chieh 節,
also meaning a "section" of the bamboo), and for this
quality they are likely to be cut by Ling Lun, musician
of the Yellow Emperor, to be "carved" (given courtly
polish) and used in celebrations of the immortals (those
at court). However, Ch'en Tzu-ang's narrative allegorical

treatment of the topic is quite different than the treatment given by T'ai-tsung and Yü Shih-nan, who simply
allude to these various aspects of bamboo. Ch'en's poem
is much closer to Lo Pin-wang's allegorical "Floating
Log": in both cases the ethical and political message of
the allegory puts the poems in the camp of the opposition
poets, despite the ornateness of the style.

What separates Lo's poem and the poem above from the
average court poem may be Ch'en's concept of hsing-chi
興寄 , translated freely as "deeper significance." Such
terms are virtually impossible to translate literally,
but essentially it means that the surface level of the
poem is a "vehicle" (chi, a "sending" or "entrusting")
for some personal response to a thing or event (hsing).
Thus, as in allegory, the logic of the surface is subordinate to the "meaning." In the case of "The Long
Bamboo," the narrative that evolves out of the yung-wu
lore has very clear autobiographical implications. Ch'en
is the bamboo, an exemplar of purity and steadfastness,
the "dragon species" to be exact. He is brought to court,
not of his own volition but because of his outstanding
qualities, where he receives "polish." He suggests to
Tung-fang Ch'iu that he would like to rise even higher
in court circles, to be closer to "Heaven," the emperor
(or in this case Empress Wu, perhaps suggested in the
allusion to the "maid of Ying's terrace," the daughter
of the Duke of Ch'in who flew on a phoenix to heaven—
the imperial position—with her lover, the pan pipe
player).

In Chinese literature a useful distinction can be made
between general and topical allegory. The distinction is
not absolute: all topical allegory may be read generally,
while much general allegory has topical overtones.
However, there is an important distinction between a
poem in which bamboo is used as a general symbol of
integrity, such as Yü Shih-nan's or T'ai-tsung's, and

a poem in which the bamboo stands for the integrity of a given individual. This distinction in the treatment of allegory bears directly on the account of literary history in the preface: topical allegory flourished during the Eastern Han and Wei, followed by a tendency toward general allegory during the Chin and Liu-Sung.[8] Therefore, during the great age of court poetry, the allegorical implications of an object were usually subordinated to its presence at hand (from "this object represents" to "about this object we may summon the following associations"), or they served only as building blocks in a rhetorical exercise. This is what we find in T'ai-tsung's and Yü Shih-nan's poem on bamboo, even though the reference is general rather than topical. The use of topical allegory in the T'ang is a consciously archaizing technique, dignified both by its antiquity and by its implications of Confucian morality.

In Ch'en Tzu-ang's work of the 680s in Lo-yang can be seen a growing mastery of the descriptive couplet, not the stately and static formality of the Shang-kuan t'i, but a kind of energetic brilliance which at times plays counterpoint to the inherent restraint of the parallel couplet. The following poem was written during Ch'en's term as Corrector of Characters, between 684 and 689.

ENTERING CH'IAO GORGE AND AN-CHÜ CREEK: THE
SOURCE OF WOOD-CHOPPING CREEK WAS HIDDEN
FAR AWAY, FORESTS AND PEAKS BRIGHTENED
ONE ANOTHER—A WONDROUS EXPERIENCE.

入峭峽安居谿
伐木谿源幽遠林
嶺相映有奇致焉

I whistled to companions, sang "Chopping Wood,"

嘯徒歌伐木

Oars raced the skiff bouncing the ripples.

驚栧漾輕舟

On a long, winding course I followed the waters,

靡迤隨波水

Splashing through current, upstream in the shallows.

潺湲泝淺流

Misty sands split the two shores,

烟沙分兩岸

Dew-drenched isles flanked by pairs of shoals,

露島夾雙洲

Dense forests of ancient trees reaching the
   clouds,

And floating peaks, criss-crossed, fallen
   upon the waters.

Cliff and pool cast lovely light upon each
   other,

Stream-filled valleys circle round and round.

The road is far, light presses urgently on me,

The mountains deep, my mood still more withdrawn.

Evening—chill brooding of deer and squirrels;

Autumn—sunset sounds of gibbons and birds.

I vow to give up my plans in the Royal Library,

Go travelling in the hermit land of cassia.

Thus I write to take leave of friends and loved
   ones,

For a thousand years I'll search for Fairy Hill.

[04463]

古樹連雲密
交峯入浪浮
巖潭相映媚
澗谷屢環周
路迥光踰逼
山深興轉幽
麋鼯寒思晚
猿鳥暮聲秋
誓息蘭臺策
將從桂樹遊
因書謝親愛
千歲覓蓬丘

"Chopping Wood" is the title or <u>Shih</u> #165, associated
with seeking companions in the traditional Mao interpretation. Line eleven primarily refers to the setting sun
making him aware of the necessity to return, but it is
difficult to resist the visual image of the literal
translation.

Ch'en Tzu-ang's descriptive technique is distinctive
and generally more energetic than that of his contemporaries. As we saw in the poetry of Lu Chao-lin, there
is a growing tendency to narrative order in the arrangement of the couplets; Ch'en is moving further and further
upstream into the mountains as day turns to evening and
is lured by the temptation not to return. Despite this
tendency to narrative order and the poem's eremitic
message, the form is basically tripartite, with the
opening and closing response expanded to two couplets
instead of one. Running alongside the tripartite form
are rapid shifts in mood, from exuberant speed and
companionship to a brilliant but solitary landscape of

misty shoals, shining peaks, and sparkling reflections, and from there to a melancholy mood of reclusion in which the poet yearns to escape from the world of human society.

Twice Ch'en Tzu-ang accompanied Chinese armies on campaigns against the nomadic tribes of the North. The first of these campaigns was to the northwest and lasted from 686 to 687; the second, some ten years later, was directed against the Khitan in the north and northeast. Ch'en's talents found a more congenial outlet in his campaign poetry, but even so there is a striking difference between the poetry of his first campaign and that of his second. The poetry of the 685 campaign is much closer to court poetry: it is dense, mannered, and less emotional than the poetry of the Khitan campaign, but its descriptive flashes reveal the Early T'ang at its best.

CROSSING GORGE-MOUTH MOUNTAIN: TO THE
    REMINDER CH'IAO CHIH-CHIH AND WANG
    WU-CHING

度 峽 口 山 贈 喬 補
關 知 之 王 二 無 競

Gorge-mouth, south of the Great Desert,

峽 口 大 漠 南

Stretches sharply before me: a border for our Middle Land.

橫 絕 界 中 國

First chaotic masses of ragged stone,

叢 石 何 紛 糺

Then small mountains that swell with blazing light.

小 山 復 嶜 岒

Seen from afar, it teems with many faces,

遠 望 多 異 容

Up close, its appearance is unvaried.

迫 之 無 異 色

Half craggy heights where lone peaks loom broken,

崔 崒 半 孤 斷

A circuitous path, twisting, then going straight.

逶 迤 屢 迴 直

It locks us indeed against the attack of Tartar horses,

信 關 胡 馬 衝

Blocks also the gateways to the Chinese frontier.

亦 距 漢 邊 塞

But we do not rely on a fastness of mountains and rivers,

豈 依 河 山 險

Rather we bring compliance by the glory of Imperial Virtue.

將 順 休 明 德

When things are most forceful, they surely
    decline,
Forms mighty as these easily reach their
    limit.
The continuous winding is suddenly gone,
There are vast stretches, level without end.
You gentlemen, with bodies as of gold,
How are you here in this wild uncivilized
    region?
By the Cloud Terrace there are many officers,
They await you beside the Royal Courtyard.

物壯誠有衰
勢雄良易極
邐迤忽而盡
泱漭平不息
之子黃金軀
如何此荒域
雲臺盛多士
待君丹墀側

[04396]

Cloud Terrace was the ceremonial location in the capital
where frontier generals were honored. It seems at first
that Ch'en Tzu-ang is tacking an incongruous social
compliment onto a beautiful landscape description, but
he is in fact transposing the technique of "reading the
landscape," practiced by Hsieh Ling-yün 謝靈運 (385-433)
into an occasional mode. The characteristic Hsieh Ling-
yün landscape poem observes the landscape, draws philosophical conclusions from its structure, and closes with
a personal response to the hidden order which the poet
has discovered.[9] In Ch'en's poem, his passage through
the ever higher mountains and then out onto the level
desert is interpreted in terms of Chinese cyclical theory:
as things reach some extreme, they inevitably return to
a "level" condition. The formal "response" of the poem
is that the fortunes of Ch'en's friends will likewise
return to stability after the hardships of campaign.

    In 689 Ch'en received a ceremonial post in the Imperial
Guard, a rank only slightly higher than his earlier post
in the Secretariat. In 691 he returned to Szechwan on
the death of his mother and returned to the capital in
693. One need only compare the opening of the following
poem, written on his return to the capital, with his
earlier poem on Ch'iao Gorge to see how little change

had occurred in his occasional style:

SETTING OUT FROM WAN-CHOU AT DAWN AND LETTING
  MY BOAT RIDE THE FLOODS: SENT BACK TO MY
  FRIENDS AND RELATIVES IN SZECHWAN

萬州曉發放舟乘
漲還寄蜀中親友

A drizzly sky, then rain clears from the cliffs   空濛巖雨霽
And, sparkling brightly, dawn clouds return.   爛熳曉雲歸
I whistle to fellow travellers, set out with   嘯放來明發
  the light,
Speeding oars race past broken jetties.   奔楫鶩斷磯
Vast stretches of forests and peaks wind around,   蒼茫林岫轉
Continuous billows fly over the floods.   駱驛漲濤飛
From distant shores lone clouds emerge,   遠岸孤雲出
Behind far peaks the sunlight is faint. ...   遙峯曙日微

                        [04462]

Once back in Lo-yang, Ch'en was made Reminder of the
Right, an office which, though low in rank, involved a
certain honor because of its proximity to the throne.
Service in Empress Wu's court was not without its perils,
and in 694 Ch'en was imprisoned because of a factional
struggle in the court. The following year he was released,
and in 696 Ch'en was made Grand Counsellor on the staff
of General Wu Yu-yi in his campaign against the Khitan.
It was on this campaign that Ch'en wrote many of his best
and most famous poems. The style of these poems differs
sharply from Ch'en's earlier work and looks forward to
one of the many faces of High T'ang poetry. It is difficult to say what factors were responsible for this
change. Lu Ts'ang-yung attributes Ch'en's famous "Song
on Yu-chou Terrace" to the poet's depression at a demotion, earned by Ch'en's repeated warnings to the inept
Wu Yu-ying about the impending military disaster.

    The "Song on Yu-chou Terrace" (04415) is preserved
in Lu's biography of Ch'en Tzu-ang and is probably Ch'en's
most famous work:

I look back—I do not see the ancients;   前 不 見 古 人
I look ahead—can't see the generations to come. 後 不 見 來 者
I brood on the endlessness of Heaven and Earth, 念 天 地 之 悠悠
And tears stream down—I stand alone.   獨 愴 然 而 涕 下

Ch'en is more remembered for these simple lines than for
all his elegant descriptions of landscapes. The poem is
a straightforward and moving description of the isolation
of the individual in space and time, cut off from past
and future, dwarfed by the immensity of the universe.
Man stands in time facing backward; the first couplet
reads literally:

I do not see the ancients in front of me/from before 前 不 見 古 人
I do not see those to come behind me/afterward.   後 不 見 來 者

The poem is best characterized as a variation on the
huai-ku, one of Ch'en Tzu-ang's favorite forms. Yu-chou,
with its many historical associations, first becomes the
occasion for Ch'en to articulate the ubi sunt theme: "I
look back—I do not see the ancients." But the center
of interest in the ubi sunt theme is quickly inverted
from the vanished glory of the past to the isolation of
the present, from the future as well as from the past.
All human beings are reduced in size, life span, and
significance by the "endlessness," both in space and time,
of Heaven and Earth. The archaic "response of tears" is
completely in place here, with its associations of simplicity and deep feeling.
     For all the beauty and pathos of its directness, the
poem is based largely on a passage from the Yüan-yu 遠遊
in the Ch'u-tz'u:

When I consider the eternity of Heaven and 惟 天 地 之 無 窮 兮
  Earth,
I bewail human life's long suffering.   哀 人 生 之 長 勤
Those gone before I shall never reach,   往 者 余 弗 及 兮
Of those to come I shall hear nothing.[10] 來 者 吾 不 聞

The poet of the Yüan-yu, whom Ch'en believed to have
been Ch'ü Yüan, resolved his grief over human mortality
by a flight through the heavens to a state of transcendence; Ch'en Tzu-ang resigns himself to solitude and
tears, but the pathos of the situation is heightened
by the background of the Yüan-yu. The flight through
the heavens is the expected response which is not there.

Despite the fact that three of Ch'en Tzu-ang's four
simple lines can be traced to this single passage, the
impact of the poem is in no way reduced. The isolation
of the lines, the failure to take the expected resolution,
and the biographical and occasional contexts all change
Ch'en's poem substantially from the source. One might
make the analogy to a painter who bases the style of one
of his own paintings on a detail of another, large painting. As we have seen earlier, new poetry is created by
reaching back into the past, using it, and altering it.

From the same period comes the following series of
poems, also considered to be representative of Ch'en Tzu-
ang's departure from the Early T'ang style. I translate
the preface and the first two poems.

VIEWING THE PAST AT CHI HILL: TO THE
   RECLUSE LU TS'ANG-YUNG, SEVEN POEMS
   WITH A PREFACE

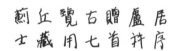

697. On a campaign in the North, I have passed through Chi
Gate and viewed the former capital of the state of Yen, whose
walls, moats, and all traces of its former hegemony have sunk
beneath the weeds. I was deeply moved, but repressed my sighs.
I remember its glory of long ago when Yüeh Yi, Tsou Yen, and
a host of worthy men visited this place. Thus I came to
climb Chi Hill and wrote seven poems to express myself on
the subject. I send these to the recluse Lu of Mount Chung-
nan. There were also traces of the Yellow Emperor here.

THE YELLOW EMPEROR'S TERRACE

軒轅臺

To the North I climbed Chi Hill for the view,

北 登 薊 丘 望

Seeking the past on the Yellow Emperor's
  Terrace.

求 古 軒 轅 臺

His winged dragon is nowhere to be seen,

應 龍 已 不 見

Where horses were pastured, now only brown
  dust.

牧 馬 空 黃 埃

Yet still I imagine Kuang-ch'eng-tzu,

尚 想 廣 成 子

Who has left his traces in the folds of
  white clouds.

遺 述 白 雲 隈

[04388]

The Yellow Emperor's Terrace was supposed to have been
located on the spot where that mythical emperor defeated
the equally mythical bandit Chih-yu. In this encounter
the Yellow Emperor rode a winged dragon. The fourth line
refers to a story in chapter twenty-four of the Chuang-
tzu in which the Yellow Emperor asked a herd-boy how to
govern the empire; the boy replied that, like pasturing
horses, it simply required that one do nothing to harm
the horses. Now in the desolation of warfare's dust,
there is no more of that pasturing, which teaches good
government. Kuang-ch'eng-tzu was a recluse, of whom the
Yellow Emperor asked about the perfection of the Way.
The absence of the winged dragon and grazing horses in
Ch'en's vision suggests not only the ubi sunt theme, it
also points to Wu Yu-yi's military failure. This first
poem of the series seems to be directed particularly to
Lu Ts'ang-yung, who as a recluse would probably be more
interested in the Yellow Emperor than in the historical
scenes that follow. The closing reference to Kuang-
ch'eng-tzu suggests that although there is no longer any
winged dragon to defeat the bandits—the Khitan—the
ideal recluse represented by Kuang-ch'eng-tzu still
survives today in men like Lu Ts'ang-yung, far away "in
the folds of white clouds." The further implication is
that Wu Yu-yi would do well to emulate the Yellow Emperor

in perfecting the Way before attempting any more campaigns. This sort of selective historical analogy would fall under Ch'en's idea of hsing-chi. "deeper significance."

KING CHAO OF YEN

To the South I climbed to the Lodge of Chieh Rock
And gazed afar to the Terrace of Gold.
The tomb mounds are grown over with tall trees,
But King Chao—where is he now!
His plans to be hegemon are finished now—
I drive my horse back down again.

[04389]

This ubi sunt poem succeeds through a directness and simplicity like that of "Song of Yu-chou Terrace." Included in the Ming anthology T'ang shih hsüan 唐詩選, this is certainly the most famous poem of the series. King Chao of Yen had the Lodge of Chieh Rock built for his advisor Tsou Yen; the Terrace of Gold was built to accomodate other advisors. Here again Ch'en Tzu-ang seems to be consciously echoing an earlier poem, the thirty-first piece in Juan Chi's "Singing My Feelings." In the following poem Juan uses the Warring States Kingdom of Wei as an analogue for his own Wei dynasty.

I rode out from the capital of Wei,
Gazed south to the Flute-watching Terrace.
The music of fifes and pipes lingers,
But King Liang—where is he now!
Their soldiers ate the brewer's dregs,
Their worthies found homes in wilderness.
For before their songs and dances were done,
Ch'in's army was upon them.
Hsia Wood is no longer ours,
Now dust rises from the crimson palaces.
Their army fell beneath Hua-yang,
Their bodies became dust and ashes.[11]

While Juan Chi's huai-ku has clear topical, contemporary intent, it would be difficult to interpret Ch'en Tzu-ang's poem in any terms but the general ubi sunt theme. Juan Chi criticizes the excessive luxury of the Kingdom of Wei and suggests that it was the cause of their destruction by the state of Ch'in; the moral for his own Wei dynasty is obvious.

The other poems of the series also concern the state of Yen and the famous personages associated with it. The aesthetic qualities that gave these poems such strong appeal to later Chinese readers depended on a literary historical context which is impossible to reproduce in translation. Their emotional directness appears as a compelling artlessness in one of the most important Chinese mimetic modes—the imitation not of actions or the world, but of inner states of emotion. The historical vision gives these emotions legitimacy: they are fully serious and not the trivial emotions of purely private concerns.

Ch'en Tzu-ang's occasional poetry of this period is more conventional, as occasional poetry must be, but we can see something of the energetic, emotional style of the huai-ku even in the context of a social occasion.

CLIMBING THE TOWER ON CHI HILL: SENDING OFF
  OFFICER CHIA ON HIS WAY TO THE CAPITAL

登薊丘樓送賈兵曹入都

Eastern mountains have been my abiding desire,
A campaign north was not to my heart.
Alone, back turned on the wish of my life,
Stirred now to tears which soak my robes;
At sunset I climb atop Chi Tower,
Gaze ever at the peaks of Yen's mountains.
The Sea of Liao floods far and wide,
While Tartar sands fly deep and thick.
O-mei Mountain, far and faint as a dream,
How shall I search the immortals there?

東山宿昔意
北征非我心
孤負平生顧
感涕下露襟
暮登薊樓上
永望燕山岑
遼海方漫漫
胡沙飛且深
峨眉香如夢
仙子昌由尋

I strike my sword, rise, and sigh,   擊劍起歡息
And the bright sun sinks suddenly westward.   白日忽西沈
I hear you are being sent to Lo-yang,   聞君洛陽使
By you I will send word southward.   因子寄南音

[04408]

Although it was entirely proper to affix the "message" to the last couplet in social occasional poetry, one cannot miss the awkward incongruity of the last couplet here. The tripartite form in which personal response followed objective scene "worked" somehow; when Ch'en Tzu-ang fills in the middle of the poem with a delineation of his personal feelings, the appropriateness of the structure breaks down.

One of Ch'en Tzu-ang's finest huai-ku was perhaps written on the journey back to Lo-yang from the Khitan campaign. The poem alludes to the great Ch'in general Po Ch'i, lord of Wu-an, who inflicted a decisive and terrible defeat on the army of the state of Chao at Ch'ang-p'ing. It was while visiting the site of this battle over a hundred years after Ch'en Tzu-ang that Li Ho wrote his famous "Song of the Arrowhead at Ch'ang-p'ing" (20843).

CLIMBING THE NORTH TOWER ON THE WALL OF   登澤州城北樓宴
    TSE-CHOU FOR A BANQUET

For most of my life, weary of travels,   平生倦遊者
Long observing the endlessness of Change,   觀化久無窮
Then coming here, climbing this city,   復來登此國
And looking down, together with you.   臨望與君同
Just now I see the forts of the troops   坐見秦兵壘
    of Ch'in,
And have heard remotely of the Chao   遙聞趙將雄
    general's valor:
Where now is the army of Lord Wu-an?—   武安軍何在
The events at Ch'ang-p'ing have turned to   長平事已空
    nothingness.

Sing for a while the song "Black Clouds,"   且 歌 玄 雲 曲
Wine on your lips, dance "Fragrant Wind."   銜 酒 舞 薰 風
Do not let the students in their blue robes   勿 便 青 衿 子
Sigh for you, white-haired old men!   嗟 爾 白 頭 翁

                    [04411]

"Black Clouds" was a Han ceremonial song celebrating the
emperor's choice of wise advisors; "Fragrant Wind" is a
verse attributed to the sage-king Shun:

The fragrance of the South Wind   南 風 之 薰 兮
Can melt my people's woes.   可 以 解 吾 民 之 慍 兮
The season of the South Wind   南 風 之 時 兮
Can help my people's fortunes.[12]   可 以 阜 吾 民 之 財 兮

The topical circumstances that surround this poem add to
its complexity. In the opening Ch'en assumes a detached,
philosophical viewpoint as the "observer of Change";
although this stance is uncommon in Ch'en's occasional
poetry, it is one of the dominant stances of the Kan-yü,
which we will discuss shortly. From this detached view
point Ch'en can see a historical analogy to Wu Yu-yi's
present military fiasco in the defeat of Chao at Ch'ang-
p'ing. But from the same detached viewpoint Ch'en also
sees the meaninglessness of the defeat in the impermanence
of things. In response to this, Ch'en urges his companions
to sing two songs which suggest hope that the emperor (or
empress in this case) will choose good advisors and that
the troubles of the nation will be alleviated. They are
not to be pitied as failures, but are rather to show the
next generation of officials, the "students in their blue
robes," a kind of Confucian heroism. Change, which brings
defeat, renders defeat meaningless by its constancy and
promises better times. Like "Crossing Gorge-Mouth Mountain," this poem is a complex consolation in social occasional poetry, not simply a celebration or commiseration.
Unlike the earlier poem, which is based on the philosophical

landscape poetry of Hsieh Ling-yün, this poem uses the
"bold melancholy" (pei-chuang 悲壯 , a modal term used
in T'ang criticism and associated with the poetry of the
Chien-an and Wei) of the huai-ku to work out the consolation.

In the autumn of 697 Ch'en returned to Lo-yang where
he resumed his post as Reminder of the Right. It was
probably in the next year that he withdrew from office
on the grounds of his father's failing health and returned
to his native Szechwan.

I clasp my robes crossing Han Pass,	攬衣度幽谷
Holding back tears, I gaze to the streams of Ch'in.	衕涕望秦川
The gates to Shu begin from here,	蜀門自茲始
Clouds and mountains stretching far and wide.	雲山方浩然

[04395]

Shortly after his return, Ch'en's father died, and Ch'en
himself was in failing health. The poems of Ch'en Tzu-
ang's last years lack the intensity of his poetry written
on the Khitan campaign, but many of them have a distinctive
strength which looks forward to a different face of the
High T'ang.

LYING SICK IN MY HOME GARDEN   臥疾家園

In this world, the Master Without Fame,	世上無名子
Among mortals my years and months grow longer.	人間歲月賖
I have cast from me all my plans and strategies,	縱橫策已棄
In perfect stillness the Way is my home.	寂寞道為家
As I lie sick, no one comes to call on me,	臥疾誰能問
I dwell in peace, the year flowers in vain.	閑居空物華
I still remember my friends of the Spirit Terrace,	猶憶靈臺友
As I lodge in Purity, hermit in great roseate clouds.	棲真隱大霞
Refine the cinnabar, let the sun-carriage speed on,	還丹奔日御

Return to youth, swallow the "sprouts of clouds." 却 老 餐 霞 芽
Who would have guessed that the guest at White 寧 知 白 社 客
  Temple
Would never weary of Green Gate's melons. 不 厭 青 門 瓜

[04459]

The "Spirit Terrace" refers to the capital; the association probably came to mind through the phrase "dwelling
in peace," <u>hsien-chü</u> 閑居, the title of a <u>fu</u> by the Chin
poet P'an Yüeh 潘岳 (d. 300), in which the Spirit Terrace
is mentioned. "Sprouts of clouds" was a kenning for tea.
The White Temple was where one Tung Ching lodged in Lo-
yang when eager to have an interview with the great men
of the day: here it simply means that Ch'en had been eager
for office. "Green Gate's melons" refers to the story of
the Marquis of Tung-ling mentioned earlier in the notes.
Tu Fu was to echo the last line of this poem affirming
his own reclusion in his famous sequence "Autumn Wastes"
(11491):

The autumn wind blows on staff and table— 秋 風 吹 几 杖
I shall never weary of North Mountain's bracken. 不 厭 北 山 薇

North Mountain's bracken refers to the story of Po Yi and
Shu Ch'i, a sterner purity and more ominous reclusion than
that of the Marquis of Tung-ling.

   In 702 Ch'en Tzu-ang died. According to his friend
and biographer Lu Ts'ang-yung, he was imprisoned by a
rapacious local official who wanted to get his hands on
the family wealth. Some modern scholars have suggested
that Lu, who gave up the life of a hermit to chase public
success in the capital, was covering up a murder instigated
by an antagonistic court faction. In 702 Wang Wei and Li
Po were both only infants; the High T'ang was still several
decades away.

13

THE KAN-YÜ

In his poem (10709) written on a visit to Ch'en Tzu-ang's former dwelling, Tu Fu closes with the couplet:

You have proven your loyalty and virtue
  forever—
We have, left for us, the Kan-yü.

終古立忠義
感遇有遺編

Although Ch'en Tzu-ang may have been best known for his brief effusion on Yu-chou Terrace, none of his works were taken as seriously by discriminating readers as the thirty-eight poems entitled Kan-yü 感遇, "Stirred by My Experiences." They were the kind of works deemed worthy of mention in the author's biography in the official history and were included in the important early Sung fu-ku anthology, the T'ang-wen-ts'ui. They were first singled out in Lu Ts'ang-yung's preface to Ch'en Tzu-ang's collected works: "When it comes to stirring others, to abrupt strength of style, to the subtle becoming clear and the obscure becoming manifest, with a view to seeing the subtleties of Change and thereby to reach the very borders of those in heaven, then we have the Kan-yü.[13] On the other hand, none of the Kan-yü are represented in the surviving anthologies compiled in the T'ang itself, anthologies which for the most part follow popular taste in poetry.

We cannot be sure whether the Kan-yü were considered serious poetry because of the overt philosophical and moral content of many of the pieces or because of the topical political allegory that was later read into them. The great Ch'ing allegorist Ch'en Hang 陳沆(1785-1826) would read Tu Fu's phrase "loyalty and virtue" 忠義 as implying that Tu Fu saw topical, political comments in

the series.[14] However, one might just as easily take
Tu Fu's reference to Ch'en's character in general terms.
Lu Ts'ang-yung's comments, on the other hand, tend to
suggest a more general, philosophical reading of the
poems, but this too is suspect: Lu might well have sought
to suppress a topical, political interpretation of the
Kan-yü. Furthermore, phrases such as "those in heaven"
may just as easily refer to those at court as to the gods
and immortals.

   The Kan-yü are usually filiated to Juan Chi's Yung-
huai, "Singing My Feelings," which we have discussed
earlier. This filiation is first credited to the late
eighth-century monk Chiao-jan 皎然.[15] The Yung-huai
certainly were read as political allegory during the
T'ang, but if we read the Kan-yü closely, we can see that
Ch'en Tzu-ang made only indirect use of the Yung-huai, if
he used them at all. Some of the Kan-yü are almost certainly political allegory; some are clearly not. The
majority of the poems lie in that difficult middle ground,
and we must weigh whether topical allegory is present on
a case by case basis.

   The question of the presence of allegory extends even
to the title of the series. The allegorists read Kan-yü
as "Stirred by the problem of 'meeting one's time,'"
taking yü 遇 in its political sense as "success," to
appear in history at a time when one's talents are appreciated by a virtuous prince. Clearly the implication is
that Ch'en Tzu-ang is "stirred" by appearing at the wrong
time in history. One may also take the title in much the
same way as Yung-huai, "Singing My Feelings," in which
Kan-yü would be "stirred by what I encounter," "stirred
by my experiences."

   Certain biographical inconsistencies appear in most
of the topical allegorical interpretations, even in those
poems which are certainly allegorical. Many do seem to
attack the empress and the Wu clan; however, we should

remember that Ch'en was a loyal servant of the empress
for much of his career, the author of "A Praise of the
Great Chou Receiving the Mandate."[16] One can always
resolve the problem by assuming that such attacks were
written early in his life, late in his life, or at some
time when Ch'en was out of favor with the ruling powers;
Ch'en Hang, for example, often engages in such specula-
tions on the flimsiest of grounds. Nevertheless, with
a few exceptions, our best topical interpretations can
be only guesses.

While filiation to a Wei poet such as Juan Chi may be
preferable in establishing a fu-ku pedigree for Ch'en
Tzu-ang, a number of the poems belong thematically to
the kind of poetry written during the Eastern Chin, the
abstract and abstruse poetry of hsüan-hsüeh 玄學, "Dark
Learning." Most hsüan-hsüeh poetry has been lost, but
enough survives to see its main characteristic was neo-
Taoist speculation in a highly abstract terminology.[17]
A consistent trait of Chinese poetry through its long
development has been a preference for concrete imagery
over abstraction, and shortly after its heyday, hsüan-
hsüeh poetry fell into extreme disfavor. With the
exception of some quaint imitations of hsüan-hsüeh
poems by Chiang Yen, the court poets carefully avoided
it.[18] Hsüan-hsüeh poetry received equally rough treatment at the hands of the early fu-ku theorists: even
Ch'en Tzu-ang himself condemns the poetry of the Chin
in the preface to "The Long Bamboo." And yet the poetry
of hsüan-hsüeh was the only model for serious, philosophical poetry that was available to Ch'en. The tradition
of hsüan-hsüeh poetry is only one important source from
which Ch'en drew: echoes of Kuo P'u's poetry on immortals,
various prose forms, the tradition of border poetry, and
even yüeh-fu can be heard in lines or whole poems of the
series.

There is no overall thematic or philosophical unity

in the Kan-yü: Confucian and Taoist sentiments are mixed
unreservedly. Nor does the series as a whole have any
artistic unity: the first poem does seem to be an "opening
piece," and here and there one can see pairs of poems
that should be read together, but there is no unifying
structure. This fits Ch'en Hang's contention that the
poems do not represent the work of a single period but
rather were written throughout Ch'en's life.[19] An earlier
tradition maintained that they were all works of Ch'en's
youth, but this is clearly wrong. Like the tsa-shih 雜詩
of the Wei, these poems probably represent the "unclassified" portion of Ch'en's output, those poems not
written for a specific occasion or whose occasion Ch'en
did not dare specify.

Though poems like "Lying Sick in My Home Garden" bear
a resemblance to some of the Kan-yü, as a whole the
styles of the Kan-yü are quite different from the usual
style of occasional poems.[20] Although some of Kan-yü
reject completely the formal, tripartite pattern of court
poetry, many of the poems retain it in some concealed
form. Those poems which reject it altogether often lack
the structural tightness and subtlety of implied relationships which are to be found in more conventional poems.

For convenience the Kan-yü can be divided into two
groups: first there are border poems and a small group
of poems on the topics most commonly associated with
fu-ku—bird and plant allegories and huai-ku. The second
group, constituting the majority, may be classed as variations on the theme called hsien-jen shih-chih 賢人失志,
"the virtuous man disillusioned."[21] The theme is basically
that the virtuous man contemplates and renounces, either
directly or allegorically, the corruption of the world
and its impermanence; grieved or outraged by what he
sees, he condemns the world of evil and transience, sings
his sorrows, and may, as a final gesture, seek to become
a hermit or immortal. This is a very old and complicated

theme in Chinese literature, touching some deep ritual
strains in the Chinese tradition and some strong psychological chords in the character of the official class.

The Confucian tradition forced young intellectuals
into its social mold with ruthless determination; however,
those same moral standards which a young man was taught
to apply to society might ultimately become his means to
escape from society. If society failed to measure up to
his moral standards, he could reject it to uphold his
principles. Or, as was often the case, if society
rejected him, if he failed in some way, he could translate that failure into a failure on the part of society
to recognize his worth.

The hsien-jen shih-chih was a protean complex of ideas
and sentiments that underwent continuous change through
the course of Chinese intellectual history; it never
crystalized enough to define simply. It began to take
form in the Ch'un-ch'iu Period with the legends of ancient
hermits who refused to serve the state. On several occa-
tions Confucius speaks favorably of those who refused to
serve in times of misgovernment. In the fourth century
B.C. this merged with Ch'u-tz'u themes of ritual purity,
renunciation of the corruption of human society, and a
flight through the cosmos, David Hawkes's tristia and
itineraria. In various secular, religious, and allegorical
forms, the hsien-jen shih-chih was one of the most popular
themes of the Han and of the Period of Disunion before
the advent of court poetry. The theme had both purely
Confucian and purely Taoist forms, but most often it
appears in the grey region between the two. Despite
its hazy allegiances, it was an almost religious theme
to many Chinese intellectuals for it appealed to many
facets of their experience.

Those Kan-yü that fall within its broad boundaries,
treat the hsien-jen shih-chih theme either in its complete
form—from denunciation of the world to flight from it—or

in some part. Some of the poems are direct, general
treatments of the theme, while others are clearly topical
allegory, condemning specific events or figures from the
reign of the empress.

The fifth <u>Kan-yü</u> gives a good overview of the theme.
Like several other poems in the series, it is divided
into two equal parts, the first representing the world
rejected and the second representing the ideal world to
which the poet aspires. This simple structure is a step
backward from the tripartite form of the court poem, which
permitted complex relationships between the lines of a
couplet, between the couplets themselves, and between the
descriptive center of the poem and the closing response.
Clear value distinctions had always been something of an
obsession to Confucian thinkers, and this symmetrical
"praise and blame" pattern gives structural form to a
moral dichotomy. The ultimate source of this structure
lies in the symmetrical <u>ch'ang-tuan</u> 長短 persuasions of
the pre-Ch'in and Han periods, with which Ch'en Tzu-ang
must have been familiar. In such persuasions the good
points of the position for which one argues are balanced
against the negative points of the position against which
one argues.

The highest value in this poem is to become an immortal,
but as we said earlier, Taoist and Confucian values were
seldom clearly differentiated: other poems of the series
renounce the quest for immortality or suggest its futility.
The assumption of an evaluative stand itself is more
significant than the philosophical contents of that stand.

Men of the marketplace boast their cunning,
Yet in the Way they show child's foolishness.
Crawling over each other in boasting and show,
Unaware of the end they shall meet.
How could they see the Master of Mystery,
Observing the world in his flagon of jade,

市人矜巧智
於道若童蒙
傾奪相誇詑
不知身所終
詎見玄真子
觀世玉壺中

Fading away, leaving Heaven and Earth,
Riding Change into the Never-Ending?

窅然遺天地
乘化入無窮

[04351]

Both Confucians and Taoists despised the "men of the market-place," who represented a different class of society. Ch'en Tzu-ang's immortals are more appealing and convincing than the "feathered people" of the Chin dynasty, when poetry on immortals was especially popular. Cold, bemused, and aloof, Ch'en Tzu-ang's immortals represent more a point of view than actual transcendent beings. They are usually alone and possess a minimum of physical presence, in contrast to the jeweled chariots, swirling robes, and variegated palaces of earlier poetry on immortals. An interesting footnote on this poem is that probably through it, the name "Master of Mystery" 玄眞子 was adopted as a pseudonym by the High T'ang poet Chang Chih-ho 張志和.

Ch'en Tzu-ang showed particular talent in heaping invective on the crassness of the everyday world. His genius in this is without precedent in the shih tradition: instead one must look for its antecedents in the satric fu of the Eastern Han such as Chao Yi's 趙壹 "Lampooning the World and Hating Evil," Ts'e-shih chi-hsieh fu 刺世疾邪賦. The tenth Kan-yü is a delightful piece of invective, whose rhetoric had an influence on later fu-ku poets such as Meng Chiao 孟郊.

I dwelled deep in seclusion, observing the basis of Change,	深居觀元化
How men struggle, swollen with resentment, licking their chops.	悱然爭朵頤
They gobble each other up with calumnies,	讒說相噉食
For profit and harm, mistrust everywhere.[22]	利害紛嶷嶷
Plump and portly, those servile fawners,	便便夸毗子
Maintaining in turn each other's splendor.	榮耀更相持
Wu Kuang yielded up the empire,	務光讓天下

While merchants compete, sharp as awls and
    knives.
It's all over—I'll go pick magic herbs,
Ten thousand ages exist at the same moment.

商賈競刀錐
已矣行采芝
萬世同一時

[04356]

Like the preceding poem, this poem is built out of a
series of evaluative juxtapositions: the calm observer
of the nature of things is set against the contentious
world he observes; the ancient hermit Wu Kuang is set
against the merchants; the vicious pettiness of human
society is set against the final transcendence of time.

These evaluative juxtapositions are probably a conscious
structural feature of the poem; if we look more deeply, we
find that the structure is more conservative. The phrase
"observing Change," kuan-hua 觀化, appears in the opening
of many of the Kan-yü: this initial abstraction, peculiar
to the Kan-yü, serves the same function as the opening
statement of setting or context in a tripartite court
poem. Just as the court poet sets up the occasion whose
natural surroundings he describes in the middle couplets,
so Ch'en Tzu-ang begins by setting the conditions under
which he observes the pettiness of the world. Nor is
there any more subordination in Ch'en's enumeration of
the world's vices than in the enumeration of landscape
features in the middle couplets of a court poem. The
resolution to "go pick magic herbs" occupies a function
analogous to the personal response in the tripartite
form: Ch'en is, in fact, responding emotionally to what
he has seen. A poetry very different from court poetry
is being built out of a modification of the old tripartite
form: the statement changes, but the "grammar" remains
the same.

In Kan-yu XXIV (04370), Ch'en turns his genius for
invective against a more specific target, the great
ministers of the court.

Who are those fellows with pint-sized brains,
In pretty court robes, decked out for green
   spring?
On the fifteenth each month the moon may be
   full,
But doesn't treasure its own full splendor.
In great halls they waste the gold and the jade;
Ten tons hanging from a slender thread.
How can they carry the great tripod of state?—
When it's snatched from them, they'll be
   laughingstocks.

挈 瓶 者 誰 子
姣 服 當 青 春
三 五 明 月 滿
盈 華 不 自 珍
高 堂 委 金 玉
微 縷 懸 千 鈞
如 何 負 公 鼎
被 奪 笑 時 人

The image of "ten tons hanging from a slender thread" was
borrowed from a Han dynasty letter to describe an extremely
precarious situation. Carrying the "tripod of state"
refers to the great responsibilities with which these
ministers have been entrusted. Such sarcasm and mockery
represents only a minor strain in the tradition of Chinese
social criticism; more often writers prefer to describe
sympathetically those who have suffered from misgovernment.

   One of the marks of Ch'en Tzu-ang's genius in the Kan-
yü is his ability to create effective poetry without the
complex description of the physical world which one comes
to expect in Chinese poetry. Most short Chinese poetry
is presented to the mind through the senses, a scene for
contemplation. Rarely does one find the mind projecting
a wholly imaginary scene, except in poems on historical
periods and in poems with highly conventional themes such
as border yüeh-fu. From conventional allegory such as
"The Long Bamboo," Ch'en proceeds to highly imaginative
allegory as in the closing of the following poem, Kan-yü
XXXVIII (04384):

Confucius investigated the basis of Change,
How the Dark Immense is followed by Bright and
   Gentle:
In the Great Cycle is Expansion and Contraction,
Springs and autumns come and go in succession.

仲 尼 探 元 化
幽 鴻 順 陽 和
大 運 自 盈 縮
春 秋 遞 來 過

Then blinding gales suddenly scream in rage,   盲 飈 忽 號 怒
All things of the world rend each other apart. 萬 物 相 分 劘
Oceans dark and vast rumble and swell,   溟 海 皆 震 蕩
How then shall the lone phoenix survive?   孤 鳳 其 如 何

The "Dark Immense" refers to the elemental nature of
winter, while the "Bright and Gentle" refers to spring.
Although we now consider Confucius primarily a social
philosopher, the "Ten Wings" of the <u>Yi-ching</u>," cosmological
tracts in the form of commentaries, were traditionally
attributed to him: thus Ch'en Tzu-ang sees him investigat-
ing the cosmos order. This poem seems to speak of a
cataclysmic disruption of the cosmic order. The idea
of the world being "in flood" had long been a favorite
image of universal corruption and dissension or, depending
on your viewpoint, a positive image of natural flux.
Clearly defined bodies of water such as rivers with
their fords could represent the Confucian Way; Taoists
often preferred the undifferentiation of the sea, which
stood for a primal chaos transcending values and was
opposed to Confucian concepts of value differentiation
and order. From this tradition Ch'en Tzu-ang projects
an imaginary, allegorical scene: the moral dissolution
of the world's order becomes a raging sea in which the
phoenix, the emblem of the sage, finds himself helplessly
tossed about.

In <u>Kan-yü</u> XXII we find a similar closing image of a
lone creature tossed about in the violent chaos of an
ocean storm. In this case the disintegration is of the
year rather than of the universe; the poem is an "autumn
meditation." Autumn was a season traditionally associated
with destruction and dissolution, and the final image here
suggests a close connection between the moral disintegration of the universe and the physical disintegration of
nature with the onset of autumn. In the <u>hsien-jen shih-
chih</u> theme, evil and impermanence are strangely associated:

in fleeing one, the hermit-immortal also flees the other.

By faint frost know the year comes to a close,　微霜知歳晏
The axe handle once was green and leafy.　　　　斧柯始青青
Still more, this evening of fall's metallic skies,　況乃金天夕
When floods of dew soak the crowds of blossoms.　浩露沾羣英
Climb a mountain, gaze upon the universe,　　　登山望宇宙
The bright sun has already darkened in the west.　白日已西暝
Then the cloudy seas froth in gales—　　　　　　雲海方蕩潏
How shall the lone fins find any peace?　　　　孤鱗安得寧

[04368]

It is unclear whether the "fins" (literally "scales")
refers to an ordinary fish, a dragon, or a whale.

In Kan-yü Ch'en Tzu-ang shows a fascination for vast,
cosmic panoramas; it is the scope of vision of that
transcendent eye which "observes Change." Ch'en does
not concern himself here with the unique forms of nature,
its "wonders," which the court poet captures in his
parallel couplets. Rather Ch'en observes the generalities
of the autumn landscape. In doing so and in choosing the
theme of impermanence, Ch'en is aligning himself with the
poetry of the Chien-an and Wei in their treatment of
autumn. But while Ch'en may be trying to capture something of the Chien-an and Wei manner, he never truly
sounds like a Chien-an and Wei poet. Their autumn
landscapes were constructed out of a fixed repertoire
of elements which were followed according to an almost
formulaic pattern. Ch'en, on the other hand, is a self-
conscious, structuring poet who uses his material for
original ends.

In its rhetorical question, the closing couplet uses
one of the standard response devices of the tripartite
form, but it is also one of those closing images designed
to stir a response in the reader. In both this and the
preceding poem a solitary creature is reduced to tininess

and helplessness in the midst of a vast, turbulent landscape. This technique of making something appear tiny
and helpless by setting it alone in a immense, inanimate
scene was effective, and it was to become a favorite
closing device of Tu Fu. To cite just two of the most
famous examples, in "Night Travels: writing my feelings":

Wind-tossed, what am I like?—　　　飄飄何所似
A lone sand gull between Heaven and Earth.　天地一沙鷗
                    [11433]

and in the seventh "Autumn Meditation" (11554): "Lakes
and rivers fill the earth—one old fisherman" 江湖滿地
一漁翁. Though the technique is the same, Ch'en Tzu-
ang's allegorical beasts in their allegorical storm
contrast sharply with Tu Fu's visionary symbolism.

  Despite Ch'en Tzu-ang's extravagant claims for it,
there was not really much "new" (or in Ch'en's terms, so
old that it seemed new again) in "The Long Bamboo"; Ch'en
topicalized and personalized the allegory, but this kind
of ornate allegory had never completely disappeared during
the age of court poetry. Lo Pin-wang, for example, wrote
many such poems. On the other hand, the kind of allegory
in the two poems above was truly new and made a powerful
impression on a few contemporary and many later readers.
It was the Kan-yü that were remembered and not "The Long
Bamboo." At times Ch'en's imagination slips into an almost
maniacal frenzy as in Kan-yü XX (04366):

The dark, mysterious heavens are hidden and　玄天幽且默
   silent,
The crowds dispute—mocking, raucous laughter.　羣議曷嗤嗤
Yet the teaching of the Sage endures　聖人教猶在
While the world's cycles have long rolled high,　世運久陵夷
   then low.
One rope—to what can it be tied?　一繩將何繫
Nor can we hold to drunken melancholy.　憂醉不能持

Off, off!—go pick magic herbs,   去 去 行 採 芝
Do not be cheated by the dust of this world!   勺 爲 塵 所 欺

Again we see Ch'en's fascination for violent juxtapositions: above are the heavens whose purpose is both
mysterious and unknowable; beneath is an ugly, raucous
world of turmoil. In this unstable world the only constants are the models of the sages and the laws of Change
itself ("the teaching of the Sage" can also refer to the
cosmology of the _Yi-ching_ commentaries specifically).

     Ch'en's abrupt shifts in subject and his brief flashes
of powerful imagery give a picture of mental imbalance
rather than decorous control. From Ch'en's more conventional poetry we can see that this is an assumed role
rather than a necessary condition of Ch'en's writing.
It is in the tradition of the "virtuous incoherence" of
the sage, who seems unbalanced by the degeneracy of his
age. One of the most famous examples of this is _Analects_,
XVIII. 5:

     Chieh-yü, the madman of Ch'u, passed by Confucius singing:
     "Phoenix, O Phoenix! How low virtue has fallen! Those gone
     cannot be reproved, but those to come may still be saved.
     Finished! It is finished! Those now in government are in
     danger!" Confucius dismounted desiring to speak with him, but
     Chieh-yü fled, and Confucius did not get to talk with him.

The virtuous madman with his intense, exclamatory denuncia-
tions of the age belongs to a minor, but enduring tradition
in Confucianism with tangential relations to the _hsien-jen_
shih-chih theme. The unbalanced sage is closely allied
to the figure of the crazy old Taoist, beneath whose
foolishness and seeming incoherence is supposed to lie
deep wisdom.

     Released from the courtly demand to describe only the
scene at hand, many forms of fantasy were possible for
the poet. Old themes such as the spirit journey through

the heavens reappear in new guises, as in the following poem, Kan-yü XXXVI (04382):

Just now in a wild, free mood I yearn,
But for what?—for Mount O-mei in my own Shu;
I long to be with the madman of Ch'u,
To meet him in white clouds, endlessly far away.
The times must be wrong! I grieve that I've missed mine,
And tears trickle down in an endless stream.
I dreamed I climbed to the caves of Mount Sui,
Then to the south gathered herbs on Mount Wu,
Investigated the Basis, observed all things in Change,
Left the world, chasing a dragon in the clouds.
But when its undulations would seem to last forever,
I awoke. I could not see it.

浩然坐何慕
吾蜀有峩眉
念與楚狂子
悠悠白雲期
時哉悲不會
涕泣久漣洏
夢登綏山穴
南采巫山芝
探元觀羣化
遺世從雲螭
婉孌將永矣
感悟不見之

The reinactment of the spirit journey in a dream journey was to become an important theme in the poetry of the eighth and ninth centuries. Though the themes themselves remain constants, each poet's treatment was to be highly individuated: Li Po's dream flights tend to be dazzlingly colorful and well developed. Again, in contrast to eighth-century treatments of identical themes, Ch'en Tzu-ang's versions are brief, stark, and abstract. The highly original poetic closure here heightens the effect by its abruptness.

As the T'ang brought back many of the older themes of Chinese literature, it often rationalized them for a new age. We suggested earlier that Ch'en's immortals represent a state of mind more than the physical beings of religious Taoism (though it might be pointed out that Li Po's immortals are quite physical). The spirit journey through the cosmos, associated with ancient Ch'u shamanism, is rationalized into the dream journey. Ch'en certainly

longed for some form of transcendence, but it seems
unlikely that he could believe in the gods and immortals
in the same way some earlier poets had.

This rationalization of fantasy may be connected to
be presumed nonfictionality of occasional poetry, which
had become the dominant mode of poetry during the preceding centuries. Court poetry had insistently kept the
poet concerned with the world "at hand." It was in this
world of physical presence that the poet sought "wonders"
and not in the imagination. The presumption of nonfictionality is an important feature of later Chinese
poetry, and it is grounded in the practice of court
poetry. There was a need to seek out a historical,
nonfictional frame of reference for consciously fictional
poetry such as allegory and yüeh-fu, hence the later
tendency to topical interpretation. Both allegory and
yüeh-fu provided important outlets for the fiction-
making imagination, but even in the remarkable fantasy
of the Kan-yü we can see now and again the need to ground
that fantasy in a real occasion, a need to say "I dreamed
. . ." Dreams have an occasional, historical reality
which is lacking in straight fantasy.

At times the abstract meditations of the Kan-yü
approach incomprehensibility. The following poem, the
eighth of the series, is unique in its heavy use of
Buddhist terminology. Although Ch'en speculates that
Buddhist nihilism might offer release from universal
decline, the poem leaves the reader with the same sense
of cosmic disorder as some of the preceeding poems.

I have observed Change from Mount K'un-lun,	吾 觀 崑 崙 化
Sun and moon lighting up Darkness as they sank,	日 月 淪 洞 冥
And in the interaction of shadow and shining Essence,	精 魄 相 交 構
Heaven and Sod arise in their own order.	天 壤 以 羅 生
Confucius investigated the Absolute,	仲 尼 推 太 極

Lao-tzu honored the Mysterious Dark,

The Metal Immortal of the West, the Buddha,

Had lofty principles concerning Ignorance of Self.

When Appearance and Vacuity have both been
  extinguished,

Then how can Cause and Karma form?

But the Doctrine of Names is in hopeless
  confusion,

And neither life nor death have yet ceased.

[04354]

K'un-lun was an actual mountain in the northwest, but its
primary significance here is as the dwelling place of
immortals, particularly of Hsi-wang-mu, the great goddess
who entertained King Mu on his travels (as we shall see
in another of the Kan-yü). What begins as a visual scene
turns visionary as Ch'en perceives the generation of the
cosmos through the interaction of Light and Dark, of Yin
and Yang. "Shadow and shining Essence" refer here specifically to the light and dark portions of the moon.
Buddha, appearing in the guise of the God of the West,
moves the poem toward the expected evocation of transcendence, but in this case the goal is Buddhist Extinction, chi-mieh 寂滅 , transcending both life and death.
Ch'en clearly delights in strings of abstract terminology;
underneath the terms the argument is actually quite
simple, and their intent seems rather to mystify.[23]

Though the preceding poem seems to be using Buddhist
thought sympathetically, the nineteenth poem (04365) of
the series is genuinely caustic in its attack on Buddhist
secular wealth. The arguments used are the standard ones
of anti-Buddhist polemics, but their effective use in
poetry is something new.

The sage seeks no advantage for himself,

Feels worry, gives succour to the masses.

The Yellow Canopy was not the will of Yao,

Much less the tyrant's Terrace of Jade;

Yet I have heard of this Western Teaching

Whose Way of cleansing the soul is greatly honored.

Why is it, then, they use up gold and jade,

Carving them into something they think worth worship?

Mountain forests are gone for temples in the clouds,

They press for precious paintings, feathers, pearls.

What even the work of demons could not do,

How can human effort accomplish?

They boast their heedlessness of worldly things—entanglements only increase;

They vaunt their wisdom, but the Way grows ever darker.

瑤臺安可論
吾聞西方化
清淨道彌敦
奈何窮金玉
雕刻以為尊
雲構山林盡
瑤圖珠翠煩
鬼功尚未可
人力安能存
夸愚適增累
矜智道逾昏

The "Yellow Canopy" was one of the imperial insignia, a modest luxury compared to the Terrace of Jade built by the tyrant Chou, last ruler of the ancient Shang dynasty. Empress Wu was particularly devoted to Buddhism, and the poem may be topical rather than a general attack on Buddhist secular wealth.

In the grand opening of the poem above we can see an attempt to recreate in poetry the kind of moral authority possessed by classical prose. Remarkable too is the overt social criticism, representing the ethical focus long sought by fu-ku theorists in poetry. Only the biting irony saves the poem from being a versified memorial. Again Ch'en uses the "praise and blame" structure, first setting forth the ideal, then following it with an attack.

The potential for topical social criticism is clear in the preceding poem; in some cases Ch'en's meditations on cosmic change and the transcendence of change do seem to have topical as well as general significance. The cosmic symbolism used in speaking of the imperial court

makes such topical, political interpretations particularly
believable. In these cases, deliberate obfuscation, which
we saw in the eighth poem of the series, can serve the
useful purpose of shielding the poet from the consequences
of more direct criticism. Empress Wu's dominance of the
court and her later seizure of the throne makes an easy
target beneath the thin veil of cosmic-sexual dualism,
as in the sixth poem of the series (04352).

I have observed the dragon's transformation,	吾觀龍變化
And now understand the essence of pure Yang.	乃知至陽精
How dense and dark is the forest of stone	石林何昊密
And the hidden cave where no one tarries.	幽洞無留行
Those who found the immortal Way of old	古之得仙道
Were truly the match of the basis of Change.	信與元化并
The feelings of Mystery—no childish knowledge—	玄感非蒙識
Who can plumb the engulfing dark?	誰能測渝冥
Men of this world are limited by what their eyes see,	世人抱目見
Drunk with wine, they laugh at the cinnabar classics.	酣酒笑丹經
But on Mount K'un-lun there are trees of jade—	崑崙有瑤樹
How can we get to pluck the blossoms?	安得採其英

The "cinnabar classics" are Taoist works on the cult of
immortality. While most of the poem does not lend itself
to allegorical interpretation, the first couplet with
its "dragon transforming" and its "essence of pure Yang"
make it difficult for the allegorist to resist. With an
empress (female Yin principle) on the throne, all references to the male Yang principle become suspect. I will
quote Ch'en Hang's interpretation of the poem in full as
an example of topical, allegorical interpretation, which
Ch'en applies throughout the series.

This poem tells how the Mandate of Heaven, though lost, will
return again. The inchworm has its time to expand and its time

to contract; none can fathom the transformations of the holy
dragon. Since ancient times these have been used to stand for
the ruler facing south and receiving the mandate. In this case
it refers to the T'ang royal house and the imperial throne. From
its hidden and dormant state it will leap into view, nor can it
be held in check by the many forces of Yin [presumably referring
to the empress]. As they accord with the Cycle and have their
restoration [chung-hsing 中興], they will be in complete agree-
ment with the Mandate of Heaven, and this is not to be accomplished
by human effort. It is, in fact, exactly like an immortal attaining the Way and ascending to the sky, something that is always
indicative of his complete unity with the forces of Creation.
The average people of the world see only with their eyes and
know nothing of the Mandate of Heaven; they understand only that
decline attends upon glory. If you speak to them about this,
they will laugh and not believe. May it come to pass some day
that the flying dragon will find it advantageous to reveal himself
again, that the myriad phenomena may all see him reigning again
on K'un-lun and wandering through the Supreme Clarity.[24]

We need not accept this Ch'ing scholar's interpretation
with any special authority; we have seen in earlier poems
that Ch'en Tzu-ang is quite capable of writing general,
nontopical meditations on change and immortality. We
know that topical allegory can be present in the Kan-yü,
but it is often impossible to determine with any certainty
that it is. Even if we can determine that it is present,
it is even more difficult to be certain what the allegory
refers to. The mere fact that a topical interpretation
"works" does not make it true: topical interpretation
demands a kind of intentional, historical validity which
most other forms of interpretation do not demand. Too
many referents are available for the traditional symbols:
the dragon might refer to the T'ang royal house, to an
ambitious official, or, stretching the metaphor to fit
unusual political circumstances, to Empress Wu herself;

in the latter case, Empress Wu demonstrates a transformation of the dragon (emperor) by leaving her hidden Yin-
female state and showing herself to be in fact the
"essence of pure Yang."

Some poems like Kan-yü VII (04353) hang uncomfortably
between being topical allegory and being a meditative
poem on impermanence.

The same bright sun never returns,
Spring, season of green and Yang, hath ended
  indeed.
On what vast, uncertain vision do I brood?—
Lying in the forest, I observe Nonbeginning.
Crowds of blossoms lost in the season's darkness,
The cry of the shrike pains my ear.
The state of Chaos broke up long ago,
Who now knows the Nest Father?

白 日 每 不 歸
青 陽 時 舊 矣
茫 茫 吾 何 思
林 臥 觀 無 始
衆 芳 委 時 晦
鵙 鵙 鳴 悲 耳
鴻 荒 古 已 頹
誰 識 巢 居 子

"Nonbeginning" is a Taoist term referring to the state
before creation when nothing commenced and therefore
nothing came to an end. Chaos (hung-huang 鴻荒,) is not
specifically a Taoist term, but refers to much the same
condition as "Nonbeginning." The Nest Father was a famous
hermit at the time of the mythical sage-king Yao.

The allegorists would associate the sun with the
emperor, ignoring its even more common function as a
marker of the passage of the day, and hence as a symbol
of impermanence. In the allegorical interpretation the
kenning for spring, "green-Yang" (freely translated above
as "Spring, season of green and Yang"), assumes special
significance: the Yang would be associated with a male
emperor no longer on the throne. However, since the
next season, summer, is the time when the Yang is at its
height, it would be difficult to connect this end-of-
spring poem with the ascendence of the forces of Yin.
The shrike is associated with the fall of spring's flowers
as well as with evil courtiers and slanderers, following

the allegorical interpretation of the <u>Li Sao</u>.[25] The same
question arises in regard to the closing resolution to
become a hermit: we do not know if he is fleeing the
world of impermanence or the evils of the court.

Meditation on the impermanence of the phenomenal
world had been an important topic in the poetry of the
Chien-an and Wei. We should remember that it was this
poetry which was held up as the stylistic ideal in the
preface to "The Long Bamboo." While not necessarily
bound up with the <u>hsien-jen</u> <u>shih-chih</u> theme, the meditation on impermanence may serve as an allegory of the
disillusioned scholar's response to political and moral
decline. In the <u>Li Sao</u>, Ch'ü Yüan first laments that his
ruler, the "fair one," has rejected him and then complains
that time is fleeting. Fair flowers are good men, known
by their reputation, their "fragrance"; weeds are evil
courtiers. The associations of certain key phrases will
usually signal the reader whether to look for allegory
or not; the shrike in the preceding poem is such a word,
leading us to revaluate the natural description in the
first part of the poem. In this case we might decide
that the shrike is not allegorical and echoes the <u>Li Sao</u>
only in its surface associations with the fall of spring
flowers. The impermanence of the world is an important
theme in its own right.

Ch'en Tzu-ang does not subscribe to the cheerful
Taoism of Chuang-tzu in which death is deprived of meaning
through the constancy of Change (<u>Kan-yü</u> VIII is an exception here); Ch'en sees instead a world of entropy and
decline, which leads him to long for transcendence, the
"Nonlife" of the following poem. This is the thirteenth
poem of the series (04359) and was probably written during
his last years in Szechwan.

Dwelling in the forest, long sick,   林居病時久
Wood and water wipe clear my lone purity.   水木淡孤清

The Kan-yü

Calmly I lie, observing the Change of things,　　閑 臥 觀 物 化
Depressed by eternity, brood on Nonlife.　　　　悠 悠 念 無 生
Green spring no sooner sprouts into being,　　　青 春 始 萌 達
Then Red Fire, summer's element, is at its peak.　朱 火 已 滿 盈
From this time on, the passing and the falling—　徂 落 方 自 此
Stirred to sighs, when shall I find peace?　　　感 嘆 何 時 平

Instead of the elegant parallel couplets in which Ch'en
cast many other landscapes he had seen, here nature
resolves into its constituent elements—wood, water, and
fire—and the processes which inform their alternation.
This elemental landscape is natural for the intellectual
vision of the calm observer of Change. But a tension
exists between this detached stance and the implicit
horror which the poet feels at what he sees, whether it
be the contentious world of human society or the inherent
entropy of nature.

It is difficult to say what makes this a Kan-yü,
whereas a poem like "Lying Sick in My Home Garden" is
not. Both poems probably come from the same period in
the poet's life, and both are in much the same style.
Here and there among the Kan-yü occasional subgenres
appear in a new guise. The thirty-second poem of the
series (04378) concerns longing for old friends, a common
enough lyric topic, but Ch'en places it in the Kan-yü
context of a meditation on impermanence.

How many days now, living in seclusion, in　　索 居 獨 幾 日
　solitude?—
Blazing summer is suddenly in decline.　　　　炎 夏 忽 然 衰
Bright colors in sunlight all shaded and covered,　陽 彩 皆 陰 翳
Friends and relations—strayed, gone different　　親 友 盡 睽 違
　ways.
Climb a mountain, gaze, cannot see them,　　　登 山 望 不 見
Tears trickle down in an endless stream.　　　涕 泣 久 漣 洏
All my life stirred by their faces' beauty,　　宿 昔 感 顏 色
As though fixing a time to meet the white clouds　若 與 白 雲 期

Proud young men on horseback,
Galloping after each other in dumb confusion.
In the mountains of Shu, by the rivers of
  Ch'u—
When again shall we join hands?

馬 上 驕 豪 子
驅 逐 正 蚩 蚩
蜀 山 與 楚 水
携 手 在 何 時

Ch'en Hang interprets this poem as an allegory for the
poet's longing for his ruler; this is clearly a poem
where such political allegory is out of place. Ch'en
Tzu-ang begins with the same sort of detached meditation
on Change that he has used in many other poems, but in
this case the specific application of the process of
Change is the separation of friends and relatives. Notice
that the sixth line of this poem is identical to the sixth
line of the thirty-sixth poem of the series; Ch'en uses
repeated phrases and similar phrases throughout the
series. It may be that the function of these repetitions
is to approximate the lyric formulae of Chien-an and Wei
poetry: tears trickling down is the most well-worn response
in poetry of those periods, but it belongs at the end of
the poem rather than in the middle.

   Ch'en Tzu-ang's tendency to shift subjects abruptly
makes part of his poems difficult to interpret. We
presume that he is imagining the faces of his friends
and relatives back in Szechwan who are growing old without
him. But the sudden intrusion of "proud young men on
horseback" leaves us wondering whether he is referring
to his own youthful circle or to the heedless youth of
the present among whom he is a stranger. The former
seems more likely, but Ch'en Hang evidently favors the
latter, interpreting the image as referring to those
scrambling for power.

   The poems on the impermanence of things in the natural
world have a human counterpart in the huai-ku; human
history was interpreted in terms of cyclical change whose
laws might be observed in nature. We have already seen

how closely this theme was associated with fu-ku. Like
the seasonal imagery in the preceding poems, historical
incidents may be used in a variety of ways, ranging from
exempla in larger poems to topical analogies for contemporary events to pure huai-ku in which the past is interesting for its own sake. In most cases, the elegiac tone
which Ch'en adopts shows that the emotional focus of the
poem is on the past itself, whatever exemplary, analogical
function it may also serve.

   Kan-yü XXVII and XXVIII represent two different kinds
of huai-ku: the first is an occasional huai-ku, the poet's
meditation set in the context of biographical experience,
travelling past Wu Mountain; the second is more properly
a historical poem. Both concern the ancient state of
Ch'u, and both allude to the famous story of the goddess
of Wu Mountain (see p. 137).

At dawn I set out from Yi-tu Isle,

Longing for home flooded over me.

But now my home is not to be seen,

My path has gone past Wu Mountain's south
   slope.

The colored clouds engulf Wu Mountain,

The high hill, now faint and indistinct.

A long, long time I've stood here gazing,

Tears stream down, soaking my robes.

This is not just the sorrow of leaving home,

For I remember King Hsiang of Ch'u long ago.

The "morning clouds" are nowhere to be seen,

The state of Ch'u has also perished.

朝發宜都渚
浩然思故鄉
故鄉不可見
路隔巫山陽
巫山綵雲沒
高丘正微茫
佇立望已久
涕落霑衣裳
豈茲越鄉感
憶昔楚襄王
朝雲無處所
荊國亦淪亡

[04373]

From the style and circumstances of this simple poem, it
is tempting to place it in 681, on Ch'en's first journey
to Lo-yang. It is more rambling than many of the later
Kan-yü, and it lacks their stark, quickly shifting
imagery. As Ch'en passes Wu Mountain on his journey

down the Yangtze, he looks back toward his home, to find
his view blocked by Wu Mountain. Since Wu Mountain is
within his view, he begins a huai-ku on the legend of
the goddess. The "morning clouds" suggest an ephemeral
sexual experience whose beauty cannot be recaptured
(see p. 137), but Ch'en fuses the image with the state
of Ch'u itself, whose existence now seems just as
ephemeral. The "high hill" of line six is where the
goddess told King Hsiang she lived; it also refers to
the barrow of a ruler. Here also, in the hazy distance
of the poet's vision, the two situations are interwoven.
The position taken by Ch'en Hang, that sexual indulgence
led to the fall of Ch'u and this refers to the relationship between Kao-tsung and Empress Wu, is simply not
warranted by the poem.

On the other hand, Kan-yü XXVIII uses the story of
Chang-hua Terrace, where King Ling of Ch'u used to hold
his orgies.[26] In this case there is a precedent for
topical criticism through historical analogy: thus is
the "Chang-hua Terrace Fu" by Pien Jang 邊讓 (d. ca. 208).
Ch'en Tzu-ang would have been familiar with the introduc-
tory note to this fu in the Later Han History (c. 80b),
which says that Pien Jang's fu was "like the indirect
criticism (feng) of Ssu-ma Hsiang-ju." Thus Pien Jang's
work would be criticizing the Han emperor Ling through
the figure of King Ling of Ch'u.

Long ago they feasted on Chang-hua,
The King of Ch'u loved debauchery.
Rainbow banners, a kingfisher awning,
As he shot the wild ox in Yün-meng Forest.
Then back he went to the Kao-t'ang pavilion,
Gazed in sorrow toward the peak of Yün-yang.
His valiant plans—where are they now?
Only the sparrows chant on in vain.

昔荊霓射竭悵雄黃
日王旌兕來望圖雀
章樂翠雲高雲今空
華荒羽夢唐陽何哀
宴溪蓋林觀岑在吟

[04734]

Although this poem may be topical allegory, it does have
an elegiac <u>huai-ku</u> ending, remarkably similar to the
ending of Lu Chao-lin's poem on Ssu-ma Hsiang-ju's Lute
Terrace (02781), though the birds are different. Except
for the criticism implied in the first couplet, the poem
is not unlike many of Ch'en's <u>huai-ku</u>, contrasting past
glory with present decline and responding with the
characteristic <u>ubi</u> <u>sunt</u>: "His valiant plans—where are
they now?"

A topical interpretation is inescapable in several of
the <u>Kan-yü</u> on historical events. While the appropriateness of a topical referent is not enough to prove its
presence in a poem, it would be difficult for a contemporary reader to avoid the kind of analogies to the
situation of Empress Wu that <u>Kan-yü</u> XXI seems to demand.
Queen Hsüan, wife of King Chao of Ch'in, managed to
secure top positions in the government for many of her
relatives: her younger brother Wei Mao became the Marquis
of Jang. Obvious parallels exist here with Empress Wu,
who likewise installed her relatives in high positions
In the case of Queen Hsüan, a wandering rhetorician from
the east named Fan Chü made a caustic comment to King
Chao about his reputation for uxoriousness among the
feudal lords. This so enraged the king that he gave Fan
Chü the authority to check the abuses of Queen Hsüan and
her relations. Obviously the analogy works best if we
assume that the poem was written during Ch'en's youth
when Kao-tsung was still on the throne and there remained
a chance to check the empress' power, but we might also
read the poem as Ch'en looking back on Kao-tsung's failure
to check her power.

The dragonfly wanders between Heaven and Earth,	蜻 蛉 遊 天 地
At heart it fears harm from no other creature.	與 物 本 無 患
It flies and flies, cannot get away,	飛 飛 未 能 去
The sparrow has pounced upon it.	黃 雀 來 相 干

The Marquis of Jang was rich in Ch'in's favor,
Felt his joys and companions were as metal and
   stone.
In and out he went in the capital Hsien-yang,
None of the feudal lords dared say a word.
Little did they know that a wanderer from
   Shan-tung
Would stir the Ch'in king's heart to rage.
A commoner he was, becoming minister—
A thousand years and it causes bitter grief.

                              [04367]

寵歡秦富侯穰
裏交比石金
出入咸陽
諸侯莫敢言
寧知山東客
激怒秦王肝
布衣取丞相
千載為辛酸

The last line here is grounds for presuming the presence
of topical allegory in this poem: such grief is felt in
the present because the ancient example is not being
repeated in the T'ang.

   Perhaps the most interesting aspect of this poem is
the relationship between the opening story of the dragonfly and the rest of the poem. This sort of brief parable
opening was used occasionally in the poetry of the Chien-
an and Wei as a parallel or contrast to the main body of
the poem. The parable itself comes from a compound
analogy in the Chan-kuo ts'e (chüan 17, Ch'u 4) in which
Chuang Hsin tells King Hsiang of Ch'u of a series of
creatures and men who wander carefree, heedless of their
fate, until some greater figure destroys them. The
warning is that King Hsiang must remove two of his
favorites or he will suffer the same fate at the hands
of Ch'in. It is none other than the Marquis of Jang
who will be deputed by Ch'in to bring destruction on
King Hsiang.

   On one level of the poem, Ch'en Tzu-ang is obviously
extending the analogy of the Chan-kuo ts'e so that the
final destroyer, the Marquis of Jang, will himself be
destroyed. On another level, Ch'en Tzu-ang is complicat-
ing the analogy. The dragonfly is identified with the
marquis, both proud and carefree, each destroyed by a

more powerful figure. The natural sympathy we give to
the dragonfly must, through the analogy, be transferred
to the marquis. But our analogical sympathy conflicts
with the historical evaluation of the marquis and the
closing of the poem. The effect is strange—sympathy
for the fall of a powerful, but morally negative character—and without parallel in other seventh-century
poetry.

Usually Ch'en Tzu-ang is more direct in his use of
historical examples, consonant with the idea of uncom-
promising moral honesty which Confucian writers praised
so highly. In <u>Kan-yü</u> IV (04350) the moral significance
of each of the exempla is clear; complexity is achieved
through the juxtaposition.

Yüeh Yang was a general of Wei,	樂 羊 為 魏 將
Eating his son in his greed for martial glory.	食 子 殉 軍 功
If one cares so little for one's flesh and blood,	骨 肉 且 相 薄
How could one be loyal to another?	他 人 安 得 忠
Yet I have heard that the Minister of Chung shan	吾 聞 中 山 相
Was connected to the old man that freed the fawn.	乃 屬 放 麑 翁
If one could not bear to harm a lone beast,	孤 獸 猶 不 忍
How much more true in serving one's lord to the end?	況 以 奉 君 終

Like several of the <u>Kan-yü</u> translated earlier, this poem
is made up of two equal and antithetical situations, in
this case contrasting historical exempla. The first
story is of the Wei general Yüeh Yang, who attacked the
state of Chung-shan where his own son was being held
hostage; Chung-shan returned the boy to his father in
a stew, which Yüeh Yang unwittingly ate. The second
story is of Meng Sun, the minister of Chung-shan, who
captured a fawn and sent it back to his residence to be
cooked. The doe followed the fawn crying out, and the

old man who had been entrusted with the task released the fawn out of compassion. The two stories are perfectly matched and are just the sort of exempla one would find paired in a prose argument. In both cases an offspring is threatened with destruction, and the parents react differently. In the first case what seems on the surface to be extreme loyalty to one's ruler is suspect, while in the second case what seems to be disobeying the commands of a superior is, in fact, an example of inner morality which promises higher loyalty. Again it is possible that a topical point is being made; Ch'en Hang suggests the execution of Crown Prince Hung by the empress, but the situation seems more complicated than that.

A good case can be made for topical allegory in the twenty-sixth poem of the series: it appears to be directed against the emperor's neglect of his palace ladies on account of the empress. If this is true, then the poem probably dates from the reign of Kao-tsung, but it might also be from the first reign of Chung-tsung, who shared the throne with the empress (his mother) for some years after Kao-tsung's death. The vehicle for political satire is the legend of King Mu of Chou who visited Hsi-wang-mu, the "Queen Mother of the West," who lived at "Tiered Walls" on the top of Mount K'un-lun. Mu's palace ladies, of course, were less than pleased with his peripatetic nature.

Rude and wild, Mu, Son of Heaven,	荒哉穆天子
Longing to meet with the white clouds.	好樂白雲期
His palace ladies always resent his leaving,	宮女多怨曠
And that Tiered Wall has blocked their moth eyebrows.	層城閉蛾眉
Each day more addicted to Jade Terrace's joys,	日耽瑤臺樂
He does not grieve for the season of peach and plum.	豈傷桃李時
In vain they fall on the green moss, gone,	青苔空萎絶
As white hair grows behind the curtains of gauze.	白髮生羅帷

[04372]

The "white clouds" here refers specifically to the song
sung by Hsi-wang-mu to King Mu as he feasted with her by
Jade Pool:

White clouds in the sky,   白 雲 在 天
Hills and mounds emerge,   丘 陵 自 出
The road so long,   道 里 悠 遠
Mountains and streams will divide us.   山 川 間 之
I wish you to be immortal—   將 子 無 死
You may still come again.[27]   尚 復 能 來

Jade Pool 瑤池 was part of Hsi-wang-mu's residence, but
Jade Terrace 瑤臺 was often used as a general term for
immortal palaces and carried particularly unsavory
associations as the name of a terrace built by the
tyrant Chou of the Shang dynasty. Peaches and plums
represent things of transient beauty, in this case Mu's
palace ladies. Both blossoms and ladies must be appreciated while thay are in flower, and Mu, with his insa-
tiable quest for immortality, will lose just such beautiful
but impermanent things of his own world. Again Ch'en
Tzu ang is making a revision of a well-established topic,
the complaint of the palace lady. This form, unpopular
with <u>fu-ku</u> writers, has been made respectably by topical
allegory.

In 690 Empress Wu did away with the T'ang dynasty and
proclaimed a new dynasty, the Chou. The following poem,
<u>Kan-yü</u> XIV, is clearly topical and must have been written
after that date. The poem is based on the story of Chi-
tzu, a virtuous prince of the fallen Shang-Yin dynasty.
On his way to the court of Chou (the same character is
used for Empress Wu's upstart dynasty), Chi-tzu passed
the ruins of the old Yin capital; at the sight of wild
grain growing in the ruins he was so moved that he wrote
a song called "The Grain is Ripe."[28] The Yi and Ku are
rivers near Lo-yang; the tripod was the symbol of the

dynasty. The Jade Terrace, the hermits of West Mountain
(Po Yi and Shu Ch'i), and the Marquis of Tung-ling have
all been discussed earlier.

At the crossroads I wept for the Way in the
  world,
Heaven's mandate is far beyond our ken.
Long ago a prince of the house of Yin,
On a jade white horse was going to court at Chou;
The jeweled tripod has sunk in the Yi and Ku,
The Jade Terrace has become an ancient mound.
Feel pain at the thought of West Mountain's
  loyal hermits,
At the former Marquis of Tung-ling too.

臨岐泣世道
天命良悠悠
昔日殷王子
玉馬遂朝周
寶鼎淪伊穀
瑤臺成故丘
西山傷遺老
東陵有故侯

[04360]

Beneath its wealth of historical references this is a
very moving poem, suggesting the kinds of conflicts which
officials must have felt when Empress Wu dropped all
pretense of supporting the T'ang and founded her own
dynasty. Like most members of the court, Ch'en chose
to stay with the empress. While the example of Chi-tzu
provided some consolation, the higher examples of Po Yi,
Shu Ch'i, and the Marquis of Tung-ling must have been
nagging sources of guilt.

   The lure of escape from the morally compromising
service to the new Chou dynasty seems to have increased
Ch'en's predisposition for the life of the hermit and
the cult of immortality. By renouncing his official
career, Ch'en could resolve not only the genuine ethical
problems posed by the empress' usurpation of the throne,
but also his own sense of failure in not having achieved
high office. This is the final stage of the hsien-jen
shih-chih theme: one lives in an evil world which is
getting worse, so that the only thing for a good man to
do is to give it all up. The sense that the world has
been getting ever more corrupt and the Way is becoming

lost is nothing new in Chinese intellectual history, but
it was felt with particular intensity by many T'ang
fu-ku writers.   This sense of universal decline adds a
dimension to the huai-ku that often makes it more than
a simple lament for the impermanence of things.

Bluntness had long been one of the highest values
praised in Confucian ministers: while he may not have
enjoyed it, T'ai-tsung put up with a great deal of direct
criticism.   In virtually the same breath he would to told
that it was the mark of a great monarch to endure such.
Empress Wu, while tolerant in some matters, had committed
a number of ghastly crimes in her rise to power, and
these might not be mentioned.   Bluntness was no longer
a virtue, and the sycophant flourished.

Kan-yü XVIII sets up the idea of refusal to take
office in a world where honest behavior is not tolerated.
Ch'en Chung-tzu of Wu-ling in the state of Ch'i was once
approached by an emissary from the state of Ch'u and
asked to serve in Ch'u.   When Ch'en asked his wife what
she thought of the offer, she advised him that honest
men did not survive long near the throne.   Ch'en declined
the offer and fled.   Chang Chih (Chang Ch'ang-kung),
mentioned in the last line, was forced to leave office
because of his direct behavior.

Long has deviousness been the trend,
By now the Way of bluntness is at its end.
Certainly some are stirred by it now,
But the fashion of the age would destroy this
    practice.
Watering gardens is a low position indeed,
But in Wu-ling it showed radiant purity.
The ways of his age had no place for him—
Alas! Poor Chang Ch'ang-kung.

[04364]

Despite his fascination with the idea of transcendence

and the cult of immortality, in most cases Ch'en Tzu-ang
cannot completely accept it as a consolation.   The
eleventh poem is a praise of the model hermit Kuei-ku-
tzu, "the Master of Ghost Valley," yet the poem closes
on a note of futility.

I love the Master of Ghost Valley,

By his blue creek no foul vapors of this world.

In his sack he tied up the Way of world
    governing,

Left his body behind, now among white clouds.

Seven mighty powers then fought like dragons,

The world was in turmoil and without a lord.

He found glory hollow, a thing of no value,

Wrote "yield, preserve self, hide in a dark
    age."

Spread it out, it fills the universe—

Roll it up, it won't make an inch.

But how can we hope for the life of the
    mountain tree?

In vain do we flock with the deer.

[04357]

The "seven mighty powers" are the Warring States; the
"it" of lines nine and ten is, of course, the Way.
Despite the counterstatement of the final couplet, the
praise of the hermit dominates the poem.   The manner of
treatment resembles many High T'ang poems on the same
topic.   The bold declaration of the first line was
imitated several decades later by both Meng Hao-jan
(07764) and Li Po (08153).   The syntax is straightforward, particles are used freely, and perfect parallelism is avoided.   The effect is of a spontaneous,
energetic outburst, a quality sought after by many High
T'ang poets.   To the western ear, the idea of "energy"
may sound like a particularly elusive concept, but
traditional Chinese critics of poetry took it very

seriously and saw it in many distinct forms—"pent up,"
"expansive," "bold melancholy." Such terms describe an
identifiable quality of emotion which infuses a poem.

  Even in this piece, the most positive of the Kan-yü,
Ch'en closes on a despairing note. The pessimism of the
Kan-yü is pervasive: vast storms of chaos rage, the
natural world is falling, and the way of bluntness and
honesty has been lost in human society. Ch'en's broad
philosophical vision encompasses the universe, and he
sees it in a state of entropy. Kan-yü XVII is one of
the most powerful poems of the series, a quick review
of Chinese history showing the principle of entropy at
work. Ch'en Hang reads the promise of restoration into
Ch'en's poems on cyclical decline; cyclical theory does
promise glory after fall, but Ch'en's vision sees only
the fall.

I live hidden away, observing the Great Cycle,
Brood on the endlessness of all living things.
Since earliest times rise and fall alternate,
With them neither sage nor hero can contend.
With Nan of Chou perished the last ancient
   dynasty,
Seven mighty powers fell to the Ying of Ch'in,
Then I've heard how the Red Spirit of Han
Lifted his sword entering Hsien-yang.
But when the Fiery light had lost all form,
Then Chin and the nomads made pact and alliance.
When the Way of Yao and Yü grew dark,
Gloom and tyranny were released upon the world.
Do you think there were no heroes then?
No—Heaven's Way was with the Tartars!
Gasp with shock—what can we say?
The times grew drunk and never sobered.
Confucius was in straits in eastern Lu,
Lao-tzu fled to the Western Ocean.

幽居觀大運
悠悠念群生
終古代興沒
豪聖莫能爭
三季淪周赧
七雄滅暴嬴
復聞赤精帝
提劍入咸陽
炎光既無象
晉虜復縱橫
堯禹道既昧
昏虐世方行
豈無當世雄
天道與胡兵
咄咄安可言
時醉而未醒
仲尼溺東魯
伯陽逝西溟

The Great Cycle has gone on like this forever,　　大運自古來
Why should a single person sigh?　　　　　　　　　孤人胡嘆哉
                              [04363]

The royal house of Ch'in was surnamed Ying; Ch'in conquered the "seven mighty powers" of the Warring States.
The Han's element was fire, hence the "Red Spirit" and
the "Fiery light." After the Han broke up into the
Three Kingdoms, the Chin briefly reunified China, but
soon lost the North to a series of non-Chinese kingdoms.
As different as this kind of poetry is from court poetry,
as soon as we look beneath the message, we see Ch'en
stating first the circumstances, then listing a series
of historical examples, and closing with a personal
response.

   From the preface to "The Long Bamboo" we know that
allegorical yung-wu were closely associated with fu-ku.
Because the various plants and animals which were the
subjects of such poems already possessed rigidly fixed
associations, allegorical yung-wu was the most stylized
of the fu-ku subgenres. The second poem of the series
(04348) is an excellent example of a traditional yung-wu
allegory.

Orchid and turmeric grow in spring and summer,　　蘭若生春夏
How richly flowering in their prime!　　　　　　　芊蔚何青青
Hidden, alone, their beauty in deserted forests,　幽獨空林色
Vermilion blossoms covering purple stems.　　　　朱蕤冒紫莖
Gradually then the bright sun turns evening,　　　遲遲白日晚
With trembling, with quivering the autumn winds　嫋嫋秋風生
  rise.
When the year's flowering has all fallen away,　　歲華盡搖落
What becomes of their fragrant intentions?　　　　芳意竟何成

Orchid and turmeric stand for men of talent and virtue
who live out their lives in the wilds, their virtues
never appreciated. The "fragrant intentions" are, in

human terms, "virtuous intentions."

   <u>Kan-yü</u> XXIII (04364) is a bird parable, illustrating
the Taoist precept of the dangers of too much beauty.

The kingfisher nests by the South Sea,	翡 翠 巢 南 海
Male and female in forests of pearl trees.	雄 雌 珠 樹 林
How could they know of a fair lady's whim?—	何 知 美 人 意
That she was doted on like shining gold.	嬌 愛 比 黄 金
Their bodies perish in that Blazing Land,	殺 身 炎 州 裏
Their feathers fall in the shade of some marble hall.	委 羽 玉 堂 陰
A dense plumage to make hairpins glisten,	旖 旎 光 首 飾
Lush down to leave brocade coverlets sparkling.	葳 蕤 爛 錦 衾
Certainly they were far enough away,	豈 不 在 遐 遠
But still were sought by outstretched nets.	虞 羅 忽 見 尋
Too much worth is indeed an encumbrance,	多 材 固 為 累
Alas, I sigh for this precious bird.	嗟 息 此 珍 禽

   Five of the <u>Kan-yü</u> are border poems. As we have seen,
border poetry had been written throughout the period of
court poetry and had no special attachment to fu-ku.
The presence of these poems in the <u>Kan-yü</u> necessarily
complicates our notion of what the series was meant to
be. If poems on cosmic change do not fall comfortably
within any of the usual subgenres, border poems and <u>yung-
wu</u> do. It is significant that Ch'en has no <u>yüeh-fu</u> in
his collection, and it is into that category that border
poems would most easily fall. While they may have occasional, topical referents, the <u>Kan-yü</u>, like <u>yueh-fü</u>, tend
to speak of types and universal situations rather than
specific occasions. Unlike most <u>yüeh-fu</u>, the <u>Kan-yü</u> add
a moral, political, or philosophical dimension to the
universal treatment. This is also true of the border
poems in the <u>Kan-yü</u> and may account for their inclusion
in the series.

   The third <u>Kan-yü</u> is a straightforward piece on the
sufferings of the Chinese troops on the frontier.

A blue sky over the passes to Ting-ling,
Past and present, roads stretching far into
    wilderness.
Crumbled battlements of frontier forts,
Bones bleaching in the sun, no bodies whole.
Yellow sands rise south of the Gobi,
As the bright sun sinks under the western
    horizon.
Three hundred thousand Chinese troops
Have indeed done service against the Hsiung-nu.
One sees only the dead of the battlefields—
No one pities those left alone on the frontiers.

蒼蒼丁零塞
今古緬荒途
亭堠何摧兀
暴骨無全軀
黃沙幕南起
白日隱西隅
漢甲三十萬
曾以事匈奴
但見沙場死
誰憐塞上孤

[04349]

Ch'en seems here to be countering the traditional yüeh-fu
concern for those dead on the frontiers by shifting the
focus to those left alive and alone on the frontier.
Those "alone" are literally "orphans," and it is unclear
whether these are real orphans, raising a social issue,
or figurative "orphans," the survivors of the battles.
The emotional response to the dead is called for and
given, but Ch'en extends the implications back into the
world of the living.

   The thirty-fourth poem of the series is another piece
on the futility of border warfare. The figure of the
young hothead who goes out to fight the nomads and win
glory for himself only to end up a white-haired private
was already a stock figure by Ch'en Tzu-ang's time. But
Ch'en's treatment of the theme is both distinctive and
moving.

A north wind blows the trees by the ocean,
They moan and rustle: the border is autumn.
Who is that fellow in the pavilion there,
Filling the moonlit halls with his lament?
He tells us he is a wanderer in Yu and Yen,
Who tied up his hair and went on far travels.

朔風吹海樹
蕭條邊已秋
亭上誰家子
哀哀明月樓
自言幽燕客
結髮事遠遊

With his sling he killed some local clerk,
With bare blade took vengeance on some private
  enemy,
Then fleeing he came to the sea,
Impressed into service in this border land.
His home three thousand miles away,
Yet the Liao's waters go on and on forever.
Always he rages when Tartar troops invade,
Thinks this a shame to our Chinese land.
How could he have known that after seventy
  battles
He'd have white hair, and not yet be a lord?

[04380]

東邏上州
赤丸殺公私
白刃報私讎
避仇至海上邊
被役此邊千里
故鄉三千悠悠
遼水復悠悠入
每憤胡兵入羞
常為漢國羞
何知七十戰
白首未封侯

Of all the Kan-yü this is closest in spirit to the yüeh-
fu. The preceding poem aimed for universality in the
timeless generality of its treatment; this poem approaches
it by means of a normative type.

In other border poems Ch'en Tzu-ang adopts a persona
in the first person. It is tempting to read such poems
as purely personal, but as we read them, we can see that
Ch'en's persona is also a normative type, no less universal than the preceding poems.

I'm the child of a noble family,
All my life I've admired talent.
Stirred by the times, I longed to serve the
  state,
Grasped my sword and rose up from the wilds.
To the west I galloped to Ting-ling's passes,
To the north I climbed the terrace of the Khan.
Went up a mountain, gazed a thousand miles,
Meditating on the past, my heart was grieved.
No one can claim that I fear my end,
To be ground away into grains of dust.

[04381]

子才國萊塞臺里哉禍埃
本為貴公
平生愛報萬
感時思報萬
拔劍起丁零
西馳上單于
北登山見心
登山懷古
懷古言未滅成塵
誰言滅成

Here in Kan-yü XXXV much is left unsaid: the "meditation

on the past" which depresses the persona must concern
the kind of historical fatalism and sense of futility
that appears so frequently in the Kan-yü. He will
achieve no glory; the borders will never be pacified.
Such fatalism undercuts the meaning of self-sacrifice
for the state; as Ch'en wrote in Kan-yü XXII:

Do you think there were no heroes then?	豈無當世雄
No—Heaven's Way was with the Tartars!	天道與胡兵

The grisly affirmation of courage in the closing couplet
is necessary: he must explain that his grief is due to
this sense of futility rather than to cowardice. The
undaunted courage of the border poem and the melancholy
of the huai-ku are in collision.

   Kan-yü XXXVII (04383) is a beautiful meditation on the
physical closeness but fundamental opposition of civilization and barbarism.

At dawn I entered Yün-chung Commandery,	朝入雲中郡
To the north I gazed to the terrace of Khan.	北望單于臺
How closely Ch'in adjoins Tartary!	胡秦何密邇
Bold indeed is the spirit of the sandy northland.	沙朝氣雄驕
Scattering in confusion, the "darlings of Heaven,"	籍籍天已興
Then in a wild charge they come back again.	猖狂已復名
The guardian wall gives rise to famous generals,	塞垣空崔嵬
Frontier forts thrust high into the sky.	亭堠嗟吾何
But now I sigh, and what is it for?	咄嗟吾何
That the border poeple's paths grow over with	邊人塗草萊
weeds.	

The "darlings of Heaven" refers to the nomads: a khan
once replied haughtily that if the Chinese emperor was
the "Son of Heaven," "then the nomads were Heaven's
favorite children, its darlings." Paths are not only the
physical markers of civilization, they are physical
manifestations of the Way—they show people how they

should go. At this juncture between the barbarian north
and China, represented as Ch'in, the forces of civilization are losing, the paths are being overgrown with
weeds.   It is characteristic of Chinese poetry in general
and T'ang poetry in particular that the physical world
and the world of ideas are not clearly differentiated.
Looking at the physical world one can see ideas manifested; looking at a "way," one sees the Way.   Ch'en
Tzu-ang was successful in creating a powerful poetry
using abstract ideas, but the real future of T'ang
poetry lay precisely in the identification of the world
of things and the world of ideas.   The purely sensual
world of much court poetry could be transformed by making
the sensual world also "mean."

PART FOUR

THE COURT POETS OF EMPRESS WU AND CHUNG-TSUNG,
680–710

INTRODUCTION TO PART FOUR

In rhetoric Sung and Shen boasted changing
   the rules,

沈宋裁辭矜變律

Wang and Yang flourished their brushes,
   found good friends.

王陽落筆得良朋

In those days they claimed the master's
   touch—

當時自謂宗師妙

But today we see only a knack for parallelism.

今日惟觀對屬能

      Li Shang-yin, "Offhand Poem" I [29538]

    To the poets and critics of the eighth and ninth cen-
turies, only a very few names stood out among the hundreds
of Early T'ang poets: the "Four Talents of the Early
T'ang" (Wang Po, Yang Chiung, and their "good friends,"
Lu Chao-lin and Lo Pin-wang) would have probably been the
first to come to mind, along with Ch'en Tzu-ang, who possessed unassailable credentials as a <u>fu-ku</u> writer. After
these would come the two court poets of Empress Wu and
Chung-tsung, Sung Chih-wen 宋之問 and Shen Ch'üan-ch'i
沈佺期, who were credited with perfection of the regulated
verse ("changing the rules"). A complicated and sophisticated poet of the Late T'ang such as Li Shang-yin 李商隱
could look back at even the best poets of the Early T'ang
and see only competent craftsmanship, a "knack for parallelism." The Early T'ang poet's work sounded hollow, his
style and imagery hackneyed by two centuries of use.

    Few generations can admire their ancestors until those
ancestors are far enough in the past that they cease to
threaten the present. Beneath the complacent confidence
of Li Shang-yin's cruel and contemptuous epigram lies the
fundamental continuity of many elements of Early T'ang
poetry. The eighth and ninth centuries produced greater
poets than the seventh, but the seventh century gave them
their forms, themes, and stylistic conventions. Not only
was the regulated verse created by the Early T'ang, most
of the major occasional subgenres of the eighth and ninth

227

centuries took on their mature forms and conventions
during the Early T'ang. The reason that Li Shang-yin
felt that he and poets of his generation were writing
"better" was because in certain fundamental ways they
were writing poetry "of the same kind."

Our clearest picture of court poetry and its conventions comes from the last years of Empress Wu's reign and
from the second reigns of Chung-tsung and Jui-tsung, her
successors. The simplest reason for this is that more
poems survive from these two decades than from the seventh
century. The picture is not only clearer, it is also more
attractive: certain changes and developments were taking
place that were to lead into the style of the High T'ang.
It may be that some factors of literary sociology had an
influence on these changes in court poetry. Much of the
continuity with the court poetry of the Southern Dynasties
had been lost: the great southern literary families, which
had produced poets if not many high officials through
T'ai-tsung's reign, gradually fell out of sight as
Empress Wu raised men of little-known background to
positions of favor in the court. Not only was the continuity of literary families disrupted, the continuity
of "poetic lineage" was broken: once a young promising
poet would go to the capital to win the praise and become
the protégé of some elder, established poet, a fact that
would be duly recorded in his biography. Many of T'ai-
tsung's poets, we may remember, could trace their literary
ancestry back to the Liang: in his youth Yü Shih-nan
dazzled Hsü Ling and Chiang Tsung, and each of them in
turn had dazzled some notable in their youths. Although
this is biographical convention, it does represent a
genuine interest in literary continuity. In Empress Wu's
reign young poets began to attach themselves instead to
the entourages of court favorites such as Chang Yi-chih
張易之, men who could not make such subtle discrimina-
tions of propriety as Yü Shih-nan. One interesting

survival of the older tradition of "hereditary talent"
is to be found in the position of Shang-kuan Wan-erh,
Shang-kuan Yi's granddaughter, who was made arbiter in
court poetic competitions.

The disruption of the continuity of court poetry,
begun in the middle of the seventh century, inevitably
resulted in the intrusion of individuality into court
poetry. Earlier court poetry, with its rigid codes of
decorum and normative convention, demanded technical
skill and abhorred individuality. Wang Po and Lu Chao-
lin show some individuation; Lo Pin-wang and Ch'en Tzu-
ang have marked personal styles. Another factor was that
during this period an increasing amount of personal poetry
and informal occasional poetry appeared.[1] This in turn
influenced the taste of the court. While court poems
proper and formal occasional poems still dominate the
last decades of the seventh and first decade of the
eighth century, they sound subtly different than the
monolithic courtly style which stretched from Shang-kuan
Yi back a century and a half.

14

THE LITERARY ESTABLISHMENT

In the <u>Anecdotes on Poems from the Entire T'ang</u> (<u>Ch'üan T'ang shih-hua</u> 全唐詩話) and in the <u>Records of Occasions in T'ang Poetry</u> (<u>T'ang-shih chi-shih</u> 唐詩紀事) we are given a complete list of the literary establishment of the court, the Hsiu-wen-kuan 修文館, for the year 708.[2] While this list omits a number of important figures, some of whom died before 708, and while it includes a number of nonentities, it is still our best source for the major literary figures of the latter part of Empress Wu's reign and the reign of Chung-tsung. The Hsiu-wen-kuan had previously been the Hung-wen-kuan 弘文館, mentioned in an earlier chapter. Also known as the Ch'ung-wen-kuan 崇文館, it was officially part of the Chancellory and should be distinguished from the Han-lin Academy 翰林院, a less formal and not strictly literary office which achieved prominence and provided a place for some of the best poets during the reign of Hsüan-tsung.

At the top of the Hsiu-wen-kuan hierarchy were four Grand Scholars 大學士: Li Chiao 李嶠, Tsung Ch'u-k'o 宗楚客, Chao Yen-chao 趙彥昭, and Wei Ssu-li 韋嗣立. Wei Ssu-li was a clansman of Empress Wei and the brother of one of Chung-tsung's ministers; it was at his famous villa that many of the outings of the court were held. Li Chiao (644-713), the most important literary figure among the Grand Scholars and perhaps the most represent- ative of this era of court poetry, had been a major figure since the 670s.

Next in rank were the eight Scholars 學士: Li Shih 李適, Liu Hsien 劉憲, Ts'ui Shih 崔湜, Cheng Yin 鄭愔, Lu Ts'ang-yung 盧藏用, Li Yi 李乂, Ts'en Hsi 岑羲, and the completely unknown Liu Tzu-hsüan 劉子玄. Of these

Li Shih (663-711), Ts'ui Shih (671-713), and Li Yi (647-714) are the most noteworthy. Lu Ts'ang-yung appears here in the avatar of elegant court poet; in the last section we saw him as Ch'en Tzu-ang's hermit friend and biographer.

Finally there were twelve Auxiliary Scholars 直學士: Hsüeh Chi 薛稷, Ma Huai-su 馬懷素, Sung Chih-wen 宋之問, Wu P'ing-yi 武平一, Tu Shen-yen 杜審言, Shen Ch'üan-ch'i 沈佺期, Yen Chao-yin 閻朝隱, Wei An-shih 韋安石, Hsü Chien 徐堅, Wei Yuan-tan 韋元旦, Hsü Yen-po 徐彥伯, and Liu Yün-chi 劉允濟. Among these are the three men who are generally considered the best poets of the period: Sung Chih-wen (656?-712), Shen Ch'üan-ch'i (656?-714), and Tu Shen-yen (648?-708). Their work is generally broader in scope and contains more personal poetry than other poets of the period. Hsü Chien (659-729) may be remembered as the compiler of the Ch'u-hsüeh-chi during the early reign of Hsüan-tsung.

In addition to the members of the Hsiu-wen-kuan, there were a number of other important poets who predeceased 708: Ts'ui Jung 崔融 (653-706), Su Wei-tao 蘇味道 (648-705), and the fourth of the "Four Talents," Yang Chiung 楊烱 (ca. 650-sometime after 693). Among the poets whose work spans the reign of Chung-tsung into the early part of Hsüan-tsung's reign were Su T'ing 蘇頲 (670-727), Chang Yüeh 張說, and Chang Chiu-ling 張九齡. Chang Yüeh will be treated in chapter 15. Shang-kuan Wan-erh 上官婉兒 (or Chao-jung 昭容), a favorite in the courts of Wu and Chung-tsung, has been mentioned earlier.[3]

The total corpus of poems by the poets of the Hsiu-wen-kuan, along with the poems of Ts'ui Jung, Su Wei-tao, and Yang Chiung, amounts to almost a thousand poems. Of these about six hundred can be accounted for in the collections of Li Chiao, Sung Chih-wen, Shen Ch'üan-ch'i, and Tu Shen-yen. But this is by no means the total output of the period: there were a host of other minor poets, both belonging to and outside of court circles. In

addition, sizeable parts of the large collections of Su
T'ing, Chang Yüeh, and Chang Chiu-ling belong to this
period, not to mention the hundred and thirty-odd poems
of Ch'en Tzu-ang.

HOW TO WRITE A COURT POEM IN 708: FORMS, GENRES, AND SUBGENRES

As we examined in an earlier chapter, court poetry was a formalized art in its structure, in its range of topics and vocabulary, and in its exclusion of intense moral, political, and private sentiments. This formalization was largely a product of the circumstances under which court occasional poetry was composed. Our evidence of the practice of court poetry in earlier centuries is fragmentary, but enough material—poems, complete poem series, and anecdotes—survives from the second reign of Chung-tsung (705-10) to build a relatively complete picture.

The composition of poetry on outings of the court was not a disinterested undertaking. Following a long-established banquet tradition, the courtier who was last to finish his poem on such occasions was required to drink a forfeit of a certain amount of wine. Though this is mild indeed, we may be sure that a certain amount of embarrassment was attached to poetic sluggishness. Our chronicles of court outings do mention who was first to finish his poem and who was last. Therefore, a premium was set on being able to produce graceful verses quickly on demand. Nothing aided swift composition as much as a generous store of appropriate conventions and a fixed form in which to cast them.

This need was addressed by the "tripartite form": first, there is an opening section, usually one couplet, setting the occasion, followed by an expandable middle section of parallel descriptive couplets. The final section is the "message" of the poem, some intrusion of personal wish or sentiment, some witty idea, or some observation that casts a new light on what precedes.

Sometimes the closing couplet will simply describe the
end of the occasion. Theorists of regulated verse have
made more complicated subdivisions of these three parts,
but these later divisions are descriptive rather than
prescriptive.[4] The more basic tripartite form predates
and transcends the limitations of regulated verse. A
large percentage (though not all) poems of the period are
in the tripartite form; in an even greater percentage
the tripartite form stands as the norm from which they
vary or toward which they tend.

The regulated verse, lü-shih 律詩 , grew out of a
gradual fusion of the very common eight-line poem, certain
rules of tonal decorum, and the tripartite form. Perfect
regulated verses, such as Wang Chi's "View of the Wilds,"
appear throughout the seventh century, but the form did
not become strict and regular until sometimes during the
reigns of Wu and Chung-tsung. At that time the final
requirement of the genre developed: two basic tonal
patterns for the couplet existed, and it was determined
that those two couplet patterns should alternate through
four couplets of the poem. Earlier there had been a
tendency to alternation, but it was not a fixed requirement. The tripartite form was also usually followed in
the developing p'ai-lu: there the form was identical to
regulated verse, except that the middle descriptive
couplets exceeded two.

As a convenience in this volume, we will use the term
"regulated verse" for all proto-regulated verse forms,
both perfect and imperfect, but it whould be stressed
that to refer to "regulated verse" at any time in the
Early T'ang is, strictly speaking, an anachronism. What
later became a conscious, formal genre was then only an
amalgam of proprieties. Because poems that set out to
answer those proprieties could be judged formally on how
well they fulfilled them, we have an implicit genre, which
by the first decade of the eighth century had reached the

form that was later to become the conscious genre "regulated verse." In both its earlier, looser form and in
its later, fixed form, this proto-regulated verse stood
in opposition to poetry that ignored its proprieties or
avoided them. This other poetry, associated with the
pre-Southern Dynasties style, was later to become another
conscious genre, ku-shih 古詩 , "old style poetry."

The tripartite form dominated not only the proto-
regulated genres, it also dominated much poetry in the
developing ku-shih genre. Where the tripartite form is
not followed exactly, it often retains its power to shape
poetic structure: nondescriptive, nonparallel couplets
may occur in the middle part of the poem, but they will
often be paratactic enumerations, like parallel descriptive couplets, and will form the body of information to
which the closing couplet or couplets respond. Ku-shih
began its development after the proprieties of the courtly
style had begun to form in the Southern Dynasties. The
two genres, so to speak, "grew apart, side by side": as
poets became aware of the increasing formalization of
poetry, they reacted against it—the fu-ku impulse. They
sought primitivism and spontaneity through consciously
avoiding the tonal regulations of formal occasional
poetry. Though poets like Ch'en Tzu-ang did try different
structural principles in poetry, of all the proprieties
of the courtly style the tripartite form was the most
difficult to avoid. The same pattern of setting, scene,
and response was still all-powerful in the ninth century,
so that a poet like Li Shang-yin might see his generation's relation to the Early T'ang as one of "progress"
rather than as "difference."

The development of the tripartite form in Chinese
poetry is part of the history of the pentasyllabic shih
from its origins. The earliest element was the idea of
the closure as a personal response to what precedes. In
the poetry of the Chien-an and Wei a statement of intense,

personal emotion—a desire or exclamation of sorrow—was
used as a mark of poetic closure. After choosing one of
a number of conventional openings, poets would often run
through a series of lyric formulae and close by saying
how they were grieved or stirred by the situation. A
more positive closing would tell how the poet wished to
be or do something that would resolve his grief. Ts'ao
Chih's first "Unclassified Poem" 雜詩 is an excellent
example of this early stage; here the closure is complicated by the use of both the wish and the statement of
sorrow; the poet wishes the bird to carry the message of
his longing, and when that fails, he expresses his sorrow.

Over high terraces are strong and mournful winds,	高臺多悲風
The dawn sun shines on the northern grove.	朝日照北林
That person is thousands of miles away—	之子在萬里
Lakes and rivers, far and deep.	江湖迥且深
How can my double boat reach him?	方舟安可極
Thoughts of one parted are always hard to bear.	離思故難任
A lone goose flies on its journey south,	孤鴈飛南游
Giving a long and mournful cry as it passes my courtyard.	過庭長哀吟
I let my thoughts fly up to it, longing for him far away,	翹思慕遠人
Desiring to send him word thereby.	願欲托遺音
Its form and shadow are suddenly not seen—	形影忽不見
Its swift flight wounds my heart.[5]	翩翩傷我心

In the hands of a major poet such as Ts'ao Chih, the
lyric conventions of the <u>yüeh-fu</u> theme "longing for one
far away" are handled with individuality and sophistication. "Wounds my heart" is a characteristic phrase of
poetic closure, as is the wish to send a message of one's
longing by a bird. Moreover, the one other "response"
line of the poem is line six, which marks a major break
in the poem.

     In the latter part of the Wei and during the Chin,

parallelism and verbal ornamentation play an increasingly
important role in the <u>shih</u>. The couplet was becoming a
self-contained unit, and parallel couplets were tending
to cluster in the middle of poems. The aesthetic motives
for this are not difficult to guess: the intense emotion
of the closing response would be undercut by the symmetrical balance of the parallel couplet. Parallelism
in the opening couplet is common, but it tends to make
the poem mechanical. An early example of the perfect
tripartite form is in the famous first <u>Yung-huai</u> of Juan
Chi:

In the night I could not sleep—	夜 中 不 能 寐
Rising, then sitting, I strummed my lute.	起 坐 彈 鳴 琴
The thin curtains mirror the bright moon,	薄 帷 鑒 明 月
A clear wind blows the flaps of my robe.	清 風 吹 我 襟
A lone goose cries in the wilds outside,	孤 鴻 號 外 野
Hovering birds sing in the north woods.	翔 鳥 鳴 北 林
I pace about—what do I see?—	徘 徊 將 何 見
Melancholy thoughts wound my solitary heart.[6]	憂 思 獨 傷 心

In its length and in the position of its parallel couplets,
this poem is accidentally close to regulated verse, which
may account for some of its popularity in later ages.
We find here the normative structure of setting, scene,
and response: the first couplet, nonparallel, sets the
context of the experience by describing the poet's un-
accountable restlessness; the middle two couplets, parallel,
describe the scene with relative objectivity, first inside,
then outside; then comes the emotional response, using the
same "wounded heart" as the Ts'ao Chih poem. The poet is
actively present in the first and last couplets and
"absent" in the middle two.

    In the centuries that followed, the best poets learned
to manipulate this structure for their own purposes. The
landscape poet Hsieh Ling-yün may insert an intellectual

meditation on the landscape between scene and response
to clarify the relation between the two.   In a two-part
poem such as "Entering P'eng-li Lake," he will use the
closing response as a device to mark a shift in the poem's
direction.[7]   In a poem like "Winter Day" Pao Chao may give
a response of consolation and endurance to a scene of
impermanence instead of the usual cry of despair.[8]   The
forms that the response may take increase and complicate,
but they are still a personal reaction to the preceding
scene.

By the Liang dynasty the tripartite form had become
increasingly fixed, both in court occasional poems as
well as in the poems on other topics.   To give one example
from among hundreds, there is Yü Chien-wu's 庾肩吾 (fl.
520) "Following the Rhymes of the Crown Prince's 'Leaving
Mystery Garden': to command":

Spring light rises in the lovely mansion,	春光起麗譙
Clog-wearing footsteps ascend the mountain peak.	屣步陟山椒
The tower's shadow hangs over the flying canopy,	閣影臨飛蓋
Orioles' voices have entered the open flutes.	鸞鳴入洞蕭
Waters turn back, mounting up former beaches,	水還登故渚
Trees grow tall, shading the bridge before them.	樹長隆前橋
Green lotuses grow filagree leaves,	綠荷生綺葉
Cinnabar vines send up thin tendrils.	丹藤上細苗
In compliance I look back, shamed to muster my eloquence,	顧循懃振藻
What use for me to imitate the finest jade?[9]	何用擬瓊瑤

The last couplet may be paraphrased: "In compliance with
your command, I look back and describe the scene, but my
own meager talents are shamed by comparison to your poem,
my Prince, which is like the finest jade."   The opening
couplet is parallel and descriptive, but it does describe
the general location and time, in contrast to the specific
details described in the middle couplets.   Here we see the
tendency, characteristic of court poetry, to fragment the

description into a string of unrelated items. When the poet enters with his closing response, he shows the new artistic self-consciousness of the court poet: he responds to his poem as a poem rather than to be scene itself. He is not just "stating his intention" (<u>yen-chih</u> 言志); he is creating an artistic object that will be judged against others of its kind.

The style of a banquet poem by Shang-kuan Yi almost a hundred and fifty years later is indistinguishable from that of Yü Chien-wu.

BANQUET AT AN-TE MOUNTAIN POOL

The highroad arrives at a P'ing-chin Lodge,
The rear hall has arrayed a great banquet.
With close friends begin familiar pleasures.
Lovely mats spread out on a fragrant morning.
Windblown mists gather in dense trees.
The lotus blooms anew on the winding pools.
Rain clears—a rainbow bridge in the evening;
Flowers fall—a phoenix terrace in spring.
Kingfisher hairpins sink toward the dancing mats,
Grained pearwood beams scatter the dust of song.
Now I regret that our flowing goblets are full—
Evening birds have left the city gates.[10]

上路抵平津
後堂羅薦陳
綺交開狎賞
麗席展芳辰
密樹風煙積
迴塘荷荑新
雨霽虹橋晚
花落鳳臺春
翠釵低舞席
文杏散歌塵
方惜流觴滿
夕鳥去城闉

[02708]

The opening is clearer here than in Yü Chien-wu's poem, while the closing combines the expected emotional response ("now I regret") with the variant banquet closing that it is evening and the party is over. P'ing-chin Lodge was built by one Kung-sun Hung of the Han dynasty to entertain virtuous scholars. The tenth line refers to a commonplace that singing stirs the very dust on the beams to movement.

As poets like Wang Po and Lu Chao-lin began writing

more personal poetry, they carried the tripartite form
with them. Even the long ballads on the capital use a
variant of the pattern. Not until the Kan-yü of Ch'en
Tzu-ang was there anything like a conscious attempt to
break free of the tripartite form. When Ch'en Tzu-ang
tried to break radically away from the tripartite form,
the poem usually became mechanical and artificial in its
structure, as some of the "praise and blame" poems of the
Kan-yü; as we have seen, in the more successful of the
Kan-yü Ch'en often is writing a variant of the old formula;
for example, substituting historical exempla for descriptive couplets. Kan-yü XXIX, directed against a campaign
in Szechwan, contrasts strongly with the preceding banquet
poem by Shang-kuan Yi; it answers the goal of the opposition poetics by taking a moral stand on a topic of contemporary concern. All the same, the tripartite form underlies Ch'en Tzu-ang's argument and helps make the poem one
of the finest of the Kan-yü.

The year 687 is coming to a close;	暮歲云丁 兵事甲亥
In the Western Mountains men labor at warfare.	西山
Hampered by provisions, they circuit the road of Ch'iung,	羸糧臣道 城
Halberds over shoulders, strike fear in barbarian cities.	荷戟驚先
The dead of winter, the shrouding fog is heavy,	嚴冬嵐陰勁 生
From empty caves, oozing clouds appear.	窮岫泄雲
A gloom so heavy you can't tell day from night,	昏曀無晝夜 驚
Yet again and again, dispatches call them to arms.	羽檄復相
Clamber and crouch over thousand-yard drops,	攀蹐競萬仞 冥 裏 行
Tumble from sheer places, rushing into deepest blackness.	崩危走九冥
Scattered in confusion among peaks and gorges,	籍籍峯壑裏
They lament, marching through ice and snow.	哀哀冰雪行
Our Sage Ruler steers the Universe,	聖人御宇宙
And I've heard the Great Stair is level.	聞道泰階平

The great lords, the meat-eaters, have fouled
  up in their plans,

And those who live on greens must go on far
  campaigns.

肉食謀何失
藜藿鎮縱橫

[04375]

The Great Stair is a constellation that symbolizes the
imperial social order: that it is "level" indicates that
the world should be in order and at peace. The first
couplet here is clearly the setting, the context. While
the middle couplets are not parallel and have been arranged
in something like a narrative order, they still form the
physical "scene" to which the closing response reacts.
Finally, instead of a gracious compliment or polite
regret at the close of a banquet, Ch'en reacts with
indignant criticism of the government, but this is still
the "message" of the poem, the internal response of the
poet to the preceding scene.

   The major poets of the eighth and ninth centuries
inherited the tripartite form, codified generically in
the regulated verse and appearing more loosely in other
forms. Like Ch'en Tzu-ang, they learned to integrate
the form, to counter the tendency of the pattern to
degenerate into a series of poorly related fragments.
Sometimes they would make a narrative order out of the
middle couplets, as in the preceding poem; sometimes they
would play one couplet off against another—the tripartite
form was open and succeptible to many variations. They
also developed new forms of poetic closure, such as the
objective scene designed to stir a response in the reader,
which we have seen in the poetry of Wang Po. But the
tripartite form remained at the heart of the Chinese
lyric, which was often conceived as a structured "scene"
(ching 景) followed by an emotional "response" (ch'ing 情).

   In court poetry the parallel couplet was the center
of stylistic interest. The "knack for parallelism" was
the primary requisite for quick composition; once the

technique was mastered, the courtier could run swiftly
through the middle of the poem, saving his intellectual
energies for the clever closing. This applies only to
technically correct parallelism; genius in parallelism
was difficult and beyond the rules.

Parallelism has been a metrical device in many major
literatures at some period in their development, but
never was it elaborated, refined, and rationalized with
such seriousness as it was in Chinese literature. In
early prose parallelism served to reinforce analogical
arguments of dubious logic. It appealed to the Chinese
fondness for balance and symmetry, and indeed it was
justified in terms of the bilateral symmetry of nature by
Liu Hsieh in the Wen-hsin tiao-lung:

> Creation fashioned the forms of things; limbed bodies need be in
> pairs. The Transcendent Order works it thus; matters do not
> stand alone. Thus when the mind gives birth to literary works,
> it channels and casts all men's cares; high and low require each
> other, and through their own natures become parallel.[11]

Liu Hsieh's own prose style is beautifully parallel. Liu
Hsieh not only uses bilateral symmetry as a natural analogy
to parallelism, he also uses another, more subtle argument
which echoes an important strain of Chinese philosophical
thought. Like the concepts "high" and "low," all things
can be defined only in relation to something else, something which is at once different and at the same time
commensurate. The parallel couplet defines a scene by
mutual context: each line highlights aspects of the other
by similarities and differences.

Such a sophisticated theory of parallelism was far
less important to poets than the actual practice of
parallelism. Liu Hsieh himself sets up a fourfold classification of parallelism: (1) verbal, (2) historical or
mythical allusion, (3) direct, and (4) antithetical. As

mentioned earlier, Shang-kuan Yi was credited with a
sixfold and an eightfold classification system. But
these practical guidelines were hindsight: parallelism
was learned by practice. Habits grew up, such as matching "Heaven" with "Earth," balancing a line describing
a mountain scene with one describing a water scene; so
many conventional antitheses were available that if one
sought only technical "correctness," one five-syllable
descriptive line virtually wrote its match.

In the early stages of the development of the pentasyllabic shih, parallelism is often no more than a formal
device, as in the second couplet of the first Yung-huai:

The thin curtains mirror the bright moon,   薄 帷 鑒 明 月
A clear wind blows the flaps of my robes.   清 風 吹 我 襟

Because of the poor matching here between the corresponding words of the two lines, later critics would probably
not allow this syntactic parallelism to be "true" parallelism—yet the impulse is clear. The moonlight and the
clear wind are both conventional elements of the "autumn
mode" from which Juan Chi is drawing, but they bear no
necessary relation to each other: they do not define one
another. The solitary wild goose in the following couplet
is also part of the "autumn mode," but this couplet shows
a more sophisticated use of parallelism, which in the
relationship between the corresponding words of the lines
more closely approximates later ideas of "true" parallelism.

A lone goose cries in the wilds outside,   孤 鴻 號 外 野
Hovering birds sing in the north woods.   翔 鳥 鳴 北 林

The noble "lone goose" is set against the ordinary "birds."
Since it is night, the birds should be roosting, and it
seems almost as though the cry of the passing goose has
set them into flight, reminding them of autumn and the
time of migration. All are correlates to the poet's own

restlessness. To a certain extent, the more complex
relationships between the lines of a parallel couplet
were predicated on the technical demands to match things
of "the same kind." The opposition of "thin curtains"
and "clear wind," which do not belong to the same category,
does not provide as clear a mutual definition as the
opposition of "lone goose" and "hovering birds."

The more sophisticated parallelism became, the more
demands it made upon the reader to fill in the ellipses
and decipher the hidden relationships. Parallelism
engendered a particular way of reading poetry, matching
scene against scene to discover the similarities and
differences. In the Shang-kuan Yi poem quoted above,
we read:

Rain clears—a rainbow bridge in the evening;　　雨霽虹橋晚
Flowers fall—a phoenix terrace in spring.　　　　花滋鳳臺春

In the phrase "rainbow bridge" it is not at all clear
whether Shang-kuan Yi is describing a rainbow that seems
like a bridge or a bridge that seems like a rainbow. The
uncertainty lingers in the reader's mind until he reads
"phoenix terrace": this would tend to demand a real bridge
in the first line of the couplet. The transition from
"Is it a rainbow or a bridge?" to "It's a bridge" is a
process of visual revelation that goes along with the
main thrust of the couplet. Because we have a double
example of the relationship, we know that each line is
an implicit conditional construction; because the rain
has cleared up, (we can see) the rainbow bridge in the
evening; because the flowers have fallen (from the trees,
we can see) the phoenix terrace in spring. Other elements
of the two lines draw together, sometimes simply as in a
"spring evening," sometimes more complexly as we associate
the rain with the fall of the flowers, both as a causative
agent and as a parallel movement.

As an example of genius in parallelism, let us look at the middle couplets of one of Sung Chih-wen's finest poems, "Mountain Villa at Lu-hun" (03252):

源 source spring	水 water	看 look at	花 flowers	入 enter
幽 secluded secluding	林 woods	採 pick	藥 herb	行 walk
野 wilds	人 person	祖 mutually	問 ask	姓 surname
山 mountain	鳥 birds	自 of themselves	呼 call out	名 name

Sung Chih-wen's tonal pattern here is an acceptable variant of a standard pattern. The couplets may be translated:

To look at flowers I follow in to the source of the waters;
To pick herbs I walk in the secluded forest.
Greet men of the wilds, exchange clan names,
But mountain birds call out their own first names.

Two of the most significant contributions of parallelism to Chinese poetic diction were in making syntactic experimentation possible and in facilitating variation of word class, that curious phenomenon of literary Chinese which allows words that normally serve as transitive, intransitive, or causative verbs, adjective, adverbs, or nouns to shift their word class according to their position in the sentence. The first of these, syntactic distortion, occurs in the first couplet above. The most natural way to construe the first line above would be: "I look at flowers entering the waters of the spring." But the second line of the couplet must be read: "I walk the secluded forest picking herbs." Therefore, the reader reinterprets the first line of the couplet as: "I enter [that is, go deep into the woods to] the source of the

waters of the spring to look at the flowers." Usually
one line of a couplet is unambiguous, and its pattern may
be imposed on a more problematic matching line. Sometimes, as above, it involves reinterpretation of a line;
sometimes, as in the case of the Shang-kuan Yi couplet,
it involves definition of an ambiguity. In a simple
form, the straightforward line precedes the difficult
line, allowing the reader to make his adjustments in the
natural course of reading; in more complex cases, as here,
the resolving line follows the difficult line, forcing us
backward to call into question the relationships and
"correct" our first reading. In the hands of later
couplet-masters such as Tu Fu, both lines may be difficult,
or one line may try to force an impossible interpretation
on another line.

It must be emphasized that in most cases of reinterpretation or definition of ambiguity, the process is
unconscious. The adjustment which must be made in the
reading of the first line above is not radical and can
be made automatically by a reader accustomed to parallelism. Such ambiguities impinge on the reader's consciousness only as a feeling of indefiniteness in the
line, but the ambiguity is meaningful because, as we
shall see later, he is also seeing the flowers fall into
the spring. The result of this device of parallelism is
often a strange tentativeness in the Chinese poetic
language: the objects are present but their relation
to one another is shifting and ill defined.

As we reconstrue the first line of this couplet to
its new meaning, we have the poet "entering [the woods]
to the source of the waters." Purposeful action ("in
order to look at flowers") may be implied and it may not.
Implicit in "entering to the source" is the notion that
he followed the stream, and hidden here is the reason
that he knew he would find flowering trees at the source—
he followed the trail of blossoms upstream, having deduced

from the blossoms floating in the water that flowering
trees lay ahead. This in turn echoes the story of "Peach
Blossom Spring" by T'ao Ch'ien, in which a fisherman
discovers a utopian village by following a trail of peach
blossoms upstream. And of course when he enters to the
source of the waters, he finds the blossoms entering the
spring—the first interpretation which the reader was
forced to abandon.

This first couplet concerns reclusion, associated
with a symbolic "return" to one's home and a personal
"return" to one's basic nature; "return" is specifically
mentioned in the first couplet of the poem, which was not
quoted above, and it is an implicit association of the
"source" of the spring. Seclusion cuts one off from the
world of human society, and through it a person is stripped
of the false motives of public life. The "source" is the
object of "return." How is this process of return realized in the structure of the couplet?

The two verbs of human activity, "looking at" and
"picking," are placed in parallel to one another. This
juxtaposition intensifies the ways in which these two
words are different: the first is a passive activity,
performed by someone who is outside nature, observing
but not participating in it; the second is more active,
the human interacting with the natural world. This
transition is part of the process of "return" as is the
transition between the second pair of verbs juxtaposed
in the couplet, "enter" and "walk." The first implies a
previous position outside the natural scene, from which
the human "enters" and becomes secluded; in contrast to
"enter," which is an end-directed activity, "walk" is
not directed to some spatial goal but rather refers to
free movement. In later couplets one often finds verbs
that imply goals juxtaposed with verbs which do not point
to the idea of spontaneity, the theme that dominates the
second of the couplets quoted above.

An analogous transition occurs between "flowers" in
the first line of the couplet, traditional symbols of
impermanent beauty, and "herbs," used to concoct an
elixir to prolong life. As in the hsien-jen shih-chih
賢人失志 theme, reclusion and immortality are connected.
The juxtaposed associations of impermanence and immortality
are given depth by the Peach Blossom Spring theme, whose
inhabitants were treated as immortals by T'ang writers.
Thus the transition implied in the juxtaposition of these
two lines is a movement from a position outside nature
into seclusion, a return to the "source" where one may
hope to live more healthily and happily.

In this state of nature the poet meets hermits and
other woodland figures, "men of the wilds." There is a
freshness to these chance encounters, because these men
are always strangers—he must "ask their surnames."
Unlike in the public world of official society he need
not know their rank or office. But there is a transition
to an even greater freshness and spontaneity in the second
line of this couplet. First, Sung plays on the fact that
many birds were known popularly by onomotopoetic names
imitating their calls, as in the English "whippoorwill"
and "bobwhite." Thus the birds call out their own "names,"
ming 名 , which is both the generic word for "name" as
well as the "given name" of an individual. The "given
name" aspect is playful parallelism to match the "surname"
in the preceding line, while the generic "name" is what
they are calling out. The couplet involves a transition
from relatively natural behavior to truly spontaneous
behavior: the hermits need to be asked their names, while
the birds spontaneously tell theirs. The hermits tell
only their family names, while birds show spontaneous
familiarity in telling the poet their "given names."

At this point the skeptical reader will surely ask
how much of this was "intended" by the poet. Certainly
the ambiguity of the first line of the first couplet and

the witty play in the second couplet _were_ intended. As
for the subtler juxtapositions which were discussed in
the first couplet, they were probably not consciously
intended, but they are the means by which the couplet
makes its point, a transition from a state outside nature
to seclusion. Couplets like these were beyond the powers
of the majority of court poets, and the complex juxtapositions they set up look forward to the best of the High
T'ang. The poetic language was becoming increasingly
laden with intellectual and affective associations, while
parallel juxtapositions drew attention to the relationships between these richly connotative words. Thus
whether such complex meanings were intended or not, they
inescapably became the final result of the reading process.

   With the discussion of the tripartite form and the
couplet in mind, here we will look at a complete court
poem. The following is a heptasyllabic regulated verse;
though this genre did not have the long gestation period
of the pentasyllabic regulated verse, it achieved a fixed
form at about the same time, in the first decade of the
eighth century. It is Shen Ch'üan-ch'i's "A Banquet at
Hsing-ch'ing Pool" (05060), composed on the sixth day of
the fourth month in 710.

碧	水	澄	潭	映	遠	空
emerald	water	clear	pool	reflect	distant	void/sky
紫	雲	香	駕	御	微	風
purple	cloud	fragrant	carriage	ride	faint	wind,
漢	家	城	闕	疑	天	上
Han	house	walls	palace gate	seem	Heaven	on
秦	地	山	川	似	鏡	中
Ch'in	land	mountain	streams	as though	mirror	in
向	浦	廻	舟	萍	已	綠
face to	shore	turn	boat	waterweeds	already	green
分	林	蔽	殿	槿	初	紅
divide	forest	conceal	hall	hibiscus	first	red
古	來	徒	羨	橫	汾	賞
antiquity-since	in vain	yearn		crossing	Fen	pleasure

今	日	宸	游	聖	藻	雄
this	day	imperial	excursion	Sage	ornateness	mightier

A clear pool of emerald waters reflects the distant void,
A scented wood carriage in a purple cloud rides the faint breeze.
Wall and towers of the House of Han seem as though in Heaven,
Mountains and streams of the land of Ch'in are as in a mirror.
The turning boat faces the shore—waterweeds already green;
A hall in the midst of the forest, hidden—the hibiscus are turning red.
Since ancient times men have yearned in vain for the joy of crossing the Fen,
But on the royal excursion today, His Majesty's rhetoric is stronger.

One of the proper ways to open a court banquet poem is with the arrival of the emperor in all his majesty; this is often done with established clichés of imperial majesty, such as having him come "shaking the earth" (for example, 03701). In this poem Shen Ch'üan-ch'i begins with a touch of drama; a still pool reflects the empty sky, which fills abruptly with color and movement as the imperial purple aura and the imperial carriage made of scented wood arrives. Shen is playing on the most popular of conventions to describe the emperor and the court—they are the immortals of heaven. As the poet looks into the pool's reflection, he "mistakes" the arrival of the court party for a vision of immortals in heaven. The emperor comes in a "cloud" set in the reflection of the empty sky, and his carriages "ride the wind" 御風, a phrase used in the <u>Chuang-tzu</u> to describe the apotheosis of the immortal Lieh-tzu.

The next fortuitous delusion suffered by the pool-gazing poet is the appearance of the palace compound in reflection; since these are superimposed on the reflected sky, he mistakes them for the palaces of heaven, but "corrects" his metaphor by indicating they are the palaces of "the House of Han." Shen's scope of vision fills and broadens, from the empty pool to the arrival of the

imperial party to the palace compound, all seen in reflection. Next the poet sees the entire landscape of the
capital region in his "mirror." As we have seen earlier
in the Kan-yü, there is a need to rationalize old fic-
tions—here the identification of the court and heaven;
the solution is a popular form of metaphor in T'ang poetry,
the "delusory metaphor," in which the poet tacitly or
explicitly admits the fictionality of his metaphor.
Instead of saying "X is Y," the poet says "it seems to
me" or "I mistakenly thought X was Y."

   In their directness, in their dramatic order, and in
their grand tone, these first four lines approach the
High T'ang style. The narrow, specific scene of the
third couplet could be found both in earlier court poetry
and in the High T'ang. Here the poet looks up and first
sees the scene around the pool, then sees the forest
beyond. The sixth line suggests an outbuilding of the
palace, appearing in the midst of the wood, but partially
hidden by the flowering hibiscus. Notice that Shen uses
the verb fen 分 , "to split," as did Ch'en Tzu-ang, to
describe the appearance of something that disrupts a
visual continuity. In court poetry the time of year is
often established by the order of the flowering plants:
often, as here, one plant is "already" in one condition
(here "green"), while another is "only now" beginning to
blossom. Another popular time balance is "already" set
against "not yet" (wei 未) in the second line of the
couplet.

   The last couplet refers to Han Wu-ti's "Song of the
Autumn Wind," written at a pleasure outing after the
Sacrifice to Earth at Fen-ying, described in Li Chiao's
ballad.

The autumn wind rises,   秋 風 起 兮
     white clouds fly,   白 雲 飛

The leaves of trees and grasses yellow and fall,
    geese journey south.
The orchids blossom,
    the chrysanthemums bud,
I take my fair one by the hand,
    cannot forget her,
I sail my towered barge
    across the river Fen.
Cutting across the midstream current,
    raising white waves,
Pipes and drums ring out,
    a rowing song is raised.
My joy is at its peak,
    but gloomy feelings grow,
How long can youth last,
    who can halt old age?[12]

草木黃落兮

鴻雁南歸

蘭有秀兮

菊有芳

攜佳人兮

不能忘

汎樓船兮

濟汾河

橫中流兮

揚素波

簫鼓鳴兮

發櫂歌

歡樂極兮

哀情多

少壯幾時兮

奈老何

The gracious comment to Chung-tsung's poetry in the last
couplet of Shen's poem brings back the imperial theme,
but instead of mere identification with Han Wu-ti as we
might expect, Chung-tsung outdoes him in the "mightiness"
(hsiung 雄, "virile strength") of his poem. For a thousand years other rulers had tried to equal the joy of
Wu-ti crossing the Fen, but Chung-tsung has succeeded.
The delicate little boating scene of the third couplet
transcends the strong feelings of Wu-ti. Considering
the quality of Chung-tsung's extant poetry, Shen's compliment is more than generous.

    The basic subgenres of T'ang poetry had reached almost
their full complement during the Southern Dynasties.[13]
A few of the poetic occasions popular during the High
T'ang appear only rarely before the eighth century—poems
on meeting someone on the road, on overnight gatherings,
on informal visits to assorted pavilions, lodges, etcetera.
But in all cases the proportion of personal poetry and
informal occasional poetry increases dramatically early

in the eighth century. If we exclude the poets who have
relatively large collections surviving—Li Chiao (209
poems), Sung Chih-wen (196 poems), Shen Ch'üan-ch'i (157
poems), and Tu Shen-yen (43 poems)—the majority of extant
poems from the reigns of Wu and Chung-tsung were written
to imperial command on imperial outings, banquets, and
ceremonial partings. Li Chiao presents a special case
because of his large yung-wu collection, but a substantial
proportion of the noncourtly poems of Sung, Shen, and Tu
were written during their southern exiles. Thus while
there is a long but fragmentary tradition for most of
the informal occasional subgenres, court occasions were
still the dominant center of poetic composition.

After courtly occasional poetry the next most popular
forms were yung-wu and yüeh-fu, each of which had a fixed
range of narrower themes. Though yung-wu and yüeh-fu
were among the oldest shih categories, in this period
they retained the themes and manners of treatment which
they had acquired during the Southern Dynasties. Many
objects were never used as topics of yung-wu poems; others,
hardly ever. Noncourtly banquet poems share the conventions of court banquet poems, but the diction varies
greatly according to the status of the participants and
the formality of the occasion. Verse letters (chi 寄 ,
tseng 贈 , ta 答 , etcetera) also had a very old tradition;
when addressed to high officials, these were among the
most stylized and ornamented poems written. Parting
poems had been written since the Chien-an, but they
increase sharply in number during this period to become
the most popular occasional subgenre later in the T'ang.
The various forms of poetic lament were another old and
stylized group. Other subgenres existed—poems on temples,
music, and so forth—and all subgenres could be "rhyme-
matched," one poet using the same rhymes or rhyme category
as another. Perhaps the most personal poems of the period
were the travel poems, a subgenre dating formally back to

the Chin, but even in travel poems poets were apt to be
carried away by their considerable descriptive powers.

Finally, it seems that Empress Wu in particular had
a fondness for heptasyllabic songs. Some of these were
written for court occasions, and many others were written
privately. They are some of the most interesting and
lively poems of the period, and played an important role
in the creation of the High T'ang style. Each subgenre
had its own range of styles and its own set of conventions,
though there was considerable overlap between them. Indeed
during the entire period of court poetry, with the exception of a few unconventional writers such as Wang Chi,
Lo Pin-wang, and Ch'en Tzu-ang, it is easier and more
appropriate to describe subgeneric styles than individual
styles.

16

POETRY IN THE LIFE OF THE COURT

In the <u>Records of Occasions in T'ang Poetry</u>, following the list of the members of the Hsiu-wen kuan, there is a brief description of the poetry outings of Chung-tsung. The unknown author speaks with both wistfulness and censure:

> Whenever the Son of Heaven would go on picnics or pleasure out-
> ings, he would be accompanied only by his ministers and the
> Auxiliary Scholars. In spring His Majesty would visit the Pear
> Orchard and attend the Purification Ceremony at the Wei River,
> at which he would present circlets of willow to ward off the
> pestilence. In summer he would hold banquets at the vineyards
> and present red cherries. In autumn he would climb to the Buddha
> of the Temple of Compassionate Mercy, and there he would be
> offered chrysanthemum flower wine with a wish for His Majesty's
> long life. In winter His Majesty would visit Hsin-feng, passing
> through the White Deer Pavilion, and climbing Mount Li, where he
> would permit a bath in the Warm Springs. There he would grant
> fragrant powders and orchid oils. To those of his retinue he
> would present horses from the Soaring Unicorn Stables, and to
> each of his officials, a yellow robe.
>   Whenever the emperor was moved by something, he would write a
> poem, and all the Scholars would follow suit using the same rhyme.
> This indeed was what men of that age took delight in and yearned
> after. Thus it happened that everyone in the retinue grew overly
> familiar, glib, and brimming with flattery, and they forgot the
> rules of propriety that obtain between a ruler and his courtiers.
> Only through literary genius did men gain Imperial Favor: men
> such as Wei Yüan-tan, Liu Yün-chi, Shen Ch'üan-ch'i, Sung Chih-
> wen, Yen Chao-yin, and others were known for this and nothing
> else.[14]

These occasional poem series took various forms. They
seem to have usually been competitions, the object being
speed or quality. When the criterion was literary quality,
the standards of judgment were extremely subtle. The
reward for the victor was often a piece of brocade, and
in later poetic diction, the phrase "to get the brocade"
meant to achieve poetic renown. The loser was required
to drink a specified amount of wine as a forfeit.

Such poems are generally designated "to imperial command" (ying-chih 應制). In some cases the courtiers
would "respectfully follow the rhymes" (feng-ho 奉和)
of His Majesty's poem, while in other cases the emperor
would set the topic and give different rhymes to different
poets, including himself (fen-yün 分韻). Prefaces were
probably added to all the series; one survives written
by Chung-tsung himself. Ordinarily such prefaces would
set the scene, bring up some of the allusions used, and
enumerate the poets.

We do not know if poems were chanted aloud as they
were completed or simply handed in for judgement, but in
many of the series we can see poems that seem to respond
to one another; for example, they will contain couplets
of the pattern "Who would say X? [something said in
another poem of the series]/Rather we should say Y."
This would suggest that poems were recited upon completion. The same myths, allusions, and themes will be used
throughout a series, and the ability to pilfer from
follow-poets surely facilitated quick composition.

Both the list of the members of the Hsiu-wen kuan and
the elegiac memoir of Chung-tsung's court outings come
from a long prose passage under the poet Li Shih in the
Records of Occasions in T'ang Poetry. There is no apparent reason for its inclusion at that point. After the
passages already quoted, there follows a short chronicle
of over forty occasions of the court between 708 and 710.
Along with the date and the occasion, there may be appended

a noteworthy couplet or a mention of who finished their
poem first or last. We have more poems preserved from
these occasions than from any other similar period of
court occasions in the T'ang. Almost all the extant poems
of these occasions are preserved in the Records of Occasions and in the Wen-yüan ying-hua. It seems likely that
the compilers of the Wen-yüan ying-hua and Chi Yu-kung
計有功, the author of the twelfth-century Records of
Occasions, had available a collection of imperial poem
series between the years 708 and 710. The prose passage
mentioned above was probably the preface to that collection.

Many of these poem series are too long to quote in
their entirety, while others have only a few poems surviving. I will translate seven of the eight surviving poems
under the title "Early Spring: His Majesty Visits the
Southern Villa of the Princess T'ai-p'ing 初春辛太平
公主南莊, written on the eleventh day of the second
month in 709. I follow the order and attributions of
the Wen-yüan ying-hua (176.9a-10b); the order, at least,
follows roughly the status of the participants in the
Hsiu-wen kuan and may indicate that the order of composition was according to rank. The poem omitted is attributed
to both Wei Ssu-li (04838) and Chao Yen-chao (05242).

Li Chiao:

Our host's mountain mansion appears, touching the very sky,	主家山第接雲開
The Son of Heaven on spring excursion comes shaking the earth.	天子春遊動地來
Here and there see Horse Guards circle beyond the flowers,	羽騎參差花外轉
Rainbow banners flap in the breeze, turning beside the sun.	霓旌搖曳日邊回
Have this stony rill play in concert with the tunes of the lute,[15]	還將石溜調琴曲
And take red clouds from peaks to fill our cups of wine.	更取峯霞入酒杯

The bird-belled coach has left the isles
   of magpies and of rooks,

鸞輅已辭烏鵲渚

Yet sounds of their piping still swirls
   around Phoenix Terrace.

簫聲猶繞鳳皇臺

[03701]

The "sun" in line four may refer to the emperor as well
as to the real sun. "Red clouds" were one of the wondrous
foods supposed to confer long life; Li Chiao has the
imperial party imbibing them through their reflections
in the wine.

    Su T'ing:

To our host's mountain mansion early
   spring returns;

主家山第早春歸

The royal palanquin on spring excursion,
   surrounded by azure mists.

御輦春遊繞翠微

They purchased the land, spread out gold
   that was once an enclosure.

買地鋪金曾作埒

Searched the river to get their stones
   that had held up the loom.

尋河取石舊支機

Among the clouds bright color of trees,
   with thousands of flowers filled,

雲間樹色千花滿

In the bamboo the voice of a stream, a
   hundred courses flying.

竹裏泉聲百道飛

Of course we have the tune of the phoenix,
   melody of the gods,

自有神仙鳴鳳曲

And should all use our songs and dances
   to repay the radiance of His Majesty's
   favor.

佇將歌舞報恩暉

[05056 under Shen Ch'üan-ch'i]

Notice that Su T'ing uses phrases from Li Chiao's poem
in his opening couplet. What the "gold" of line three
refers to is unclear, but it may refer to flowers.
Reference to the stones that "held up the loom" are made
in several of the poems: briefly, the story goes that a
man was once searching for the source of the Yellow River
and came upon a lady washing silk. He asked her where
he was and she told him he was in the "River of Stars,"

the Milky Way. She presented him with a stone, and he returned. Later he asked the diviner Yen Chün-p'ing about the stone and Yen informed him that it was the stone which held up the loom of the Weaving Girl, a personified constellation. Since Princess T'ai-p'ing is connected with "heaven," the court, she has access to such stones. This story is based on an ancient belief that the ocean flows up into heaven, into the "River of Stars," and then back down again in the west forming the Yellow and Yangtze rivers. A second, related story, which merges with the preceding story in some of the poems, concerns a man who lived by the Yangtze, and every year in the eighth month a raft came floating past him, going out to sea. One year he got on the raft. After seeing the dwellings and denizens of heaven (and not knowing where he was), he returned to Szechwan and asked the diviner Yen Chün-p'ing how he got there. Yen Chün-p'ing answered that he remembered there was a wandering star in the Herdboy constellation that year, and the man realized he had made the circuit of the Milky Way.

The song of the phoenix in the eighth line refers to the story of Nung-yü, the daughter of Duke Mu of Ch'in, and the pipemaster. The pipemaster taught her to play the song of the phoenix on the panpipes, then they summoned a phoenix and eloped off to heaven on its back. The "Phoenix Terrace" of Li Chiao's poem may also refer to the same story. Thus Su T'ing and his fellow poets have the music which will carry them to "heaven."

Shen Ch'üan-ch'i:

Our host's mountain mansion's gates rise
    by the River Pa,

The scenery of the royal excursion enters
    the new year.

Beneath Phoenix Hall cross the weapons
    of the Guard,

By Magpie Bridge they spread imperial
    banquet mats.

主第山門起灞川
宸遊風景入初年
鳳皇樓下交天仗
烏鵲橋頭敞御筵

Everywhere among the flowers we meet
  with colored stones,

往往花間逢綵石

And oftentimes among bamboo we see those
  streams of red.

時時竹裏見紅泉

This morning the royal retinue is beside
  a P'ing-yang's Lodge,

今朝扈蹕平陽館

None yearn to ride that fabled raft to
  the cloudy River of Stars.

不羨乘槎雲漢邊

[04030 under Su T'ing]

Shen Ch'üan-ch'i draws on even more fabulous lore: The
Weaving Girl constellation (mentioned in the story of
getting the stones) and the Herdboy constellation (mentioned in the story of riding the raft to the Milky Way)
were popularly seen as lovers, allowed to meet only once
a year when mapgies would form a bridge for them to cross
over the heavens to one another. The "lovers" here are
probably Princess T'ai-p'ing and her husband Prince Ting.
The "streams of red" are streams filled with fallen
flowers. Han Shou, the Marquis of P'ing-yang, was the
husband of Han Wu-ti's elder sister and here clearly
stands for Prince Ting.

  Sung Chih-wen:

The road from Green Gate touches the
  Phoenix Terrace,

青門路接鳳凰臺

A royal excursion by the pale Ch'an,
  dragon outriders come.

素滻宸遊龍騎來

Brook plants by nature welcome the
  scented carriage—they bow;

澗草自迎香輦合

Cliff flowers surely attend on the
  imperial banquet—they blossom.

巖花應待御筵開

Our writings move round the Northern Dipper,
  form the stars' configurations,

文移北斗成天象

The wine is held toward South Mountain
  as a wish for long life.

酒近南山作壽杯

This day too attendant courtiers take
  a stone away—

此日侍臣將石去

All are pleased that our Discerning
  Prince presents gold on his return.

共歡明主賜金回

[03312]

The wit of the second couplet is based (1) a visual
observation that the plants "fold up," ho 合, seeming
to do obeisance to the imperial retinue; and (2) a pun
on k'ai 開, meaning both to "blossom" and to "spread a
banquet." The fifth line obscurely tells us either that
the emperor is the central subject of the courtier's
poems or that the emepror's poem (no longer extant) sets
the pattern for the accompanying poems of his courtiers
just as the Northern Dipper determines the position of
the other stars. It echoes Analects, II. 1: "The Master
said, 'Who governs by Virtue may be compared to the
North Star which maintains its place while other stars
do obeisance to it.'" Presumably all the courtiers held
their cups in the direction of South Mountain, a traditional symbol of longevity, to convey their wishes to
the emperor.

Li Yi:

Beyond P'ing-yang's Lodge there is the home of an immortal,	平 陽 館 外 有 仙 家
In this garden by the Ch'in, nature's beauty is in splendor.	沁 水 園 中 好 物 華
The land rises up from East Moor, turning back the sun's chariot,	地 出 東 郊 迴 日 御
The walls look down on the Southern Dipper, cloud coaches cross over.	城 臨 南 斗 度 雲 車
Harmonies of windblown springs circle bamboo of hidden groves,	風 泉 韻 繞 幽 林 竹
Light shakes on rain and sleet among flowers of different trees.	雨 霰 光 搖 雜 樹 花
Your Majesty has been wished the fortune of a million years span—	已 慶 時 來 千 億 壽
And when you return at sunset, you will indeed be "nine layers" distant.	還 言 日 暮 九 重 賒

[04875]

In his first couplet Li Yi ingeniously brings in a third
river of the capital region to vary Shen Ch'üan-ch'i's Pa
and Sung Chih-wen's mention of the Ch'an; surely Princess

T'ai-p'ing's villa was far less watery than the scene
would suggest. Line three suggests that the mountain
region south of Ch'ang-an is so high that it forces the
sun-chariot to turn back in its course and it looks down
on the constellations. The last couplet depends on a
play on the "nine layers," referring both to heaven and
to the palace.

Li Yung 李邕:

I've heard of the stone that held the loom in that silvery "river"	傳聞銀漢石支機
And have also seen the golden palanquin emerge from the Tzu-wei star.	復見金輿出紫微
Crows and magpies cross before the Weaving Girl's Bridge,	織女橋前烏鵲起
Over a hall of the immortals, phoenixes fly.	仙人樓上鳳皇飛
A current of wind reaches our seats, the singing fans flutter,	流風入座飄歌扇
A cascade's water encroaches on stairs, splashing the dancing robes.	瀑水侵階濺舞衣
Again today as when someone intruded between Ox and Dipper,	今日還同郎牛斗
And like him, on a raft we will follow the sea's ebb homeward.	乘槎共逐海潮歸

[05522]

The same references are used here as in the preceding
poems, with the addition of the Tzu-wei star, where the
palace of heaven was supposed to be located.

Shao Sheng 邵昇:

The loveliness of this garden by the Ch'in surpasses P'eng-lai and Ying-chou,	沁園佳麗奪蓬瀛
Azure cliffs and streams of red encircle the capital.	翠壁紅泉繞上京
Our two sages suddenly go travelling from the luan-bird palace,	二聖忽從鸞殿幸
A pair of immortals descends from phoenix hall to greet them.	雙仙正下鳳樓迎

Flowers swallow the foot palanquin
  as it emerges from the void,

Trees mix with tent palaces, complete
  as in a painting.

There is no way to ride that raft, spy
  the isles of the River of Stars,

To no purpose we ask the diviner, go
  to Yen Chün-p'ing.

花 含 步 輦 空 間 出

樹 雜 帷 宮 畫 裏 成

無 路 乘 槎 窺 漢 渚

徒 知 訪 卜 就 君 平

[03907]

P'eng-lai and Ying-chou were the two islands of the
immortals in the Eastern Ocean. The "two sages" are
Chung-tsung and Empress Wei, while the "pair of immortals"
refers to Princess T'ai-p'ing and her husband, Prince
Ting. It must be kept in mind that beneath these dulcet
verses, the Princess T'ai-p'ing and her husband were as
unscrupulous a pair of ogres as that unscrupulous age
produced. Chung-tsung's principal talent was in staying
alive, which was no mean feat for a member of the royal
house in those days; having survived the reign of his
mother, Empress Wu, he might well be treated as "immortal."

The repetition of certain phrases and the repeated use
of a limited number of allusions is evident. The first
couplets of five of the poems set the scene with the
mention of an imperial visit, many using the same phrases;
the other two poems begin with a general description of
the scenery, tying it in some way to an "immortal" (royal)
presence. The poems group themselves by twos and threes.
The first three poems all have a variation of the phrase
"our host's mountain mansion" in the first line. With
Sh'en Ch'üan-ch'i a series of river names begins, each
poet trying to work a different river of the capital into
his opening couplet. Clearly no strict rules are in
operation here: each poem seems to pick one or more
strands from the preceding poems until they feel a topic
is played out. It is significant that the poem that
violates the tripartite form by first describing nature

and then in the second couplet introducing the imperial
visit is by Shao Sheng, the least noteworthy of the poets
participating; this is his only poem extant. Shao Sheng's
poem is weak in a number of ways: he opens with the trite
"surpassing" topos, and his closing does not say what he
wanted it to say—he probably meant to say what Shen
Ch'üan-ch'i said at the end of his poem, that no one
needs to visit heaven because the joys of heaven are to
be found here on earth. But somehow Sheng's phrasing
has him saying the wrong thing: one cannot get to heaven
and therefore we ask a Yen Chün-p'ing where we have been
in vain.

The middle couplets of the poems are descriptive; the
third couplet in particular seems to demand a certain
kind of treatment, mentioning several of the following
elements: bamboo, clouds, streams, flowering trees, and
stones. Sung Chih-wen's marvellously ornate third couplet
departs from this pattern. Most of the poems close with
some clever twist. At least three of the poems mention
the emperor's return, a proper banquet closing.

A nice contrast can be made between the poem of Li
Chiao, the grand old man of court poetry, and that of
Sung Chih-wen, a member of the younger generation. Li
Chiao's poem is gracious and subdued: the wit of Li's
third couplet scarcely ruffles the flow of the poem—the
reader expects the sounds of water to mingle harmoniously
with the banquet music and is accustomed to some play on
the idea of reflection. The last couplet leaves the
reader with a delicate sense of immortal music lingering
in the air with faint hints of the themes of the Herdboy
and Weaving Girl and Nung-yü and the pipemaster. It possesses all the decorum of earlier court poetry in the
new heptasyllabic regulated verse. Sung Chih-wen's poem
is more aggressively clever. The descriptive second
couplet has the plants and flowers bowing and spreading
banquets in the most contorted syntax. The third couplet

also demands some mental gymnastics on the part of the reader to fill out the metaphor. Finally Sung ingeniously combines allusion to the story of "taking away the stone" with a compliment to imperial largesse. Wit was, of course, desirable to a certain extent in court poetry, but it is not difficult here to sense the rumblings of individuality as the poet truly competes, refuses to lose his identity in the anonymity of convention.

Imperial command poems were not confined to banquet pieces. Official partings and other occasions were also topics on which the attendant courtiers might sharpen their wits. Even the huai-ku could be the topic for a poem series as in "His Majesty Visits Wei-yang Palace in the Old City of Ch'ang-an" 幸長安故城未央宮, written on the thirtieth day of the twelfth month, 708. Wei-yang Palace was a Han palace, then in ruins.

Li Chiao:

A former palace built by a worthy minister,
To the new park here our Sage Ruler comes.
The Cycle moves on, walls and fosses interchange;
Deep in years, the beams and roofs have crumbled.
In its rear pools the water is no more,
The halls in front have long ago turned ashes.
No one can tell where was once the Pavilion to the Winds,
In vain we hear stories of the Plates to Catch the Dew.
Yet royal hearts may meet across a thousand years,
An imperial verse, another Chiu-shao appears.
Today where poem after poem is written,
One might imagine us still on Po-liang Terrace.

[03705]

The Chiu-shao 九韶 is the music of the sage-emperor Shun, here recreated by Chung-tsung. As mentioned earlier, Po-liang Terrace was the site of a famous party given by

Han Wu-ti at which (Li Chiao would have believed) the emperor and his courtiers each composed a heptasyllabic couplet in the first "linked verse" of Chinese literature.

Chao Yen-chao:

Mounting at dawn, the royal retinue moved forth,	鳳駕移天驛
And leaning on railings, we observe the Han capital.	憑軒覽漢都
Chill mist recedes from the purple-fringed residence,	寒煙收紫禁
Spring's beauty fills the Yellow Plan.	春色繞黃圖
Here ancient histories have left their traces behind,	舊史遺陳迹
How former kings lost the hegemon's right.	前王失霸符
From mountains and rivers only an inch of earth is gone,	山河寸土盡
But palaces and pavilions—not a foot of their beams survives.	宮觀尺樑無
Greatness resideth in Virtue alone,	崇高惟在德
How could one scheme for such mighty beauty?	壯麗豈為謨
These thatched cottages are a mirror for Your Majesty,	茨室留皇鑒
In the "Fragrant Wind" there is much to be considered.	熏歌盛有虞

[05245]

Chao Yen-chao begins a moralizing approach that is picked up in the later pieces. Line three refers to a purple mist that surrounds a certain star, here indicating the purple aura that surrounds the emperor and departs with him when he goes out on an excursion. The "Yellow Plan" in the following line is a diagram describing the auspicious arrangement of buildings in the palace compound; here it simply stands for the palace area. The "Fragrant Wind," mentioned earlier in conjunction with a poem by Ch'en Tzu-ang, is a song attributed to the sage Emperor Shun that expresses his concern for his people. The last line may suggest that Chung-tsung heed the ancient example of Shun if he wants to keep his throne; it may also suggest that the courtiers' poems are like the "Fragrant Wind" of old, teaching the same lesson. The latter alternative is indicated in Liu Hsien's response (if we accept the <u>Wen-yüan ying-hua</u> order):

After a thousand years to the palace of Han,	漢宮千祀外
His Majesty's carriage has come for a visit.	軒駕一來遊
Eternally here in its tranquil calm,	夷蕩長如此
But that awesome force of spirit lingers no more.	威靈不復留
From the heights an imperial appreciation emerges,	憑高睿賞發
Meditating on the past, Our Sage's heart has seen all.	懷古聖情周
The chill gathers in toward South Mountain,	寒向南山斂
Spring passes by the north Wei floating.	春過北渭浮
The deeds of earthenwork were splendid of old,	土功昔云盛
Now the flower of mankind visits it today.	人英今所求
Blessed to hear this song of the "Fragrant Wind,"	幸聽薰風曲
We now know the shame of the Hegemon's way.	方知霸道羞

[03942]

The "Fragrant Wind" song referred to here may be either Chung-tsung's opening piece or Chao Yen-chao's moralizing poem. Liu seems to be taking Chao Yen-chao to task for his comment on the "Hegemon's right" (literally the "Hegemon's tally"): from the context of his poem Chao Yen-chao was probably not casting aspersion on the Han's legitimacy but rather simply referring to their power in his use of "hegemon." The word, however, has very bad moral overtones, suggesting rule by power rather than by right; Liu gracefully suggests that if the T'ang is to be like the Han or better than the Han, it too must reject the "Hegemon's way." Chao's and Liu's moralizing seems to have irritated Sung Chih-wen:

The King of Han had not yet ceased his wars,

When Minister Hsiao constructed this palace.

Yet its mighty beauty was gone in one morning,

Its awesome force of spirit absent for a
   thousand years.

His Imperial Wisdom grieves for these traces
   of the past,

He sets out wine to feast his courtiers.

The chill is light beyond the pennoned pikes,

Spring emerges amid the tent city.

Our joyful thoughts turn back the sinking
   sun,

Our songs continue the "Great Wind."

This morning the glory of our emperor

Has no need of a Shu-sun T'ung.

[03319]

Sung responds to the preceding poems in a number of ways.
Though the Han may have ruled by right, Sung reminds the
party that the Han was still at war when this palace was
constructed. He continues by reiterating the theme of
glory and sudden decline, but in the face of this evidence
of impermanence, Sung suggests that the joy of the banquet
"turns back the sinking sun." The "Great Wind" was the
poem of Han Kao-tsu, expressing self-satisfaction at
his new empire and his power. Shu-sun T'ung was the
Han ritualist who was largely responsible for Han Kao-
tsu's state sponsorship of Confucianism; we may remember
T'ai-tsung's irritation at Wei Cheng's remonstrating
example of Shu-sun T'ung (see p. 33)—Sung Ch'ih-wen may
have also remembered it. Chao Yen-chao and Liu Hsien
were beginning to sound like Wei Cheng in their moralizing; Sung reprimands them, reminding them that this is
an occasion to celebrate imperial glory as Han Kao-tsu
did. Since Chung-tsung already represents Confucian
virtue incarnate, he has no need of a pair of Shu-sun
T'ung's to remind him about the path of virtue and the

wrong of the "Hegemon's way."

   We can see in this exchange something of the tension
that surrounded Confucian morality in court literature.
The huai-ku, a subgenre with close links to fu-ku sentiments, led Chao Yen-chao irresistably to moralizing.
Once the moral-evaluative mode was begun, it was difficult
to escape: Liu Hsien was led to "correct" Chao Yen-chao's
careless use of the term "hegemon." Sung Chih-wen tried
to end the dispute by the oldest argument against constant
moralizing, that certain occasions are simply for pleasure,
but he is careful to put this argument in a form that is
safe from attack: Chung-tsung is enjoying himself like
a great Han Kao-tsu and is so moral already he needs no
moralists, no "mirror of history."

   The courtiers are competing not only in the realm of
Confucian platitudes, they are also competing aesthetically. A clear example of this is in the descriptive
couplets that match "chill" with "spring"—for example,
Chao Yen-chao in an ornate but dull couplet:

Chill mist recedes from the purple-fringed residence,	寒煙收紫禁
Spring's beauty fills the Yellow Plan,	春色繞黃圖

As he "corrects" Chao's terminology, so Liu Hsien cannot
resist outdoing Chao's couplet:

The chill gathers in toward South Mountain,	寒向南山斂
Spring passes by the north Wei floating.	春過北渭浮

Sung Chih-wen·cannot resist showing off, not only outdoing Liu Hsien in ingenuity, but also putting his couplet
in the same position in the poem as Liu's.

The chill is light beyond the pennoned pikes,	寒輕綵仗外
Spring emerges amid the tent city.	春發幔城中

Not only is "light" a more interesting qualification of

the chill than its "receding" or "gathering in," the
couplet is more internally coherent, the chill fleeing
the circle of springtime warmth which emerges in the camp
through imperial effulgence and the brightly colored
pennons of the retinue.

I will spare the reader the last extant poem of the
series, a generously allusive piece by Li Yi. He seems
to do trying to smooth over Sung Chih-wen's excessive
rebuttal of his superiors by commenting on the series
of poems as a whole:

Each in turn makes a bow to Shu-sun T'ung's
  rites,   代捐孫通禮
Our court may boast the talents of Chia Yi.   朝稱賈誼才
                    [04883]

This is a remarkable group of poems for in it we see the
influence wielded by the conventions of a given subgenre.
The same poets who were accustomed to turn out banquet
poems like those on the visit to Princess T'ai-p'ing's
villa, now turn their attention to the rule of Virtue
and the "mirror of history" which is to be found in the
ruins of the Han capital of Ch'ang-an. The capital theme
of the 670s has made its way into court poetry along with
the fu-ku didacticism that was associated with the huai-
ku. Since a relatively plain style is appropriate for the
huai-ku, the normal contortions and periphrases of court
poetry have been stripped away in these pieces, giving
remarkably sober results.

In poetry competitions judgement by quality is mentioned less often than judgement by speed of composition.
An interesting passage in the Records of Occasions gives
us a notion of what such competitions must have been like.

On the last day of the first month [709], Chung-tsung visited
K'un-ming Pool and composed a poem on the occasion. The courtiers
then composed more than a hundred pieces to imperial command. In

front of the royal tent a brightly colored frame tower was set
up, and His Majesty commanded Shang-kuan Wan-erh to select one
poem as the new imperial composition. He then had his courtiers
gather beneath the tower, and in an instant papers started flying
down. As each competitor recognized his own poem, he clasped it
to him. This went on until only the poems of Shen Ch'üan-ch'i
and Sung Chih-wen had not been tossed down. More time passed and
a piece of paper came fluttering down. Everyone rushed to look
at it and it was Shen's. Then they heard Shang-kuan Wan-erh's
evaluation: "Both poems were equally matched in craftsmanship,
but Shen's last couplet went:

This humble courtier would carve rotting stuff,　　微 臣 彫 朽 質
And is shamed to perceive the material of　　　　　羞 觀 豫 章 材
　　Camphor Terrace.

[In vain I labor at poetry: considering my lesser talent, it is
like carving rotten wood—the craft is there but the genius is
not. Thus I am ashamed before the others here, including His
Majesty, who possess more talent—better timber—than I.]

In my opinion the energy of his lines stops here. Sung's poem
closed:

I do not grieve that the bright moon is gone,　　不 愁 明 月 盡
For the pearl that shines by night comes in　　　自 有 夜 珠 來
　　its stead.

[Even though the moon is gone, the luminous genius of the verses
composed here may take its place.]

This ends the poem on the upbeat." Shen Ch'üan-ch'i submitted
and did not dare contest the matter.[16]

  T'ang evaluative and descriptive comments on poetry
often sound strangely rarified to us, though they are
relatively crude compared to the subtle judgements in
Japanese utaawase. The tradition of such poetic evaluations in the eighth and particularly the ninth centuries
may well have begun with the competitions of court poets.
Another thing we learn from this passage is the importance
of the last couplet, the "point" of the poem. The "craft-
manship" in which the two poets were equal may refer to

their adherence to tonal regulations, although it may
also refer to the craft of the middle couplets. As long
as the "craft" was perfect, the clever twist at the end
of the poem was more susceptible to judgement.

17

A PRIVATE BANQUET AT MR. KAO'S PAVILION

By the end of the seventh century the tradition of Chinese banquet poetry was already very old. Legend carried this tradition back to the parties of King Hsiang of Ch'u and his honey-tongued courtier Sung Yü; most of this legend is imaginative extrapolation from frames of _fu_ written during the Han. The early Han prince Hsiao of Liang and his courtiers Tsou Yang, Mei Sheng, Chuang Chu, and Ssu-ma Hsiang-ju form another legendary banquet party; whatever truth there may have been to their meetings, their revels were blown out of all proportion by later embellishments. There is even an apocryphal collection of short _yung-wu fu_ supposedly written at their banquets.[17]

The earliest banquet collection of _shih_ of which we have firm knowledge is the early third-century "Gathering in Yeh" (_Yeh-chung chi_ 鄴中集) with a preface by Ts'ao P'i 曹丕. The collection itself does not survive, but an imitation of it by Hsieh Ling-yün is preserved in chapter 40 of the _Wen-hsüan_. If Hsieh is holding faithfully to the form of the original, as seems likely, then we know that the essential elements of the banquet collection were present by the third century. There is a preface followed by a series of poems, one by each of the men present. In Hsieh's imitations the poems use different rhymes, and this common feature of banquet poems probably did not appear until the Southern Dynasties.

The Chin dynasty produced two collections famous for their prefaces, the "Golden Valley Garden Poems" 金谷園詩, with a preface by Shih Ch'ung 石崇, and the "Orchid Pavilion Collection" 蘭亭集, with a preface by the famous calligrapher Wang Hsi-chih 王羲之. A few of the poems

survive. The prefaces to such banquet collections were
often more enduring works of literature than the poems
themselves: one does not invite friends to a party on
account of their poetic talents, but one does choose the
most gifted among them to write the preface. These
prefaces usually take the form of first setting the
occasion, then describing the joys of the party, often
followed by a meditation on the impermanence of the beauty
and pleasures they are then enjoying, the desire to preserve these moments of joy in writing, and closing with
the details of who was present or how many were present,
and, in later times, what rhyme was used. The prefaces
to the "Golden Valley Garden Poems" and the "Orchid
Pavilion Collection" were not only the prime models of
later prefaces, they provided a storehouse of allusions
for both the prefaces and the poems themselves. I quote
an abridged version of the "Golden Valley Garden Poems"
as an example:

In the sixth year of the Yüan-k'ang Reign [296]. . . . I have a
villa in the Golden Valley of Ho-yang County. There are clear
streams and thick, burgeoning woods, orchards, groves of bamboo
and cypress, and all kinds of herbs. Perfect indeed this place
is as something to give the eyes joy and the heart pleasure. At
this time Wang Hsü, Libationer and Grand General of the Western
Campaign, is about to return to Ch'ang-an, and I, along with a
group of other worthy gentlemen, am sending him off. We have
gone into the stream valley, strolling and feasting day and night.
Frequently we move along—at times climbing high places to look
down, at times sitting in a row along the river bank. Then
sometimes we take our zithers, our mouth-organs, and lutes
together in coaches and play them in concert on the road, or
halting we play them in alternation with fifes and drums. At
this point everyone is writing a poem to describe his innermost
feelings, and when someone cannot, he is obliged to pay the
forfeit of drinking three pints of wine. Stirred that life does

not last forever, fearing the unpredictability of ruin, I have
set forth the date, the official titles and names of the men
present on this occasion. I have also copied out the poems as
follows. I hope those who take an interest in such things in
later ages will look them over. In all there were thirty participants.[18]

The "Golden Valley Garden Poems" belong to an important
subcategory of banquet collections, those composed for
parting banquets. Though they conventionally brood over
the impermanence of the world, such banquet collections
are themselves notable for their impermanence. From
scattered prefaces and single poems throughout the T'ang,
we know that there were once hundreds, perhaps thousands,
of such collections for parties and partings. It is unlikely that more than a few ever achieved wide circulation.
The quality of the vast majority of such occasional poems
cannot but make us grateful for the disappearance of these
collections, but they are an important fact in the composition of T'ang poetry. Any number of surviving parting
poems and banquet poems might be far more comprehensible
if we possessed the collection of which they once formed
a part. Again thanks to the Records of Occasions we have
one such collection, though it has also survived independently.[19] This collection consists of the works written
at three parties held at the forest pavilion of one Kao
Cheng-ch'en 高正臣. Ch'en Tzu-ang wrote the preface
(04445).

PREFACE FOR A BANQUET ON THE LAST DAY OF THE MONTH AT MR. KAO'S
    FOREST PAVILION

Since ancient times the excursions, banquets, and pleasures have
been many indeed, on the fine mornings and in the lovely scenes
of this world, among its gardens and groves, pools and pavilions.
So if a place be secluded and solitary, one cannot spy the glory
of the Royal Dwelling and occasions are missed, friendships

perish, and the roads of an age of peace are usually blocked.
How can such a situation compare with the brilliant opening of
the dawn, enjoying the pleasures of court and wilds. . . . The
choicest delicacies are laid before us on finely wrought mats—
pearls, kingfisher, and onyx; strings and pipes are played in the
fragrant gardens—the dulcimers of Ch'in and the zithers of Chao.
A stately multitude of caps and ribbons, many guests have been
invited from the In-laws Ward; luan-birds and phoenixes ring out,
there being present visitors who are among the masters of literature. They describe a view that takes in all the capital domain,
on through to the towers and terraces of the Park of Han; glancing
to the side they rein in the Yi and Lo, looking down on the shores
of gods and immortals. Then there are the men and ladies of the
capital, wandering bravos and catamites who emerge, riding bit
to bit from out of the Golden Market, four-horse terms entering
the avenues of the Bronze Camels. Carriages of aromatic woods,
brocaded hubs, breezes rising in gauze and damask, jeweled awnings,
wrought saddles, pearls sparkling like the sun.

At this time the t'ai-tsu pitchpipes are ending [that is, the
close of the first month]; the air is fresh and clear in the
capital, mountains and rivers are showing the spring, and the
weather is clearing over the splendid scene. The walls and
palace towers are beautiful, and the year's radiance is at its
fullest. Here we linger to take our pleasure, enjoying the
flowers and birds so much we forget to return; we never weary
in our appreciation, finding some personal satisfaction facing
the woods and brooks. Magnificent indeed!—surely this is the
grandest scene of the Royal Domain. How can we allow those
talents of the Chin capital alone, Wang Hsi-chih and Shih Ch'ung,
to set the standards for visits by the River Lo, or let the many
grandees of the House of Wei, Ts'ao P'i and his group, monopolize
parties in Yeh? Best that we should express what is on our minds
to commemorate this fine excursion. Together we chose a single
rhyme, hua.

I will quote just a few of the extant poems, the first by

Kao Cheng-ch'en (03952):

The First Month accords with a fine festival,
In spring we enjoy the flowering of things.
Forget our cares in a goblet of wine,
Mold our characters growing used to this
    mountain home
Willows azure, leaves holding in the mist,
Plums fragrant, flowers bearing snow.
But passing time will do us no favors
And gradually the sinking light slants
    downward.

正月符嘉節
三春玩物華
忘懷寄尊酒
陶性狎山家
柳翠含煙葉
梅芳帶雪花
光陰不相借
遲遲落景斜

Ch'en Tzu-ang (04445):

Searching out spring, we strolled up the
    highroad;
Seeking a banquet, we enter this mountain
    home.
A lord's mansion filled with hatpins and
    ribbons,
The scene of the Royal Domain is splendid.
Jade pools first spurting out their currents,
Pearled trees beginning to open their flowers.
Our pleasure is not yet at its fullest,
When from over the forest tower lingering
    red clouds scatter.

尋春遊上路
追宴入山家
主第簪纓滿
皇州景望華
玉池初吐溜
珠樹始開花
歡娛方未極
林閣散餘霞

Ts'ui Chih-hsien 崔知賢 (03954):

The premier month in the land of Ho-yang,
On this fragrant morning the scene is splendid.
With cheeps and flutters, birds of the season
    change,
Sparkling bright, spring's red clouds rise.
Willows wave their beauty where the wind is,
Plums scatter their flowers before the sun.
Lingering here, evening by Lo-yang's walls,
Songs and piping in Shih Ch'ung's home.

上月河陽地
芳辰景物華
綿蠻變時鳥
照曜起春霞
柳搖風處色
梅散日前花
淹留洛城晚
歌吹石崇家

Han Chung-hsüan 韓仲宣 (03958):

If you wish to know the joys of excursions,
Our fragrant goblets face the flowering of
  things.
This land touches P'an Yüeh's county,
The garden is of Shih Ch'ung's home.
Where the willows are, clouds seem to be
  leaves;
Among the plums, snow resembles the flowers.
As the sun sets the homeward road is far,
But we linger, companions of mists and red
  clouds.

欲 知 行 有 樂
芳 尊 對 物 華
地 接 安 仁 縣
園 是 李 倫 家
柳 處 雲 疑 葉
梅 間 雪 似 花
日 落 歸 途 遠
留 興 伴 煙 霞

The similarity of these poems to court banquet poems is
inescapable, though they are hardly as well-wrought as
the works of a Shang-kuan Yi or Sung Chih-wen. The
language is simpler, the range of allusion narrower, and
there is no attempt at great cleverness. These and the
many other poems of Mr. Kao's three banquets are far more
significant as documents of literary sociology than as
literature: they represent the quality of average occasional poetry in the T'ang, fully competent but utterly
uninspired. The majority of poets participating in the
three series that comprise this banquet collection have
no other extant poems: they were ordinary educated men,
middle-level bureaucrats and certainly not the sort to
be found in court competitions. They were invited to a
party and expected to turn out a poem. They ran through
a base of conventional images and ideas on which great
poetry had been written before and would be written again
later, but they make no attempt to use this conventional
base for their own ends. Except for Ch'en Tzu-ang's
poem, the third couplet in each of the poems (and in
other poems in this series) set a line on willows against
a line on plums: willows are always mixed with mist or
resemble mist; plum blossoms always seem like snow. Had

we discussed all the poems of this series, we could have
taken out all the clichés and, reserving certain topics
for certain couplets, could have tossed them together
at random to turn out a credible addition to the series.

Ch'en Tzu-ang's poem presents the picture of a major
poet writing a poem every bit as vapid as those of the
other officials at the party. This poem is not included
in the earliest form of Ch'en's collected works; that is,
it was included in an appendix, and it source was probably
this banquet collection. While poets did preserve many
of their occasional poems, they probably willingly left
the majority to the ravages of time. But the poem does
show us the power of a subgenre to subvert originality
and bring those of great talent and those of no talent
to about the same level. Indeed, a virtuoso piece by a
poet like Sung Chih-wen would have sounded a discordant
note in the series as a whole, which flows from poem to
poem with a harmonious blandness.

18

THE COURTLY YUNG-WU

Yung-wu 詠物, "poetry on things," was one of the most
stable and enduring of the poetic subgenres. Because
yung-wu were more closely associated with fu than other
subgenres, the rigid conventions of the yung-wu fu
carried over into the yung-wu shih. During the first
half of the Six Dynasties the allegorical element in
yung-wu poetry had been dominant, but in the hands of
late fifth-century poets such as Hsieh T'iao 謝朓 (464-
99) the traditional allegorical associations of objects
were reduced to mere attributes of the thing itself. The
yung-wu became simply a descriptive poem, for example,
the bamboo would no longer stand for a man of resolute
integrity, but associations of resolution and integrity
would play a role in the description of bamboo. Allegorical yung-wu were still written, but they were a relatively minor tradition. During the sixth and seventh
centuries yung-wu were usually rhetorical exercises,
often delightful ones. As the scope of poetry broadened
in the latter part of the seventh century, the old yung-wu
tradition was also put to new uses. Ch'en Tzu-ang returned
to allegory; other poets liberated themselves from the
rigid conventions of description and turned out imaginative
yung-wu ballads: Lu Chao-lin's "Hard Travelling" looks
forward to these in its treatment of the withered tree
theme. Still other poets took the cleverness expected
in yung-wu and tried to make it intellectually significant as well as entertaining.
   Even more than the banquet poem, yung-wu provided a
poet an excellent opportunity to display his ingenuity.
Throughout the T'ang one finds anecdotes in which a
poet's talents are tested by being asked to compose an

extempore poem about some object. The following anecdote
about Su T'ing may be apocryphal, but it gives a good
indication of the kind of cleverness demanded in yung-wu:

> Su Kuei [a minister in Chung-tsung's reign and Su T'ing's father]
> at first knew nothing of Su T'ing's talent. One day a guest
> arrived at Su Kuei's and was waiting in the guest room when Su
> T'ing came along the veranda plying his broom. A scrap of writ-
> ing fell from Su T'ing's robes, and the guest picked it up to
> look at it. It was Su T'ing's "On a Black Slave Boy," and con-
> tained the lines:
>
>   His fingers are like ten black ink-sticks,   指 如 十 挺 墨
>   His ears are like a pair of wide spoons.   耳 似 兩 張 匙
>
> The guest thought this was exceptional. After a while Su Kuei
> came out and lingered with his guests, chatting and chanting
> poems. The guest then asked who was the person responsible for
> the poem he had found, sure as he was that it must be one of Su
> Kuei's kin, whether a legitimate son or a concubine's child. Su
> Kuei then told the guest about the boy, and the guest expressed
> surprise and admiration, asking Su Kuei to treat the boy with
> more respect and to recommend him, for he was certainly an out-
> standing child of the Su family. Little by little Su Kuei grew
> more fond of him. Someone presented the family with a rabbit and
> it was hung on the porch. Su Kuei summoned Su T'ing to write a
> poem about it, and T'ing wrote:
>
>   The rabbit died, its spirit spent,   兔 子 死 蘭 彈
>   They brought it slung on a bamboo pole.   將 來 掛 竹 竿
>   Just hold it to a mirror.   試 將 明 鏡 照
>   And its no different than what you see in   無 異 月 中 看
>   the moon.[20]

It should be explained that the Rabbit was one of the
several mythical denizens of the moon; it was a rabbit
form rather than an "Old Man" that was seen there. The
function of this Rabbit-in-the-Moon was to pound the
elixir of immortal life. The comparison of a dead rabbit
in the mirror to this Rabbit-in-the-Moon—the moon was

often compared to a mirror and vice versa—is ingenious
enough to delight any reader, but it serves no more
complicated function in the poem. The potentially rich
irony of a dead piece of game becoming the immortal Rabbit
who grinds the elixir of immortality is not exploited.
If it is genuine, this poem probably dates from the late
680s or early 690s. We might contrast it with a poem
written in 713 by the fifteen-year-old Wang Wei, "On a
Friend's Mica Screen":[21]

Take your mica screen,	君 家 雲 母 障
Set it up in your wild courtyard:	持 向 野 庭 開
Mountains and streams will merge with it naturally,	自 有 山 泉 入
Coming not on account of the brightly colored painting.	非 因 采 畫 來

Like Su T'ing's youthful effort, this unassuming poem by
Wang Wei depends on a clever twist: the art of the landscape screen is so close to nature that it will merge
with the real landscape and become one with it. This is
hardly a startling notion in Chinese theory of art and
it becomes a commonplace in later poetry on painting,
but in this poem the wit is functional, as it was not in
Su T'ing's poem. At its best art was supposed to lose
its artifice, to intrude into the real world. We may
remember that in landscape couplets a spatial continuity
is often expressed verbally as an "entering" 入 ; Wang Wei
breathes life into this dead metaphorical verb—"merge"
is literally "enter"—as the outlines of the real mountains
and rivers actively link with their counterparts in the
painted screen. The landscape actively "comes," forming
a unit with the screen because it is not aware of the
screen's artifice. Likewise, in this poem the artifice
of Early T'ang wit disappears in the comment Wang Wei
is making about art and nature.
        In the Early T'ang yung-wu topics are amplified in a

predictable number of ways. Descriptive techniques were
the most important. Four of the most common of these
are: (1) enumeration of attributes, paired in couplets
(the simplest of the techniques); (2) resemblances—either
metaphors or similes marked by the rich vocabulary of
simile, ju 如 , ssu 似 , jo 若 , lei 類 , t'ung 同 , and yi 疑
("one wonders if it might not be . . ." or "it seems to
be . . . "); (3) contextual descriptions which seek the
unusual "wonders" of the thing in some setting; and (4)
description through effects, in which case the name of
the object is usually avoided. In the couplets these
descriptive techniques can be divided up into cumulative
descriptions (X; and Y) and transitional descriptions
(X; then Y). In most couplets these two forms are difficult to distinguish, but often transitional descriptions
are marked by stock pairs of grammatical particles; for
example, cha 乍 . . . , huan 還 . . . , "suddenly (it seemed
X), but then (it seemed Y)."

The second important technique of amplification was
the use of historical, mythical, or intellectual associations of a given object. In the case of some common
topics, a set of associations will be so strong that a
poem which ignores them seems somehow wanting. An example
might be the association of bamboo with integrity, in
which the fact that it stays green through the winter
should be mentioned, often with a pun on its chieh 節 ,
"joints" or "integrity." Another example, which we shall
see later in this chapter, is the necessity of mentioning
the statues of the bronze immortals and their dew pans
when writing a poem on dew. These commonplace associations made up a body of literary "lore," which was set
forth neatly in encyclopedias such as the Ch'u-hsüeh chi.
Occasionally a poet will display his erudition by coming
up with a particularly recherché reference to his object.
Often, couplets using the proper poetic lore will be
mixed with the descriptive techniques mentioned above.

Most yung-wu contain only one or two such lore couplets,
but some, including many by Lo Pin-wang, are made up
entirely of historical and mythical associations.

These techniques of amplification were to continue
through the eighth and ninth centuries, but in better
poetry they were integrated into some unified interpretation of the object. In contrast, Early T'ang yung-wu
tend to be paratactic, filling out the required space
with an unsubordinated itemization of descriptions and
associations. In the ninth century this enumerative
technique reappeared as a subform of yung-wu, the most
famous examples of which are Li Shang-yin's "Tears"
(29411) and Peonies" (29260). These poems closely
resemble the yung-wu of Lo Pin-wang, but put the density
to more sophisticated literary ends.

Another Early T'ang subform which can also be found
in later centuries is the yung-wu made up entirely of
the effects of the object; these sound somewhat like
riddle poems in the medieval West and have a Chinese
antecedent in some of the fu of Hsün-tzu. The following
example (03729) is by Li Chiao:

WIND

It knows how to bring down late autumn's leaves,	解落三秋葉
And can make mid-spring's flowers open.	能開二月花
When it passes the river, thousand-foot waves—	過江千尺浪
When it enters bamboo, thousands of stalks slant.	入竹萬竿斜

Generally, the yung-wu of the second half of the
seventh century are more dense, ornate, and artificial
than those of the first half of the century. As might
be expected, the first poet in whose work this appears
is Lo Pin-wang. Lo has one yung-wu series and some
other yung-wu that may or may not form a series. These
are masterpieces of dense, precious Early T'ang rhetoric.

I will give a literal translation of one (04193), followed
by a paraphrase.

SNOW

Dragon clouds: jade leaves rise,

Crane snow: auspicious/jade-tally blossoms/flakes
   renew.

Its shadows in confusion: the Bronze Raven
   blowing,

Its light melts: Jade Horse Ford.

Full of radiance, it brightens white-silk seal-
   script,

Hiding its traces, it shows the well-omened orb.

One cannot pair the Secluded Orchid with it,

In vain it would avoid Bright Spring.

龍 雲 玉 葉 上
鶴 雪 瑞 花 新
影 亂 銅 烏 吹
光 銷 玉 馬 津
含 輝 明 素 篆
隱 迹 表 祥 輪
幽 蘭 不 可 儷
徒 自 繞 陽 春

Dragon-shaped clouds [or clouds which follow dragons] resembling
leaves of jade, rise, and then snow renews in blossom-flakes
which take the shapes of jade tallies or auspicious signs. This
is a "crane snow," a snow like the one about which two crows
chatted under a bridge in A.D. 374, one saying to the other,
"The cold this year is not a bit less than it was the year Yao
died." [A Taoist joke, of sorts: cranes, being immortal, could
make weather comparisons across two and half millennia.] The
shadows of the snowflakes are scattered in disorder on the Bronze
Raven weathervane of the Imperial Observatory; the weathervane
shakes in the wind. However, the bright snowflakes melt when they
touch water such as that at White Horse Ford [here called White-
Jade Horse Ford to provide a better parallel for the "Bronze
Raven"]. The reflected light which seems to be given off by the
flakes could illuminate seal characters inscribed on white silk
such as might have been read by Sun K'ang, who was so poor that
his family could afford no oil for his lamp and therefore he
studied at night by moonlight reflected on the snow. Yet its
very traces disappear, and that fact is revealed when the auspicious orb of the sun appears. When it appears in an ancient song
entitled "The White Snow," the snow should not be paired with the

Hidden Orchid melody, as was done in the "Snow Fu" by Hsieh Hui-
lien and earlier in the "Fu of Criticism" by Sung Yü: this is
wrong because the context of the "Fu of Criticism" is lascivious,
while "The White Snow" is a virtuous ancient song. Furthermore,
the real white snow does not belong in the same season as the
real hidden orchid. On the other hand, "The White Snow" tries
in vain to avoid being paired with the song "Bright Spring"—the
two songs are often spoken of together, both being virtuous
ancient songs. "White Snow" tries to avoid it because "Bright
Spring" will cause it to melt.

Such an involute interweaving of allusions, associations,
wit, and metaphors is the hallmark of Lo Pin-wang's distinctive, if painful, talent. The parts do not form an
integrated whole, but they are not really expected to;
the interest of the poem lies in dazzling the readers
line by line. The nine poems that comprise Lo's "On an
Autumn Morning: following the rhymes of Administrator
Mao of Tzu-chou" (04196-04204) are equally memorable
pieces of allusive periphrasis, treating nine objects of
autumn: wind, clouds, cicadas, dew, moon, water, fireflies, chrysanthemums, and wild geese.

The Early T'ang poet whose name is most strongly linked
with yung-wu is Li Chiao. Li Chiao has an independent
collection of one hundred and twenty yung-wu entitled
the "Miscellaneous Songs," Tsa-yung 雜詠 arranged roughly
according to the classification system of the encyclopedias: celestial phenomena, terrestial phenomena, "fragrant plants," "fine trees," "wondrous birds," and
"auspicious beasts." The "Miscellaneous Songs" has
been preserved independently in Japan, with a preface
by Chang T'ing-fang 張庭芳 dated 747.[22] Chang's preface
is one of the rare examples of a High T'ang writer giving
his opinion on the work of a court poet. He praises the
collection in terms of poetic rhetoric, diction, and
euphony and emphasizes its pedagogic value:

> I hope that it will be of aid in the crafting and polishing of
> verse, so that one may avoid sluggishness. I would have it shown
> to youths, but would not dare offer it to future worthies.[23]

The disclaimer that a work is only for students and not
for discriminating readers is a prefatory trope (for
example, Li Po's preface to the "Fu on the Great Bird"
大鵬賦), but one which applies when offering one's own
work to the public and not that of another. Chang T'ing-
fang seems to be serious here. The implication is that
poetry as a learned craft is appropriate for students,
but that serious poetry for mature readers is something
more. Behind his gracious praise, Chang T'ing-fang's
High T'ang attitude is only slightly less condescending
than Li Shang-yin's in the quatrain quoted earlier.

Li Chiao's was probably not the first such collection;
we possess what may be a fragment of such a yung-wu collection by Tung Ssu-kung 董思恭, who flourished in the
660s and 670s. This group of poems (03781-03789) represents a good coverage of the heaven section: sun, moon,
stars, wind, clouds, snow, dew, fog, and rainbows. Since
Li Chiao was active during the same period, the two series
may be roughly contemporaneous: Li Chiao's yung-wu in the
"Miscellaneous Songs" sound very much like youthful
exercises and show none of the masterful grace of his
poetry written during Chung-tsung's reign. Tung Ssu-
kung's yung-wu are generally superior. Both collections
may be something in the nature of exercise books, either
to try one's hand at a full range of yung-wu topics or
present a group of textbook examples to other poets. It
is possible that, like banquet collections, there were
once many such yung-wu collections which now survive only
in scattered fragments.

I will quote three poems on dew, by Lo Pin-wang, Tung
Ssu-kung, and Li Chiao respectively. All three poems
allude to the statues of the bronze immortals, set up by

Han Wu-ti; in their hands these statues held pans to catch dew from which an elixir of immortality was to be made.   Lo Pin-wang:

At Jade Pass the chill air comes early,	玉關寒氣早
To Golden Basin the colors of autumn return.	金塘秋色歸
Floating on palms of immortals, its light gets ever purer;	沒掌光逾淨
Filling the lotus, its dripping is still faint.	添荷滴尚微
Changing to frost, the dawn spittle hardens;	變霜凝曉液
Receiving the moonlight, it casts a circular reflection.	永月奉圓輝
But it also appears on the Terrace of Wu,	別有吳臺上
Where it must be soaking the Ch'u courtier's robes.	應浥楚臣衣

[04199]

After describing the haunting physical beauty of the dew, in the last couplet Lo introduces a menacing vision of the dew, alluding to the story of Wu Pei, a courtier of the Han Prince of Huai-nan.   When the prince was plotting a rebellion, Wu Pei warned him that he had a vision of the thorns growing in the prince's palace and the dew soaking his old robes.   Tsung Ssu-kung:

Its night color freezes on the immortals' palms,	夜色凝仙掌
Its morning sweetness descends in the emperor's courtyard.	晨甘下帝庭
Before we know it, the last month of autumn has come,	不覺九秋至
And far away it falls at Three Perils.	遠向三危零
On reed isles the flowers are just turning white.	蘆渚花初白
In gardens of mallow the leaves are still green.	葵園葉尚青
It dries in the sunlight, once its largesse is sprinkled,	晞陽一瀼惠
And then wishes to swell the dark sea.	方顧益滄溟

[03787]

Among the commonplaces used in this poem is the reference

to the "sweet dew" 甘露, a sign of heaven's favor and imperial benevolence. Likewise, the sunlight in which the dew dries is a sign of imperial favor. Three Perils is a place where the most beautiful water in the world is supposed to be found. Li Chiao:

Dripping it brightens the flower garden,
Rolls sparkling down lush clumps of bamboo.
Jade—it hangs beneath cinnabar thorns;
Pearls—it is heavy on the green lotus.
By night it startles the thousand-year-old crane,
By dawn it dries in the wind of the eighth month.
It longs to freeze in the palms of the immortals,
To serve forever at Wei-yang Palace.

滴瀝明花苑
葳靃法竹叢
玉垂丹棘下
珠湛綠荷中
夜警千年鶴
朝晞八月風
顧凝仙掌內
長奉未央宮

[03586]

The first couplet consists of effects; the second is metaphorical. The last couplets play on traditional associations. The immortal crane of line five is frightened by the dew, associated with autumn, the season of destruction. In the last couplet if the dew freezes, it will not evaporate, thus approximating the immortality it is supposed to confer. Its "service at Wei-yang Palace" may simply be expanding the theme of immortality from the preceding line, but it may also refer to the "sweet dew" that fell at Wei-yang Palace during the reign of Han Hsüan-ti; at this sign of heaven's favor, the emperor proclaimed a general amnesty. "Sweet dew" is another commonplace association, given in the Ch'u-hsüeh chi.

Lo Pin-wang's poem is by far the most original and learned, and its closing couplet shifts perspective on the dew. The speculative "it must be" (ying 應) provides an element of personal reaction on the part of the poet. Both Tung's and Li's poems are more conventional, and

both close with a common variety of yung-wu closure, a
wish on the part of the object described.

By the time of Sung Chih-wen we can already see the
old treatment as rhetorical exercise giving way to a new
symbolic treatment. In contrast to the consciously wooden
allegories of Ch'en Tzu-ang, the symbolic yung-wu retains
its identity as a "thing" as well as signifying something
more. A beautiful example of this is Sung Chih-wen's
"On Old Chang's Pine Tree" 題張老松樹(03189); the pine
tree had long been a symbol of solitary rectitude, but
Sung Chih-wen handles the theme with exceptional power.

The year grows late beneath the eastern cliff,　　歲 晚 東 巖 下
I peer all around—how desolate it seems!　　周 顧 何 悽 惻
The sun sinks in the shadows of western
　　mountains,　　日 落 西 山 陰
And from all plants rises the visage of the
　　cold.　　眾 草 起 寒 色
In their midst there is a tall pine,　　中 有 喬 松 樹
Which brings me to heave a long sigh.　　使 我 長 歎 息
A hundred feet up without a single branch,　　百 尺 無 寸 枝
By nature a lifetime straight and alone.　　一 生 自 孤 直
　　　　　　　　[03189]

Fifty years later a poem like this would be undistinguished,
but in the context of the period it is exceptional. The
first two couplets fall comfortably into the tripartite
form, but Sung interjects a personal reaction in the third
couplet, and closes with one of those descriptive couplets
designed to stir the reader's emotions. Sung's use of the
plain style is effective and contrasts sharply with the
ornateness of the preceding poems.

Yung-wu quatrains, which had relied on wit even more
than longer yung-wu, also show this tendency to complex
symbolization during the last decades of the seventh and
first decade of the eighth centuries. There are seven
particularly fine quatrains attributed to Kuo Chen 郭震

(d. 713) which exemplify this change.[24]   Each of following three poems treats a different aspect of the theme
of the unappreciated man of virtue, part of the hsien-jen
shih-chih theme.

FIREFLIES   螢

When autumn winds are biting chill and the   秋風凜凜月依依
   moonlight's faint,

They fly past in the shadow of the tall plane 飛過高梧影裏時
   tree;

Where it's darkest they seem to teach others   暗處若教同衆類
   of their kind—

In this world they struggle to make someone   世間爭得有人知
   know of them.

            [03844]

CRICKETS   蟀

You deeply sadden whoever has left his home,   愁殺離家未達人
   who hasn't reached his goal;

Your every note reaches his pillow to be   一聲聲到枕前聞
   heard.

But don't take your bitter chanting to the   苦吟莫向朱門裏
   red gates of the rich—

Songs and piping fill their ears—they will   滿耳笙歌不聽君
   not listen to you.

            [03845]

A WELL IN THE WILDS   野井

Even though no one draws from it, its taste is 縱無汲引味清澄
   fresh and clear,

Its chill soaks the cold sky and the orb of   冷浸寒空月一輪
   the moon.

But if they had dug it beside some important   鑿處若教當要路
   highway,

For its lord it might serve to aid the men   爲君常濟往來人
   who come and go.

            [03847]

In the following brilliantly descriptive poem on clouds
(03846), Kuo Chen fuses perfectly a complex visual scene

and echoes of several traditional themes. Foremost among these is the image of the solitary wanderer as a cloud.

CLOUDS   雲

In the emptiness they cluster and scatter,   聚散虛空去復還
  go off, return again,

A man of the wilds leans calmly on his staff   野人閒處倚筇看
  watching them.

He never knew a body could be such a rootless   不知身是無根物
  thing—

Hiding the moon, covering the stars from   蔽月遮星作萬端
  thousands of different directions.

19

OTHER OCCASIONAL SUBGENRES

The vast majority of informal occasional poetry from the
reigns of Wu and Chung-tsung has been lost. Most of what
survives is in the large collections of Li Chiao, Sung
Chih-wen, and Shen Ch'üan-ch'i, and to a lesser degree
in the smaller collections of Tu Shen-yen, Yang Chiung,
Ts'ui Shih, and others. Yet there were any number of
literary figures who once had collected works in ten or
twenty chüan, at least a few chüan of which must have
been poetry, and who now have less than twenty poems
extant. The majority of those extant poems are banquet
poems and poems to imperial command. The anthologists
of the Wen-yüan ying-hua, the primary source of much of
the poetry of the period, strongly preferred court poems
to informal occasional poetry when selecting poems from
this period; this is quite the opposite of their practice
when anthologizing the poetry of the eighth and ninth
centuries.

Parting poems are an interesting case in point since
they constitute the largest of the Wen-yüan ying-hua
categories of shih: in this section the Early T'ang is
very poorly represented in comparison with parting poems
of the eighth and ninth centuries. Yet it was in the
Early T'ang that the basic characteristics of the T'ang
parting poem were taking form. Parting poems (sung 送
"sending off," pieh 別 and liu-pieh 留別 "parting from,"
and chien 餞 "holding a parting banquet for") are one
of the easiest subgenres to characterize. The pentasyllabic regulated verse and its earlier "imperfect" forms
are the preferred genre, forming a slight majority over
all other genres combined. There is a wide stylistic
range, and not unexpectedly, the elaborateness of the

style increases in direct proportion to the formality of
the occasion and the distance in rank of the addressee
above the poet. Very formal parting poems tend to be
ku-shih or p'ai-lü.

Many of the conventions of later T'ang parting poems
developed during the three decades from 680 to 710. The
tripartite structure is strong in such poems. As in
banquet poetry the most common way to open a parting poem
was with a general description of the scene, but the subgenre was already evolving some of its own opening conventions, all of which set different kinds of general contexts
for the specifics of the rest of the poem. Here are
examples of some of the more common openings:

   1. The cause for leaving:

The Northern Barbarians wish an alliance,   北狄顧和親
And from the Eastern capital an envoy emerges.   東京發使臣
       Tu Shen-yen, "Sending Off Chamberlain Kao on His Mission
          North" [03753]

His Majesty worries for the northern commanderies, 帝憂河朔郡
And in the south opens up the Hai-ling granaries. 南餽海陵倉
       Sung Chih-wen, "Sending Off Yao of the Censorate on a
          Mission to Chiang-tung" [03271]

   2. Here versus there—the starting point and destination of a journey:

At the crossroads, parting in late autumn,   岐路三秋別
The Yangtze fords are ten thousand miles far.   江津萬里長
       Yang Chiung, "Sending Off Magistrate Fang of Lin-chin"
          [03164]

   3. The hardships of the journey ahead:

I would ask of the roads of Liang's mountains—   借問梁山道
Jagged peaks in how many layers?   巘岑幾萬里
       Sung Chih-wen, "Sending Off Yang Wang to Chin-shui" [03330]

4. "Take consolation in this moment":

At the crossroads you are now a traveller,   岐路方為客
Let this sweet cup of wine cheer your face for a   芳尊暫解顏
    while.

                          Li Chiao, "Again Parting" [03560]

Typically the middle couplets of the parting poem will describe particular aspects of the scene at hand, aspects which involve the emotions stirred by parting. But there is more liberty in the parting poem to explore the emotions of those present, to elaborate on the causes of the journey, or to speculate on the future. A few conventional juxtapositions begin to emerge such as a line on the wine set in parallel with a line on songs or parting poems in the third couplet of a regulated verse.

The varieties of poetic closure are more numerous than opening conventions, and are often more relevant to the particular situation; for example, the official going to take his provincial post will be encouraged to govern well (03264) or the person going on a diplomatic mission or military campaign will be wished successful completion of his mission (03721, 03733) or that he return victorious, entering the passes or capital with "songs and dances" (03262, 03715). The traditional response of tears was a popular form of closure in parting poetry, as in Yang Chiung's "Sending Off Tutor Li on His Retirement" (03173):

Once I send you off by the pools of the Pa,   灞池一相送
Facing mist and roseate clouds my tears will stream   流涕向煙霞
    down.

We may remember Wang Po's famous inversion of the response of tears in one of his parting poems (03456):

Let us not, at this crossroads,   無為在岐路
Like a young boy and girl soak our robes with   兒女共霑巾
    tears.

Here we can see how a convention grows: Wang Po's original
invension of a very old response becomes itself a convention of closure, usually in the form of an admonition.
With no little incongruous humor Shen Ch'üan-ch'i admon-
ishes a military man not to weep on his armor (05095).
Reasons for this closing admonition are elaborated in
later poetry, as in Kao Shih:

Those with talent must always use it,   有 才 無 不 適
So go on then! Don't trouble yourself in vain.   行 矣 莫 徒 勞
                    [10445]

The admonition may be transferred to other subgenres, as
in Han Yü:

Let us not behave like some young boy and girl,   無 為 兒 女 態
All depressed, brooding over poverty.   憔 悴 悲 賤 貧
                    [17811]

The closing may leave the friends staring at the landscape,
emptied of the traveller who is then out of sight, as in
Li Chiao:

After parting, out beyond the green mountains,   別 後 青 山 外
I gaze toward you among the white clouds.   相 望 白 雲 中
                    [03714]

This is much the same thing that Lo Pin-wang saw earlier
in one of his parting poems:

I gaze back, out beyond Green Gate,   還 望 青 門 外
And see only the white clouds drifting.   空 見 白 雲 浮
                    [04185]

These are, of course, all _natural_ responses to the situation of parting, but they are hardly the only responses
possible. Some responses we might expect such as "When
will I see you again?" become conventional closures for

parting poems only in the High T'ang.

Since many travellers journeyed by boat, it is not surprising that water metaphors were a common form of closure in parting poems and that the metaphor was so successful that it was used whether the traveller was going by water or not. The inexorable eastward movement of the waters suggests impermanence and the thought that one may never see one's friend again; that the waters flow on forever is like the sorrow that the men parted will feel. Since one can go either direction on the waters, they stand for the "parting of ways" and the ancient "division of the Way" theme:

I heave a great sigh at the eastward flowing
   waters—
What now fills my cup can never be lifted again.
        Shen Ch'üan-ch'i, "Sending Off a Friend to Take His Post
          in K'uo-chou" [04969]

太息東流水
盈觴難再持

The bitterness of parting is, it seems, endless:
Before my gate the Cassia River's waters slant
  away.
       Yang Chiung, "Sending Off the Recluse Yang"   [03168]

別恨應無限
門前桂水斜

Inexorably the waters of the royal moat,
From this point on go either east or west.
       Li Chiao, "Sending Off Li Yung" [03359]

殷勤御溝水
從此各東西

I cannot gaze at the parting pavilion—
There the moat waters go either west or east.
       Yang Chiung, "Sending Collator Liu Off on a Campaign" [03170]

離亭不可望
溝水自東西

Moonlight is another popular closing image: the poet may speculate that he will at least share the moonlight with the person leaving (03553), or it may be combined with the water imagery:

As I send you off, back to your home district,
The bright moonlight fills the river before me.
       Yang Chiung, "By Night: Sending Off Chao Tsung" [03183]

送君還舊府
明月滿前川

Verse letters, being less specific in content than parting poems, cover an even wider range of topics. There can be elaborate autobiographical sketches, requests for preferment, praises, and self-justifications, addressed to high officials and friends of equal status alike. The <u>Wen-hsüan</u> tradition was particularly strong in this subgenre, especially in elaborate pieces addressed to those of higher rank. But in some cases verse letters left more room for personal sentiments than prose letters, and among them can be found some of the most beautiful poems of the age. Leaving office Kuo Chen writes:

TO COLLATOR LIU

寄劉校書

A low clerk for three years—why even mention it?

俗更三年何足論

Ever knowing glory or shame could fall in the space of a day.

每將榮辱在朝昏

When talent is slight, it's easy to grow old in the wind-blown dust,

才微易向風塵老

When your state is low, you cannot repay a dear friend's kindness.

身賤難酬知己恩

The last orioles in the royal park sing in the setting sun,

御苑殘鶯啼落日

A fine rain by Yellow Mountain Palace soaks my homeward carriage.

黃山細雨涇歸軒

I look back to the Minister's Bureau of the Great House of Han—

迴望漢家丞相府

Since yesterday I wonder who has been sweeping the tiers of gates.

昨來誰得掃重門

[03830]

The psychological subtlety of the last line, lying between amusement and regret, is close to that of the best High T'ang poetry. Kuo wonders about his successor sweeping the gates to success, pitying his wasted efforts but wondering if he, the succeeding sweeper, will be the one to find success in the "space of a day."

Because the verse letter was one of the most appropriate outlets for intense personal emotion, its quality soared

when poets had some serious personal matter to communicate.
Such an occasion was offered in 705 when Chung-tsung
assumed the throne, and the Chang brothers, favorites
of the empress, fell from power. Most of the empire's
best poets had been associated with the Chang brothers,
and in the ensuing purge of their entourage, South China
received more than its share of poetically gifted admin-
istrators. Men such as Su Wei-tao, Ts'ui Jung, Tu Shen-
yen, Sung Chih-wen, and Shen Ch'üan-ch'i all were banished
to the far south. Those who survived the arduous journey
were soon recalled, to be banished again some five years
later. We will discuss some of these verse letters in
later chapters.

Travel poems were often also verse letters, but many
were written for the poet himself. Like the verse letter,
travel poetry became a principal outlet for the impulse
to personal poetry. Otherwise undistinguished poets might
rise occasionally to greatness in such poems: a case in
point is that of the Auxiliary Scholar, Liu Yün-chi, though
it is perhaps unfair to compare his travel poems with his
other poetry in that only four poems survive out of his
ten chüan collected works. However, both his travel
poems are excellent. The following poem (03797) is hardly
typical of the subgenre but merits inclusion for its unusual topic.

SEEING A DEAD MAN BY THE ROADSIDE[25]

A brooding chill—in vain you see the sun;
A dark silence—how could you tell the year?
Your soul I cannot ask what happened,
But I'm sure you were straight as a bowstring.

見道邊死人
淒涼徒見日
冥寞詎知年
魂今不可問
應為直如弦

His other travel poem represents another extreme: it is a
magnificent, formal ninety-six line descriptive poem
(03794) that is too long to quote here.

Although travel poetry could be as elaborately descriptiv

as any court poem, it was also the subgenre in which we
most often find the _fu-ku_ attempt to recapture the plain
style of the Chien-an and Wei. We may remember that many
of Ch'en Tzu-ang's _fu-ku_ poems were technically travel
poems. A typical case is that of the Auxiliary Scholar
Hsüeh Chi (649-713). Most of Hsüeh's fourteen surviving
poems are court and banquet pieces; however, a poem by
Tu Fu, "Viewing a Wall with the Calligraphy and Painting
of Hsüeh Chi, Junior Guardian of the Crown Prince" (10715),
begins:

The Junior Guardian had the "old style"	少 保 有 古 風
To be found in his poem on Shan Moor;	得 之 陝 郊 篇
But alas, fame and fortune were perverse,	惜 哉 功 名 忤
And now we see only his paintings and calligraphy.	但 見 書 畫 傳

We have few enough references as to exactly what constituted the theoretical "old style"; the poem Tu Fu is referring to is Hsueh's "Returning to the Capital on an Autumn
Day: written ten miles west of Shan-chou" 秋 日 還 京 陝 西
十 里 作 (04914).

I drive my carriage across the moors of Shan,	驅 車 越 陝 郊
Look back north over the Great River.	北 顧 臨 大 河
As I gaze toward my home beyond the river,	隔 河 望 鄉 邑
Autumn winds raise waves on the water,	秋 風 水 增 波
To the west I mount the Hsien-yang road,	西 登 咸 陽 途
Toward sunset my melancholy brooding grows.	日 暮 憂 思 多
Fu Cliff twists windingly upward,	傅 巖 既 紆 鬱
Shou-yang Mountain also juts high.	首 山 亦 嵯 峨
Gone is the old man who labored at building,	操 築 無 昔 老
But the song "Picking Bracken" survives.	採 薇 有 遺 歌
On my journeys the seasons revolve—	客 遊 節 回 換
How long can human life last?	人 生 能 幾 何

The last line of this poem is a conscious use of a Chien-
an and Wei formula. The story of Fu Cliff alluded to is

of the Shang king Wu-ting (reigned 1324-1265 B.C.), who
dreamed of a sage who said his name was Yüeh. When the
king sent his emissaries to look for the old man, they
found him in a chain gang, building a rammed earth rampart
on Fu Cliff. Wu-ting made him his minister. "Picking
Bracken" was the song sung by Po Yi and Shu Ch'i when they
refused to serve the Chou, choosing to starve themselves
to death by eating bracken on Shou-yang Mountain. Taken
together the allusions suggest that Hsüeh sees little hope
of preferment and that he is disturbed about serving a
new dynasty. This almost certainly refers to Empress Wu's
Chou dynasty, though it is possible that it refers to the
restored T'ang of 705. This sort of personal meditation
on one's position in the political world was out of place
in most of the occasional subgenres; the solitude of the
travel poem accomodated it easily.

We do not have space here to go into other of the older
subgenres such as laments, and many of the newer subgenres
such as visiting poems and graffiti (t'i 題) had not yet
developed strong subgeneric conventions. In the early
eighth century the number of occasions that demanded a
poetic response increased—poems on paintings, poems
complimenting some object owned by a friend, poems of
gradditude, visiting someone and not finding them at home,
etcetra. Eventually all of these developed their own
conventional themes and range of diction.

20

THE NEW SONGS OF EMPRESS WU'S REIGN

The heptasyllabic meter had more "popular" and fewer
literary associations than the pentasyllabic meter. Before
the High T'ang the diction of heptasyllabic poetry was
generally less ornamented, its syntax more straightforward,
and its subject matter often that of yüeh-fu, although as
we have seen in the capital poems, it easily accommodated
lush, epideictic description. Its intrusion into court
poetry proper during the last decades of the Early T'ang
suggests a popularization of courtly taste. During the
reign of Chung-tsung, the use of the heptasyllabic meter
became widespread in regulated verse and became subject
to the kind of ornamentation practised in pentasyllabic
court poetry. But even before then, during the reign of
Empress Wu, the heptasyllabic meter was popular in songs,
often with trisyllabic and pentasyllabic lines mixed in.
A number of anecdotes survive which suggest that Empress
Wu was particularly fond of heptasyllabic songs, and it
is not surprising that someone like Empress Wu, who lacked
the literary education of an accomplished courtier, would
prefer their flashy energy to the stiff formality of
pentasyllabic court poetry.

We have one such song to commemorate a visit by the
empress to Lung-men, the Buddhist temple complex at Dragon
Gates. As a heptasyllabic song to imperial command, it
is unique in the period, but an accompanying note suggests
that it was one of a whole series of such poems.

Empress Wu was visiting Dragon Gate and ordered her courtiers to
compose poems on the event, promising a brocade gown to the one
who finished first. Tung-fang Ch'iu, the Historian of the Left,
completed his poem first and took the prize. However, the courtiers

303

were uneasy about this, and while Sung Chih-wen's poem was finished afterward, it was of great beauty in both style and content. Not one of those present failed to praise its excellence, so they stripped Ch'iu of the brocade gown and clothed Sung Chih-wen in it.[26]

Mercifully Tung-fang Ch'iu's poem has been lost. Ironically Tung-fang Ch'iu's niche in literary history has been assured by Ch'en Tzu-ang's preface to "The Long Bamboo," in which the courtly style is roundly denounced. Sung Chih-wen's poem (03222) survives.

DRAGON GATE   龍門應制

Last night's rain has cleared the pall of dust,   宿雨霽氛埃

And drifting clouds pass over the high gate towers.   流雲度城關

By the river levee willows put on new azure,   河堤柳新翠

On trees in the park the flowers come out early.   苑樹花先發

Flowers and willows of Lo-yang,
  heavy with moisture this season,   洛陽花柳此時濃

Mountain and river, tower and terrace,
  shine layer upon layer.   山水樓臺映幾重

A crowd of nobles brushes through fog
  to the soaring Phoenix's court,   羣公拂霧朝翔鳳

Her Majesty takes advantage of spring
  to visit the dragon caves.   天子乘春幸鑿龍

The dragon caves are right close by,
  just out of the royal city,   鑿龍近出王城外

A swollen stream of feathered guards
  crowds in on the carriage awnings.   羽從淋漓擁軒蓋

When the cloudlike retinue had just come
  to the bridge over royal waters,   雲蹕繞臨御水橋

Her Holy Robes had already reached
  the party on Fragrance Mountain.   天衣已入香山會

Mountain cliffs, steep and craggy,
  breaking off, then continuing,   山壁嶄巖斷復連

Clear streams, transparent and pure,
  looked down into the Yi.   靖流澄澈俯伊川

Pagodas' reflections far, far in the distance
  over the green waves,
雁塔遙遙綠波上

Niches sparkling like stars
  at the edge of the blue mists.
星龕奕奕翠微邊

Layered ridges where long had grown
  those thousand-foot trees,
層巒舊長千尋木

Remote valleys into which first fly
  hundred-yard cascades.
遠壑初飛百丈泉

Now pennoned pikes and rainbow banners
  circle the fragrant towers,
絲仗蜺旌遶香閣

She alights from Her palanquin, climbs a high
  spot to gaze on the Yellow River and Lo.
下輦登高望河洛

Tower and palace of the Eastern City
  seem as stars in their turnings,
東城宮闕擬昭回

The canals and banks of the South Fields
  interlock in arabesques.
南陌溝塍殊綺錯

In the groves a holy fragrance
  from the Terrace of Seven Precious Things,
林下天香七寶臺

On the mountains, spring wine,
  cups for toasts—"Live Forever!"
山中春酒萬年杯

Once the faintest breeze rises,
  auspicious flowers fall,
微風一起祥花落

And when immortal music begins to play,
  portentous birds come.
仙樂初鳴瑞鳥來

The birds come, the flowers fall
  in their endless bounty,
鳥來花落紛無已

We raise our cups to wish Her long life
  in the scented roseate clouds.
稱觴獻壽煙霞裏

And our songs and dances linger on
  as the sun begins to sink,
歌舞淹留景欲斜

While among the stones there still remain
  immortal coaches of five-colored clouds.
石間猶駐五雲車

Bird-banners soar and flutter,
  stay in the scented grass,
鳥旗翼翼留芳草

Dragon outriders charge on past,
  shine among evening's flowers.
龍騎駸駸映晚花

With a thousand carriages, ten thousand riders,
  the ringing palanquin goes forth,
千乘萬騎鑾輿出

Waters calm, mountains deserted—
  a stern ban clears commoners,
水靜山空嚴警蹕

But beyond the capital moors
  a tumult draws the onlookers,
郊外喧喧引看人

The whole capital fixes its gaze southward
  on the dust of the carriages.

傾都南望屬車塵

Boistrous sounds roll in the wind,
  hearing the Course of Yellow Radiance,

囂聲引颺聞黃道

The royal aura circles about
  and enters the Purple Mist Residence.

王氣周迴入紫宸

Former kings took the Tripod,
  our mountains and rivers secure,

先王定鼎山河固

Now the Precious Mandate falls to Chou—
  all things are renewed.

寶命來周萬物新

Our Empress has nothing to do
  with the pleasures of Jasper Pool,

吾皇不事瑤池樂

With the seasonal rains she comes to observe
  the springtime of the farmers.

時雨來觀農扈春

A few terms require explanation: the "Course of Yellow
Radiance" is the course of the sun and therefore of the
ruler; the tripod is the symbol of dynastic legitimacy.
Jasper Pool was where King Mu feasted with Hsi-wang-mu
and suggests here either the quest for excessive splendor
or sexual indulgence.

    Sung Chih-wen uses much the same technique to praise
the empress' outing as was used earlier in the songs on
the capital; however, Sung's use of the epideictic descriptive style is more sophisticated as he strings it into
something like a narrative. In borrowing <u>fu</u> structure for
their poems on the capital, the poets of the 670s rounded
off their praises of sensual beauty with some sort of
remonstrance or negative reaction. Clearly such a closing
would be out of place, even dangerous, here; however, the
need remains for the poet to end the piece with some sort
of ethical comment. Thus Sung Chih-wen closes with praises
for the legitimacy and moral force of the empress' Chou
dynasty.

    We can also see the habits of the courtly banquet poem
appearing here and there in the poem: the first heptasyllabic couplet (lines five and six) is not parallel, but as
the poet begins to describe the landscape, the couplets

are perfectly matched. Nor can Sung resist a long description of the end of the banquet, setting sun and
lingering delight, as is appropriate in the banquet poem.
This lush, sensual descriptive style must have been
immensely entertaining, and when Tu Fu recalled the lost
splendor of the T'ang after the An Lu-shan rebellion, he
would often echo elegiacally this courtly descriptive
style.

   Another, widely anthologized heptasyllabic song is
said to have received the direct praise of the empress in
a rather amusing anecdote. The poem is "The River of
Light" (03221), the Milky Way, using the conventional
identification of the court and heaven.

> At that time Sung Chih-wen had wanted the post of Scholar of the
> North Gate, but the Empress would not grant it. Thus we find in
> the poem allusion to "riding the raft" and "visiting the diviner"
> [the story of the man who voyaged through the Milky Way on a raft
> and eventually returned to Szechwan]. When the empress saw his
> poem, she told Ts'ui Jung, "I had no idea he was so talented; I
> refused his request only because he had such bad teeth." Sung
> Chih-wen felt humiliated by this to the end of his days.[27]

THE RIVER OF LIGHT   明河篇

Chill wind in the eighth month,
  the air in the heavens is crystal,   八月涼風天氣晶

No clouds in the sky for thousands of miles,
  the river of stars is bright.   萬里無雲河漢明

At dusk it appears by the southern towers,
  shallow it is and clear,   昏見南樓清且淺

Toward dawn it sinks into western mountains,
  spreads north and south and up over.   曉落西山縱復橫

The walls and towers of Lo-yang
  rise up into the heavens,   洛陽城闕天中起

And every night that long river runs
  through the palace's thousand gates.   長河夜夜千門裏

Tiered walkways, layered tiles,
  hide it, cover it over,   複道連甍共蔽虧

The painted halls and marble gates
  are set just right for it.
畫堂瓊戶特相宜

There on the mica screens,
  the "river" first floods over,
雲母帳前初泛濫

And beyond the crystalline latticework
  it gets further and further away.
水精簾外轉逶迤

Wondrous, those shining revolutions,
  blanched white as silk,
倬彼昭回如練白

Then again coming out of the Eastern City
  and touching the southern paths.
復出東城接南陌

On the southern path a traveller
  goes off, not to return,
南陌征人去不歸

In whose home tonight are they pounding
  the winter clothes?
誰家今夜擣寒衣

Over mandarin ducks on the loom,
  sparse fireflies pass,
鴛鴦機上疏螢度

Past the magpie bridge,
  a lone goose flies on.
烏鵲橋邊一雁飛

The goose flies on, the fireflies pass—
  sorrow without end,
雁飛螢度愁難歇

And now I see that river of light
  gradually dimming, sinking.
坐見明河漸微沒

It has been able to grow and shrink
  at the will of the drifting clouds,
己能舒卷任浮雲

And does not begrudge that its radiance
  must yield to the bright moon.
不惜光輝讓流月

You can gaze at the river of light,
  but you cannot approach it,
明河可望不可親

Though I wish to find the raft to ride
  and ask the way over.
願得乘槎一問津

Then shall I take the stone that supports
  the Weaving Girl's loom,
更將織女支機石

And return to search out the man who sells
  auguries in Ch'eng-tu.
還訪成都賣卜人

As allusive and laden with traditional allegory as the
poem is, it is an excellent description of the Milky Way
over the capital. Sung was the most ingenious of the
court poets and works the river metaphor into the poem
brilliantly; for example, the light reflected on the mica
screens becomes a "flooding over" of the "river." As the
poet leaves the capital in despair, he echoes the tradi-

tional metaphor of a man seeking recognition by his ruler
as a spurned lover: the mandarin ducks promise "conjugal"
bliss; the "magpie bridge" allows the Herdboy star to
visit the Weaving Girl across the Milky Way, but he is
the lone goose which can only fly past it. Finally he
turns to the two stories of riding to the heavens on a
boat, used in an earlier chapter in the poems written at
Princess T'ai-p'ing's villa.

If the occasion cited for this poem is correct, it is
earlier than "Dragon Gate." Though the topic of description is different from that of the capital poems, it
follows basically the same formula, closing with a plea
for for preferment like that of Lo Pin-wang in "Imperial
Capital," rather than moralizing. The style of this poem
is close to that of Lo Pin-wang in a number of ways: the
compound allusions, the use of fu-ku metaphors such as
the lone goose in an elaborate context, and the peculiar
combination of stylistic density and personal expression.
As such, "The River of Light" is a transition piece between
the songs of the 670s and those of the later seventh and
early eighth centuries.

Though special conditions might necessitate a change
in the closing message of the song, the old form of praise
followed by censure lingered on. The unusual topic of the
following piece by Shen Ch'üan-ch'i (04987) makes it a
historical poem, like the capital poems of Lu Chao-lin
and Lo Pin-wang. However, the tradition of such historical
poems makes it clear that the referent of Shen's poem is
topical, concerning some excess in Wu's or Chung-tsung's
court.

AIRING CLOTHES ON THE SEVENTH NIGHT　　七夕曝衣篇

Haven't you seen in days of old
  by Yi-ch'un Park, by T'ai-yeh Pool,　君不見昔日宣春太液邊

How the painted towers of P'i-hsiang Palace
  reached up into the sky?　披香畫閣與天連

There the lamp flames sparkled,
  the candelabras shone,

The smoke of incense swelled,
  and "compound fragrance" burned.

On this very night when the stars are dense
  and the "river" is at its whitest,

People tell how the Herdboy
  and Weaving Girl wander.

In the palace there is commotion
  on the Clothes-Airing Tower,

And in heaven, there is such loveliness
  on the mats where the rouge is applied.

Where do they air the clothes
  when the skies are turning orange?—

Where brightly clothed palace maids
  are lifting trunks of jade.

Pearled slippers scurry up
  the orchid staircases,

Gilded steps wind around and around,
  up above plumwood beams.

Into heaven's scarlet river

Emerald smoke rises,

Paired flowers and crouching rabbits
  on painted screens,

The four masters and coiling dragons
  hold up miniature panels.

They unroll gauze, shake out damask,
  clouds and fog appear,

Strung with jade and dangling pearls,
  the river of stars turns.

Red clouds of dawn scatter their colors,
  shaming the clothesracks,

The evening moon divides its beams,
  makes Mirror Terrace seem poor.

Above there is the immortal's gauze sash
  of eternal life,

In the middle see an embroidery
  where the Jade Girl meets her love.

In the tortoise shell casements
  are spring seasons all their own,

And behind the coral windows
  it turns dawn instead of dark,

燈火灼爍九微映
香氣氛氳百和然
此夜星繁河正白
人傳織女牽牛客
宮中擾擾曝衣樓
天上娥娥紅紛席
曝衣何許曛半黃
宮中綵女提玉箱
珠履奔騰上蘭砌
金梯宛轉出梅梁
絳河裏
碧煙上
雙花伏兔畫屏風
四子盤龍擎斗帳
舒羅散縠雲霧開
綴玉垂珠星漢回
朝霞散彩羞衣架
晚月分光劣鏡臺
上有仙人長命綹
中看玉女迎歡繡
玳瑁簾中別作春
珊瑚窗裏翻成晝

Into Pepper Chambers and Gilded Rooms
  favor has flowed anew,

Manners haughty and wasteful,
  not acting on their own.

Wen-ti of Han was right to regret
  Dew Terrace's expense,

Wu-ti of Chin has need to burn
  the furs before palace halls.

椒房金屋寵新流

意氣嬌奢不自由

漢文宜惜露臺費

晉武須焚前殿裘

The seventh night of the seventh month was when the Herdboy and Weaving Girl were supposed to meet. Shen Ch'üan-
ch'i's frugal closing sounds oddly incongruous after his
lush confusion between the "river of stars" and the bright
clothing of the palace ladies, which forms "clouds and
fog," sparkles like stars, reveals scenes of heaven, and
shifts the season and time of day at will. The ability
of artifice to invert the natural order (for example,
lines twenty-three and twenty-four) is a complex theme
in Chinese literature: sometimes it suggests the power of
art and human invention, but often it betokens a dangerous
perversity. In this poem its use is deliberately ambiguous,
standing between admiring description and moral remonstrance.
A similar inversion of nature underlies the following poem
by Fu Chiao-mo.

    Fu Chiao-mo 富嘉謨 was certainly one of the strangest
poets of the Early T'ang, and his only surviving poem (of
a collection once in ten chüan), "The Luminous Ice," is
one of the strangest of the heptasyllabic songs. Fu and
his friend Wu Shao-wei 吳少微 were felt to have created
an independent style, opposed to the style of court poetry.
Though not entirely outside the circle of court poets, Fu
Chiao-mo and Wu Shao-wei seem to have had an affinity for
the opposition poetics. Chang Yüeh, whose work we shall
discuss in the next section, paid a beautiful impression-
istic tribute to Fu Chiao-mo's style:

  Like a lone peak, a sheer slope, a mile-high cliff from which
  dense clouds swell up, from which both thunder and lightning emerge.

Truly terrifying—if displayed in the halls of government, it
would cause a shock.[28]

如孤峯絕岸, 壁立萬仞, 濃雲鬱興, 震雷俱發, 誠
可畏也。若施於廊廟, 駭矣。

The metaphor of a sheer or precipitous place for an unusually daring poetic style was to become a commonplace
of poetic criticism. Wu Shao-wei's work has fared better
than that of the more famous Fu Chiao-mo: six poems of
his have survived out of a collection once in ten chüan.
Two of these poems are romantic ballads much like those
of Liu Hsi-yi (04940, 04941); another is a fine piece in
the "ruined city" tradition, "On Passing a Former City of
the Han" (04939); yet another is a lament for Fu Chiao-mo
in which Wu praises his friend as a restorer of Confucius.
On one level, Fu's "The Luminous Ice" is courtly celebration, but on its symbolic level, the Yin element of ice
suggesting the empress, the poem should probably be read
as veiled criticism.

THE LUMINOUS ICE   明冰篇

In the northland's vast reaches
  oceans and rivers freeze,   北陸蒼茫阿海凝

South Mountain flashes with ice,
  both by day and by night,   南山闌干晝夜冰

A pale radiance looming high
  as the bright moon ascends.   素彩峨峨明月升

Deep in the mountains, at the ends of valleys,
  not revealing itself,   深山窮谷不自見

How could it know they would chop and gather it
  to present to Her Majesty,   安知採斲備嘉薦

Leave it frozen solid in a dark room,
  covered by cooling fans?   陰房洞沍掩寒扇

In the second month of bright spring,
  just as the dawn first brightens,   陽春二月朝始暾

And spring light rolls in the waves
  past the palace's thousand gates,   春光潭沱度千門

Then timely the luminous ice is brought out
  and offered to the Most High.   明冰時出御至尊

The vermilion courtyard flashes,
  the nine grades of officers there,

彤 庭 赫 赫 九 儀 備

Dazzling dangling of jade from waists
  as the thousand courtiers serve,

腰 玉 煌 煌 千 官 事

Luminous ice the whole year through,
  ever in its place.

明 冰 畢 歲 周 在 位

Remember before in the sandy north
  where the chill winds overflowed,

憶 昨 沙 漠 寒 風 漲

On the long Yellow River by Mount K'un-lun
  the ice first hardened,

崑 崙 長 河 冰 始 壯

Vast stretches of sheer craggy tiers
  swelling with watchtowers.

漫 汗 崚 嶒 積 亭 障

Now the wild geese give their mournful cries
  coming over the Yangtze,

嗈 嗈 鳴 雁 江 上 來

On the pooled terraces of the royal park
  the ice thaws again,

禁 苑 池 臺 冰 復 開

Quaking blue and drenching green
  reflect mansions and terraces.

搖 青 涵 綠 映 樓 臺

In the Songs of Pin, the "Seventh Month,"
  the beginning of the Royal Airs,

幽 歌 七 月 王 風 始

There they dug out ice and stored it away,
  reflected the order of things,

鑿 冰 藏 用 昭 物 軌

For the four seasons will not err
  for a thousand million years.

四 時 不 忒 千 萬 祀

[04935]

Ostensibly this is a descriptive poem marvelling at the
practise of storing ice away for springtime; however,
contradictory topical impulses lie just beneath the surface. Line twelve, for example, may translate in part
"ever in its place," but it also says quite plainly "the
Chou is on the throne." The "Seventh Month," Shih 154,
does indeed talk of chopping ice and storing it away, but
the "beginning of the Royal Airs" (Wang-feng 王風) in the
Shih-ching is a lament for the ruins of the Chou capital.
And how can "digging out the ice and storing it away," a
violation of seasonal progression, "reflect the order of
things?" This phrase is as incongruous in line twenty
as the "beginning of the Royal Airs" is in the preceding
line, and it is tempting to take each half of these lines

as responding to the corresponding half of the other
lines: the "reflected the order of things" goes with the
lament for the ruins of the Chou capital. Or do they
"reflect the order of things" by storing the ice, knowing
that spring must surely come. This and a score of other
hidden references in the poem point strongly to a topical
interpretation, but the poem is frankly baffling: we can
not be sure if it is a praise of the Chou, a prophecy of
the Chou's downfall, or a praise of Chung-tsung for his
sequestration of Empress Wu, as one hides away the Yin
element ice in the springtime. One other curiosity of
this poem is its unusual form: it is written in tercets.

"The Luminous Ice" is fundamentally a yung-wu poem,
and some of the finest yung-wu of the period were written
in the heptasyllabic song form. The traditions of the
heptasyllabic song allowed more freedom and imagination,
and in this form poets were able to transcend the rigid
techniques of amplification for pentasyllabic yung-wu.
The stilted treatment of the "sword" in Li Chiao's independent collection of yung-wu (03618) contrasts sharply
with the energetic treatment of the subject in the following heptasyllabic song (03534):

THE PRECIOUS SWORD   寶劍篇

Wu's mountains open,   吳山開
Yüeh's streams dry up,   越溪涸
Three metals fuse together
  to form this precious blade,   三金合冶成寶鍔
Tempered in green waters,   淬綠水
Mirroring clouds of red,   鑒紅雲
Five-colored flames rise,
  light swelling in the stream.   五采焰起光氲氳
On its back an inscription made
  to last ten thousand years,   背上銘為萬年字
Its front is marked with
  the pattern of seven stars.   胸前點作七星文
Mottled like a tortoise shell,
  White Rainbow's color,   龜甲參差白虹色

Golden ornament twining round
  as on a well pulley.

A startled rhino breaks through the center—
  no match for its sharpness;

A herd of fine steeds gallops headlong—
  no peer for its straightness.

The shivering chill of wind and frost,
  clear over its scabbard,

Yet its soul lies far, far away,
  bright in the Dipper.

Fleeing disaster at dawn it pierced
  the Chin emperor's room,

Escaping the fight one night it entered
  the Ch'u king's city.

One morning it found its match,
  met a great immortal,

Tigers roared and dragons screamed
  as it mounted to the skies.

The Emperor of the East lifted it
  at his place in the Tzu-wei Star,

The King of the West strapped it
  on at Red Walls fields.

In this age of peace we have long ceased
  the use of weapons,

But fortunate we are to get this,
  now all things military and civil are complete.

It eliminates troubles, averts disasters—
  fit for a ruler,

To increase his span and extend his years
  longer than Heaven and Earth.

轆轤宛轉黃金飾
駭犀中斷寧方利
駿馬羣騑未擬直
風霜凜凜匣上清
精氣遙遙斗間明
避災朝穿晉帝屋
逃亂夜入楚王城
一朝邂偶逢大仙
虎吼龍鳴騰上天
東皇提昇紫微座
西皇佩下赤城田
永平久息干戈事
儌倖得充文武備
除災辟患宜君王
益壽延齡後天地

This poem is replete with sword lore. The sword itself
is described in terms of, perhaps identified with, one of
the three legendary swords forged by Blacksmith Ou, a
famous metalworker of the southeast in antiquity. It has
the "seven star" pattern of the hero Wu Tzu-hsü's sword;
it is like White Rainbow, a famous mythical sword; buried,
its spirit shines in the heavens as a portent, the means
by which Lei Huan once found two ancient swords. Although
more formal yung-wu also use such historical and legendary
references, they do not use them in quite such an exuberant

way.   Likewise, lines eleven and twelve are "resemblances,"
but their violent, kinetic mode distinguishes them from
the more formal resemblances of the pentasyllabic yung-wu;
for example, Li Chiao's pentasyllabic yung-wu on the sword,
describes its brightness:

On the blade lotuses stir,   鍔上芙蓉動
In its scabbard, brightness of frost and snow. 匣中霜雪明
                         [03618]

In the song, Li begins with an imaginative description
of the forging of the sword, followed by a description
of its appearance; he then tells its fantastic history,
culminating in its apotheosis in the hands of the various
rulers of the celestial regions. But bringing the sword
back to earth, Li must somehow reconcile it with the
civil virtues. Schooled in courtly evasions, Li gracefully
explains that the sword averts trouble and therefore
promises to extend the ruler's life.

    Kuo Chen, whose yung-wu quatrains we have discussed
previously, has an equally energetic ballad on a sword.
This poem was singled out for praise by Tu Fu (10714)
and was reputedly a favorite of Empress Wu's.[29]

AN ANCIENT SWORD   古劍篇

Haven't you seen how in K'un-wu they melt the
    iron, how the flames and the smoke fly,   君不見昆吾鐵冶飛炎煙

How crimson light and purple vapors
    flash brightly together?   紅光紫氣俱赫然

How many years did it take in all
    for the master smith to refine it,   良工鍛練凡幾年

To cast himself a precious sword
    by the name of Dragon Stream?   鑄得寶劍名龍泉

Dragon Stream's appearance
    was like the frost and snow,   龍泉顏色如霜雪

And the master smith heaved a sigh
    for its wondrous rareness.   良工咨嗟歎奇絕

Its case of crystal and jade,
    spurting flowers of lotus,   琉璃玉匣吐蓮花

Its golden guard with the spiral inlay
  shines like the bright moon.

Now in a time when the world lacks
  the windblown dust of war,

We're lucky to have it to fully defend
  a good man's body.

The light of its spirit in darkness
  is the blue snake's color,

Its pattern is in scales
  like a green tortoise shell.

If it hasn't formed a bond
  with some wandering bravo,

Then surely it has been the darling
  of some hero of a man.

Who would have thought it would be cast
  away in the middle of the road

Or have fallen and been buried beside
  some ancient prison?

But though it be buried in dust again,
  no place now to be used,

Still night after night it will make its
  spirit strike against the skies.

錯鏤金環映明月
正逢天下無風塵
幸得周防君子身
精光黯黯青蛇色
文章片片綠龜鱗
非直結交游俠子
亦曾親近英雄人
何言中路遭棄捐
零落漂淪古獄邊
雖復塵埋無所用
猶能夜夜氣衝天

[03828]

Both this poem and the preceding poem allude to the story
of Lei Huan. During the reign of Wu-ti in the Chin dynasty
there was a portent of purple mists in the heavens. Lei
Huan identified this as the aura of a precious sword lying
buried and unappreciated. Digging by the prison wall in
Feng-ch'eng, Lei Huan found the two most famous swords
of antiquity, Dragon Stream and T'ai-an. Among Early
T'ang poets, Kuo Chen's work most strongly foreshadows
the High T'ang style: unlike Li Chiao, Kuo does not try
to reconcile the clash of values embodied in the praise
of a sword in an age of peace. He begins a resolution
similar to Li Chiao's in line ten, but moves away from
it, leaving the sword's aura striking the heavens in
frustration.

    The following yüeh-fu by Sung Chih-wen gives some
indication why the T'ang felt so strongly that their

poetry had restored the style of antiquity. The original
ballad, possibly from the third century, cheerfully
described the wanderings of the immortal Wang-tzu-ch'iao
up and down through the clouds where he joined a banquet
of the gods.[30] This original ballad was written in a
combination of tri-syllabic and heptasyllabic lines.
There are two rather stodgy versions of the ballad by
Southern Dynasties court poets, Chiang Yen and Kao Yün-
sheng 高允生 , written in pentasyllabic meter. Both are
competent pieces of versification, neatly parallel in the
middle couplets, describing Wang-tzu-ch'iao's apotheosis
with all the poetic lore proper to the subject. A version
of the ballad by a Northern Dynasties poet, Kao Yün 高允 ,
returned to the irregular meter of the original and captured something of its exuberance, but also made full use
of the lore of heavenly flights as the Southern Dynasties
poets did. In the first part of his poem, Sung Chih-wen
completely recaptures the energy of the original, but his
closing complicates the theme in a characteristically
T'ang way.

WANG-TZU-CH'IAO   王子喬

Wang-tzu-ch'iao   王子喬
Loved the immortals—   愛神仙
On the seventh day of the seventh month   七月七日上賓天
  he went up to visit heaven.
The white tiger strummed the zither,   白虎搖瑟鳳吹笙
  the phoenix blew the mouth organ,
And he rode along on vapors of cloud   乘騎雲氣吸日精
  sipping the essence of sun.
Sipped the essence of the moon,   吸月精
Never ever returned,   長不歸
His temple is still here, but the man is   遺廟今在而人非
  gone.
In vain I gaze at the plants on the hills,   空望山頭草
The dew on the grass soaks a man's robes.   草露溼人衣

                  [03224]

The original ballad had Wang-tzu-ch'iao soaring around in
a "free and easy wandering" before visiting the gods in
heaven; Kao Yün's ballad treated Wan-tzu-ch'iao's journey
to heaven more strictly as an apotheosis. Sung Chih-wen
brings back the casualness of the original as Wang-tzu-
ch'iao simply goes to "visit" heaven and chances never
to return. However, the closing human perspective changes
and complicates the ballad; the dew, a traditional symbol
of impermanence, soaks men's robes as a chilling reminder
of the difference between ordinary men and immortals.

Both Sung Chieh-wen and Shen Ch'üan-ch'i begin to use
the heptasyllabic song for personal poetry and occasional
poetry. Sung has a piece in mixed pentasyllabic and
heptasyllabic lines on releasing a white pheasant, and
Shen uses the heptasyllabic meter for an idyllic travel
poem (04988).

ENTERING SHAO-MI CREEK VALLEY　　　　　入少密溪

Cloudy peaks and mossy cliffs
　surround the creek slanting,　　　　雲峯苔壁繞溪斜

My river road in the fragrant wind,
　flowers lining the shore.　　　　　江路香風夾岸花

Where the trees are dense, I could scarcely
　believe that a bird could get through,　樹密不言通鳥道

Then a cock crowed and I realized
　that here was someone's home.　　　雞鳴始覺有人家

The human dwellings were further on
　deep where it opened onto a cliff,　人家更在深巖口

The stream waters flowed all around
　in front and behind the cottages.　澗水周流宅前後

Fish flashed darting past
　a pair of fisher boys,　　　　　　遊魚瞥瞥雙釣童

The crack of axe chopping wood—
　one old woodcutter.　　　　　　伐木丁丁一樵叟

They told me they were just fleeing the
　bustle and not fleeing Ch'in,　　　自言避喧非避秦

Hemp robed, plowing, digging their wells—
　people of Yao's times.　　　　　薜衣耕鑿帝堯人

They asked me to stay, to wait a while
  until chicken and wheat were ready,

相 留 且 待 雞 黍 熟

And by evening I rested deep in the mountains
  in a spring of moonlight through the vines.

夕 臥 深 山 蘿 月 春

Poetry like this is to all intents and purposes High T'ang
poetry. Shen echoes a number of pastoral motifs in this
poem, but the predominant one is T'ao Ch'ien's "Peach
Blossom Spring," which the villagers deny ("not fleeing
Ch'in") but fully embody.

    The tradition of poetic descriptions of music was old
and well established in the fu. Poems on music were
particularly popular during the eighth and ninth centuries,
and some of them are among the greatest poetry of the
T'ang. Since music was a nonverbal medium, description
of music allowed the poet a wide scope of imaginative
metaphor, describing the scenes evoked or emotions stirred
by the sounds. Like the dream poem, the music poem came
from a "real" occasion which by its nature demanded imaginative treatment. Shen Ch'üan-ch'i was one of the first
T'ang poets to fully exploit the poem on music in the
following heptasyllabic song on a lutanist whose music
evoked thunder. "The Thunder-rumble Song" was originally
a literary yüeh-fu of the Liang which described real
thunder; in contrast to Sung Chih-wen's return to the
original yüeh-fu in "Wang-tzu-ch'iao," Shen's treatment
of his yüeh-fu theme is completely original.

THE THUNDER-RUMBLE SONG

霹 靂 引

In the seventh month of the year

歲 七 月

The Fire Element recedes and Metal rises.

火 伏 而 金 生

Among my guests was one who had
  played the lute at my gate,

客 有 鼓 琴 於 門 者

Who played thunder-rumble on the note
  shang.

奏 霹 靂 之 商 聲

First he tapped the note yü—
  things came rending apart;

始 戛 羽 以 駴 者

Last he struck the note kung—
  there was a peal of thunder.

終扣宮而研驖

Lightning blazed and flashed,
  dragons leapt through the skies,

電耀耀兮龍躍

Thunder boomed crashing,
  and the rains came dark.

雷闐闐兮雨冥

Vapors gaped and moaned,
  matching his ode,

氣鳴唅以會雅

Music and storm blew in gusts,
  rising before me.

態㩧翁以橫生

And it seemed like a thousand banners
  galloping,

有如驅千橷

All weapons marshalled,

制五夬

Splitting wild serpents,

截荒虺

Beheading the long leviathan.

斬長鯨

Now who would compare this
  to Hsi K'ang's lost Kuang-ling song?

孰與廣陵比

And its mood is entirely different
  from those spirits, companions of cranes.

意別鶴儔精而已

But it causes my hero's soul to stir,

俾我雄子魄動

Brave men's hair stands on end,

毅夫髮立

Their thanks for His Grace, not shallow,

懷恩不淺

For the rules of war men unite in pairs.

武義雙輯

Look down on the Tartars as trifles,

視胡若芥

Cut through the Chieh as a harvest.

剪羯如拾

These are not just strong feelings at a
  party—

豈徒慷慨中筵

They are the full magnificence of all
  pleasure.

備舉娛之翁習哉

[04989]

From summoning up a thunderstorm, Shen's lutanist stirs
up all manner of martial feelings among the guests, a
music different from the refined music of a Hsi K'ang or
of the immortals. By the end of the performance the
guests seem ready to go off to the frontiers to obliterate
the enemies of the empire in gratitude for the emperor's
grace.
    One of the staple themes of palace poetry and yüeh-fu

might be best described in its most general form as women
without men: this may take the form of a neglected wife
or palace lady, a wife whose husband was fighting at the
frontier, and other less common subthemes. This theme
was quite popular, especially in heptasyllabic songs.
Shen Ch'üan-ch'i, for example, has two such poems (04985,
04986). One poet whose work was closely identified with
this theme was Ch'iao Chih-chih 喬知之 , a contemporary
and friend of Ch'en Tzu-ang. One of Ch'iao's poems is a
ni-ku 擬古 , "imitation of the ancient style," addressed
to Ch'en Tzu-ang. Though this does show the association
of the "ancient style" with Ch'en, the poem is simply a
conventional meditation on the hardships of military
campaigns.

     Ch'iao Chih-chih is famous because of his tragic exper-
ience with his concubine Pi-yü, "Green Jade." Pi-yü
caught the eye of a powerful clansman of the empress, Wu
Ch'eng-ssu. The story goes that after Wu abducted the
girl, Ch'iao addressed the following poem to her. On
reading it, Pi-yü killed herself, leaving the poem on her
corpse. Wu Ch'eng-ssu found the poem and contrived the
death of Ch'iao Chih-chih as a revenge. The female persona
that Ch'iao uses is Green Pearl, the concubine of the Chin
intellectual Shih Ch'ung, the host of the Golden Valley
banquet. When a powerful official maneuvered to obtain
the girl, Shih Ch'ung resisted and got in trouble. Green
Pearl thereupon committed suicide by throwing herself from
a high building. If Ch'iao Chih-chih did in fact write
this poem, holding up the example of Green Pearl to Pi-yü
was a cruel act, forcing her to choose between humiliation
and suicide.

GREEN PEARL   綠珠篇

In the Shih clan's Golden Valley   石家金谷重新聲
   they love the popular songs,
And for ten baskets of bright pearls 明珠十斛買娉婷
   they bought a fair girl.

"I love this day, sir,
　that you promised yourself to me,

I rejoice in this day
　that I gained your heart.

The towers and chambers of your home
　were never kept locked,

And you always let the others
　watch my songs and dances.

Their spirits were haughty and proud,
　not men of reason;

They boasted of their power,
　attacked you as they pleased.

To leave you, to go from you—
　this I could never bear,

In vain I tried to hide behind my sleeves,
　ruining my rouge.

A lifetime's parting now,
　here on this high tower—

In one morning my youthful face
　will end itself for you."

此 日 可 憐 君 自 許

此 時 可 喜 得 人 情

君 家 閨 閣 未 曾 關

常 時 歌 舞 借 人 看

意 氣 雄 豪 非 分 理

驕 矜 勢 力 橫 相 干

辭 君 去 君 終 不 忍

徒 勞 掩 袂 傷 鉛 粉

百 年 離 別 在 高 樓

一 旦 紅 顏 為 君 盡

[04298]

As is the case with many famous poems in the T'ang, the
biographical, occasional circumstances make the poem
interesting and poignant. Without them the poem is simply
maudlin.

An unnaturally large proportion of Ch'iao Chih-chih's
poetry is made up of yüeh-fu using female personae. Cases
like this in which a body of poems neatly conforms to a
single, famous biographical incident should make us suspicious. There are three possibilities. The first, which
most nearly conforms to the traditional biographical
approach, is that Ch'iao Chih-chih had an unusual fascination for women which is revealed in his poetry and which
culminated in the Pi-yü episode. A second possibility
is that because of the Pi-yü episode, anthologists assigned
anonymous poems to him because they believed he was the
type to write such poems. The third possibility is perhaps
the most plausible: because of the fame of the Pi-yü

episode, anthologists preserved that part of his collection which dealt with women. Not enough of Ch'iao Chih-
chih's poetry survives to make any judgement on the basis
of style.

   One of the best of these poems is the "Ballad of the
Singing Girl" 倡女行 (04300):

Pomegranate wine,	石榴酒
The brew of the grape,	葡萄漿
Scent of orchid and cassia,	蘭桂芳
Fragrance of dogwood.	茱萸香
I beg you, sir, to halt your golden saddle	願君駐金鞍
And share a while with me the year's sweetness;	暫此共年芳
I beg you, sir, to take off my blouse of gauze,	願君解羅襦
Get drunk with me and share this couch.	一醉同匡牀
For when Cho Wen-chün was newly widowed,	文君正新寡
She set her mind on being a singing girl.	結念在歌倡
Last night behind my lace curtain, I welcomed Han Shou,	昨宵綺帳迎韓壽
This morning with my gauze sleeves I led in Master P'an.	今朝羅袖引潘郎
I never play the northern flute and wake the neighborhood,	莫吹羌笛驚都里
And I won't play the p'i-p'a, make a hubbub in these chambers,	不用琵琶喧洞房
I'll just sing a new song of the night,	且歌新夜曲
Nor strum the "Ming-kuang" song of Ch'u—	莫弄楚明光
This song is sensual and full of bitterness,	此曲怨且豔
And its sad notes will break a person's heart.	哀音斷人腸

The widow Cho Wen-chün later married Ssu-ma Hsiang-ju,
while Han Shou was known for eloping with the daughter of
his employer. P'an Yüeh was famous for his good looks.
But beneath the layer of allusions this poem has an un-
restrained sensuality uncommon in this period.

21

TU SHEN-YEN

After the preeminent Ch'en Tzu-ang, Tu Shen-yen, Shen
Ch'üan-ch'i, and Sung Shih-wen were clearly the most
talented poets of the last decades of the seventh and
first decade of the eighth century. Although none of the
three developed a truly personal style, as a group their
work shows the growing private side of court poetry. As
we said earlier, most of the informal occasional poetry
of the period is found in their collections or in Ch'en
Tzu-ang's. All three were caught up in the banishments
of 705 when the Chang brothers fell from power and Chung-
tsung resumed the throne. Most of Tu Shen-yen's surviving
works date from before his exile, but Sung and Shen were
transformed as poets by the emotional impact of their
banishment to the far South.

Tu Shen-yen was born in the mid to late 640s and passed
the chin-shih examination in 670. It should be remembered
that Tu Shen-yen, Sung Chih-wen and Shen Ch'üan-ch'i were
roughly contemporary to the "Four Talents," but did not
achieve fame until several decades later. With the possible exception of Sung Chih-wen's "River of Light," the
three have no datable poems of the 670s, and the bulk of
their work belongs in the first decade of the eighth
century. All three began in minor official posts and
rose to prominence through the patronage of the Chang
brothers.

Tu Shen-yen began his career as a ninth-grade chief of
employees (wei 尉) in Hsien-ch'eng county in modern Shensi.
Next he held a somewhat higher post in Lo-yang, but became
embroiled in a factional dispute and was exiled to a provincial administrative post in Chiang-hsi. After his
recall to the capital, he attracted the attention of the

Chang brothers and held several middle-level posts in the
capital. Little is known of Tu Shen-yen's character
except that he had a reputation for exceptional arrogance.
By this time Tu already had achieved some fame as a poet
and was known together with Li Chiao, Ts'ui Jung, and Su
Wei-tao as one of the "Four Friends of Literature" 文章
四友. In 705 Tu Shen-yen was exiled to the far South,
farther than most of his friends, but not quite as far as
Shen Ch'üan-ch'i. Tu was sent to Feng-chou, just upstream
from modern Hanoi. In the general amnesty declared shortly
thereafter, Tu returned to the capital to serve as a registrar in the Academy and, of course, as an Auxiliary
Scholar in the Hsiu-wen-kuan.

Tu Shen-yen is often given special consideration in
histories of T'ang poetry because he was the grandfather
of Tu Fu. In his preface to Tu Shen-yen's collection,
Yang Wan-li 楊萬里 cites numerous parallels between the
poems of the grandfather and those of the grandson.[31] It
is probably no great exaggeration to say that Tu Fu's
unusual fondness for the style of court poetry has something to do with his admiration for his grandfather. But
though Tu Shen-yu represents a transitional style between
the Early T'ang and High T'ang, he is certainly not the
first figure in a Tu Fu "school" as some anthologists
would place him.[32]

Tu Shen-yen was something of a genius in a narrow scope.
Had he lived in a period when the range of poetry was
broader, or had he possessed a more rebellious and adven-
turesome poetic personality, he might well have become a
major poet. As it stands, he managed to infuse his works
with an openness and grace that few other court poets
possessed. Above all, Tu Shen-yen was a stylist, and
the particular virtues of his work—well-chosen words
and slight syntactic shifts—do not come through in translation. Even his formal occasional court poems sparkle
with a fludity that makes many other court poets seem wooden.

MATCHING THE RHYMES OF WEI CH'ENG-
  CH'ING'S "VISITING PRINCES YI-YANG'S
  MOUNTAIN POOL" [second of five]

和 韋 承 慶 過
義 陽 公 主 山 池
五 首 之 二

The path twists as sheer peaks press on it,

The bridge slants down and the gaping bank
  blocks it.

Jade streams shift wine's flavor along,

Stalactites in exchange for the scent of
  rice.

Green twigs supplely bind the fogs,

Purple vines long to drag up the winds.

And as, in this way, our joy in the feast
  grows less,

We go off instead to the rear pool and ponds.

逶 轉 危 峯 逼
橋 斜 缺 岸 妨
玉 泉 移 酒 味
石 髓 換 粳 香
縮 霧 青 條 弱
牽 風 紫 蔓 長
猶 言 宴 樂 少
別 問 後 池 塘

[03742]

The first couplet of this poem was cited as an exemplary
couplet in the "Couplet Construction of T'ang Poets,"
T'ang jen chü-fa 唐人句法 , preserved in the Sung critical
anthology Jade Chips of the Poets, Shih-jen yü-hsieh 詩人
玉屑 .[33] As an opening couplet it is startling; its style
and subject, the dominance of the forms of the landscape
over human construction, would be more appropriate in a
middle couplet. The second couplet moderates Tu's initial
daring, bringing in the party, where wine cups are floated
in the stream, and the theme of immortality, stalactites
being boiled for an elixir of eternal life—at least this
is what Tu Shen-yen imagines as he sniffs the scent from
the rice cooker.

    The third couplet has willow fronds or insect floss
hanging in the fog, seeming to "bind" it, while the
hanging vines, fluttering in the wind, seem to be pulling
the wind along. This metaphorical inversion of causality
was to be a popular technique in regulated verse and was
used frequently by Tu Fu. The last couplet is a disap-
pointingly conventional closing. With the exception of
the last couplet, each couplet in the poem is a gem, but

the couplets are unrelated gems, strung together by rhyme
and the actual circumstances of the banquet.

The fourth poem of the series (03644) is another unusually graceful and clever court poem.

Masses of stone lean just at the balustrade,
A waterfall passes the window in flight.
Fawns butt against the mats of the singing
  girls,
Baby cranes tug at the servant boys' robes.
Fruits in the orchard—hard to taste them
  all;
Lotus in the pond—plucked but not yet few.
Now we raise curtains, await the moon before
  it rises,
When we should be returning home in our
  drunkenness.

This poem also opens with a couplet that would be appropriate in a middle position (though it might be pointed
out that the first poem of the series has a proper opening couplet). The closing couplet here inverts the conventional "now it is evening and time to return" closing;
rather the partygoers cannot bear to leave the scene
though they know they should.

The most famous of Tu Shen-yen's poems is a pentasyllabic regulated verse "Matching the Rhymes of Assistant
Lu of Chin-ling's 'Early Spring Excursion'" 和晉陵陸丞
早春遊望 (03746). Although this poem is also attributed
to the eighth-century poet Wei Ying-wu 韋應物, it is not
part of the main body of Wei's collection and the Wen-yüan
ying-hua clearly attributes it to Tu Shen-yen. The stylistic play and certain phrase patterns which recur in Tu
Shen-yen's other poems suggest that it is indeed Tu's.
It is an anthology piece, but justly so.

Alone, men on official journeys
Are most startled by the renewal of things
  and the season:

Rose and white clouds, the brightness emerging
   from the sea,

Plum and willow, springtime crossing the river.

The clear air urges on the orioles,

And the sky's light makes the green watergrass
   coil.[34]

Suddenly I hear an old melody sung,

And thought of return makes me ready to soak
   my kerchief with tears.

雲霞出海曙
梅柳渡江春
淑氣催黃鳥
晴光轉綠蘋
忽聞歌古調
歸思欲霑巾

The sense of displacement that men on official travels
feel upon seeing the springtime is a consequence of their
realizing that another year has gone by and that they,
unlike the year, have not "come full circle." The very
freshness of the natural world makes them feel a singular
oldness and brings on longing to return to their homes.
The second couplet of this poem is a particularly fine
example of ambiguous syntax and can be understood in a
number of ways, of which the translation above offers
only one. Here the descriptive central couplets are
justified in the overall unity of the poem; they are
that "wondrous" beauty of the new year that so disturbs
the traveller. The songs of the birds, associated with
spring, are contrasted to the "old melody." The standard
"response of tears" is subtly varied by Tu's use of "ready
to" 欲 ; like some other sophisticated forms of poetic
closure then developing, "ready to" avoids the finality
of poetic closure and casts the reader forward to a time
beyond the text of the poem. The tripartite structure
is particularly strong in this poem: the general case of
"being startled" is not made an intense personal response
until the last line where the poet is about to weep. But
this transition from simply being amazed to weeping is a
natural outcome of what the poet sees in the middle couplets, viewed in the context of the "old melody."

   A wittier treatment of the theme of return can be
found in the following heptasyllabic regulated verse

(03764), anthologized by the famous Ming critic Chin Sheng-t'an 金聖歎 in his <u>Sheng-t'an hsüan-p'i T'ang ts'ai-tzu shih</u> 聖歎選批唐才子詩:[35]

MY FEELINGS ON A SPRING DAY IN THE CAPITAL   春日京中有懷

This year in my travels I travel alone in Ch'in,   今年遊寓獨遊秦

Viewing the spring with sad thoughts, I cannot face this spring.   愁思看春不當春

In the emperor's Shang-lin Park flowers blossom in vain,   上林花裏花徒發

In front of Thinwillow Camp leaves pointlessly renew.   細柳管前葉漫新

By the young nobles' south bridge, I'm sure their pleasure is fulfilled,   公子南橋應盡興

And in the generals' western mansions, how many guests are detained?   將軍西第幾留賓

I send word to Lo-yang, to roads of fine scenery—   寄語洛城風日道

Next year spring's beauty will doubly bring the man home.   明年春色倍還人

Tu is in Ch'ang-an, longing to return to Lo-yang. The ornamental repetitions of the first couplet are character-istic of Early T'ang heptasyllabic verse, which we have seen earlier in Wang Po's quatrains and in the capital poems. The second couplet uses the popular theme of nature's indifference to the feelings of men, renewing itself without bringing any joy to the poet. The dis-harmony between the poet and the season resolves itself in the last line into a pressure which the spring scene exerts on the poet to return to Lo-yang: undissipated, the pressure will be "double" next year, driving the poet home under its force.

Tu Shen-yen is particularly well represented in the mid-eighth century anthology, the <u>Kuo-hsiu chi</u> 國秀集 The five poems there (03747, 03749, 03755, 03758, and 03772) show elements of Tu Shen-yen's work that look forward to the High T'ang style. Four of the five poems are pentasyllabic regulated verses.

ON A SUMMER DAY, PASSING BY THE MOUNTAIN
  LIBRARY OF MR. CHENG

To share this joy in the cup
I have come seeking the mouth of your valley.
Through layers of hanging vines the mountain
  path enters,
Amid lotuses in the creek your pavilion appears.
The sunlit air holds the last of the rain,
And the shade of clouds sends off evening
  thunder.
But when the bells and drums of Lo-yang reach
  me,
Carriage and horses turn back slowly, unwilling.

[03755]

"The mouth of your valley" (ku-k'ou 谷口) plays on the
toponymn "Valley-mouth", associated with another Cheng,
the Han recluse Cheng Tzu-chen 鄭子真.

  Though this poem is far more direct than the average
formal banquet poem, we might notice Tu Shen-yen's use
of the standard banquet closing—"now it is evening and
I must go home."

ON AN AUTUMN NIGHT: BANQUETING AT THE COTTAGE
  OF MAGISTRATE CHENG OF LIN-CHIN

Moving or resting in a palce so high there is
  nothing below,
To invite or visit there is only you.
In our wine we endure this string of months,
Beyond us are only the drifting clouds,
The dew is white—night bells pierce through;
The wind clear—the waterclock's drip can be
  heard at dawn.
We sit hand in hand till the last of our
  pleasure is gone,
And it seems once again we had never left
  the crowd.

[03747]

In contrast to the preceding poem and Tu's formal banquet pieces, the couplets of this poem form a narrative unity, first setting up their past friendship and then indirectly describing the passage of the night until they "wake up" at dawn and return to the ordinary world. The dreamlike unity of mood is partially achieved by eliminating precise description of the physical scene: there is only the dew and wind in "a place so high there is no land below" (wu-ti 無地, literally "no land"), making their party strangely ethereal.

Tu Shen-yen's gift as a stylist was such that he could write powerful and moving poems even when he was not personally engaged. In the following piece Tu Shen-yen molds the conventions from P'an Yüeh's "Lament for my Wife" (Tao-wang 悼亡) into a very moving poem written on behalf of a higher official for a deceased lover.

LAMENT FOR A LOVELY GIRL: ON BEHALF   代張侍御傷美人
OF CHANG THE CENSOR

At sixteen the gates of the Yellow Springs   二八泉扉掩
    have closed,

Behind the bedcurtains the fondness and   帷屏寵愛空
    love is gone.

Traces as of tears melt away the night's   淚痕消夜燭
    candle,

Skeins of sorrow tangle the spring wind.   愁緒亂春風

With her coy smile she seems yet to survive,   巧笑人疑在

In fresh makeup her songs weren't yet   新妝曲未終
    finished.

I know you must feel sorrow for scent of   應憐脂粉氣
    powder and oil in the air,

Still lingering on her dancing robes.   留著舞衣中

                    [03752]

"Skeins" 緒 of line four probably refers to the willow floss or insect silk fluttering in the breeze, but it also suggests "something that touches one," an occasion for an emotion.

In some of the poems of Wang Po and Ch'en Tzu-ang we
have seen the new beginnings of a descriptive landscape
poetry. Experiencing the spectacular landscapes of
South China in their various exiles, Tu Shen-yen, Shen
Ch'üan-ch'i, and Sung Chih-wen wrote a number of dazzling
descriptive landscape poems. The following piece (03768)
is from Tu Shen-yen's first exile in Chiang-hsi.

CROSSING STONEGATE MOUNTAIN   度 石 門 山

Stonegate—a straight drop a thousand feet,   石 門 千 仞 斷

Where spurting waters fall in the distant   迸 水 落 遙 空
  sky.

The road binds half the overhanging slope,   道 束 懸 岸 半

And bridges slant into sheer ravines.   橋 欹 絕 澗 中

When scaling this, a person often rests,   仰 攀 人 屢 息

Now straight below a rider comes through.   直 下 騎 纔 通

Mud packs the paths where serpents dart,   泥 擁 奔 蛇 徑

Clouds bury the brush where wild beasts   雲 埋 伏 獸 叢
  crouch.

The stars' path: north of Dipper and Ox;   星 躔 牛 斗 北

A vein of the earth: east of Elephant's   地 脈 象 牙 東
  Tusk.

Opening, then blocking, changing as I move   開 塞 隨 行 變
  on;

Heights and depths alike, wherever my gaze   高 深 觸 望 同
  alights.

The sound of the river joins with a sudden   江 聲 連 驟 雨
  shower,

Sunlit air embraces the last of a rainbow.   日 氣 抱 殘 虹

And before red and brilliant summer changes   未 改 朱 明 律
  on the calendar,

The winds bear autumn's white dew.   先 含 白 露 風

If firm and pure of heart, no terror at   堅 貞 深 不 憚
  these depths,

Yet it seems this rough country will never   險 澀 諒 難 窮
  end.

Here there's a difference from the pleasure   有 異 登 臨 賞
  of high vistas—

Simply because of Creation's great deeds.   徒 為 造 化 功

Despite the brilliance of many of Tu's couplets, the
landscape here has no philosophical significance as did
Ch'en Tzu-ang's description of Gorge-mouth Mountain. Tu
is simply crafting the "wonders" of the landscape into
fine parallel couplets and letting us know that travelling
over such a landscape is no easy matter. The following
landscape poem (03732) was written by Tu during his exile
of 705.

WRITTEN AT JUMBLE-ROCK MOUNTAIN BY THE   南海亂石山作
    SOUTH SEA

The Sea of Chang swells to the very
    sky,
And a host of mountains rear up high from
    the earth.
They tell me this place is called Jumble-rock,
The charts and classics tell nothing of it.
Its sheer overhangs are all frightening,
Great or small, none of ordinary kind.
At once it will reach out to cloudy isles,
Then back up to link with the river of
    stars.
Suddenly jutting up as though in flight,
Then hanging over sharply on the point of
    falling.
Dawn's glow makes it blush purple and crimson,
And in moonlight it gleams blue and turquoise.
On the towering summits fog and rain gather;
Sequestered there, fairies and spirits hide.
Ten thousand yards up a crane's nest hangs,
A gibbon's arm dangles over a thousand-foot
    drop.
When I left home before, seasonal winds moved
    forth;
By the time I've reached here, the third
    month has come.
Observing this place, I sing my song,
For long I'll imagine the strangeness of its
    spirits.

As in the preceding poem, the tripartite form is strong
here. Since the description of awesome landscapes played
little role in court poetry, a poet may borrow from
earlier poetry and _fu_ to reorganize his piece: Sun Ch'o's
孫綽 fourth-century _fu_ "Wandering on Mount T'ien-t'ai"
遊天台山賦 , preserved in the Wen-hsüan, provided an
excellent source for landscape poetry. In this _fu_ Sun Ch
Ch'o makes a point to tell the reader that the canonical
geographical treatises do not describe T'ien-t'ai, giving
his imagination free reign by permitting him to avoid the
requisite list of traditional associations proper in
writing about a given location. Through Tu Shen-yen's
poem or perhaps directly from Sun Ch'o's _fu_, this convention returns to T'ang landscape poetry. Han Yü, for
example, uses it in his long poem "South Mountains"
(17790).

A large part of Shen Ch'üan-ch'i's and Sung Chih-wen's
poetry comes from their periods of exile in the South.
Their exile poems mark a clear turning point in their
work to a bolder, more personal style. In contrast, Tu
Shen-yen has relatively few exile poems, and these are
a culmination of his earlier work rather than a change.
The counterexample which Tu's exile poetry offers is
helpful in showing that Shen and Sung were, in fact,
being original and personal in their exile poems and
not simply following a tradition of "exile poetry" (though
such a tradition became firmly established later). Tu
Shen-yen is decorous, descriptive, and firmly in control.

LODGING IN ANNAM   旅寓安南

In Chiao-chih the weather is strange,   交趾殊風候
The cold comes slowly, the warmth hurries   寒遲暖復催
  back again.
In mid-winter mountain fruits are ripe,   仲冬山果熟
In the first month wildflowers blossom.   正月野花開
Dusky fogs arise from the monsoons,   積雨生昏霧

Light frosts bring down peals of thunder.   輕霜下震雷
My homeland, over ten thousand miles away—   故鄉踰萬里
Thoughts of it twice what they once were.   客思倍從來

[03750]

The opening of this poem is an excellent example of an
Early T'ang rhetorical exposition of a topic. We have
seen a similar rhetorical order in Ch'en Shu-pao's
"Watering My Horse by the Great Wall." This system,
which might be called a "breakdown amplification," fits
smoothly into the first two parts of the tripartite form.
The poet gives an initial statement, then divides it into
parts with ever greater specificity. The first line sets
forth a general proposition, that the "weather is strange":
the second line gives two specific examples. Each half
of the second line, the slow coming of the cold and quick
return of warm weather, is expanded to a full line in the
second couplet, giving a more specific example. It is
not clear in what season the "monsoon" belongs, but the
third couplet may be an inversion of the antithesis, the
early warmth and late cold; in any case it offers yet
another example of the "strangeness" of the weather. The
personal response to this strangeness is longing to return,
an emotion quite natural whenever the poet is away from
home, but have doubled by the alienness of this landscape.
As we saw earlier in "My Feelings on a Spring Day in the
Capital," "doubling" is a decorous intensification of
emotion, easily calculable and contrasting with the
"grief without limit" one finds so often in High T'ang
poetry.

    If anything sets Tu Shen-yen's exile poetry apart
from his court poetry, it is a heightening of the tendency
toward simplicity, already apparent in contrasting his
work with those of other court poets. He retains much
that is good in court poetry, the syntactic complexity
and careful choice of words; on the other hand, he rids

his work of the excessive and ornamental periphrasis
that was the base of court poetry.

LONGING TO RETURN ON A SPRING DAY

The heart is wounded by my homeward gaze,
Spring's arrival is different from years past.
Mountains in rivers seem to mirror the gate
    of Wei,
The mulberries, the catalpa remind me of Ch'in's
    streams.
Flowers mingle with birds in the budding garden,
Winds join the mists over green plains.
Again I long for the land of joy and pleasure,
The houses and carriages of the Lo River
    Bridge.

春 日 懷 歸

心 是 傷 歸 望
春 歸 異 往 年
河 山 鑒 魏 闕
桑 梓 憶 秦 川
花 雜 芳 園 鳥
風 和 綠 野 煙
更 懷 歡 賞 地
車 馬 洛 橋 邊

[03751]

The "gates of Wei" refer to the capital, but it is unclear whether Tu is longing for Ch'ang-an (suggested by
line four) or for Lo-yang, suggested in the last line.
In the first case, it is his first exile; in the second
case, his exile of 705. Although exile did not change
Tu's poetry, it sobered it; the Early T'ang poet looked
over the landscape for some element to fashion a witty
metaphor, but in exile the landscape sends less cheerful
messages:

ON CROSSING THE RIVER HSIANG

As the sun sinks amid groves and gardens
    I grieve for travels past,
But this spring the birds and flowers
    make the grief of the frontier.
Alone, I yearn for the capital as I hide
    out in the South,
I am not like that River Hsiang whose
    waters flow ever northward.

渡 湘 江

遲 日 園 林 悲 昔 遊
今 春 花 鳥 作 邊 愁
獨 憐 京 國 人 南 竄
不 似 湘 江 水 北 流

[037773]

The translation of the third line of this poem is a sad

compromise that destroys the beautifully ambiguous syntax
of the original. With a strong caesura violation the
line becomes, "Alone I pity that a man of the capital
must hide out in the South." Another way to interpret
the line is with zeugma, the verb lien 憐 accounting
for both his "longing" for the capital and his "pity" for
his own condition: "Alone I yearn for the capital, pity
myself that I must hide out in the South."

22

SHEN CH'ÜAN-CH'I

Shen Ch'üan-ch'i (ca. 650-713), the second figure in our
triad of late seventh- and early eighth-century court
poets, passed the chin-shih in 675. Shen rose through a
series of minor posts until, like Tu Shen-yen, he became
a favorite of the infamous Chang Yi-chih in the first
years of the eighth century. With the fall of the Chang
brothers and the empress, Shen was banished to Huan-chou
in Vietnam, even further south than Tu Shen-yen. In the
general amnesty that soon followed, Shen returned to the
capital to take the post of Diarist under Chung-tsung,
serving also as Auxiliary Scholar in the Hsiu-wen kuan.
Eventually he rose to the post of Grand Secretary in the
Secretariat and later held a position in the bureaucracy
of the heir apparent.

Shen Ch'üan-ch'i's name is traditionally associated
with the perfection of the heptasyllabic regulated verse.
Although Shen does have one of the few perfect heptasyllabic regulated verses datable before the eighth century,
he probably did not "invent" the form, but was simply
the most talented of its early practitioners. His "Banquet at Hsing-ch'ing Pool," which we have discussed at
length in an earlier chapter, represents the court poem
at its best. In this form at least, Shen is superior to
his friend and rival Sung Chih-wen, to whom Shang-kuan
Wan-erh gave the "brocade prize" for his pentasyllabic
poem.

Shen's lone seventh-century heptasyllabic regulated
verse is interesting in that its topic conforms to the
notion of heptasyllabic verse as a popular form; later,
in the first decades of the eighth century, heptasyllabic
regulated verse becomes strongly associated with formal

court poetry with a few fine exceptions. The seventh-
century example is a <u>ku-yi</u>, "old theme," concerning a
woman whose husband is fighting on the frontier. The
poem (05065) is addressed, appropriately, to Ch'iao Chih-
chih, whose work so often uses a female persona.[36]

OLD THEME: TO THE REMINDER CH'IAO
  CHIH-CHIH

古意呈補闕喬知之

A young wife of the Lu household in
  her turmeric chamber,

盧家少婦鬱金堂

Sea seallows roost in pairs on her
  tortoiseshell inlaid beams.

海燕雙棲玳瑁梁

Late autumn when chill washing blocks
  speed the leaves of trees falling,

九月寒砧催木葉

Ten years of campaign duty—she
  remembers Liao-yang.

十年征戍憶遼陽

From north of White Wolf River the
  news is cut off;

白狼河北音書斷

Here south of the red phoenix walls,
  autumn nights are long.

丹鳳城南秋夜長

Who understands the grief she bears?—
  "alone, not seeing him";

誰謂含愁獨不見

Then she lets the bright moonlight
  shine on the "flowing yellow."

更教明月照流黃

Shen weaves together numerous <u>yüeh-fu</u> associations of
frontier warfare and the deserted wife. The "Lu household" simply stands for a wealthy household; even there
the pairs of swallows remind the solitary woman of the
absence of <u>her</u> mate. The "red phoenix walls" refer to
the palace. The phrase "alone, not seeing him" (<u>tu pu</u>
<u>chien</u> 獨不見) is a <u>yüeh-fu</u> title and may refer speci-
fically to a song she sings or hears. The enigmatic
last line contains another echo of the <u>yüeh-fu</u> in the
"flowing yellow," a kind of silk associated with women
with absent husbands. Though it follows the rules of
middle couplet parallelism and tonal anthithesis, this
poem is much closer to <u>yüeh-fu</u> than it is to regulated
verse; it is a mood piece, evoking the ambiance of the

deserted wife, rather than an attempt to describe a
physical world and a personal response to it.

Sung Chih-wen and Shen Ch'üan-ch'i were the dominant
figures in court poetry during the reign of Chung-tsung.
Of the two, Sung had the more complicated intellect; he
was a wit and a master of courtly rhetoric whose genius
was less at ease within the rules. Shen had a richer
imagination, greater stylistic control and powers of
description, and was ultimately a better poet than Sung
Chih-wen. In Shen's descriptive court poems much of the
stilted periphrasis of earlier court poetry disappears,
leaving something far closer to private nature poetry.[37]

RESPECTFULLY FOLLOWING THE RHYMES OF "ROYAL
VISIT TO SPRING-VIEW PALACE ON A SPRING
DAY": TO COMMAND

奉和春日幸望
春宮應制

Fragrant meadows and green plains,
  strewn with spring light,

芳郊綠野散春晴

Around tiered walkways and detached palaces
  the mist and fog rise.

複道離宮煙霧生

A thousand branches of willow fronds—
  on the point of fraying;

楊柳千條花欲綻

A hundred yards of grape vines,
  their tendrils beginning to wind.

蒲萄百丈蔓初縈

The scent of the forest, aroma of wine
  merge together as one;

林香酒氣元相入

Birds' warbling and singers' voices
  each stand separate.

鳥囀歌聲各自成

Surely this season's beauty will draw us
  from nightlong drunkenness,

定是風光牽宿醉

And with dawn we shall set forth again,
  this time to K'ung-ming Pool.

來晨復得幸昆明

[05057]

During the reign of Hsüan-tsung much of the sensuality
disappears from court poetry. The descriptive delicacy
that often appears in the court poetry of Chung-tsung's
reign contrasts sharply with the energy and emphasis on
the imperial theme of the following poem (05059), written

in 712 when Hsüan-tsung assumed the throne.

DRAGON POOL

龍池篇

The leaping dragon of Dragon Pool—
   the dragon has flown;

The Dragon-virtue foreknew Heaven,
   and Heaven does not err.

This pool reveals the river of stars,
   discerns the Yellow Course,

Its dragon heads to Heaven's gates,
   enters the Tzu-wei.

Lodge and mansion, terrace and tower,
   full of spirit and color,

Our Prince's ducks and wild geese
   possess His radiance.

To requite Him the waters of all
   the streams of the world

Come to dawn court at this very spot,
   and none go off eastward.

龍池躍龍龍已飛
龍德先天天不違
池開天漢分黃道
龍向天門入紫微
邸第樓臺多氣色
君王鳧雁有光輝
為報寰中百川水
來朝此地莫東歸

"Dragon Pool" is fraught with imperial symbolism: the
dragon is the young Hsüan-tsung who has emerged from his
growth phase and "taken flight," ascended to Heaven and
the throne. As in Shen's poem on Hsing-ch'ing Pool, the
pool's reflection allows the poet to confuse the ter-
restrial palaces and the world of heaven. The "Yellow
Course" is thus that of sun and the emperor, who moves
into the palace or the Tzu-wei constellation. The imperial
effulgence and the aura of the sun illuminate the sur-
rounding palaces and denizens of the pool alike. The
last couplet plays on the traditional metaphor for assuming the throne as apotheosis: the streams flow into
Hsüan-tsung's pool rather than following their accustomed
paths to the sea; thus the streams show not only their
respect for the emperor, they also defy the laws of
change and impermanence, represented by the eastward
flow of all waters.

   Sun Ch'üan-ch'i's official career lacks a well-docu-
mented itinerary of provincial posts to facilitate the

dating of his poems.   We know that Shen was in Szechwan,
probably before 705.   The opening of the following poem
(04973) is reminiscent of the descriptive landscapes of
Tu Shen-yen's first exile.

PASSING DRAGON-GATE IN SHU   過蜀龍門

This Dragon-Gate was not the one cut by Yü;   龍門非禹鑿
An uncanny wonder which must be Nature's
  work.   詭怪乃天功
To the southwest it comes out of the Wu
  Gorges,   西南出巴峽
Not the same as ordinary mountains.   不與眾山同
Long channels crisscross for five miles,   長寶互五里
As it twists and turns, then thrusts into
  the sky,   宛轉復嵌空
Dipping torrents make hidden stones sparkle,   伏湍照潛石
Crashing waters give rise to whirlwinds....   濺水生輪風

Shen begins his poem by dissociating the Dragon-Gate of
Szechwan from the Yellow River Dragon-Gate which was
believed to have been cut by the mythical emperor Yü.
This disavowal serves much the same function as the
rejection of traditional geographical sources in Sun Ch'o
and Tu Shen-yen: it emphasizes the strangeness of the
place, the uncommon "wonders" which the poet will describe.

     Even before his exile, Shen was a master of the less
formal subgenres such as visiting poems.   The following
pentasyllabic regulated verse (05036), anthologized in
the Southern Sung Poems in Three Genres (San-t'i shih
三體詩), was written while Shen was in Lo-yang.

VISITING SHAO-LIN TEMPLE   遊少林寺

Singing long I visit the precious land   長歌遊寶地
And pace about, facing its trees of pearls.   徒倚對珠林
Wind and frost of the past on Wild Goose
  Pagoda,   雁塔風霜古
Its Dragon Pool too is deep in years.   龍池歲月深

The skies of its purple gardens clear in
   evening,
And its emerald halls cast autumn shadows.
A homeward road through a night of mists
   and rose clouds,
The mountain cicadas chanting everywhere.

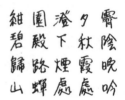

Poems on visiting Buddhist temples had their own conventions and formed virtually an independent subgenre—indeed,
the Wen-yüan ying-hua treats them under a single heading.
Certain kinds of references to Buddhist lore, such as
the "precious land" and the "trees of pearls" here, were
expected. The use of such references varies from the
abstruse (for example, 04230) to poems like the above,
which is not much different than a banquet poem. The
closure here is essentially a transformation of the "let's
go home; it's evening" closing of the courtly banquet
poem; however, this is achieved through an objective
scene which evokes solitude and autumnal melancholy.
The culmination of the poet's experience in the temple
is one of clarity (line five) associated with enlighten-
ment, but soon afterward the poet faces the growing
darkness and lengthening shadows of evening, finally
moving home into an isolating world of mists and clouds.

   Many of the conventions of formal court poetry were
taken over and transformed in informal occasional poetry
and in personal poetry. The court poem was the poet's
basic material. The poet-courtier constantly beheld
heaven's manifestation here on earth in the persons of
the emperor and his court; looking into a mirroring pool,
Shen could conveniently confuse the reflected image of
the skies and that of the setting of the banquet. Spending the night alone on his travels, Shen might experience
the awe and wonder of his high mountain lodging: this
feeling of transcendence becomes an intrusion of heaven
into the world of earth, just as the "River of Light"
flowed into the palaces of Lo-yang.

I wandered alone across a thousand and more
  miles,

Slept high, west of Seven-Twist Ridge.

The dawn moon looked down on my window,
  nearby,

And the river of heaven flowed low into my
  door...

獨遊千里外
高臥七蟠西
曉月臨窻近
天河入戶低

[05039]

In the courtly banquet poem, the poet is fascinated by
the point of contact or the fusion between human things
and things of the natural world, how the forest's scent
merges with the aroma of wine or how the songs of the
birds are juxtaposed with those of the singing girls
(05057). In the following poem (05035) Nature merges
with a Buddhist temple rather than an aristocratic outing,
forming a complex consolation for the poet in exile.

WHITE CRANE TEMPLE IN LO-CH'ENG

樂城白鶴寺

The sutra library opens onto the emerald sea,

碧海開龍藏

A "wild goose" hall rises into blue clouds.

青雲起雁堂

The surf's voices greet the dharma drums,

潮聲迎法鼓

And rain-filled air soaks the holy incense.

雨氣溼天香

Its trees join the darkness of mountains
  ahead,

樹接前山暗

Its creek receives the chill of a cascade's
  waters.

溪承瀑水涼

Let us not speak of banishment to a far land—

無言謫居遠

Purified, I have found the Lord of the Void.

清淨得空王

The courtier in Shen cannot resist having a "wild goose
hall" actually "rise" into the clouds as though it were
flying away. Later in T'ang poetry one finds similar
temples that seem to take flight (with their "wings"),
representing their aspiration toward transcendence (for
example, 19761).

     In addition to the personalization of courtly tropes,
there is another aspect of Shen's poetry that points

strongly to the High T'ang: this is the range of his
poetry. The thematic and stylistic range of most court
poets was severely limited; poets like Wang Chi who
reacted against the courtly style either did not or
could not write court poetry. Even the great Ch'en Tzu-
ang did not have mastery over a full range of contemporary
styles. Shen Ch'üan-ch'i and Sung Chih-wen, like the
great High T'ang poets, could be courtiers, bucolic poets,
song writers, or fu-ku moralists at will. The dissociation of literary style from life style was an important
factor in a poet's ability to gain mastery over conventional styles, most of which involved a distinct role or
persona. As they gained distance from their poetic
personae, they were able to shape them for their personal
needs. Here I am not suggesting that poets were not
sincerely engaged in the poetic persona they chose, but
simply that they had more mobility between them. Like
other poets of his day, Shen firmly mastered the most
decorous and formal style of court poetry (for example,
05081 or 05082), but he also could write poems with some
of the playfulness of a Wang Chi.

FISHING POLE

The sun gathers in the red mists at dawn,
And I dangle my line here by the dark green
    stream.
The man seems to be sitting in heaven,
While the fish seem hung in a mirror.
Now and then they leap up to avoid the oars,
They're suspicious of the hook—I always tug
    it too soon.
The torrent bank was steep, my carriage hard
    to control,
Then placid pools which try to make my boat
    linger on.
In vain, sir, are you fond of fishing for
    wealth,

釣竿篇
朝日斂紅煙
垂竿向綠川
人疑天上坐
魚似鏡中懸
避檝時驚透
猜鉤每誤牽
湍危不理轄
潭靜欲留船
釣玉君徒尚

Shen Ch'üan-ch'i

I find no virtue in the quest for gold.
Just watch now how the fragrant bait sinks—
They take it greedily, but can they miss
   the trap?

徵 金 我 未 賢
為 看 芳 餌 下
貪 得 會 無 筌

[05078]

Set in this leisurely, gently humorous personal narrative, even Shen Ch'üan-ch'i's favorite witty mirror illusion in line three does not seem out of place. The prefect parallelism of the second, third, and fourth couplets does not fragment the poem into disparate scenes, but rather the poem unfolds in a smooth linear progression. The closing moral which the poet draws from his fishing scene is more playful than grimly Confucian. Descriptive couplets like the third and fourth are not conventions but are based on observation of nature.

At other times Shen can put on the robes of the fu-ku poet and write with the moral indignation of the Kan-yü.

WRONGFULLY IMPRISONED [first of two]

I love that child of the Tseng household
Whose mother threw down her shuttle when
   he was doubted.
I love the Chi clan's Duke of Chou
Who didn't lack a poem on the owl.
The subject expends his loyalty, the son,
   his filial love,
Yet ruler and parent are deluded by
   falsehood.
A tissue of lies splits flesh and blood—
Holding in my sorrow, I am stirred to
   these verses.

枉 繫 二 首 之 一
吾 憐 曾 家 子
昔 有 投 杼 疑
吾 憐 姬 公 旦
非 無 鴟 鴞 詩
臣 子 竭 忠 孝
君 親 惑 讒 欺
孝 斐 離 骨 肉
含 愁 興 此 辭

[04980]

Although Shen uses lien 憐 rather than ai 愛 ("love"), in the opening of this poem, we hear clearly an echo of the eleventh Kan-yü. The first couplet refers to a story about Confucius's disciple Tseng Shen: another man by the same name had committed a murder, and the authorities mistakenly went to tell Tseng Shen's mother; at first she refused to listen, then threw down her shuttle and fled the house, unwilling to hear lies about her son. When the Duke of Chou's brothers were executed for plotting rebellion against King Ch'eng of Chou, suspicion fell on the Duke of Chou; in response he wrote a poem entitled "Owl" protesting his innocence and loyalty—this is the traditional topic allegorical interpretation of Shih 155.

In his quatrains Shen can display the "closed" ending of earlier court poetry (for example, 05111) and put witty closure to personal ends.

COLD FOOD FESTIVAL   寒 食

Everywhere under the sky flames are extinguished,   普 天 皆 滅 焰
All around the earth smoke is hidden.   匝 地 盡 藏 煙
So I know not then from whence this fire   不 知 何 處 火
Comes to set a wanderer's heart ablaze.[38]   來 就 客 心 然

[05106]

The fireless festival should mean joy and companionship; to the wanderer it only emphasizes his isolation. Not only is his "burning" a metaphor for his misery, the disparity between this state and that of the rest of the world parallels his external condition. But Shen can also use the more modern "open" closure, a suggestive descriptive ending.

MOUNT MANG   邙 山

On North Mang Mountain the tombs and   北 邙 山 上 列 墳 塋
  graves are ranged,
For all times, a thousand autumns facing   萬 古 千 秋 對 洛 城
  Lo-yang.
When the sun goes down songs and bells   城 中 日 夕 歌 鐘 起
  ring out in the walls,
But on the mountain hear only the sound   山 上 唯 聞 松 柏 聲
  of wind in the pines.

[05115]

North Mang was the traditional burial spot in Lo-yang.
The poet leaves it to the reader to define the relation
between the last two lines, the sounds of revelry in the
city and the chill wind over the tombs. A similar juxtaposition was employed in many of the capital poems, but
the brevity here gives quite a different effect: the
capital poems must resolve the ambiguity which this poem,
with its undefined juxtaposition, allows to remain—one
may read it as a comment on the foolishness of human life
in face of the inevitability of death or as carpe diem
(in the later case, we remove "but" from line four).

In his yüeh-fu Shen Ch'üan-ch'i was at his most conservative; although many are particularly fine examples of
late seventh-century yüeh-fu, their style is indistinguishable from that of poets like Yang Chiung or Sung Chih-
wen. In fact, a number of Shen's best yüeh-fu are also
attributed to Sung Chih-wen. If anything distinguishes
them from the yüeh-fu of the sixth and early seventh
centuries, it is a unity of argument replacing the older
unity of rhetorical amplification, which we saw earlier
in Ch'en Shu-pao's yüeh-fu and in Tu Shen-yen's exile
poem. In the older form the poet generates a series of
independent, descriptive scenes out of an opening line or
couplet; in the newer form each line is a precondition for
what follows.

LUNG-T'OU'S WATERS

On Lung Mountain the leaves flutter and fall,
As the geese of Lung Mountain cross the cold
   sky.
In grief he sees the waters of late autumn
Split into streams running through two lands:
One flows west into barbarian commanderies,
The other, down east to the rivers of Ch'in.
The campaigner turns his head again and again,
His heart full of helpless sorrow.

[05013]

In the following poem (05014) the course of the moon on
one night strangely parallels a Chinese military victory.

MOON OVER THE PASSES   關山月

A Chinese moon rises over the Sea of Liao,   漢月生遼海
Faintly growing a half radiance emerges.   朦朧出半暉
At dusk it is over Black Rabbit Commandery,   合昏玄兔郡
By midnight above the Po-teng Siege.   中夜白登圍
Then its halo sinks far behind western
    passes,   暈落關山迴
Frost and sleet bear the faintest of its
    beams.   光含霜霰微
When the general hears the dawn bugle blow,   將軍聽曉角
The battle steeds are on the point of
    returning southward.   戰馬欲南歸

The tranquility of the moon's silent passage over the
violent battlegrounds of the North creates a ghostly mood.
The moon is a "Chinese moon" because it is the same moon
seen in China, observed both by the frontier soldier and
his wife back in her chambers at home.

UNCLASSIFIED POEM [last of three]   雜詩三首之三

I've heard tell that at the Yellow Dragon
    garrisons   聞道黃龍戍
War has not stopped for several years now.   頻年不解兵
Alas, that the same moon over the lady's
    chamber   可憐閨裏月
Hangs ever over the camps of the House
    of Han.   長在漢家營
The young wife's thoughts this spring,   少婦今春意
Her husband's emotions last night.   良人昨夜情
Who can take those banners and drums   誰能將旗鼓
And once and for all take Dragon City?   一為取龍城
                           [05024]

The older, more fragmented structure did survive and often
proved a better medium for descriptive couplets. In such

poems a unity of mood rather than rational argument was
developing.

GOING OUT THE PASSES

出塞

Ten years through the Great Desert,
Ten thousand miles from Ch'ang-p'ing.
A cold sun grows over halberds and swords,
Dark clouds brush the pennons and banners.
Hungry crows scream over the ancient forts,
Weary horses yearn for the deserted walls.
Bitter suffering, north of the Kao-lan
    garrison,
Where Tartar frosts have crushed the
    troops of Han.

十年通大漠
萬里出長平
寒日生戈劍
陰雲拂旆旌
飢烏啼舊壘
痕馬戀空城
辛苦皋蘭北
胡霜損漢兵

[05020]

There are difficulties in dating Shen Ch'üan-ch'i's poems
written in the capital; it is often impossible to tell
whether a poem was written before his 705 exile or after
his return. However, as is the case with Sung Chih-wen,
the style of Shen's exile poems is radically different
from his capital style. After Shen and Sung returned to
court, they fell easily back into graceful court poetry,
but the poems written on their exiles are very much in
the energetic, personal High T'ang style. On his way to
exile in Huan-chou, Shen wrote the following poem (04972),
impressive of its kind but little different than the poem
quoted earlier from his journey to Szechwan.

UPSTREAM FROM CH'ANG-LO COMMANDERY TO WHITESTONE PEAK, THEN DOWN TO LIN-CHOU

自昌樂郡泝流至白石
嶺下行入郴州

This mountain is a border between barbarian
    and Chinese,
Nature's sheer barrier stretching across
    vast space.
The Grand Historian failed to climb and
    investigate,

茲山界夷夏
天險橫寥廓
太史漏登探

Here King Yü was halted when he opened
  our Chinese land.

A northward current drains up from the south

Through a crowd of valleys winding around
  many peaks.

Rushing waves leap like lightning,

Strike against stone like claps of thunder.

On its slopes trees linger from the age
  of Chaos,

Its torrents swell with Shen-nung's herbs,

Here stalactite caves drip steadily,

And moss and lichens swirl bright colors

The graceful curves of a rainbow in a pool,

The vague forms of cranes beside rapids.

Toward the end of the year when the Fire
  Star sinks,

The skies are high, the clouds and mist
  look frail,

Metallic west winds blow the green treetops,

Jade drops of dew wash over red sheaths of
  bamboo.

Our boat moves upstream to Shih-hsing yamen,

Then an overland climb to Kuei-yang's walls

Grapevines trail along the long slopes,

Dome melons dangle long skeins.

Forests in our path obstruct all travel,

We meet embankments, have to advance and
  go back.

Escaping such difficulties, we've no chance
  to eat;

Until it's entirely dark there's no time to
  moor.

I'm not at all afraid to bathe my feet in
  these creeks,

Nor could anyone say I hate mountain paths,

But walking among these rivers and mountains,

The steepness and swirling waters are unlike
  any others.

How can I keep these experiences to myself?—

I write this and send it to the capital.

文命限開鑿
北流自南瀉
羣峯回象塹
馳波如電騰
激石似雷落
岸留盤古樹
澗蓄神農藥
乳竇何淋漓
苔蘚更彩錯
娟娟潭裏虹
渺渺灘邊鶴
歲杪應流火
天高雲霧薄
金風吹綠梢
玉露洗紅籜
泝舟始興廨
登踐桂陽郭
蒲萄緣脩坂
芎蘿曳長絆
叢林阻往來
遇堰每前卻
救艱不遑飯
畢昏無暇泊
濯溪寧足懼
磴道誰云惡
我行山水間
湍險皆不若
安能獨見聞
書此貽京洛

A few references require explanation: Shen-nung was a
mythical emperor of antiquity whose name is associated
with herb lore. The Fire Star sinks in the seventh month,
indicating the beginning of autumn. "Bathing one's feet"
suggests reclusion, a phrase derived from the song of the
fisherman in "The Fisherman," quoted earlier.

   The poem above should sound familiar; we have seen
very similar writing in Wang Po's "Mud Gulch" and Tu
Shen-yen's "Written at Jumble-rock Mountain." As in the
latter poem, Shen disavows traditional geographical lore
in line three and describes a fantastic landscape of
bright colors, swirling waters, and overhanging cliffs.
As in Wang Po's poem and Tu Shen-yen's "Crossing Stonegate
Mountain," Shen concludes by saying that this landscape
is so difficult that it denies the enjoyment one finds in
simpler landscapes. The last line, of the "and-so-I-write-
this-poem" variety, is particularly unsatisfying and
suggests that the poet simply could not think of anything
else to say.

   "Upstream from Ch'ang-lo Commandery" was written on
Shen's way into exile; the following poem (04975) was
written on his return: its energy, imagination, and unity
set it clearly apart from the earlier poem and place it
in the High T'ang.

MOORING BY NIGHT AT YÜEH-CHOU: MEETING
   AN ENVOY FROM THE NORTH

夜泊越州逢
北使

The universe sends down its thunder and its
   rain;

天地降雷雨

Once banished, I return to the capital.

放逐還國都

Again I busy myself with winds and tides,

重以風潮事

Though the month of the year warns against
   turning the prow.

年月戒回艫

My appearance has grown old out there in the
   wilds,

容顏荒外老

My thoughts and fancies, turned foolish in the
   outlands.

心想域中愚

As I moor and rest on this very night,

憩泊在茲夜

Blazing clouds pursue the Dipper's pivot,

A cyclone swirls around the Sea God,

Thunder crackles about T'ien-wu,

The Earth-Turtle claps, a crowd of isles
   are lost,

A leviathan swallows the concourse of many
   rivers.

By chance I have met an envoy from the palace,

We join hands, soak each other with our tears.

In our hunger we gnaw the dates of Ch'i,

Sleeping, share the rushes of Ch'in.

I, going north, brood on being saved;

You, sent south—Imperial wisdom planned it.

One going, one coming—let's have no
   reproaches—

Why should we shrink from the journeys ahead?

炎雲逐斗樞
飇胸繞海若
霹靂取天吳
鼇抃羣島矢
鯨吞衆流輸
偶逢金華使
握手滾相濡
飢共噬齊橐
眠共席秦蒲
既北思攸濟
將南睿所圖
往來固无咎
何忽憚前枿

The opening theme of the rainstorm combines two contradictory associations, one for each of the travellers: on the one hand, there is the "rain" of imperial favor; on the other, the idea of the storm as adversity. Shen then continues to build a monstrous vision of the storm, populated by mythical denizens of the oceans and the Turtle that carries the earth. Finally, Shen calms the poem with his message, the bonds among men and the equanimity with which they should face their various fortunes. Of course, it is much easier for Shen to speak of equanimity on his return to the capital and it is perhaps not out of place to detect a note of perverse pleasure in the fact that someone else is going south now. The structure of this poem is fundamentally tripartite, like "Upstream from Ch'ang-lo Commandery," but the "scene" to which the poet responds is itself made up of several independent situations.

One of Shen Ch'üan-ch'i's most famous poems (05066), a heptasyllabic regulated verse, was probably written in 705 as Shen and Tu Shen-yen were going into exile by different routes.

FROM AFAR FOLLOWING THE RHYMES OF
  ASSISTANT TU'S "CROSSING THE
  SOUTHERN PEAKS"

遠同杜員外審言
過嶺

Heaven is long, Earth is vast:
  the Peaks divide them;

天長地闊嶺頭分

Leaving both family and state,
  you see the white clouds.

去國離家見白雲

What use to speak of the pang the heart
  feels for the bank of the Lo?

洛浦肝腸無用說

And I can't bear to hear of Ch'ung Mountain,
  of its plague and pestilence.

崇山瘴癘不堪聞

Floating on the Chang Sea to the south,
  where is the man?

南浮漲海人何處

Gazing north Heng-yang—
  how often the flocks of geese?

北望衡陽雁幾羣

Spring wind in both places,
  ten thousand miles between,

兩地春風萬餘里

When again shall we give greetings
  to our glorious Lord?

何時重謁聖明君

Heng-yang was reputedly the furthest point south in the
yearly migration of the wild geese. The calm and control
of this poem is unusual for Shen's exile poetry. As we
trace Shen's journey south in the year 705, we can see a
growing bitterness and irony in his poetry. The poetic
conventions first come under attack. In the following
poem's closing, Shen refuses all the appropriate responses—weeping, refusal to weep, or consolation in the
landscape.

SETTING OUT EARLY FROM CH'ANG-P'ING ISLE

早發昌平島

I loose the mooring after the spring wind
  starts up,

解纜春風後

Make the oars sing before the dawn's high
  waters.

鳴榔曉漲前

Then the sun's raven comes out from the
  oceanside trees,

陽烏出海樹

And geese in the clouds descend in the
  river mist,

雲雁下江煙

Swelling vapors dash against long isles,

積氣衝長島

Rippling light overflows the great stream.

浮光溢大川

I cannot long for the capital's gates—
All alone, the heart's pleasures are an
   icy chill.

不 能 懷 魏 闕
心 賞 獨 泠 然

[05038]

Shen's descriptive genius in the first six lines makes the
closing all the harsher. The harshness intensifies and
irony, uncommon in Chinese poetry, begins to appear, as
in line three of the following poem (05097).

ENTERING HELLGATE PASS

入 鬼 門 關

I've always heard of the road to the rivers
   of plague,
Now I myself have come to Hellgate Pass.
In this land no man ever grows old,
How many of the exiles here ever return?
Ever since I have left the capital,
My hair is falling, my face shrivelling.
By evening I lodge among poisonous insects,
By dawn I walk over mountain roads.
My horse stands poised over thousand-foot
   ravines,
My boat is menaced by ten thousand bends.
If you would ask me where my exile is—
In the southwest, where all are barbarians.

昔 傳 瘴 江 路
今 至 鬼 門 關
土 地 無 人 老
流 移 幾 客 還
自 從 別 京 洛
頹 鬢 與 衰 顏
夕 宿 含 沙 裏
晨 行 岡 路 間
馬 危 千 仞 谷
舟 險 萬 重 灣
問 我 投 何 地
西 南 盡 百 蠻

With no little black humor, in line three Shen plays on
the convention of the landscape as a world of immortals,
where the recluse "never grows old" by avoiding the contention of public life. In the South also "no man ever
grows old," but for different reasons. The plainness of
Shen's diction in this poem is effective; courtly ornament
would be out of place. The court poet could compact lines
like the fifth one here into one or two characters, but
the expanded forms, rich in particles, are appropriate
for poetry of self-expression—the "old style."
    By the time Shen reached Huan-chou, he was in complete

despair, certain that his place of exile had been chosen
with singular malice.

FIRST REACHING HUAN-CHOU

初達驩州

Banished travellers—eighteen of us—

流子一十八

But the decree for me was unlike the others.

命予偏不偶

I was exiled the furthest—to the world's
very end—

配遠天遂窮

And took longest to arrive, the last of them
all.

到遲日最後

By water I went through the Tan-erh's lands,

水行儋耳國

Then overland through jungles of tatooed
savages.

陸行雕題藪

My soul wandered to the very gate of the
ghosts,

魂魂遊鬼門

And my skeleton will be left in Leviathan's
mouth.

骸骨遺鯨口

Bearing with my hunger I lie down by night,

夜則忍飢臥

At dawn move on swiftly, carrying sickness.

朝則抱病走

I scratch out my hair in this southern
wilderness,

搔首向南荒

Brush away tears gazing at the northern
Dipper.

拭淚看北斗

Oh, what year will reprieve arrive,

何年赦書來

That I may once again drink the wine of
Lo-yang?

重飲洛陽酒

[04978]

The "gate of the ghosts" is translated above as Hellgate,
the entrance to the underworld that lent its name to a
pass in the southwest.

The harshest charge that can be levelled against the
court poets is that their verse is bloodless. This was
no season for graciousness, and in Huan-chou Shen began
to use the regulated verse as it had not been used before.

GAZING BY NIGHT IN THE SOUTH PAVILION OF HUAN-CHOU

驩州南亭夜望

Last night as I gazed from the South Pavilion,

昨夜南亭望

I dreamed clearly I was in Lo-yang.

Who could claim I had ever left home?

I was together at the table with my
children.

I awoke suddenly, still believing it real,

Then after deep thought, understood its
emptiness.

How many inches of my writhing innards survive?

I brush away tears sitting in the spring wind.

中 洛 夢 明 分
別 道 誰 家 室
同 嘗 案 女 兒
是 言 猶 覺 忽
空 悟 始 思 沈
寸 幾 餘 腸 肝
風 春 坐 淚 拭

[05043]

Parallelism is violated in the second couplet, while in
the third it is purely a formal device underlying a hypotactic sentence. Still, the response of tears returns,
a traditional echo in an untraditional poem.

Shen vented his bitterness in Huan-chou with a vigor
completely unlike his poetry of the capital.

By life and death, split from flesh and blood,

By glory and shame, rived from former
companions.

Cast off, my body alone survives,

All the troubles of my former life are
finished.

肉 骨 離 生 死
遊 朋 間 辱 榮
在 身 一 置 棄
休 事 萬 生 乎

"Moving from the Official Residence of Huan-chou to a
Creek Pavilion in the Mountains: to Governor Su" [05099]

My soul grows weary of the roads of mountain
cranes,

My heart is drunk from the springs where the
hawks swoop.

. . . . .

Who tells us the "blazing land" is broad?—

Here Earth ends and one feels that Heaven is
low.

路 鶴 山 疲 魂
溪 鳶 跕 醉 心
. . . .
廣 謂 誰 方 炎
低 天 覺 盡 地

"A Reprieve Comes but I May Not Return: written on a rock
over the river" [05100]

Phrases such as the "spring where the hawks swoop" were
probably local place names, but they take on a violent

significance for the poet in exile. But even in the power
of these lines, Shen is working through a particular
syntactic form which we have seen earlier in a milder
form in Tu Shen-yen's "Crossing Stonegate Mountain":

Mud packs the paths where serpents dart,   泥擁弄蛇徑
Clouds bury the brush where wild beasts   雲埋伏獸叢
   crouch.

Shen achieves a poetic identity, but he achieves it <u>through</u>
a poetic tradition he had received from others. The cosmology which describes the heavens as a vast dome becomes
vividly real as Shen imagines the sky over Huan-chou to
be unnaturally low.

It was natural for a poet exiled to the South to turn
to the models of Ch'ü Yuan and Chia Yi. Shen Ch'üan-ch'i
echoes Chia Yi's "The Owl," in which the Han poet questioned an owl about the vicissitudes of fate. Shen,
instead, is himself questioned by an ogre, and the poet
responds with his life's story.

ANSWERING THE OGRE: WRITTEN FOR SOMEONE   答魑魅代書寄
   AT HOME   家人

An ogre came to ask after me,   魑魅來相問
How I came to stray from the Royal Domain;   君何失帝鄉
How, wizened with years, I left the palace   龍鐘辭北闕
   gates,
And tottering, stumbling, keep to this   蹭蹬守南荒
   southern wilderness;
How I came to pity my white hair in the   覽鏡憐雙鬢
   mirror,
To regret these countless streams of tears   沾衣惜萬行
   that soak my robes;
Why I left my home, cradling my sorrows,   抱愁那去國
On the point of old age, donning the robes   將老更垂裳
   of government.
My shadow answered, "In former years I   影答余他歲
Enjoyed special favor in service in   恩私宦洛陽
   Lo-yang..."

                  [05101]

In the remainder of this very long poem, Shen reviews
his past experiences, his exile, and his present state
of mind with elegant diction.

   Among the poems of Sung Chih-wen and Shen Ch'üan-ch'i
written during the 705 exile, there was a group which
began a new subgenre, the elegiac description of the
poet's youth and better times. The tradition of the
personal narrative plays some role in this subgenre, but
the strongest influence is the tradition of the capital
poem. Rather than a Han past which points to the universal processes of glory and decline, these poems
elegiacally celebrate a more recent past, embellished
by the vagaries of memory in adversity. Tu Fu, Li Po,
and many other High T'ang poets wrote such poems after
the An Lu-shan rebellion.

ON THE THIRD DAY OF THE THIRD MONTH: SITTING
   ALONE IN HUAN-CHOU REMEMBERING PAST TRAVELS

In the two capitals, much to see and do in
   season,
The Third Day is the best for excursions.
The wind slowly rolls up under a lovely sun,
The rain gradually retires from the petal-
   strewn dust.
Red peach blossoms begin to fall to earth,
Green willows half cover the canals.
Then servant boys wear full spring livery,
And palace ladies leave off their archery
   guards.
The Lustration Hall leads through to the
   Han Park,
Purification mats circle the halls of Ch'in.
Here rhetoricians like Shu Hsi, their
   discussions subtle,
And writers like Chang Hua, their histories
   vigorous.
Not a pavilion without a horse tied to it,
Not a bank without some boat crossing over.

Sounds of dance-flutes cross the thousand gates
of the palace

On the screens and hangings painted watercourses
flow.

A golden shot arcs toward a bird,

The sweet bait is cast to meet its fish.

The clear and shallow is loved for bathing
impurities,

Meeting good fortune, they rejoice in offerings
and toasts.

Sacred straw strewn to be cast away,

The drying of the holy herbs must be finished.

Who would have thought in this season for
summoning souls,

I would be a prisoner fending off ogres instead?

My friends are gone, beyond the horizon;

My heart's pleasure must be found south of
the sun.

The Bronze Pillar stands awesome over the
Red Frontiers,

Where crimson slopes stand guard over fiery
nooks.

Blazing vapors steam from dawn to evening,

The fogs of pestilence fill winter and
autumn.

When shall I be pardoned from over the
western waters?

How can I linger here in the southland?

And with no one to face me over the wine
brazier,

How can I ease the melancholy of leaving home?

[05098]

We need not go into the extensive references made to the
purification ceremonies of the Third Day festival, but
obviously the ceremony has special meaning to Shen,
dwelling in the fetid south and longing for his crimes
to be "bathed away." Although the poem begins by "remembering past travels," it modulates into speculation on
what is being done that very day in the capital (made

explicit in line twenty-two), then contrasting their joy
with his own misery. The capital poem juxtaposition of
glory and decline is here transposed to a spatial relationship, being in the capital set against being at the
edge of the world.

When Shen's reprieve came at last (he was first transferred to a post further north before being recalled to
the capital), his joy was no less exuberant than his
misery at exile had been intense.

REJOICING AT A REPRIEVE

Last year, a wanderer lodging in the
  wilderness;
This spring, pardon granted, I return.
When the orders came through, dark valleys
  were warmed,
The bowl was lifted, the bright sun radiant.
A joyous spirit met a wronged spirit,
An official's green robes repaid the
  commoner's whites,
So let me join the leaves of Ho-p'u
And together we'll fly north to Lo-yang.

                    [05050]

Having a bowl over one's head was a cliché metaphor for
imperial disfavor, since it stopped one from seeing
"heaven" and the "bright sunlight" of imperial favor.

During his stay in Huan-chou, Shen Ch'üan-ch'i paid
a visit to the nearby Shao-lung Temple. The equanimity
which Shen shows toward his fate in this poem is quite
different than the intensity of his other exile poems.
The poem is a consolation and shows that exile had done
more for Shen's work than simply helping him break free
of conventional poetic restraints. The poem tries to
make a unified statement, integrating landscape and
emotion in a way that court poetry never could.

SHAO-LUNG TEMPLE   紹隆寺

> Preface: Shao-lung is the most wondrous temple of the far south
> and is located some twenty-five miles from Huan-chou. About to
> journey north, I spent the entire day visiting it, burning
> incense according to custom, and wrote this poem as I went back
> on the boat.

Long have I followed Sakyamuni—	吾從釋迦久
Nothing greater than to be a student of Nirvana—	無上師涅槃
I sought the Way for thirty years,	探道三十載
Found the Way on the world's southern edge.	得道天南端
Nothing is better than going to some strange place—	非勝適殊方
Where a clamor rises, turning to Truth is hard.	起諠歸理難
Thus being banished turned out a good Cause,	放棄乃良緣
Worldly cares never bother me here.	世慮不曾干
Precincts of incense circle the isles to the North,	香界縈北渚
Pagodas like flowers shade the south peaks.	花龕隱南巒
Sheer and high, the stones beneath the stairs,	危昂階下石
As mountain torrents sweep past the windows.	澒漾窗中瀾
When clouds cover it over, look at the tree-tops rising tall;	雲蓋看木秀
When the sky is empty, see the encircling vines.	天空見藤盤
Dwelling amid crudeness, strive to sit in meditation;	處俗勤宴坐
Living in poverty, store merit by circumambulation.	居貪業行壇
And through this carnal body of passions	試將有漏軀
Let me form awhile the outlook of "Nonlife."	聊作無生觀
In the end I will have investigated all the classes of things,	了然究諸品
And fully realized the peace of those who find stillness.	彌覺靜著安

[04976]

23

SUNG CHIH-WEN

The political career of Sung Chih-wen was much like that of Shen Ch'üan-ch'i: Sung also passed the chin-shih examination in 675 and later achieved prominence as a favorite of the Chang brothers. In 705 Sung was banished to Shuang-chou in Kwangtung Province. After the general amnesty he held several good posts, including Auxiliary Scholar in the Hsiu-wen kuan. Sometime after Jui-tsung took the throne, in 710, Sung was again banished, first to Yüeh-chou in Chekiang, then further south to Ch'in-chou in Kwangtung. In the year 712, Sung Chih-wen was kindly granted permission to commit suicide by the emperor. Though eighth- and ninth-century poets some-times refer to him with fondness, Sung Chih-wen's reputa-tion has been very low among historians because of his association with the Changs.

Although Sung Chih-wen's reputation as a poet exceeds that of Shen Ch'üan-ch'i, his work is perhaps less inter-esting than that of Shen. Along with Shen, Sung Chih-wen is credited with the perfection of the rules of regulated verse, but his treatment of the standard themes is some-what more conservative and his exile poems are less violently intense. His most original poems are his heptasyllabic songs, which we have treated earlier, and his "Ch'u Songs," which seem to have been popular in his own day. Sung's "Ch'u Songs" are distinguishable from heptasyllabic verse only by the exclamatory particle hsi 兮 in the fourth position in the line and certain thematic conventions. The most famous of Sung's "Ch'u Songs" was his "Song of Going Down the Mountain" (03227), which was widely imitated.

I go down Sung Mountain,
    full of brooding,
Take a Fair One by the hand,
    pace slowly, slowly.
The bright moon among the pines
    will ever be like this,
But when you go off wandering again
    when shall you return?

今思山嵩下多
今佳人遲遲佳步
今明月間松長
此如君再遊何時傻

Notice that Sung slips easily into a standard heptasyllabic line in the third line of this short poem. The
"Ch'u Song" was associated with an emotional effusiveness
that might be called "romantic." We can sense some of
the changes in literary taste in the first decade of the
eighth century in the very fact that Sung Chih-wen uses
the Ch'u meter and that his Ch'u songs were imitated.
Another such poem (03228) was dedicated to the Taoist
Ssu-ma Ch'eng-chen, who left the court of Jui-tsung in
710:

SONG OF A WINTER NIGHT

贈司馬承禎引宵冬

There is ice on the river,
    there is snow on the mountains,
Cracks plastered in northside doors,
    the travellers are gone.
I sit alone in the mountains,
    facing the moon in the pines,
I think on the Fair One,
    waxings and wanings frequent.
The bright moonlight sparkles
    in the cold pools,
Green pines secluded and dark,
    the strong winds moan.
This feeling I have shall never be told
    to an ordinary man.
To love and not to see
    is a sorrow without end.

今有冰河
今有雪山
今堪絕北广
行人獨坐山中今
對松月懷美人今
屢盈月缺的
明瀑潭中幽的
青松勁風幽
吟此情不說向
俗人而不窮見
愛恨

Ssu-ma Ch'eng-chen's reply (46721) survives.

ANSWERING SUNG CHIH-WEN

The season approaches its close,
    spring has almost returned,
The mountain forests are silent,
    I think on the Secluded one there.
I climb strange peaks,
    gaze on the white clouds,
I brood disconsolate,
    their forms are about to scatter,
White clouds going on and on,
    off and never returning,
Cold winds howl,
    blowing the sun to setting.
Not seeing that person,
    with whom shall I speak?
I go back, sit, and strum my lute,
    thoughts growing ever further.

答宋之問

時節既欲暮　春寂人兮今
山林幽　懷登奇峯兮今
望白雲逸　悵緬欲紛悠悠
象白去　寒雲不返颼颼
風日晚　吹見其人
不　誰與言　歸坐彈琴
思逾遠

The use of the "Ch'u Song" genre, popular during the Han
dynasty, parallels Ch'en Tzu-ang's resurrection of the
poetic style of the third century. The genre's stylized
but intense language of love-longing answered the need
felt for a poetry of direct emotion. Sung's formal
parting quatrain (03359) to Ssu-ma Ch'eng-chen on his
departure from the capital in 710 makes a nice contrast
with the poems above.

SENDING OFF THE TAOIST SSU-MA ON HIS
  JOURNEY TO T'IEN-T'AI

送司馬道士遊天台

Feathered Wanderer and mouth organ songs
  here must stray apart,
Here and there above parting mats
  white clouds fly.
Beneath the palace gates of P'eng-lai,
  eternal remembrance,

羽客笙歌此地違
離筵數處白雲飛
蓬萊闕下長相憶

To a mountaintop of wu-t'ung and cypress
  you go off, not to return.   桐柏山頭去不歸

This is an example of the court poet's art: Ssu-ma Ch'eng-
chen is to be complimented as a Taoist immortal and is
therefore named by the traditional kenning "Feathered
Wanderer."

   Ssu-ma Ch'eng-chen is not simply going to "leave" the
parting banquet; rather he will go "astray" of the mouth
organ music being played there. Such an elaborate phrasing of a simple situation is characteristic of court
poetry. The parting itself is referred to by the conventional synecdoche "parting mats," and the capital is
replaced by the palace, itself referred to conventionally
as "P'eng-lai," a Han palace and the island where the
immortals dwell. Although Sung Chih-wen and Shen Ch'üan-
ch'i were both exploring new modes of poetic expression,
neither poet rejected the older, more formal style when
the occasion demanded.

   Sung Chih-wen's innovations were not only in the
revival of old forms like the "Ch'u Song." He also
shows interest in setting up complex psychological situations, an interest which was to become characteristic
of some of the best High T'ang poetry. The following
poem (03348), if genuine, was written on Sung's return
to the capital from his first exile; in its style and
its concerns it is indistinguishable from poetry written
in mid-eighth century.

CROSSING THE HAN RIVER   渡漢江

Beyond the Southern Peaks,
  news of home was cut off,   嶺外音書斷

There I passed through winter
  and forged again through spring.   經冬復歷春

Now nearing my home my heart
  is struck with dread,   近鄉情更怯

And I dare not ask news
  of men coming from there.   不敢問來人

antedates the preceding quatrain by some four
ars; the new style which appears in Sung's exile
was largely a function of the situation rather than
any permanent change to a new kind of poetry. The subtle
psychological vignette was common in quatrains on palace
ladies and lonely women; here the psychological acuity is
transferred to personal poetry. Some of the most famous
quatrains of the eighth and ninth centuries were just
such psychological vignettes. Whatever psychological
acumen there is in Sung's observation that he no longer
dares to ask what he had previously yearned to know, there
is still a certain "cleverness" to the idea: like courtly
wit, it is based on an inversion of expectations—instead
of eagerly asking, he will not ask. In the hands of the
best High T'ang poets, the wit of the Early T'ang quatrain
is put to serious purposes. The Early T'ang poet was
always seeking the anomalies or "wonders" of the world;
the High T'ang poets sought significant anomalies which
revealed something about the human condition. A few
decades after Sung Chih-wen's poem above, Ho Chih-chang
賀知章 writes:

EXTEMPORE: RETURNING HOME [first of two]	回鄉偶書二首之一
I left my home when I was a youth, now aged I return,	少小離鄉老大回
My local dialect can't be changed, but my hair has turned white.	鄉音難改鬢毛衰
The little children see me, don't recognize me,	兒童相見不相識
And laughingly ask—"Stranger, where do you come from?"	笑問客從何處來

[05446]

Even closer to Sung Chih-wen's inversion of expectations
is the following famous quatrain (09877) by Ts'en Shen
岑參:

MEETING AN ENVOY ON HIS WAY TO THE CAPITAL　逢入京使

Looking eastward toward home, the road
 stretches far,

故園東望路漫漫

My two sleeves soaked, the tears never
 dry.

雙袖龍鐘淚不乾

I meet you on horseback—no paper, no
 brush,

馬上相逢無紙筆

But I trust you to take them word—tell
 them I am fine.

憑君傳語報平安

Of course, Ts'en Shen is not "fine" at all, the reader is
left to draw the inference that Ts'en is so miserable that
he feels his primary duty is to reassure his family rather
than worry them.

Sung Chih-wen's court poems are somewhat more elaborate
then Shen Ch'üan-ch'i's, though this is only a slight personal variation on what is, basically, a uniform style.
Sung's finest court poem (03242) does not seem to be an
imperial command poem at all, but rather a spontaneous
outburst of graciousness on an imperial trip in 696.

WRITTEN WITH THE IMPERIAL RETINUE ON THE
 ROAD TO TENG-FENG

扈從登封途
中作

Tent palaces swell on the towering cliff,

帳殿鬱崔嵬

Mighty, indeed, the wanderings of immortals.

仙遊實壯哉

Morning clouds link with the curtains rolling
 up,

曉雲連幕捲

Fires by night mix with the stars in the
 circuits.

夜火雜星回

Through the dark of the valley a thousand
 banners emerge,

谷暗千旗出

The mountains sing as ten thousand coaches
 come.

山鳴萬乘來

The retinue's progress is truly worth a poem,

扈從良可賦

But I lack that talent to light up the heavens.

終乏掞天才

The "ten thousand coaches" of line six is a conventional
kenning for the emperor, "lord of ten thousand coaches."
Here, however, the descriptive context restores something

of the original force of the phrase. More interesting are Sung's personal poems from the 690s. The following piece (03198) is typical of the complicated social poetry that appears often in the High T'ang.

LYING SICK AT WARMSPRING VILLA: TO YANG CHIUNG

Taking sick leave, I rest on this peak,

In utter stillness, I weary of solitude, seclusion.

But I do have Mount Sung to depend on,

From my high resting place, ever in my eyes.

Wonders and spirits lodge on that mountain

Shaded day and night by the tribes of clouds.

Just today a drizzling rain has cleared,

Late sunlight falls back on the cliffs and valleys.

The grasses are thick by mountain torrents,

And green are the trees at the mountain's foot.

My mood at this moment seems endless,

Gazing around, I'm disturbed by the wooded foothills.

The Yi and the Lo flow off forever,

Streams and plains, doubling one after another.

In the last of summer, birds and beasts teem,

And at autumn's end the grain is ripe.

Maintaining my desires, I keep to my fenced garden,

Returning to calm, I rejoice in planting and herding.

But I regret there is no one to bring wine—

All I can do is take a handful of water from the cool spring.

溫泉莊臥病，寄楊七炯

移疾臥茲嶺，寥寥倦幽獨。
賴有嵩丘山，高枕長在目。
茲山靈異族，朝夜翳雲雨。
是日濛雨晴，返景入巖谷。
冪冪澗下草，青青山畔木。
此意方無窮，環顧悵林麓。
伊川何悠悠，川原複重複。
夏餘鳥獸戲，秋末黍稷熟。
秉願守樊圃，歸閒欣藝牧。
惜無載酒人，徒把涼泉掬。

Hsieh Ling-yün's philosophical closure, that he lacks an appreciative friend to join him in his enjoyment of the landscape, here is put to persuasive, social purposes:

Yang Chiung can hardly miss the point that he is being
invited to visit Sung. We may well wonder how Sung can
be so weary of his seclusion and delight in it so thoroughly at the same time. The logical contradiction is
subordinate to the social purpose of the poem: "I'm bored
to death here, and this is a lovely spot—so come visit
me."

There is a strong eremitic strain in Sung Chih-wen's
poetry. The following poem (03185) probably also comes
from before Sung's first exile in 705.

FIRST ARRIVING AT MY MOUNTAIN VILLA IN   初到陸渾山莊
   LU-HUN

Presented winter clothes, I am stirred by   授衣感窮節
  the season's end,

And whip on my horse, up over Yi Pass.   策馬凌伊關

Return accords with my heart's inclination,   歸齊逸人趣

Aware how each day my autumn lute plays   日覺秋琴閒
  more peacefully.

Cold dew withers the northern hill,   寒露衰北阜

Evening sunlight shatters the eastern   夕陽破東山
  mountains.

With a wild song I pace through thick shade,   浩歌步檟櫪

And the evening birds follow me home.   棲鳥隨我還

The presentation of winter clothes is associated with the
ninth month, late autumn. Despite the poem's weak opening,
it is one of Sung Chih-wen's finest pieces. The metaphorical verb in the third position in a line was a characteristic device of court poetry, but Sung's bold and violent
use of "shatters" in line six is something most court
poets would not have dared.

Sung Chih-wen wrote a rather large number of landscape
poems during his exile. These typically take the form
of a description of the landscape followed by a meditation
on the poet's experiences. In some cases (for example
03206) the landscape is only an excuse for the extended

personal narrative. In other cases (such as the following
poem, 03193) the landscape dominates, and the poet's response is brief and emotional. This latter form is the
characteristic Early T'ang landscape, yet the unity of
description in the following poem makes it much closer
to the High T'ang.

FIRST REACHING YA-K'OU

初至崖口

A Ya-k'ou a host of mountains sheer off
And raise a cliff-wall looming to heaven.
Their vapors strike the red of the setting
   sun,
Their reflections fall in emerald of
   springtime pools.
The moss is woven to embroidered brocades,
Pines and rocks painted in polychrome.
Waterbirds drift leisurely with the current,
As flowers fly sparkling from the cliffs.
The faint road enters deep from this point on,
And I have come constrained in service.
Deeply grieved, and the mood not yet over,
The clusters of mountains darken in the
   growing evening.

崖口衆山斷
嶔崟聳天壁
氣衝落日紅
影入春潭碧
錦繢織苔蘚
丹青畫松石
水禽泛容與
巖花飛的皪
微路從此深
我來限于役
惆悵情未已
羣峯暗將夕

Tu Shen-yen's two landscape poems quoted earlier, "Crossing Stonegate Mountain" and "Written at Jumble-Rock
Mountain," resemble earlier landscape poems by Wang Po
in their fragmentation of description. By mixing descriptions of day and night, rain and clear weather, they do
not build any coherent scene. Ch'en Tzu-ang's "Crossing
Gorge-mouth Mountain" is a different kind of landscape:
it does not describe a scene but a rather a passage <u>through</u>
a landscape whose form parallels an intellectual principle.
In contrast to these, Sung Chih-wen's poem above is relatively unified in visual terms: he builds one scene at
one time of day, Ya-k'ou in the growing darkness. The
following poem (07631) by Meng Hao-jan shows a High T'ang

treatment of a landscape, similar to Sung Chih-wen's but
more sophisticated. The tenth line of Sung Chih-wen's
poem is identical to the thirteenth line of Meng Hao-jan's,
and both echo <u>Shih-ching</u>, no. 14. Both poets observe a
landscape changing in the moving sunlight; both poets
admire what they see but are forced to move onward.

ON P'ENG-LI LAKE, GAZING AT LU
  MOUNTAIN

彭蠡湖中望
廬山

When in the void a halo grows round the
  moon,

太虛生月暈

The boatman knows there'll be a wind
  from the heavens,

舟子知天風

So he hoists his sail, awaiting the break
  of day,

挂席候明發

Which gradually spreads over the vastness
  of the level lake.

眇漫平湖中

Then in mid-current I can see K'uang's hill,

中流見匡阜

Which stands pressing down on the power of
  Nine Rivers.

勢壓九江雄

Its murky blackness opens to the bright
  heavens

黤黕容霽色

Until it stands towering in the morning sky,

崢嶸當曉空

And when the sun first rises over Incense
  Burner Peak,

香爐初上日

Its cascade spurts into a rainbow.

瀑布噴成虹

Long have I wished to follow Shang-tzu,

久欲追尚子

And here, still more, I am moved by Hui-yüan.

況茲懷遠公

I have come, constrained in service,

我來限于役

Without the leisure to give myself ease.

未暇息微躬

My journey to the Huai and the sea, almost
  half over,

淮海途將半

From frost and stars I can tell the year
  soon ends.

星霜歲欲窮

I send word to those roosting on these peaks—

寄言巖棲者

When my pleasure changes, I'll come and
  join you.

畢趣當來同

Meng Hao-jan's poem is even more unified than Sung Chih-
wen's: he describes the <u>process</u> of sunrise with symbolic

implications of "illumination" as it reveals Lu Mountain to the poet. As a famous abode of monks and recluses, Lu Mountain's appearance leads directly to Meng's inner conflict between government service, which has brought him to the spot, and the desire to live the life of a hermit.

The theme of facing a grand landscape and feeling one must "change one's life" appears in the following exile poem (03196).

TUNG-T'ING LAKE

The Earth is gone, Heaven and water merge,
As by dawn I came to Tung-t'ing Lake.
The first sunlight bubbled out of its midst,
Nor could I see the east or west shore.
In its crystalline sparkling on what could
  my eyes rest?
In its glitter and gleam, my heart almost fled.
A holy radiance bathed the Sea God,
Drifting vapors made T'ien-wu sparkle.
Here the Yellow Emperor came to set out
  his orchestra,
Campaigning against the Miao, King Yü of Hsia
  marched through.
Sung Yü, Ch'u's courtier, here lamented falling
  leaves,
And Yao's daughter wept for Shun at Ts'ang-wu.
Its plain gathers in the moisture of Nine Rivers,
Its mountains let through a picture of the Five
  Peaks.
The winds are cheerful, the fish leap up,
Then clouds turn evening and wild geese call
  to each other.
Alone here, looking down in these gentle waves,
In its vast floods the generations of men change.
I will wash from me all foulness forever,
And to the end of my days find pure delights.

洞庭湖

地盡天水合
朝及洞庭湖
初日當中涌
莫辨東西隅
晶耀目何在
澄瑩心欲無
靈光曇海若
游氣耿天吳
張樂軒皇至
征苗夏禹徂
楚臣悲落葉
堯女泣蒼梧
野積九江潤
山通五嶽圖
風怡魚自躍
雲夕雁相呼
獨此臨沒漾
浩將人代殊
永言洗氣濁
卒歲為清娛

If you would retire only after doing great deeds, 要 使 功 成 退
You suffer as needlessly as that great lord of   徒 勞 越 大 夫
  Yüeh.

The "great lord of Yüeh" is Fan Li, who set off on the
lake in a boat after helping the kingdom of Yüeh conquer
the kingdom of Wu in the Warring States period. As the
morning light spreads over the lake, it summons up the
images of the legendary figures associated with Lake
Tung-t'ing. Sung's poem is the first memorable example
of a whole series of poems on Lake Tung-t'ing during the
T'ang. Although Sung's poem is bolder than anything Tu
Shen-yen could have done, we might compare the poem above
with the opening of a ninety-two line poem (17825) on
Tung-t'ing, written by Han Yü early in the ninth century
when he was returning from exile.

AT YÜEH-YANG TOWER: PARTING FROM TOU   岳 陽 樓 別 竇
    HSIANG   司 直

Within China's nine provinces, Lake Tung-t'ing,   洞 庭 九 州 間
In its largeness, to what would it yield?   廓 大 誰 與 讓
To the south converge streams from a crowd of   南 滙 羣 崖 水
  slopes,
In the north they gush out, how swift and   北 注 何 奔 放
  free!
It amasses them into seven hundred miles,   瀰 爲 七 百 里
Swallowing them in, each in a different   杳 納 各 殊 狀
  form.
Since ancient times never clearing,   白 古 澄 不 清
Whirling around, mixing, no place to go.   環 混 無 歸 何
Parching winds agitate it each day,   炎 風 日 搜 攪
Weird things hidden therein are tediously   幽 怪 多 兄 長
  many.
High upward huge waves rise,   軒 然 大 波 起
Even the sky's vault is too narrow and   宇 宙 隘 而 妨
  blocks them.
Wavecrests above Sung and Hua Mountains,   巍 義 扳 嵩 華
They spring upward like strong youths.   騰 踔 軼 健 壯

How its sounds echo and resound!—
The crash and rumble of thousands of
　　chariots.
And it seems as though the Yellow Emperor
Had come to these vast and empty spaces to
　　play his music,
Dragons appear as his chime-frames,
White-silken foam blows as his tent tassels.
Gods and demons, not of the human world,
Whose rhythms are wild and erratic.

聲音一何宏
轟輷車萬兩軥
猶疑帝軒就空曠
張樂露笱簴
蛟螭吹組帳
縞練鬼神非人世
師奏頠跌踢

Han Yü repeats in an expanded form many of the allusions
and topics of Sung Chih-wen's poem. The theme of the
lake's cleansing purity, which is the center of Sung's
version, is treated later in Han Yü's poem. In the context
of his own age, Sung Chih-wen's poem is boldly imaginative,
yet compared to Han Yü's torrent of metaphor and energetic
description, Sung's style seems tightly controlled. The
tripartite form lies strongly beneath Sung's version,
whereas Han Yü's poem is a complex interweaving of past
and present visions of the lake, past and present crossings
and life experiences. Though the contrast might seem to
make Han Yü's poem more attractive, it would be the balance
between freedom and control in Sung Chih-wen's poem which
would strike later critics, such as the Ming neoclassicists, as most characteristically T'ang.

　　One of Sung's most famous regulated verses (03284) was
composed as he crossed Ta-yü Peak, going into exile.

CROSSING TA-YÜ PEAK

度大庾嶺

As I cross this peak, I leave my native land,
Halt my carriage, gaze continually toward home.
My soul follows the southward winging birds,
My tears last as long as the northside branches'
　　flowers.
Now a clearing appears in the mountain rain,
And the river's white clouds almost changed
　　to rose red.

度嶺方辭國
停軺一望家
魂隨南翥鳥
淚盡北枝花
山雨初含霽
江雲欲變霞

I pray only that there will be a day of
  return—

I do not dare be bitter at Ch'ang-sha.

但令歸有日
不敢恨長沙

According to legend, when the plum blossoms on the north
slope of Ta-yü Peak were just coming out, those on the
south slope were already falling. This suggests a major
climatic division, and line four suggests an awareness on
the part of the poet that at this point he is leaving
China proper. In the last line Sung echoes the story of
Chia Yi, exiled to Ch'ang-sha.

   In a court poem, where the response is simply one of
appreciation, it was required that the scene of the middle
couplets only be "beautiful." Poems with more complex
responses tend to demand that the scene somehow "signify,"
that it stir the response which the poet gives. The
thematic diversification of poetry in the second half
of the seventh century naturally created more complex
responses in the closing couplets of regulated verses
and other strictly tripartite poems. This, in turn, put
a pressure on the middle couplets to form a tighter intellectual unity.

   The two solutions to this demand that the middle couplets "signify" appear in the poem above. The simplest
of these is represented in the second couplet: the poet
intrudes himself into the scene. The solution that
appears in the straight description of the third couplet
is more complex and tenuous: because the last couplet is
somehow a response to the third couplet, we are directed
toward its possible symbolic implications. This does not
mean that all straight descriptive middle couplets are
intentionally symbolic; rather, the need that the response
follow naturally from them directs us to seek out such
implications, if we can find them. There is a "pressure
for meaning" in the middle couplets of tripartite poems,
a phenomenon which is very strong in eighth- and ninth-

century poetry. In the above poem "clearing" suggests
the restoration of imperial favor; the "rose clouds"
(hsia 霞) suggest immortality and thereby the court.

The third couplet of the following poem (03219) is
another example of the poet starting to describe the scene
but feeling the need to integrate it with situation he
describes.

REACHING THE POST STATION AT TUAN-CHOU:
  THERE I SEE POEMS ON THE WALL BY TU
  SHEN-YEN, SHEN CH'ÜAN-CH'I, YEN CHAO-
  YIN, AND WANG WU-CHING: I WRITE THIS
  SONG IN SORROW.

至 端 州 驛 見 杜 五
審 言 沈 三 佺 期 閭
五 朝 隱 王 二 無 競
題 壁 慨 然 成 詠

Officials of the northland, put under
  severe banishment,

逐 臣 北 地 承 嚴 譴

But we assumed that in the South we could
  always see each other.

謂 到 南 中 每 相 見

Who would have thought that in the South
  the crossroads would be so many?

豈 意 南 中 岐 路 多

A thousand mountains, ten thousand
  streams divide our posts.

千 山 萬 水 分 鄉 縣

Clouds quiver, rain scatters—each flies
  dispersing;

雲 搖 雨 散 各 翻 飛

The ocean vast, the heavens long—letters
  are so rare.

海 闊 天 長 音 信 稀

What we share at each place in this landscape is malarial fogs,

處 處 山 川 同 瘴 癘

And I worry about how many of us will
  ever be able to return.

自 憐 能 得 幾 人 歸

The "each" of line five is the point of transition in the
line between the landscape and the exiles: it can refer
to the clouds or to the men. The reader's expectation
is that it refers to the landscape, but the imperfect
parallel in line six suggests that it refers to the men.
The ambiguity tends to identify the men with the clouds,
echoing the traditional association of wanderers and
drifting clouds.

The complex associative development of the following
poem (03197) written in 710 shows that Sung Chih-wen had

progressed well beyond the mechanical strings of couplets
which make up most Early T'ang landscape poems. A ceremony performed during his exile leads the poet to think
of the gods and then to the quest for the immortals; in
turn, the natural association of the immortals with the
court drives the poet to review his experiences, which
first brings consolation and then leads to an ambiguous
state of uncertainty. Though the poem lacks the symmetrical balance of rhetorical amplification, the associative
unity tries to reflect natural processes of thought, and
this in turn makes the poem seem "natural" in comparison
with earlier personal narratives. But even beyond this
structural advantage, which places the poem in the High
T'ang, the poem is an example of how poetry was again
moving away from a purely public function to serve as a
vehicle for private meditation.

A SACRIFICE TO THE SEA: THE FOURTH YEAR OF
THE CHING-LUNG REIGN

景龍四年春祠海

A stern matter, the sacrifice to the sea
in spring,

I fast by night to cleanse away my cares.

When the cock crows, I see the sun come out,

Egrets come down and are frightened by the
swift breakers.

The land is vast, the ends of the earth
are near,

As the sky turns, the hundred streams swell.

The edge of my mat touches a deserted cove,

Where beyond my eyes is only the thick fog.

Then in the warm air the images of things
appear,

As I stroll around dark and light alternate.

The beast I have brought is not the proper
"black offering,"

But in this pure sacrifice I hope for
divine radiance.

The birds sparkle by the waves' margin,

肅事祠春溟
宵齋洗蒙慮
雞鳴見日出
鷺下驚濤鷙
地闊八荒近
天回百川澍
筵端接空曲
目外唯霧霧
暖氣物象來
周遊晦明互
致牲匪玄享
禋滌期靈照
的的波際禽

Isles of trees amid the frothing, swirling
waters.

But where now is the immortal An-ch'i?

There's no path to seek Fang-chang, the
immortal isle.

The affairs of immortals are cut off from
man's world,

Searching out such mysteries is usually vain.

Four-Light Mountain turns its back on usual
peaks,

None know where its old hermits are found.

Deeply stirred, I now soothe my heart,

Since youth I've enjoyed increasing favor

And three times held a literary man's post,

Twice accepted office with the gods and
immortals.

I do sigh at having left the passes so far
behind,

But now begin to understand the joy by the sea.

Appreciation comes, often and to no purpose,

Truth wins out—who can make a metaphor for it?

I rest my oars, what am I waiting for?—

Lingering here, suddenly it's evening.

樹在路隔塵山處
慨遇林莽遠趣多
喻待暮
間今藏與世已羣辨
自思史仙關海自能
何云
島期蔑事搜明老中齡
入拜歡知來勝楫倚
泛泛安方仙冥四遺撫
弱三兩雖始賞理留徙
良杰文神出臨空執竟忽

PART FIVE

CHANG YÜEH AND TRANSITION INTO THE HIGH T'ANG

INTRODUCTION TO PART FIVE

Period styles may change in a number of ways. A change
may come about in the course of a few years with the
introduction of some new literary theory or the affirmation of an older, neglected one: such was the case in the
790s with the development of the Mid-T'ang style. In
other cases, the change over several decades may occur
so slowly and subtly that it is impossible to draw a
clear line of demarcation: such is the case in the transition from the Early T'ang period style to the High T'ang
period style.

A change in styles clearly did occur. If we compare
almost any good poem of the 740s with a poem of the 640s,
the difference is immediately apparent. The difference
is in part a function of the individuality of the poets
involved and in part a function of a process of continuous
change, occurring through the entire century. But it is
also a change in period styles, and many of the general
elements of differentiation can be traced to the three
decades between 690 and 720, which we have already examined
in our discussions of Ch'en Tzu-ang, Shen Ch'üan-ch'i and
Sung Chih-wen.

Many attempts have been made to isolate the differences
between the poetry of the Early T'ang and that of the High
T'ang. In most cases, those traits which are ascribed to
the High T'ang can be traced back to the Early T'ang or
Southern Dynasties. Though genuine differences exist,
the Early T'ang and High T'ang styles are more closely
related than is generally believed.

The High T'ang period style is built upon an Early
T'ang base: the High T'ang grew out of the Early T'ang
and did not react against it. With their fu-ku pronounce-
ments, many High T'ang poets may have believed they were
reacting against the Early T'ang, but in practice they

were dependent upon Early T'ang norms of treatment. If
anything, the High T'ang was a liberated version of the
Early T'ang. Early T'ang poems often wrote themselves:
the conventions and techniques of amplification were so
firmly entrenched that many court poets could have been
replaced by well-programmed computers. In the High T'ang,
poets had greater mastery over both their language and
the topics; they were able to use the conventions rather
than used by them. The number of private poems and informal occasional poems increases dramatically: High T'ang
poets seem to be writing because they want to rather than
because they must. Formal court poems and ornate pieces
dedicated to high officials continue to be written throughout the T'ang, but good poets show less interest in them.
We might best express this new situation in the social
aspects of poetry by saying that the center of interest
in poetry had shifted and its scope had broadened.

The tripartite structure lingers on, even though poets
are capable of varying it to suit their needs or rejecting
it completely. Still, when poets were called upon to turn
out a quick occasional poem, as they often were, they had
the tripartite structure to fall back on. In the hands
of the best poets, the tripartite form was used with great
sophistication, its parts integrated into increasingly
complex works of art. Likewise, the old poetic conventions
are still used in the High T'ang, but poets show a greater
tendency to play with them, to twist them, and to put them
to a new purposes. We saw this, for example, in Shen
Ch'üan-ch'i's exile poem in which the landscape is one in
which "no one grows old."

The kind of landscape description in parallel couplets,
developed between 670 and 710, remained relatively stable
in the High T'ang; as we saw in the last section, poets
were beginning to learn to integrate these couplets into
unified descriptions and to use them to echo the human
condition. As poetry became less and less a rhetorical

exercise, coherence and universal significance became
increasingly important to poets, and to this end poets
became increasingly bold in their innovations.

On certain occasions, most High T'ang poets were easily
capable of the wit and ornamented diction of the Early
T'ang. However, they also developed a much simpler
form of poetic diction and learned to use it effectively
along with typically Early T'ang phrases. They learned
that good poetry is not necessarily synonymous with the
elaborate, the rhetorically complex, and the clever.
This trend toward stylistic simplification began as early
as the 670s and gradually evolved into what might be called
the T'ang "grand style." Like the famous Greek "grand
style," this suggests deep thought said simply and with
dignity. For an example one could not do better than to
quote one of Wang Wei's most famous poems (05811):

PARTING

送別

I get off my horse, offer you wine,
下馬飲君酒

Ask you where you are going.
問君何所之

You say there is something troubling you
君言不得意

And go home to rest at the edge of southern
  hills.
歸臥南山陲

Be off then—I'll ask no more—
但去莫復問

White clouds for eternity.
白雲無盡時

Such a poem is inconceivable in the Early T'ang: the
language has been completely stripped of all decorative
frills, and the complexity has been transferred from the
diction to the situation. What is not said is both the
subject of the poem and its internal aesthetic center.
The conventional association of the hermit and white
clouds achieves a new dignity and depth. The generality
of the treatment reflects the traveller's failure to give
details and the poet's unwillingness to receive them.
The emphasis on what is unspoken in the relationship

between the two men leaves the poem "open."

   The style of surviving High T'ang court poems is close
but not identical to that of seventh-century court poems:
the mannered, periphrastic style continues, but the imperial
theme is given far more weight than pure description. This
version of the courtly style was still required of candi-
dates for the chin-shih examination, and the fact that
young poets, in their desire for public careers, received
their early training in this style kept the mannered
courtly style as a constant. It is not surprising that
we find the least sense of restraint in poets such as Li
Po who disdained careers in government. The formal, public
style remained a contextual background to give meaning to
the innovation and freedom which one finds in the best
High T'ang poets.

   In the following chapters we will examine first the
work of Chang Yüeh, a figure whose work spans the first
three decades of the eighth century. Then we will look
at some poetry of the first decades of the High T'ang to
see the fulfillment of those changes begun in the last
part of the Early T'ang.

24

CHANG YÜEH

Chang Yüeh 張說(667-730) was more important as a political
figure than as a poet, though if we consider him to be an
Early T'ang poet, he is the most prolific of the period.
His collected works survive in twenty-five chüan, which
include 352 poems. Because of the respect accorded their
collections, it is often the case that great ministers
leave more poems to posterity than the most famous poets
of the day. Of Chang Yüeh's time, Chang Hsü 張旭 and
Chang Jo-hsü 張若虛 are only shadowy figures whose fame
has far outrun their surviving works, while Chang Yüeh,
virtually ignored by T'ang anthologists, has a complete
collection surviving. As a favorite of Hsüan-tsung, Chang
Yüeh has a large number of court poems and ceremonial
songs, but in his more private poetry can be seen the
growth of the new High T'ang style.

A native of Lo-yang, Chang Yüeh came from a relatively
poor family, unlike the great courtiers of the early
seventh century. In 688 Chang passed one of the empress'
special examinations, designed to seek out fresh talent
for her bureaucracy: her antagonism to the great ministerial families did much to promote social mobility in the
bureaucracy of the late seventh century. At first, Chang
Yüeh held several respectable, but low positions in the
central bureaucracy. He came to fame when the Chang
brothers (of whom he was no relation) tried to make use
of him to discredit the empress' favorite, Wei Yüan-chung.
Chang Yüeh agreed to testify against Wei at court, but
when the time came, he changed his mind and instead
publicly denounced the Chang brothers and revealed the
pressures they had put on him to testify against Wei.
Wei was saved for the moment, but for his efforts, Chang

Yüeh was banished to Ch'in-chou in Kuang-tung.

When Chung-tsung took the throne and the empire's
poetic talent was sent en masse to South China, Chang
Yüeh was recalled to the capital. He held several middle
level posts in the central government, and was supposed
to have been a member of the Hsiu-wen kuan, though he is
not mentioned on our list of the members of the office.
When Jui-tsung took the throne, Chang rose even higher to
ministerial positions in the Secretariat and Chancellory.

During the reign of Hsüan-tsung, Chang was made President of the Secretariat and enfeoffed as the Duke of
Yen. However, at the height of his career, he became
involved in a factional dispute with Yao Ch'ung and was
made Governor of Hsiang-chou in Ho-nan and, later, Governor
of Yüeh-chou even further south in Ho-nan. In 716-717
Chang was transferred north to be the Governor General
of Yu-chou. As is so often the case, it was during his
tenure at provincial posts that Chang wrote most of his
best poetry. With the death of Yao Ch'ung, Chang resumed
his post as President of the Secretariat, and after a few
more ups and downs in a struggle with the infamous Li
Lin-fu, Chang died in 730 at the age of sixty-three.

Although Chang Yüeh was a political figure, he, like
many of the great T'ang ministers, exercised no little
influence on the world of literature. He and Su T'ing
dominated the literary establishment of the court during
the first part of Hsüan-tsung's reign. These were the
men whom young poets seeking recognition had to please.

For all the excellent qualities of his poetry, Chang
Yüeh clearly lacks the "knack for parallelism," which
Li Shang-yin so condescendingly saw in Chang's predecessors. In his early poems and consistently in his court
poems, Chang Yüeh can be as formal and periphrastic as
any court poet, but he simply could not master the descriptive ingenuity which was the measure of genius in
poets such as Shen Ch'üan-ch'i and Sung Chih-wen. Chang's

deficiencies as a craftsman saved his work from the paratactic fragmentation we find in many of his earlier contemporaries, and his more smoothly flowing style answered
the changes in literary taste which were occurring in the
710s and 720s; however, it seems that the ineffectiveness
of Chang's parallelism was a genuine inability rather than
a conscious stylistic trait. Chang compensated for his
disability in a number of ways: sometimes he approaches
the grand style of later decades, but more frequently he
replaces the middle, descriptive couplets of tripartite
poems with parallel couplets stating emotion or advancing
the narrative.

The reputations of poets like Sung Chih-wen and Shen
Ch'üan-ch'i rested largely on their excellent regulated
verse, and to a lesser extent on their heptasyllabic
songs. Chang Yüeh's production of pentasyllabic regulated
verse was voluminous, though it contains little that can
equal the best of Sung or Shen. Chang Yüeh wrote relatively few heptasyllabic regulated verses, though two of
those he did write are minor classics. Chang Yüeh was a
very different kind of poet from Sung or Shen, and while
he could not equal them in stylistic grace or descriptive
genius, he compensated for his deficiencies by his personal treatment of the regulated forms.

The following regulated verse (04641) was written in
703 or 704 when Chang was exiled for his part in the Wei
Yüan-chung affair. It is a conservative parting poem,
differing very little from the standard tripartite form.

TUAN-CHOU: PARTING FROM KAO CHIN   瑞州別高六戩

Both forced into hiding on alien soil,   異壤同羈竄

But happy that we've passed each other on   途中喜共過
  the road.

When sorrows are heavy, we often lift our   愁多時舉酒
  wine,

Our toiling done, we might still sing long   勞罷或長歌
  songs.

By the South Seas, winds and tides are strong,　　南海風潮壯
By western rivers, miasmal vapors thick.　　　　西江瘴癘多
Alas, our hands unclasp once again,　　　　　於焉復分手
And with this parting, how much pain?　　　　此別傷如何

The second couplet contains the standard wine-song opposition of the parting poem, while the descriptive third
couplet makes Chang's weakness in that area apparent.
Exile worked its usual salubrious effects on Chang Yüeh's
poetry; in 705 as Chang returned to the capital, he passed
Tuan-chou again and remembered his former meeting with
Kao Chin, who appears to have died in the South.

ON MY WAY HOME I REACHED TUAN-CHOU:　　　還至端州驛前
　WHERE PREVIOUSLY I PARTED FROM　　　　與高六別處
　KAO CHIN

The old post house where the rivers divide,　　舊館分江口
In melancholy I gaze on setting sunlight.　　　僂然望落暉
When we met, we gave each other food for　　相逢傳旅食
　travel,
And about to part, exchanged clothes for　　　臨別換征衣
　the road.
The mountains and streams I remember are　　昔記山川是
　these,
Now feel pain that a generation is no more.　　今傷人代非
All who come and go follow this road,　　　往來皆此路
But living and dead do not return together.　　生死不同歸
　　　　　　　　　　　　　[04666]

The complex emotions stirred by exile put new pressures
on the tripartite form. The opening couplet provides a
general setting for the occasion, but the image of dividing rivers, which remind the poet of his parting with
Kao Chin, is a metaphorical use of the landscape usually
reserved for the middle couplets of the regulated verse.
The second couplet is a narrative flashback to the time
Chang was parting with Kao Chin and suggests the mutual
regard the two men had for one another. The idea of

exchange here echoes in the closing theme of disparity
(one returning alive, the other dead in the South): it
is as though Kao's death were in some way a substitute
for his own. All the other couplets are unified by the
theme of radical division; only the second is about shar-
ing and exchange.

The fifth line unifies the flashback and the present
by the landscape, which remains unchanged, in contrast
to the man who is gone. Direct statement of emotion is
shifted up to the sixth line, while the closing couplet
suggests emotion without stating it. Playing on the word
"road" as both a physical entity and the course a person
travels in his life, Chang fuses the physical scene before
him with a maxim. On the physical level Chang is saying
that all who go to south must take this road, but only
those alive, like himself, return by it. On the metaphorical level the "road" is the path through life on
which man "returns" to nonlife, death. All men follow
this road, too, but in this case it is Kao Chin who has
"returned" and not Chang Yüeh.

Chang also compensated for his weaknesses in the
descriptive couplet by a genius for endings. The following pentasyllabic regulated verse (04621) is an example
of Chang Yüeh's mature art, written almost fifteen years
after the preceding poems, during his tenure as Governor
General of Yu-chou.

DRINKING BY NIGHT IN YU-CHOU

A chill wind blows the night rain,
And the cold forests moan swaying.
Just now I feast in the high hall,
Which helps me forget a heart growing old.
In the army sword dances are proper,
On the frontier they honor the fife's song.
If you've never been general of a border fort,
How can you know the depths of royal favor?

幽州夜飲
涼風蕭正能軍塞不誰
州風瑟有忘中上作知
夜吹動高遮宜重邊恩
雨林宴心舞音將深

The last couplet is easy enough to translate, but its
significance is complex. Chang may be using one of the
conventions of military poetry, that being sent on campaign
is a sign of exceptional imperial favor which the soldier
is bound to "requite." While this may be appropriate
enough for a common soldier, it is difficult to avoid
feeling it is ironic coming from a man who had been
President of the Secretariat. Another possibility, in-
consistent with poetic convention but consistent with
Chang Yüeh's experiences, is that Chang is contrasting
his present situation with his previous post in the
capital, now understanding the depths of favor which he
once enjoyed. The third interpretation is dangerous and
not the sort of thing that is usually said in poetry, but
it is inescapable under the circumstances: Chang may be
being ironic, at worst sarcastic, saying that his present
post is hardly a sign of imperial favor. Most likely
Chang is juggling all three of these possibilities, though
the last one must be kept in the background.

The structure of this poem shows wide divergence from
the tripartite form. The abrupt shift in mood in the
second couplet is particularly uncharacteristic. Later
theorists of regulated verse felt that if a shift in mood
was to occur, the third couplet was the proper place for
it. The poet begins with a nonparallel descriptive couplet
setting the dreariness of the external scene outside; this
serves only to heighten the pleasure of the banquet within.
The phrase "a heart growing old" (ch'ih-mu shih 遲暮心),
literally "a heart approaching its sunset" with seasonal
associations, echoes the gloomy landscape outside and
supports the last two, negative interpretations of the
final couplet. The third couplet, introducing the military
theme, seems at first out of place, but as the last couplet
unfolds its ambiguities, we can see the third couplet as
the context which might make the poet genuinely appreciate
the frontier, the "depths of royal favor" which have sent

him here. This is a necessary context for such appreciation, just as the gloomy scene outside is a necessary
context for appreciating the banquet. Instead of a tripartite structure, this poem divides into two four-line
halves.

There is a striking simplicity in many of Chang Yüeh's
regulated verses. Part of this may be due to Chang's
difficulty with the parallel descriptive couplet, but it
may also reflect the influence of relatively plain style
of poets like Ch'en Tzu-ang.

IN THE SOUTH: PARTING FROM CHIANG CHIN
   ON HIS WAY TO CH'ING-CHOU

南 中 別 蔣 五 岑
向 青 州

My aging parents rest by northern seas,
Their poor son, cast off in this southern
   wilderness.
Tears there are, always mixed with blood,
Not a sound but comes from a broken heart.
In this place I meet an old friend,
To that land I send you off homeward.
I wish I were the leaves of the maple trees,
To follow you, crossing over Lo-yang.
                              [04642]

老 親 依 北 海
賤 子 棄 南 荒
有 淚 皆 成 血
無 聲 不 斷 腸
此 中 逢 故 友
彼 地 送 還 鄉
願 作 楓 林 葉
隨 君 度 洛 陽

The simplicity of the third couplet is so extreme that it
can only be conscious; it is hardly successful enough to
be called the "grand style," but it is aiming for just
such simple dignity. One might quote one of Wang Wei's
most famous parting couplets (06139) here as an example
of what Chang Yüeh was aiming for:

I urge you, sir, take one more cup of wine—
Once you go out Yang Pass, no more old
   friends.

勸 君 更 盡 一 杯 酒
西 去 陽 關 無 故 人

We have seen the wish to go north with the leaves in
Shen Ch'üan-ch'i's poem on his reprieve. It is impossible
to say which poem was written earlier, but Chang Yüeh's

poem consciously echoes the Chien-an and Wei closure "I
wish I were ..." as Shen's poem does not.

　　Many of Chang Yüeh's poems show the influence of the
fu-ku inclination to the style of Chien-an and Wei poetry
and the old yüeh-fu. The following opening passage (from
04535) very clearly evokes the yüeh-fu manner:

A single goose came flying above the snow,
It met me on the Heng-yang road;
In its beak it held words of separation,
Sent afar, a plant called "must-return."

一 雁 雲 上 飛
值 我 衡 陽 道
口 銜 離 別 字
遠 寄 當 歸 草

This narrative manner was closely associated with fu-ku
moralizing as in the following passages from another
poem (04536):

A lone goose came flying east,
Sending me silk letters, plain and striped.
.....
When the year is cold, all other trees change,
But the heart of pine and cypress stay ever
　firm.

孤 雁 東 飛 來
寄 我 紋 與 素

歲 寒 象 木 改
松 柏 心 常 在

The theme of the wild goose as a messenger was also used
by the poets of the sixth and seventh century, but more
typically they would treat the theme indirectly, saying,
for example, that they long for home and see a wild goose
in the sky, leaving it to the reader to make the connection. Chang Yüeh's direct, narrative treatment echoes
the old yüeh-fu, just as the closing evergreen metaphor
was the kind of emblematic allegory that T'ang poets
associated with the Chien-an and Wei.

　　Extended bird metaphors were used by Lo Pin-wang and
Ch'en Tzu-ang and had strong associations with fu-ku
primitivism. Chang Yueh "domesticates" them in informal
occasional regulated verses.

Chang Yüeh   395

THE FRONT POOL IN HSIANG-CHOU: PARTING
FROM THE TWO JUDGES HSÜ CHING-HSIEN
AND CHENG SHEN-LI

A few paces out on the water of the circular
    pool
A pair of wild geese fold their wings:
One flies to the top of a tall tree,
One returns to the edge of its former woods.
Pale waters hold the autumn scene within,
Its empty brilliance embraces the disk of night.
I have no way to detain those wings leaving me,
Over the cloudy seas their thoughts are at odds
    with mine.

[04633]

The descriptive third couplet of this poem is certainly
one of the best Chang Yüeh ever wrote, but in the context
of the poem it is completely incongruous and disrupts the
continuity of Chang's argument. Many of Chang's poems
have relatively complex arguments, and descriptive couplets are largely ornament in them. The "disk of night,"
the moon, is a kind of kenning that is characteristically
Early T'ang. Chang probably invented it himself for the
sake of rhyme.

Here and there among Chang Yüeh's poems we come across
informal occasional poems in the balanced and graceful
manner of Sung Chih-wen or Shen Ch'üan-ch'i. These are
exceptions to be rule, and I quote the following (04668)
to serve as a contrast to the preceding poems.

THE NORTH PAVILION AT HSIANG-CHOU

Few are my duties in the south pavilion,
Wind and mist, full in my northern garden.
Mountain flowers hide the roads and paths,
Pond water brushes the vines and hanging moss.
Pond lilies scatter as fish leap up,
Where the woods are secluded, a bird will
    suddenly sing.

Endless, this white-cloud mood of mine— 悠然白雲意
I follow my whim, passing by, lute in arm. 乘興抱琴過

This piece is a masterpiece of smooth competence. The
tripartite form is followed exactly, the middle couplets
are correct but uninspired parallelism, and the closing
response is entirely expected. The inversion in line
five, in which the pond water "brushes" the vines rather
than vice versa, is a characteristic device of courtly
wit. Chang is "performing" a style perfected by Sung
and Shen.

   Chang is at his best when he allows himself to complicate his closing couplets. Nowhere is this more apparent
than in the following heptasyllabic regulated verse (04704),
anthologized in the T'ang shih hsüan.

MOUNTAIN TEMPLE AT LAKE YUNG   灉湖山寺

In the stillness of deserted mountains
   forms a heart devoted to the Way,   空山寂歷道心生

While far away in the empty valleys
   the wild birds are singing.   虛谷迢遙野鳥聲

Always this meditation hut has brought appreciation of things beyond the world's dust,   禪室從來塵外賞

Nor are there any secular emotions
   to be found in this fragrant temple.   香臺豈是世中情

Among the clouds a thousand yards
   of eastern ridges emerge,   雲間東嶺千尋出

Within the trees the lake to the south
   is a whole sheet of light.   樹裏南湖一片明

If the hermits Ch'ao-fu and Hsü Yu
   had shared what I feel,   若便巢由知此意

Would they not have taken robes of vine
   in exchange for these hatpins and ribbons?   不將蘿薜易簪纓

Robes of vine stand for the eremitic life, just as the
hatpins and ribbons stand for the life of an official.
By the interpretation implied in the translation above,
the poet does not feel he yet possesses the courage to
give up office, a courage which would have been shown by

the ancient hermits Ch'ao-fu and Hsü Yu. Interpretation
of anything written depends largely on the expectations
of the readers; particularly in the case of Chinese
poetry, one makes sense of a poem by knowing what the
poet ought to be saying and construing the words accord-
ingly. The preceding translation and interpretation of
the last couplet are what most readers of poetry would
have expected Chang to say, and, indeed, many commentators
take the lines this way. However, if we read the lines
without those fixed expectations, we come up with exactly
the opposite interpretation:

If the hermits Ch'ao-fu and Hsü Yu had
    had shared what I feel,   若 便 巢 由 知 此 意.

They would not have taken the robes of vine
    in exchange for the hatpins and ribbons.   不 將 蘿 薜 易 簪 纓

or, retaining the question:

Would they not have taken their robes of vine
    and exchanged them for hatpins and ribbons?   不 將 蘿 薜 易 簪 纓

In the first of these alternatives Chang is saying that
since he, as an official, is so deeply affected by the
temple, there is no real need to become a hermit; had the
hermits of antiquity understood this, they would not have
needed to renounce public service. The last version of
the line is even more shocking and perverse: in public
service one may feel such scenes all the more deeply
because one longs for the hermit's life; had the ancient
hermits understood this, they would have willingly become
officials in order to more deeply appreciate such scenes.
Even though both of these interpretations are contrary
to the reader's thematic expectations, they do answer
the reader's generic expectations: the reader will know
that the closing couplet may contain a clever twist.
    Early T'ang poets were accustomed to ingenious descrip-
tion and witty metaphor but the range of responses was

fixed; the closest they came to manipulating the response element was in choosing a response cleverly contrary to what might be expected from the scene. Choosing a contrary response is different from inventing a new one, and this is exactly what Chang Yüeh has done in both secondary interpretations of the last line. A poet is supposed to look at a beautiful landscape and long to be a hermit; he is not supposed to say that an official appreciates the landscape even more because of his longing to escape into it. This sort of manipulation of the cognitive element of a poem is related to the growing psychological subtlety in T'ang poetry, which we saw earlier in Sung Chih-wen's quatrain on returning from exile. Although it develops out of the tradition of the witty closing, it uses the tradition of wit, the perversion of expectations, to achieve mastery over the conventions and to represent more completely the full range of human responses.

The regulated quatrain, the <u>chüeh-chü</u> 絕句, became increasingly popular during the eighth century. Chang Yüeh's collection contains over fifty quatrains, and Chang's success in this genre is not surprising if we consider that the quatrain may rely far more on an ingenious idea than on descriptive technique. Thus in the quatrain Chang can show his strengths and disguise his weaknesses. Perhaps the most famous of Chang's quatrains is "On the Roads of Shu" Setting a Date for Return" 蜀道後期 (04777):

The traveller's heart competes with sun and moon,　　　　客心爭日月
In his goings and comings, sets dates for his journeys beforehand.　　來往預期程
But the autumn wind will not wait for him　　　　秋風不相待
And will be first to reach the walls of Lo-yang.　　先至洛陽城

The "sun and moon" with which the traveller competes are
also "days and months." Although this poem is probably
from early in Chang's official career, it is characteristically High T'ang in its psychological subtlety, complexity of significance, and simplicity of diction. In
what sense does the poet compete with the sun and moon?
One implication is that he competes with them in regularity,
trying to set fixed dates for reaching his destination and
coming home (line two). But this level is undercut by an
inescapable feeling that the traveller is "racing" time,
trying to get his assignment done and return home as
swiftly as possible. The second line responds to the
first of these implications, that of regularity, while
the last two lines respond to the idea of a race with
time. Though the idea of a race contradicts that of
regularity, the two implications are united in the sense
of loss and failure in the last couplet. On the one
hand, the autumn wind speeds ahead of the regularity of
the days and months, and on the other hand, it is identified with them as Time which speeds past, defeating the
traveller's desire for an early return. The autumn wind
comes from the west, like the returning poet, but reaches
Lo-yang ahead of the poet, winning the "race."

Occasional poetry was the most common form of poetry
throughout the T'ang. Instead of abandoning it in favor
of nonoccasional poetry, the High T'ang poets raised the
occasional poem to a new level of significance. With
most such poems, beneath the complexities you find a
simple occasional message. Poems manage to exist simulta-
neously in the realm of literature and in the realm of
society, as a gesture of communication. Here, underneath
the "race with time," lies a poem which Chang might have
sent back to a friend in Lo-yang: the message is "I'll
be back sometime after the beginning of autumn; I'm trying
to keep a strict schedule."

The cleverness in the last line of the following quatrain

(04821) is even less obtrusive.

FOLLOWING THE RHYMES OF YIN MOU'S
"FLOATING ON LAKE TUNG-T'ING"

知尹從事懋汎洞庭

A continuous gaze over the level lake,
  stretching upward to the heavens,

平湖一望上連天

The autumn scene falls a thousand feet
  piercing the streams.

秋景千尋下洞泉

Then suddenly I am startled at
  how light fills the water,

忽驚水上光華滿

And it seems I'm riding my boat
  to the very edge of the sun.

疑是乘舟到日邊

Courtly wit had been a decoration; it was usually tacked
on to the end of a poem with little or no regard to its
function in the poem as a whole. Chang Yüeh shows a High
T'ang sense of poetic unity here: he builds the scene
carefully for his final image. In the first line he sets
up one of the most venerable of descriptive conventions,
that the waters of the lake seem to merge with the sky
on the horizon; in the second line he brings in the theme
of darkness as the autumn landscape casts a shadowy
reflection down into the lake. These shadows prepare for
the sudden illumination in line three. As the sunlight
suddenly fills the water, the boat ride on the gleaming
lake becomes a journey through the heavens to the edge
of the sun. The convention of the first line takes on
a new significance as the poet echoes the stories of boat
rides through heaven, so popular in court poetry. As
Chang transformed a simple message into a meditation on
time in the preceding quatrain, here he transforms a
simple ride on the lake into a transcendent experience.
Yin Mou's bland, courtly original (05138) belongs in a
different age.

    During the High T'ang there was also a revival of the
casual, spontaneous manner so successfully assumed in
the poetry of Wang Chi. With the exception of Wang Chi
this style had virtually been ignored in the seventh

century; however, some of the greatest High T'ang poets
(for example, Li Po, Wang Wei, and Meng Hao-jan) were
fascinated by it. The revival of this style went hand in
hand with a revival of the poetry of T'ao Chien. Although
we cannot date Chang Yüeh's poems in this style, he was
surely one of the earliest eighth-century poets to use it.

DRINKING ON A CLEAR NIGHT   清 夜 酌

In autumn's darkness a man feels many   秋 陰 士 多 感
    stirrings,
The rain lets up, no dust this night.   雨 息 夜 無 塵
A clear goblet, just right for the bright   清 樽 宜 明 月
    moon,
What's more, my most familiar friends.   復 有 平 生 人

                    [04770]

WRITTEN WHEN DRUNK   醉 中 作

I'm drunk—my joy is boundless,   醉 後 樂 無 極
So much better than when I'm not drunk.   彌 勝 未 醉 時
Every time I move my body, it's a dance,   動 容 皆 是 舞
Every time I speak I make a poem.   出 語 總 成 詩

                    [04771]

Drunkenness is an important component of the spontaneous
manner as it had been for T'ao Ch'ien and Wang Chi.
    Chang Yüeh's transition from an Early T'ang to a High
T'ang style can be seen in the following four quatrains,
written on New Year's during his various provincial exiles.
The first (04781) is from the 703-05 exile in Ch'in-chou.

NEW YEAR'S EVE AT CH'IN-CHOU   欽 州 守 歲

The old year will be gone this night,   故 歲 今 宵 盡
Tomorrow at dawn the new one comes.   新 年 明 旦 來
In sorrow my heart follows the Dipper's handle, 愁 心 隨 斗 柄
And I too hope for spring return to the   東 北 望 春 回
    northeast.

Like Tu Shen-yen's "On Crossing the River Hsiang," the
last couplet here is a piece of typical courtly cleverness
put to relatively serious purposes: the poet, like the
Dipper's handle, has turned south this winter, and if the
analogy holds, spring will carry him north again.   The
next two quatrains are from early in Hsüan-tsung's reign
when Chang Yüeh was Governor of Yüeh-chou.

NEW YEAR'S EVE AT YÜEH-CHOU: TWO POEMS

The night winds blow my drunken dance,
The yard gate faces my tipsy songs.
My sorrow diminishes with the passing year,
My joy increases greeting the new one.

[04782]

As in the preceding poem, Chang feels some personal correlation with an element of Nature, but in this case the
wit is underplayed and inobtrusive: his increasing joy
and drunkenness are superimposed on the change of the
year, and this augurs well for the future.   The second
poem reads:

Peach branches can ward off evil,
Blazing bamboo wake one swiftly from sleep.
Songs and dances to protract this evening,
As though one were sorry that last year is
    passing.

[04783]

The first lines refer to New Year's customs to ensure
good fortune.   The second couplet is an excellent example
of courtly wit grown mature and subtle.   Since he is in
exile in Yüeh-chou, Chang is not at all sad to see the
year pass, and he notes the incongruity between this
feeling and the night's revelry which suggests that he
wants the old year to stay, to "protract this evening."
The following poem (04784) on New Year's morning is dated

in some texts to Ch'ang's year in Yu-chou.

NEW YEAR'S MORNING   元朝

My joy this New Year's day   元 日 今 歲 樂
Yields nothing to last spring's.   不 謝 往 年 春
I do know the path my heart has always followed,   知 向 來 心 道
But who was that person I was last night?   誰 為 昨 夜 人

The third line of this poem contains a strong caesura
violation: it divides 1:2:2 rather than the proper 2:3.
Notice the enjambment of the first two lines, in contrast
to the strong line divisions in the first couplet of the
preceding two quatrains. There is a wry gentleness to
the second couplet which characterizes some of the best
High T'ang poetry. The poet feels that the joy which he
feels this New Year is as great as any the preceding
year; furthermore, he is aware of some inner identity,
some continuity in his life, the "path he has always
followed." Yet imagining himself the night before, Chang
feels he is a different person. But the ending is open;
we are left with questions. Is the poet commenting humor-
ously on his drunkenness the night before? Is he making
a serious statement about the continuousness of change in
human beings, that he is growing older? Is he saying
that like the year he is "renewed," or is he commenting
on some emotional change, either happier or more pensive,
which occurred over the course of the night? The surface
of the poem is clear but the deeper references are not.
     During his 703-05 exile and during his governorship
of Hsiang-chou, Yüeh-chou, and Yu-chou, Chang Yüeh wrote
many long poems combining landscape description and meditations on his experiences. Since these are quite similar
to the landscape poems of Shen Ch'üan-ch'i and Sung Chih-
wen, it is not necessary to discuss them in detail. Chang
wrote relatively few yung-wu, but one of them (04571) is
a delightful combination of Early T'ang playfulness and

the philosophical interests of poets like Ch'en Tzu-ang.

THE GOURD

詠瓢

Fine wine poured into a hanging gourd,
One pure, one natural—both shining brightly.
A snail's shell—its hanging head curls up;
A crane's neck—it sprouts a long handle.
Tasteful colors—the pale white and yellow;
An empty heart, making it light and strong.
Surely there are those who could decorate it,
But in respect left it in its natural state.

美 酒 酌 懸 瓢
真 淳 好 相 映
蝸 房 卷 墮 首
鶴 頸 抽 長 柄
雅 色 素 而 黃
虛 心 輕 且 勁
豈 無 雕 刻 者
貴 此 成 天 性

Chang has a number of <u>huai-ku</u> and one poem in the ruined capital tradition. This latter poem on Yeh, the former capital of the Three Kingdoms state of Wei, has an economy and sentimentality that separate it from the elaborate descriptive rhetoric of the earlier capital poems.

SONG OF YEH

鄴 都 引

Haven't you seen how

君 不 見

When Wu of Wei began his struggle for heaven's throne,

魏 武 革 創 爭 天 祿

Bands of heroes fought like dogs, galloped in pursuit?

羣 雄 睚 眦 相 馳 逐

By day he would lead his strong knights and smash phalanxes,

晝 攜 壯 士 破 堅 陣

By night he would invite poets to write of the splendid chambers.

夜 接 詞 人 賦 華 屋

His capital wound around the south side of West Mountain,

都 邑 繚 繞 西 山 陽

Mulberry, elms, stretching far off in floods by the River Chang's bends.

桑 榆 漫 漫 漳 河 曲

The city, its districts turned wastelands, men's generations changed,

城 郭 為 墟 人 代 改

Only the bright moon of the western garden endures.

但 有 西 園 明 月 在

By Yeh are the high mounds where lie many noble courtiers,

鄴 傍 高 冢 多 貴 臣

And the lovely brows, the darting glances— all dust and ashes.

娥 眉 曼 睩 共 灰 塵

Just climb Copperbird Terrace, to the
   palace of song and dancing,

There is only the autumn wind and
   unbearable sorrow.

試上銅臺歌舞處
唯有秋風愁殺人

[04583]

Copperbird Terrace, where Ts'ao Ts'ao (Wu of Wei) ordered
his palace ladies cloistered after his death, was a popular
yüeh-fu topic during this period, but in a pentasyllabic
meter rather than a heptasyllabic song like the poem above.
Chang's poem is relatively concise in contrast to the
lushly epideictic capital poems of the 670s. Like Li
Chiao's "Ballad of Fen-yin," of which Hsüan-tsung was so
fond, we have here the melancholy ubi sunt of the huai-ku
rather than the moralizing ending of the capital poems.
Because of Yeh's proximity to Lo-yang, this poem may have
been written during Empress Wu's reign, in which case it
probably reflects a royal preference for the heptasyllabic
song.

   In Chang Yüeh's poetry we begin to find large numbers
of poems on indefinite occasions; that is, poems whose
titles (and often whose texts) lack reference to specific
persons or places which fix them at a given historical
moment, for example, "Early Thunder and Spring Rain"
(04762). This reflects the increasing freedom from
generic convention in eighth-century poetry. Such poems
on indefinite occasions do appear here and there in earlier
poetry, particularly in the poetry of T'ao Ch'ien; however,
the vast majority of poems stay strictly within the subgeneric classifications. The tradition and conventions
of these subgenres served as limiting factors in the
treatment of a topic. To give an example—if a poet felt
melancholy hearing the rain, he had a wide variety of
subgeneric options: he could write an elegiac tsa-shih
雜詩, a k'u-yü fu 苦雨賦 ("Fu on Suffering from the
Rain," which often carried political implications), a
verse letter, a visiting poem on the place where he was

lodging, and so on. Writing a poem simply entitled
"Depressed at the Rain" was much less likely. When a
poet chose to write in one of the established subgenres,
he was committed to a certain kind of treatment which
might have very little to do with his original intention
in writing the poem. For example, if a poet chose to
confide his feelings in a verse epistle to a friend, he
had to put in a bit of biographical background and add a
few lines relating his mood and circumstances to the
addressee of the poem. This is what we mean when we say
that conventions controlled the poets rather than vice
versa.

   The gradual breakdown of the rigid subgeneric system
led to an individuality of treatment which contrasts
sharply to poems in the established subgenres. During
the second half of the seventh century such poems on
indefinite occasions (basically "personal poems") become
increasingly common; an excellent example is Wang Po's
"In the Mountains." In Chang Yüeh's poetry they comprise
some of his best and most original work.

HEARING BELLS BY NIGHT IN THE MOUNTAINS

Lying down by night I hear night's bells,
A night so still the mountains resound with them.
A frosty wind blows the cold moon,
Far and deep away it rises in the emptiness.
The first notes have been struck,
Then the later notes sweep flashing over.
I listen for them as though I could see them.
Try to pinpoint them—no fixed form.
Now truly I understand that ultimately we
   stand at the edge of Nothingness,
But futile fantasies of life and death
   linger in my mind.

[04568]

The sounds of a Buddhist temple bell were reminders of

the vacuity of existence. The strange indefiniteness of
these sounds as they are echoed in the mountains enforces
the lesson on the poet; the sounds are both there and not
there, possessing a peculiarly spectral existence which
represents the insubstantiality of human life. The
remarkable synaesthesia of the fourth couplet, by pretend-
ing to make the sounds visible, points up that insubstantiality.

One might compare the above poem with another famous
High T'ang visiting poem (06891), also on the sounds of
a temple bell. This piece is by Ch'ang Chien 常建 and
is curiously traditional and conservative in comparison
to Chang Yüeh's poem.

WRITTEN IN THE MEDITATION GARDEN AT THE 　　題破山寺後禪院
REAR OF BROKEN MOUNTAIN TEMPLE

On a clear morning I entered this ancient 　　清晨入古寺
  temple,
When first sunlight shone on the high forest. 　初日照高林
Twisting paths took me to hidden spots, 　　　曲逕通幽處
To a meditation hut deep in the flowering 　　禪房花木深
  trees.
Mountain light delights the nature of the 　　山光悅鳥性
  birds,
Reflections in a pool void men's hearts. 　　　潭影空人心
Here all Nature's sounds grow silent, 　　　　萬籟此都寂
And I hear only the notes of a temple bell. 　但餘鐘磬音

The theme of hearing music by night from an unseen
source was to become a stock theme in eighth- and ninth-
century poetry. Besides Chang Yüeh's poem on the temple
bell, another early example of this theme is by the
problematic figure Liu Hsi-yi.

HEARING A MOUTH ORGAN ON MOUNT SUNG 　　　嵩嶽聞笙

The moon emerges east of Sung Mountain, 　　月出嵩山東
As it brightens the mountains seem still more 　月明山益空
  deserted.

A mountain man, I love this cool scene,
Let my hair down and lie in the autumn wind.
When the wind stops, the river of stars is
   clear,
A solitary night when insects sing in the
   grasses.
I cannot see the immortal,
But in the moonlight I come nearer to his
   playing.
Crimson lips inhale the magic air,
Marble fingers tune the perfect sound.
What melody lies in this perfect sound?—
Hearts of phoenixes and cranes on magic
   mountains.
Long ago I fell into the common world,
I wish then I could have heard this song.
Now I rest on the peak of Mount Sung,
What good fortune to hear these secluded notes!
The gods and immortals are pleased with my
   actions,
And the song is engraved on my preordained
   heart.

山人愛清景
散髮臥秋風
風止夜河清
獨夜草蟲鳴
仙人不可見
乘月肩近笙
絳脣吸靈氣
玉指調真聲
真聲是何曲
三山鸞鶴情
昔去落塵俗
願言聞此曲
今來臥嵩岑
何幸聆幽者
神仙樂吾事
笙歌銘夙心

[04315]

Whoever started this theme, it caught the High T'ang's fancy and soon became a commonplace topic in its own right, picking up many of the conventions of poetry on music.

    Although the two following poems have the same title, they express entirely different sentiments. They are put together in Chang Yüeh's collected works, but are kept separate in Ch'üan T'ang shih.

HEARING THE RAIN

Winter's end, all flowers finish their cycles,
During long nights a hundred troubles gather.
A sheer fortress, immense above the river,
This deserted study, chill with the entering
   rain.

聞雨
窮冬萬花匝
永夜百憂攬
危戍臨江大
空齋入雨寒

Screeching gibbons know of frequent parting,
Crying geese sense the futile shot.
My heart faces the brazier's ashes dying,
My face follows the trees in the yard fading.
Yet I feel the favor once showed me unrequited,
And expend all my courage to look in the mirror.

[04763]

The intensity of emotion and sincerity of the poet's
distress are apparent in this exile poem. Though Chang
builds his scene out of fragments related only by mood
like an Early T'ang poem, he manages a certain develop-
mental unity as each fragment of the scene adds another
level to his unease, leading to the closing statement of
public failure, too old to serve the state properly and
fearful of seeing himself in the mirror. The tripartite
structure is clear though, as he does so often, Chang
complicates the closing. The normal subgeneric classification of this poem would be a shu-huai 述懷 "expressing
feelings"; however, at this period in the eighth century
a shu-huai would demand a rougher, more archaizing treatment of the poet's situation; the relative impersonality
of the first three couplets would have been out of place.
The indefinite occasion, "hearing the rain," allows Chang
to develop his poem in his own way.

The second poem under this title (04566) is quite
opposite in sentiment; throughout it echoes phrases and
ideas of T'ao Ch'ien's poetry. Although we cannot date
it with any certainty, it probably belongs to the T'ao
Ch'ien revival in the third decade of the eighth century.

HEARING THE RAIN   聞雨

Much rain severs me from worldly matters,
The gloomy silence leads into the Supreme
    Mystery.
Shadows on the city walls divide, unite,
Dipping from the eaves ceases, then continues.

I brood on how I have troubled Creation—
It has been some fifty years now.
Wrongly I set my heart in search of physical
   things,
But recently have managed to return to Nature.
I dwell in peace, grass and trees attend on me,
Ghosts and spirits take pity on my deserted
   rooms.
There are times when fine wines are brought in,
There are times when notes float from my clear
   lute.
Its sounds are pure, not known to this world,
My heart is drunk—how can I explain?

念 我 勞 造 化
從 來 五 十 年
誤 將 心 徇 物
近 得 還 自 然
閒 居 草 木 侍
虛 室 鬼 神 憐
有 時 進 美 酒
有 時 泛 清 絃
聲 真 不 世 識
心 醉 豈 言 詮

Wang Chi's imitation of T'ao Ch'ien was a general stylistic
and thematic imitation; he borrowed far fewer specific
phrases and themes than this poem. Wang Chi was, in fact,
imitating T'ao Ch'ien's whole life style, of which his
poetry formed only a part. Chang Yüeh's poem, on the
other hand, is truly a literary imitation. The fact that
we may therefore lend more credence to Wang Chi's poetry,
betrays a prejudice in identifying consistency with sincerity. Like most T'ang poets Chang Yüeh would use a
given response to answer a specific situation; it means
neither that the great minister of state was determined
to give it all up nor that the poem is simply an "exercise"
in the T'ao Ch'ien mode. Likewise, the T'ao Ch'ien revival
does not suggest that a wide spectrum of official-poets
were becoming disgusted with state service. Rather it
is an indication of the growing stylistic and thematic
scope of poetry, able to answer a greater variety of
human situations.

   The influence of Ch'en Tzu-ang began to make itself
felt in the first decades of the eighth century. Sung
Chih-wen, like other friends of Ch'en, turned immediately
to an archaizing style when addressing a poem to Ch'en
(03260). Chang Chiu-ling, Chang Yüeh's political protégé,

imitated the Kan-yü extensively. Chang Yüeh also wrote
a few poems in the style of the Kan-yü, and nowhere can
the voice of Ch'en Tzu-ang be heard more clearly than in
the following poem (04574).

UNCLASSIFIED POEM [last of four]   雜 詩 四 首 之 四

In silent brooding a host of doubts arise,   默 念 羣 疑 起
Then understanding the Mystery, all cares   玄 通 百 慮 清
  are cleared away.
My Original Mind is rid of male pleasures,   初 心 滅 陽 豔
And now I see the heart's brightness, clear   復 見 湛 虛 明
  and empty.
Aware of Extinction, my heart is not exhausted, 悟 滅 心 非 盡
Seeking Vacuity, I see a later life.   求 虛 見 後 生
I must now take the Law of Impermanence   應 將 無 住 法
And perfect myself to incomplete Fame.   修 到 不 成 名

This poem is every bit as obscure as the most of the
Kan-yü; however, the orientation is clearly Buddhist.
Since Buddhism was later considered to be incompatible
with fu-ku, it is strange to find Buddhist meditative
poems sitting side by side with the other characteristic
themes of fu-ku poetry.

UNCLASSIFIED POEM [first of four]   雜 詩 四 首 之 一

My heart always burns—incense within me;   把 薰 心 恆 焦
My heart flutters—a banner raised to the   舉 旆 心 恆 搖
  breeze.
Heaven is eternal, Earth endures,   天 長 地 自 久
But how many dawns can our pleasure last?   歡 樂 能 幾 朝
Just look to the trees of Western Mound—   君 看 西 陵 樹
Whom are the songs and dances charming now?   歌 舞 為 誰 嬌
                     [04572]

The closing lines refer to the Copperbird Terrace theme,
"Western Mound" being the tomb of Ts'ao Ts'ao. The ubi
sunt theme of the second couplet is characteristic of

late seventh- and early eighth-century <u>fu-ku</u> poetry,
while the bold metaphors of the first couplet look forward to the <u>fu-ku</u> poetry of a century later.

25

INTO THE HIGH T'ANG

Many poets continued to write in the mannered Early T'ang
style well into the High T'ang, and it is not surprising
that these poets usually belonged to the upper echelons
of officialdom and capital society. In the court of
the Prince of Ch'i 岐王 during the first decade of Hsüan-
tsung's reign, old poets from Chung-tsung's Hsiu-wen kuan
continued the old style unchanged and taught its lessons
in stylistic control to poets of the next generation like
the young Wang Wei. One such poet who wrote in both the
Early T'ang and High T'ang style was Chang Chiu-ling 張
九齡 (678-740), a protégé of Chang Yüeh and an important
political figure in his own right. Chang Chiu-ling's
career spans the transition between the Early T'ang and
High T'ang: he was a friend of Wang Wei and Meng Hao-jan
as well as of Sung Chih-wen and Shen Ch'üan-ch'i. The
bulk of his poetry was written between 720 and 740, so
he should properly be considered a High T'ang poet. Some
of his best poems are in the High T'ang style, but taken
as a whole his collection is markedly conservative.
    Chang Chiu-ling's output of court poetry was prodig-
ious, but it was even more strongly influenced by fu-ku
sentiments than was Chang Yüeh's court poetry: the imperial
theme, Confucian ethics, and historical exempla often
take the place of gracious comparisons of princes to
immortals, though the diction remains as formal as ever.
In addition to his formal, public poetry and a few pieces
of personal poetry in the High T'ang style, Chang Chiu-
ling also wrote fu-ku poetry, of which his imitations of
Ch'en Tzu-ang's Kan-yü are the most famous. Ch'en Tzu-
ang's highly individual style was becoming an accepted
subgeneric style, and fu-ku poetry was "domesticated."

The old distinction between the courtier-poet and the outsider was broken down. This in itself may be one of the clearest indications of the end of the Early T'ang: a great statesman and courtier can, when necessary, assume the antithetical role of the hermit.

Fu-ku poetry remained quite distinct from other High T'ang subgenres, most of which were more closely related to court poetry. To show this contrast, I will translate the fourth Kan-yü (02968), a bird allegory, and a more "modern," High T'ang treatment of a similar theme.

KAN-YÜ IV   感遇四

A lone goose comes over the sea,   孤鴻海上來
Dares not cast his glance on pond or pool.   池潢不敢顧
To one side he sees a kingfisher pair   側見雙翠鳥
Nesting in the triple pearl trees.   巢在三珠樹
Though they soar high to the tip of the   矯矯珍木巔
    precious bough,
Can they fail to fear the slinger's shot?   得無金丸懼
Fine adornment calls calamity, makes men   美服患人指
    point you out;
The great feel the weight of the gods' hatred. 高明逼神惡
Now I will wander through the dark reaches   今我遊冥冥
    of space,
How shall I be desired by the hunter?   弋者何所慕

This poem is traditionally interpreted as topical allegory: Chang is the lone goose, while the two kingfishers represent his political enemies Li Lin-fu and Niu Hsien-k'o, who forced Chang out of office.[1] While I would not deny the possibility of topical references, there are serious problems with this interpretation: as President of the Secretariat, Chang Chiu-ling had just been on the "pearl trees" himself, rather than coming in from over the sea; furthermore, it seems improbable that Chang would be warning his enemies of the perils of office since they had been the ones who had so recently taught him that

hard lesson. A pair of kingfishers whose beautiful adornments call down calamity comes directly from Ch'en Tzu-ang's
Kan-yü XXIII, so the fact that there are two of them was
to be expected and need not indicate topical allegory.
The poem seems rather to be general allegory, contrasting
the freedom of being out of office with the perils of
state service.

This somewhat stilted, archaizing treatment of the
theme was the legacy of the opposition poetics. The
development of the High T'ang style is often associated
with Ch'en Tzu-ang and fu-ku; in some ways fu-ku did aid
the growth of the T'ang style, and fu-ku poetry was an
important part of it. However, the following poem (03069)
is a characteristically High T'ang treatment of a similar
theme, and it is much more in the tradition of yung-wu
court poetry.

ON THE SWALLOWS

詠燕

Look to those tiny sea swallows
Which come so suddenly with the spring:
They know nothing of the vileness, the filth,
See only marble halls open to them.
Often they enter the broidered doors in pairs,
Circle splendid balustrades round and around
   each day.
Heedless, they compete with all things,
And when the hawks gather, worry not at all.

海燕何微眇
來春亦暫來
豈知泥滓賤
祇見玉堂開
繡戶時雙入
華軒日幾回
無心與物競
鷹隼莫相猜

There are several significant points of contrast between
the fu-ku allegory and the High T'ang yung-wu treatment.
First, "On the Swallows" follows basically the tripartite
form; the last couplet is the "open" closure, discussed
earlier, which seeks to stir a response in the reader
rather than stating a response on the part of the poet.
Kan-yü IV, on the other hand, is structured more like a
narrative and closes with an abrupt shift to the counter-

example of the goose. The yung-wu treatment is more
symbolic than allegorical: the swallows are treated as
real birds in a real scene, while the wild goose and
kingfishers are emblems in an emblematic setting. The
High T'ang style yung-wu betrays court poetry's preference
for indirection: moralizing is kept largely out of the
surface of the poem (except in the third line), and a
dramatic suspense is generated by the ominous last couplet.
In contrast, the Kan-yü's fourth couplet states the moral
plainly, and when the counterexample of the wild goose's
freedom is given, the poet does not fail to point out
what its significance is: the hunters will not chase it.
As far as "On the Swallows" has evolved from the courtly
yung-wu, its origins lie there rather than in the fu-ku
poetry of a Ch'en Tzu-ang.

High T'ang poetry is often called "popular." Although
"low" topics such as farmers, fishermen, woodcutters, and
soldiers were common, High T'ang poetry was not really
popular poetry in any proper sense of the term. It is
true that many of the greatest High T'ang poets did not
follow the usual ladder of bureaucratic success and spent
most of their lives out of service; however, the great
majority of poets were officials in the central government.
Furthermore, if a poet's works circulated and survived, it
was because he had the appreciation and support of officials in the capital. At the very lowest, such poetry
was appreciated and composed by singing girls who served
the official class or circulated in wineshops that catered
to them. There probably was a certain amount of interaction between official poetry and truly "popular" poetry,
a borrowing of themes and diction by both. However, it
was not "popular" in the sense that a Yangtze merchant
or Shensi peasant would go about their work singing the
poems of Wang Ch'ang-ling. If such an event occurred,
it was a phenomenon of sufficient rarity to merit comment
in one of the numerous anecdotal collections that circulated

during the T'ang.

Nevertheless, in comparison to the seventh century,
the High T'ang definitely saw a broadening of the social
base of poetry, shifting away from the great courtiers
and the select poetic entourage of the emperor to middle
and sometimes lower level officials. The High T'ang
style had its origins outside the court, in private poetry
and in poetry between friends of equal rank where the
strictures of courtly composition could be ignored. It
began with courtiers in exile, with poets whose position
was such that they would never be called upon to compose
at a court banquet, and with poets who had never served
until their works attracted the notice of patrons in the
capital.

The fact that such poets were not great officials
creates problems in tracing the origins of the High T'ang
style: for most of them we do not possess the kind of
precise biographical information that we have for important
political figures, and thus most of their works are un-
dateable. Many of the poets who were active in the transition period lived well into the High T'ang: for example,
Chang Hsü 張旭 was well known around 720, but it is impossible to tell whether his few surviving poems date from
that period or from several decades later.

Chang Hsü was one of a group of poets known as the
"Four Gentlemen from Wu" 吳中四士 , including Pao Jung
包融, Ho Chih-chang 賀知章 , and Chang Jo-hsü 張若虛.
One of Ho Chih-chang's poems has been quoted earlier as
an example of the High T'ang style, but it dates from
late in his life, probably in the 740s. Chang Hsü was a
calligrapher and well-known eccentric, much admired by
the famous poets of the following decades. The following
poem of his (05558), if not from the transition period,
is at least characteristic of the new High T'ang style.

THE STREAM OF PEACH BLOSSOMS   桃花谿

Shadowy, a bridge soars beyond the mist   隱隱飛橋隔野煙
  of the moors,

At the west edge of the stone jetty, ask   石磯西畔問漁船
  the fishing boat.

All the day long peach blossoms drift   桃花盡日隨流水
  with the current—

"Now where on this clear stream lies   洞在清谿何處邊
  that famous cave?"

The poem is based on T'ao Ch'ien's fable of Peach Blossom
Spring, in which a fisherman follows a trail of blossoms
upstream to a cave, in which he finds a utopian society
of simple peasants. Once the fisherman leaves the village,
he can never find it again.

   Many characteristics distinguish this poem from the
majority of Early T'ang poems. First, we might note the
nature of the occasion: it would not be at all uncharacteristic for a court poet, attending an imperial banquet
in a misty landscape, to suppose that he saw the signs of
Peach Blossom Spring appearing there. However, what would
have been for the court poet a gracious compliment, subordinate to the celebratory ends of the poem, is here the
organizing theme of the poem. Chang's closing is deliberately simple; he avoids wit but instead resolves the
situation by articulating the question at which the preceding lines had been hinting. Everything is uncertain:
forms seem to appear in the mist; an unknown speaker
either asks an unknown fisherman or of a fisherman; the
trail of peach blossoms in the water seems to be leading
somewhere. The title and the second and third lines hint
at Peach Blossom Spring without referring to it directly.
Even if the question cannot be answered—and the beauty
of the poem is that it cannot be—the reader is at least
given the question. The mythical world intrudes just
enough into this world that the reader can wonder about
its presence. The poem enacts the uncertainty of the

theme, a state between knowing and not knowing, between
being able to find one's way to the immortal world and
not being able to. Like Chang Hsü, Shen Ch'üan-ch'i
perceives the world of immortals appearing on earth, but
in the court poem the theme is merely stated: the illusion
is not integrated into the form and mood of the poem.

　　Wang Han 王翰, another poet of the transition period,
died in the later 720s. The following yüeh-fu, on the
border region of Liang-chou, makes a strong contrast
with the border yüeh-fu of the Early T'ang. The poem
(07557) dates from the 720s.

SONG OF LIANG-CHOU　　　　　　　　　　涼州詞

Fine wine of the grape, cup of phosphorescent　蒲萄美酒夜光杯
  jade,

Ready to drink, the p'i-p'a plays wildly on　欲飲琵琶馬上催
  horseback.

And if I lie drunk in this desert, sir,　　醉臥沙場君莫笑
  don't you laugh at me!—

Since ancient days men have marched into　古來征戰幾人回
  battle, and how many have returned?

The exotic grape wine of the northwestern frontiers and
the barbarian p'i-p'a are modal elements of frontier
poetry. More often than in Early T'ang frontier poetry,
the troops of High T'ang poems feel the influence of
Central Asian civilization, here in a wild drinking bout
while p'i-p'a music is played on horseback. But what
really separates this poem from an Early T'ang border
poem is the energy, the wildly unconventional behavior
which incarnates the combination of desperation and
carefreeness of the soldiers on campaign. The emotions
are not stated directly, but are rather implied in the
actions. Given form in actions, the emotions of the
soldiers can become more complex and contradictory than
any limiting statement of emotion. Midway, the poem
switches to the imperative: it addresses a "you" ("sir"),

who is partially identified with the reader. The third-
person distance which we have seen in many Early T'ang
border poems disappears, and a new kind of relationship
is created between the reader and the persona of the
poem, who speaks to the reader half-jokingly, half-
violently. The situation is both laughable and deadly
serious. Like Chang Hsü's poem, "Song of Liang-chou"
acts out a situation, and the highly conventional closing
line ceases to be merely a poetic cliché, but becomes
instead a simple truth.

At least two of the major High T'ang poets were beginning to achieve recognition during this transition period:
Meng Hao-jan 孟浩然, the eldest of the major poets, and
Wang Wei 王維, a precocious favorite of the aristocrats
in Ch'ang-an. The following heptasyllabic "old style"
poem (07659) by Meng Hao-jan may be from the transition
period.

SONG: RETURNING BY NIGHT TO LU-MEN   夜歸鹿門山歌
    MOUNTAIN

The bell rings at the mountain temple,   山寺鐘鳴晝已昏
    daylight turns to dusk,

At the ford by Fishbridge Isle,   漁梁渡頭爭渡喧
    the clamor of the ferry.

A man follows the sandy shore   人隨沙岸向江村
    to a village by the river,

I too get in my boat to return   余亦乘舟歸鹿門
    to Lu-men Mountain.

The moon over Lu-men shines,   鹿門月照開煙樹
    revealing trees in the mist,

And at once I'm where P'ang-kung   忽到龐公棲隱處
    lived as a recluse long ago.

My gate on the cliff, my path through   巖扉松徑長寂寥
    the pines, deserted forever—

Only the man who lives apart   惟有幽人夜來去
    comes and goes as he wills.

The theme and the relaxed manner of Meng Hao-jan's poetry
appealed to the busy officials in the capital in the 720s.

At this time there was a revival of interest in the poetry
of T'ao Ch'ien, and while Meng Hao-jan's style is peculiarly his own, he shares a casual simplicity with the
style of T'ao Ch'ien.

Since this poem is technically "old style," parallelism
is not mandatory in the middle couplets; however the third
and fifth lines of Meng's poem are just the sort of descriptive lines which would make the reader expect a parallel matching line. In both cases Meng refuses to give
the reader what he expects. Although elsewhere in his
poetry Meng Hao-jan is perfectly capable of writing
parallel couplets, in this poem he is gently unlearning
the artifice of court poetry, passing by opportunities
to display poetic craft. The theme is the coincidence
of freedom and what is natural; an "evening return" is
natural, shared with other persons and nature, yet in
following this natural law, the poet manifests his freedom,
his ability to come and go as he pleases. In refusing to
bow to the artifice of the courtly style, Meng acts out
that freedom in the form of the poem: the poet writes
"as he wills."

In many ways the poem above represents the negative
use of the Early T'ang style. Other poets chose to
transform it, accepting its conventions and its technical
artifice, but giving them depth and handling the artifice
so that it sounds natural. The following poem by Wang
Wei (05982), from the early 720s, shows the High T'ang
style in its full naturity.

WRITTEN ON THE WALL-TOWER OF HO-PEI   登河北城樓作

A hamlet atop Fu's cliff,   井邑傅巖上

A pavilion for travellers in the clouds   客亭雲霧間
  and mist.

From high on this wall I gaze on the   高城眺落日
  setting sun,

And the far shore reflects the blue mountains.   極浦映蒼山

A fire by the bank, a lone boat spending the
    night,
Fishermen's homes, evening birds return.
In empty stillness Heaven and Earth turn
    evening,
My heart is as calm as the broad stream.

岸火孤舟宿
漁家夕鳥還
寂寥天地暮
心與廣川閒

Wang Wei is writing a meditative poem which is, until the
last couplet, purely descriptive. Ch'en Tzu-ang, Sung
Chih-wen, Shen Ch'üan-ch'i, and Tu Shen-yen encountered
marvellous landscapes and drew conclusions from what they
saw: they interpreted, sighed, or vowed to change their
lives. As Wang Wei views the landscape from the top of
the wall, he is already "as calm as the broad stream."
His eye passes impersonally from one scene to the next,
including the scene of his own landscape-viewing.

The opening presents two "items" in the poet's field
of vision, first a village on a cliff associated with
the famous Fu Yüeh (see p. 302), followed by a solitary
pavilion in the mists. The parallelism here is not merely
artifice: it is rather a full use of the technique in
which two entities define one another by their relationship. Associations of society and state service in the
first line are set in parallel with a scene suggesting
solitary travels, Wang Wei's own situation at the time.
Parallelism creates meaning by providing two mutually
defining contexts; imagine that the pavilion was placed
in parallel with a journey alone by night: in that case
the juxtaposition would make the pavilion suggest something altogether different—lodging, security, evidence
of human presence. The two "items" of this couplet are
in the opening position of the tripartite form, which
should define the poet's situation in the most general
terms. As fragments of the scene in the impersonal
surface of the poem, these lines are not the expected
general opening; however, in the associations created by
their juxtaposition, they do indeed define the poet's

main concerns, whose dichotomy the heart, "as calm as the
broad stream," overcomes.

In the second couplet the act of viewing is placed in
parallel with the reflection of the mountains, not only
associating the poet's vision with the passivity of the
reflecting surface of the river, but also objectifying
it by placing it in the descriptive middle couplets of
the tripartite form. The third, beautifully parallel
couplet brings all things home, to stability and security—
to shore, to their roosts. Everything is quiescent and
stable but the poet, who possesses a different kind of
quiescence and stability, "still," but drifting on tran-
quilly like the great river. All the little things, the
"items" of vision, are gone and the poet is left alone
with the mighty elements of the universe—Heaven, Earth,
the great river that flows on and on, and his impersonal
heart/consciousness in the growing darkness.

This is great poetry, and the tradition of court poetry
provided Wang Wei with most of the inert elements of this
poem: the tripartite form, the craft of parallelism, the
rich associations of many of the images. But it also
provided something of equal value, something which is
absent in most poetry before the age of court poetry: it
gave the poet control, a sense of distance from his art
which allowed him to see it as art. Only with this distance could a poet avoid simply stating his message and
learn to enact in the poem the truth he wanted to convey.

APPENDIX 1

A "GRAMMAR" OF COURT POETRY

The conventions, norms, and rules of decorum of court poetry constitute a narrow semiotic system, whose violable laws were to make up
the basic "language" of High T'ang poetry. Throughout this book we
have been treating court poetry as a "language" (langue) which we
have been trying to reconstruct from its multiple "utterances"
(paroles), the individual poems. In reading poetry we must understand the "language," not only the broad language which it shares
with other forms of speaking and writing, but also its structural
language.

Most Chinese poems of this period have four parts: a title and
the tripartite form. The title is of great importance because it
signals to the reader the relevant dialect, the subgenre. The title
sets up certain expectations in the reader which will either be
satisfied or frustrated in an interesting way. Those expectations
are as much a part of what is said as the actual text of the poem:
Wang Po's famous refusal to weep at the end of a parting poem signifies
fully only when the reader knows that one is supposed to weep at the
end of a parting poem.

Most systems of order are built upon linguistic analogues. The
tripartite form is itself constructed on the model of a Chinese
sentence--a topic and a comment which together form the topic of a
second comment. As in the Chinese sentence, the logical relationship
of the comment to the topic is usually implied rather than stated.
Also as in the Chinese sentence, there is a great deal of latitude in
how open and how precise that relationship is: some poems have a
clear, implicit argument, while other poems demand that the reader
make great effort to relate the various parts.

In the macrolinguistic aspect of poetic structure, the topic-
comment construction is essentially backward-looking. Almost every
couplet is a small closure of the poem, looking back to what was
said before. Along with the fact that most lines are complete

425

predicates, this feature makes many poems static. Here we can begin
to see the necessity of external structural principles like the
tripartite form: without such a priori expectations, there would be
no sense of being "in the middle" or "at the end of" a poem; that
is, the possibility of the reader structuring a poetic argument is
only realized through the tripartite form.

The second effect of the topic-comment model is that the topic
is contingent, of less significance itself than the comment. The
topic is always subject to radical revaluation in the comment; it
is not, as in much Western poetry, a necessary cause that precedes
an effect. The reader of this book may have noticed a tendency of
many poems to reverse themselves at the end or to make seemingly
incongruous statements in the middle which can be related to what
went before but which do not follow from it. On an even larger
scale, this principle appears in some ninth-century poem sequences
in which almost every poem contradicts, revaluates, the preceding
poem.

The tripartite form is a positional grammar in which we expect
certain kinds of comments to occur at fixed positions in the poem.
In the middle couplets the reader expects to be told some specifics
as a comment on the general, opening topic; at the end the reader
expects an "I-comment" on the poem as a whole. Variations on this
structural grammar of a court poem are like the rhetorical trope of
positional inversion in a poetic sentence. As in ordinary grammar
there is a law of positional primacy, creating an interesting tension
between the demands of a positional syntax and usual word class. In
poetic diction we have the common courtly variation 見花紅 "to see
the red of the flowers" instead of 見紅花 "to see the red flowers."

Positional primacy also applies in the tripartite structure. The
reader expects an "I-comment" in the final position of a poem; therefore he will personalize even an objective closing and read it
differently than he would read the same line in the middle of a
poem. We might try reading the beautiful closing of Wang Po's
"Parting by Moonlight in a River Pavilion" II—"Mountains and rivers
cold this night"—as though it were in the middle of an eight-line
poem; what is hauntingly effective at the end is quite ordinary in

the middle. The reason for this curious phenomenon is that at the
end the line is supposed to sum up the poet's intense, emotional
response to parting: we sense that the emotion is projected onto the
scene, that the chill is too powerful to express directly. In the
middle of a poem, the cold is simply cold, carrying only faint
suggestion of the loneliness of parting. Likewise, an I-comment
transposed into the middle of the poem is deprived of much of its
impact.

Parallelism is the antithetical principle to the topic-comment
construction: instead of "about X we may say Y," parallelism sets
up the pattern "X exists somehow in relation to Y; Y exists in
relation to X." Unlike the topic-comment construction, neither is
subordinate to the other. The relationship between the two halves
of the topic-comment construction may be open, but it is still
propositional (it seeks a single resolution); the relationship
between parallel lines is usually nonpropositional and therefore
complex in the extreme. However, both the topic-comment construction
and parallelism tend to close poems and parts of poems off, so that
poems tend to become closed units, vivified by internal tensions.

In making a parallel the poet selects from a very limited range
of choices. Such limitation of choice is necessary: the possibilities
of implied relationships in a parallel couplet are so open that there
must be immediately some common term to keep the juxtaposition intelligible. One may not put Heaven in parallel with "ear."

The syntagmatic (structural, syntactical) and the paradigmatic
(topical, lexical) rules of poetry all served the single purpose of
limiting the choices available to the poet. Earlier in the text we
suggested that one social motive for such limitation was the facility
of composition—making poetry a "learnable art." A second reason is
that the new aesthetics bases on the dynamics of relationships within
the poem raised an inherent multitude of possibilities which demanded
a compensating reduction of the possibilities of the langue. The
interest and focus of a poem is primarily on the parole, on how one
part may relate to another. The familiar structuralist chess analogy
applies here with particular force: an inexhaustible number of games
are possible, and interest never wanes, but to make the game possible

fixed, arbitrary rules are necessary, setting the space, the players,
the possible moves. Furthermore, there is a tendency to limit the
performance even further, to invent new quasi-rules, such as chess
openings or the habits of court poetry; for example, putting Heaven
and Earth, land and water, in parallel or juxtaposing wine and song
in the third couplet of a parting poem.

   Poetry is not chess, and the gamelike aspect of court poetry
succumbed to two pressures. First, a game is an end in itself, but
language is referential; it is contingent on something it talks
about. The more court poetry tended toward game, the more inadequate
it appeared as a sign system in comparison to language as a whole.
Second, unlike chess or most games in which the rules are fixed,
court poetry continued to invent more and more rules until the
possibilities of the form were almost exhausted. The result was
the expansion of the langue during the second half of the seventh
century and the first decades of the eithth, subverting the limiting
rules and breaking them down. By the mid-eighth century there is a
balance of interests between the "language" and the "utterance" in
a poem.

APPENDIX 2

TONAL PATTERNS

The development of the tone patterns of regulated verse has always
been a primary subject of interest in the study of Early T'ang poetry.
In the present book I have virtually ignored the problem for several
reasons: first, in the Early T'ang we are not dealing with clearly
defined genres, but rather with flexible rules of tonal propriety
which ultimately evolved into genres; second, there have been several
excellent studies of tonal patterns in the final fixed form; and,
third, the tones are only one aspect of the "new style" which ultimately became regulated verse. In the following comments I am not
trying to make any definitive statements on the development of
pentasyllabic regulated verse, but simply suggesting the way it may
have evolved. I confine my discussion to pentasyllabic regulated
verse because that is the most common and influential of the "new
style" forms.[1]

The renowned complexity of pentasyllabic regulated verse is
deceptive. Tonal violations in the first and third positions in
the line are common and will often require compensating violations
in the following line, but since the pattern tones for the first
and third positions are only habits rather than rules, I will ignore
them. The regulated verse thus comes down to three basic tonal rules:

1. The nonrhyme lines must end with deflected tones: the rhyme
   lines must end with level tones.
2. The basis of tonal alternation is the couplet of which there
   are two forms: the "A form" couplet in which the second and
   fourth line positions are - / , / - ; and the "B form" couplet
   which is / - , - / .
3. The A and B forms of the couplet must alternate.

If there is one proposition I might argue for it is that the tonally
balanced couplet is the primary unit of all regulated forms. This

429

is true of the fixed genres, but it is even more true developmentally.

In studying the use of tones in Early T'ang poetry or in any later
poetry, it is of crucial importance not to use anthologies or individual collections reconstituted from anthologies. Particularly in
anthologies from the thirteenth century onward, tonal correctness
is a criterion of choice. For example, of Wang Chi's four eight-line
pentasyllabic poems (02612-02615), the poem chosen by the T'ang shih
hsüan (02612) is tonally correct; two of the others are not, yet
they are "regulated" in the Early T'ang sense, as we shall see
shortly.

I have examined the thirty poems listed specifically as lü-shih
in the Sung collection of Wang Po's works (SPTK). The Wang Po
collection survived independently of the anthologies (Tu Shen-yen's
collection, for example, was reconstituted in the Sung), so we know
that someone in the T'ang or Early Sung considered these thirty
poems to be regulated verse, lü-shih. The proportions I get below
have been confirmed by random samplings of other poets before Sung
Chih-wen and Shen Ch'üan-ch'i.

What we find is that while the first two rules of regulated verse
given above are followed fairly consistently, the third rule—that
the two couplet forms must alternate—is only a tendency. Futher-
more, we find that every failure to alternate is with A form couplets;
never do you find two B form couplets in succession.

Of the thirty poems ten always alternate. Poems opening with B
form couplets form the slight majority: 03446 (A); 03449 (B); 03450
(B); 03451 (B); 03456 (B); 03466 (B); 03469 (B); 03772 (A); 03773 (A);
03774 (A). Of these three have a strong tonal violations in the
seventh line, which is a line that permits such: 03456, 03773, 03774.

Fourteen poems of the thirty fail to alternate couplet forms once.
Only one of these, 03455, opens with a B form couplet and therefore
fails to alternate after the second couplet (BAAB). Of the form
AABA: 03447, 03452, 03458, 03459, 03461, 03471. Of the form ABAA:
03448, 03453, 03454, 03457, 03463, 03464, 03475. A strong tonal
violation in the first couplet is found in 03464.

Three poems fail to alternate twice and all have the form BAAA:
03460, 03465, 03467. One poem does not alternate at all (AAAA) but

contains a strong tonal violation in the first line: 03468. Two of
the poems do not follow the tonal rules for couplets in at least
one couplet: 03462, 03470.

Other seventh-century "regulated" verses have roughly the same
proportions, AABA and ABAA forming a slight majority over the consistently alternating forms. For example, in the Wang Chi poems
omitted by the T'ang shih hsüan, one (02614) is a perfect ABAB, but
it is also a dull poem. The two which fail to alternate are 02613
(AABA) and 02615 (ABAA); both are among Wang Chi's best works.

The predominance of alternating poems and poems which fail to
alternate only once tell us that alternation was a strong tendency
if not a rule. By the early eighth century and the poems of Sung
Chih-wen and Shen Ch'üan-ch'i, alternation occurs consistently, and
we have "regulated verses" in the pure sense.

NOTES ON BIBLIOGRAPHY, DATING, AND THE SELECTIVITY OF SOURCES

I must apologize for the lack of a true bibliography in this volume, but such a task is best left to a more competent bibliographer than myself. There is not an extensive literature on Early T'ang poetry. I have found that those secondary sources which deal to some degree with critical and literary historical problems are either so general as to be useless for my purposes here or treat problems of a different sort than those with which this volume is concerned. I have found that the most useful secondary sources are those which deal with the problems of biography and the chronology of works: this historical framework is the backbone that makes literary history possible. In parts two and three such secondary, historical studies have been of great importance. For "The Four Talents of the Early T'ang," the most useful work has been Liu K'ai-yang 劉開揚, "Lun Ch'u-T'ang ssu-chieh chi ch'i shih" 論初唐四傑及其詩, T'ang-shih lun-wen chi 唐詩論文集 (Shanghai: Chung-hua, 1961), pp. 1-28. For Ch'en Tzu-ang, two studies have been of great use: first, Wang Yün-hsi 王運熙, "Ch'en Tzu-ang ho t'a-te tso-p'in" 陳子昂及其作品, T'ang-shih yen-chiu lun-wen chi III 唐詩研究論文集三, Chung-kuo yü-wen hsüeh-she (1970), pp. 1-30; and second, Suzuki Shūji 鈴木修次, "Ron Chin Sugō" 論陳子昂, Tōdai shijin ron 唐代詩人論 (Tokyo: Ōtori, 1973), vol. II, pp. 47-74. In the same volume, pp. 1-46, Suzuki Shūji also has a fine essay that tries to isolate some features of Early T'ang poetic rhetoric in heptasyllabic songs. In other cases, except where cited in notes, I have relied on primary sources and devised my own rough chronology of works from them.

There remains the serious problem of the selectivity of sources for poems. For the Early T'ang we have relatively few collections of poetry intact: the collections of "The Four Talents," Ch'en Tzu-ang, and Chang Yüeh are surely intact; the collections of Wang Chi, T'ai-tsung, Li Chiao, Sung Chih-wen, and Shen Ch'üan-ch'i either probably

intact or largely so. For other poets we must depend on anthologies
or on collections reconstructed from anthologies (for example, the
collection of Tu Shen-yen). The large number of court poems from the
period is primarily due to their inclusion in the Wen-yüan ying-hua
and to a lesser degree in the T'ang-shih chi-shih (probably from the
Wen-yüan ying-hua.) The danger is that we get a distorted view of
the period because the WYYH compilers may have overrepresented court
poetry, either because of its imperial aura or because they felt that
court composition was the most significant kind of composition during
the age. Of these two possibilities, the second seems the more likely:
the "imperial aura" did not provoke the WYYH compilers to preserve
many court compositions of later reigns.

It would seem we could look to those collections which are intact
to get a clearer notion of the approximate generic and subgeneric distribution of poems in the age, but we should note that most of the
complete collections are in one way or another anomalous: Wang Chi
was never really "in court" (though he did serve in the central
government), and T'ai-tsung was almost never out of it. Ch'en Tzu-ang
and "The Four Talents" (with the exception of Yang Chiung) owe their
preservation largely to the interest of later ages, and that interest
was in turn due to the fact that they had complex, private poetry
outside the context of the court Too much of Chang Yüeh's poetry
falls in the K'ai-yüan reign to be of great use, and the majority of
the datable poems of Li Chiao, Sung Chih-wen, and Shen Ch'üan-ch'i
are late, from the early eighth century (which casts doubt on their
completeness). Furthermore, the survival of Sung's and Shen's exile
poetry involves the same difficulties in regard to later preference
for private poetry that we find in the collections of Ch'en Tzu-ang
and "The Four Talents". Li Chiao's collection, if we exclude the
separate collection of yung-wu poems, is about half court composition;
but even there we have doubts about its completeness considering the
Hsin T'ang shu bibliography notice of a collection originally in
fifty chüan. There are other factors that make a clear picture of
the distribution of poetic composition complex; for example, there
is the real possibility that in the Early T'ang, when poets were
preparing their own collections or those of their predecessors, they

<u>themselves</u> tended to overrepresent court composition. In short, the
problem is so complex and the number of unknown, but potentially
determinate factors so great that the issue cannot be resolved in the
realm of literary sociology. No doubt there were a large number of
private and informal occasional poems which do not survive, but we
also know from the survival of single poems from series that a large
number of court and formal occasional compositions have been lost.

Ultimately, the issue of distribution, however interesting in its
own right, is not crucial to the question of the primacy of court
poetry and the courtly style. Since we have seen the close relationship between private poetry and court poetry time and again in this
volume, the question is whether private poetry and informal occasional
poetry grew out of the courtly style or whether the court poem itself
is an elaboration and ornamentation of less formal compositional
conventions practiced elsewhere. A number of factors suggest that
the former is the more accurate possibility. First, the conventions
of composition which inform both formal and informal poetry belonged
to capital society: outsiders like the young Ch'en Tzu-ang did not
follow them. Second, in the Early T'ang we do not find the same
value placed on the poet as an artist that we find in the High T'ang
and afterward: with the exception of figures like Wang Chi, court
service is the dominant social goal. The idea of "being a great
poet," which we find in the self-image of later poets like Li Po and
the image others had of them, is not well developed in the Early
T'ang. If poetry is largely subordinate to social goals of court
preferment, then the courtly style will be primary. Third, the
rules of composition were generated by social exigencies which would
be keener on court and formal occasions than on solitary or informal
occasions. Thus the extent to which private poetry unconsciously
follows those rules or uses them as a basis for personal variation
reveals the extent to which court and formal composition are the
norm of poetry. Fourth, the fact that most poets would choose
contemporary norms in private composition rather than earlier, more
appropriate models of private poetry shows that poets had not yet
become as "bookish" as they were to become in later poetry. To a
Ch'ing poet, "poetry" is a vast array of written texts and past

styles; to an Early T'ang poet, "poetry" is primary a social practice. In this book we have dealt at length with notable exceptions like Ch'en Tzu-ang, but the norm is Sung Chih-wen, who in the private poetry of his exile varies the courtly norms but bases his work upon them.

NOTES

Introduction

1   See Cheng Hsi-hsien, Analyse formelle de l'oeuvre poetique d'un
    auteur des T'ang: Zhang Rou-xu (Paris: Mouton & Co., 1970), pp.
    12-13.

Part One

1   Ch'üan Liang shih, 11.12b.
2   Liang shu, 25.3b. The Liang History, which praises Hsü Mien for
    his rectitude and learning, uses this anecdote in a positive
    Confucian sense, to show Hsü's wu-ssu 無私, "lack of favoritism."
3   Ch'üan Sui wen, 20.9a.
4   The term court poetry properly describes the occasional circum-
    stances of a poem's composition; here we are using the term loosely
    to denote a period style, that of the late fifth, sixth, and
    seventh centuries when the court was the center of poetic activity
    in China. A substantial proportion of the surviving poetic corpus
    was written either for the court or in the distinctive courtly
    style that evolved. "Court poetry" is to be clearly distinguished
    from "palace poetry," kung-t'i shih.
5   Chin-lou-tzu (Taipei: Shih-chieh, 1957), 4.13a.
6   Ch'üan Sui wen, 20.9a.
7   For a fuller treatment of the formal and thematic conventions of
    the court poetry, see pp. 234-73.
8   Wen-hsin tiao-lung (Hong Kong: Commercial, 1960), p. 726.
9   Ch'üan Liang wen, 53.15b-16b.
10 Ch'üan Ch'en wen, 10.9b.
11 Sui shu, 76.2a.
12 Ch'üan Sui wen, 20.8b-9a.
13 Ch'üan Sui shih, 2.2a.
14 Ibid., 2.3b.
15 Shi shu, 15.12b.
16 I am indebted to Arthur Wright for this observation on Yang-ti's
    relations with his father.

17 Ch'üan Sui shih, 1.1a-b.

18 Ch'üan Ch'en shih, 1.4b-5a. Emending 暢 to 殤 in line eight.

19 Ch'üan Sui shih, 1.2a-b.

20 Ibid., 1.2a.

21 Yüeh-fu shih-chi (SPTK), 47.1a.

22 Li P'an-lung 李攀龍 (1514-70) began his famous anthology of
    T'ang poetry, T'ang shih hsüan 唐詩選 , with "Expressing My
    Feelings." The Ch'ing critic Shen Te-ch'ien 沈德潛 (1673-1769)
    claimed that the High T'ang style had its origins in this poem.

23 Ogawa Tamaki, Tōshi Gaisetsu (Tokyo: Iwanami, 1958), pp. 30-31.

24 Wen I-to, "T'ang-shih tsa-lun" in Wen I-to ch'üan-chi (Hong Kong:
    Yüan-tung, 1968), vol. III, p. 8.

25 Ch'üan Liang shih, 12.6a-7a.

26 See Yen Yen-chih's 顏延之 (384-456) comments cited in Li
    Shan's commentary to the Wen-hsüan, c. 23.

27 See Chiang Yen's 江淹 (444-505) "Imitations" of poets of that
    period, WH, 31.

28 T'ang-shih chi-shih (SPTK), 4.9b.

29 Sui shu, 76.1a-b.

30 Ibid., 76.2b.

31 Chiu T'ang shu, 102.8b.

32 T'ang-shih chi-shih (SPTK), 1.7b.

33 Hsü Chien et al., ed., Ch'u-hsüeh chi (Peking: Chung-hua, 1962),
    p. 748. I use the Ch'u-hsüeh chi rather than the earlier Yi-wen
    lei-chü because the Ch'u-hsüeh chi contains "anecdotal parallels."

34 Ibid.

35 Ibid., p. 749.

36 Ibid.

37 Ibid.

38 Some difficult theoretical problems are involved here because
    modern western critics tend to see a poet's literary experience,
    what he has read, as necessarily the sole or dominant factor in
    poetic creation. Without getting into a theoretical argument, I
    should explain that Chinese theorists of the shih played down the
    element of fictionality in poetry: the poem was supposed to be
    primarily a record of a real experience with the real world. It

is against this concept of poetry that we may contrast the
literary of court poetry, which often could make no preten-
sions to the "sincerity" of personal experience.

39 Ch'üan Liang shih, 3.5b.

40 Ch'üan Pei-Chou shih, 2.8b-9a.

41 Ch'üan T'ang shih (Peking: Chung-hua, 1960), p. 20.

42 T'ang-shih chi-shih (SPTK), 1.2b.

43 WH, 11.

44 Ch'üan Sui wen, 9.1a.

45 See Ch'üan T'ang wen, c.131, p. 1661; c.133, p. 1683.

46 Ch'üan T'ang shih, p. 487.

47 Chiu T'ang shu, 105.18b.

48 Shang-kuan Yi is credited with these in the Shih-yüan lei-ko
    詩苑類格 , which is in turn quoted in Wei Ch'ing-chih's
    魏慶之 Shih-jen yü-hsieh 詩人玉屑 (Taipei: Shih-chich, 1966),
    pp. 165-66.

49 Ch'üan T'ang shih-yi in Ch'üan T'ang shih, pp. 10, 174.

50 Both Wen I-to and Ogawa Tamaki believe this is a fragment. See
    Wen I-to, T'ang-shih ta-hsi in Wen I-to ch'üan-chi, vol. IV, p.
    164; Ogawa Tamaki, Tōshi Gaisetsu, p. 32.

Part Two

1 Yang Ying-ch'uan chi (SPTK), 3.3a-b.

2 Lo Pin-wang wen-chi (SPTK), preface.

3 Liu K'ai-yang, T'ang-shih lun-wen chi (Shanghai: Chung-hua, 1961),
   pp. 2-6.

4 See the "Preface to the Collection of the Duke of Nan-yang," Yu-
   yu-tzu chi (SPTK), 6.3a-6a.

5 Since Lu was never in the Imperial Library, the "Orchid Office,"
   I have taken the variant title.

6 WH, 21.

7 Compare the more delicate, sixth-century versions of the ballad
   in WYYH, 200.

8 For an example of this earlier treatment of the ballad, see Pao
   Chao's version, Ch'üan Sung shih, 4.5b.

9   WYYH, 195.

10 Wang Ching-hsien, "Towards Defining a Chinese Heroism," JAOS 95
    (January-March 1975), pp. 29-32.

11 Ch'üan Hou-Chou wen, 9.5a-b; Yu-yu-tzu chi (SPTK), 1.7a-9b.

12 Wei Ch'ing-chih, Shih-jen yü-hsieh (Taipei: Shih-chieh, 1966),
    p. 72.

13 The "narrow lanes" are associated with the brothels and enter-
    tainment quarters.

14 Liang Yi's famous tower, referred to in several other poems in
    this section, was painted with pictures of the immortals.

15 The "golden columns" were erected by Han Wu-ti; they supported
    pans to collect the dew, from which an elixir of immortality
    was to be made.

16 The first story referred to here is that of Hsiao-shih, the master
    of the panpipes, who was engaged by Duke Mu of Ch'in to entertain
    his daughter. The pair fell in love; Hsiao-shih taught her to
    play the pipes, and they flew off together on a phoenix. The
    second story refers to Chao Fei-yen, a favorite of Han Ch'eng-ti,
    who studied the dance in her youth and thus attracted the atten-
    tion of the emperor.

17 The pi-mu, conventionally used as a metaphor for lovers, was a
    legendary fish with two bodies and one eye shared between them.

18 Mandarin ducks were traditional symbols of conjugal fidelty and
    happiness.

19 Swallows were traditionally associated with marital and sexual
    love.

20 Cloudlike coiffures, "cicada-wing" curls, and "new moon" eyebrows
    are the T'ang equivalents of "lips like cherries," "teeth like
    pearls," and "eyes like stars"—the metaphorical itemization of
    feminine beauty.

21 What 屍豚 refers to in this line is uncertain; I have taken one
    of the numerous speculations.

22 Crows crying by night in the Censorate, evolving from an incident
    in Han omenology to a popular song to a yüeh-fu title, may suggest
    that the Censorate, charged with ferreting out official corrup-
    tion, is idle.

23 Sparrows roosting in the Constabulary suggests corruption and
    idleness similar to that of the crows crying in the Censorate.

24 Peach and plum, here used in reference to the singing girls,
    comes from a much repeated Han proverb that, though peach and
    plum do not speak, a path forms to them; that is, people come
    to admire their beauty.

25 "Northern hall" refers to the women's quarters which were
    ritually located on the north side of a house. The young
    gallants are "like the moon" in that they come out by night
    and retire in the morning.

26 Kuan-fu was a Han general known both for his moral uprightness
    and arrogance.

27 A reference to Hsiao Wang-chih, a powerful minister at the time
    of Han Yüan-ti.

28 Yang Hsiung, one of the most outstanding Han writers and intel-
    lectuals, appears after the Han as an archetypal scholar-hermit.

29 For a more detailed and somewhat different interpretation of this
    poem see Hans Frankel, The Flowering Plum and the Palace Lady:
    Interpretations of Chinese Poetry (New Haven: Yale, 1976), pp.
    130-43.

30 Yang-tzu Fa-yen (SPTK), 2.1a.

31 When the mythical Yellow Emperor was carried to his apotheosis
    on the back of a dragon, as many of his retinue as could hold
    on to the dragon accompanied him.

32 T'ang-shih chi-shih (SPTK), 10.21a-b.

33 The usual title of this poem is "Parting from Hsüeh Hua"; however,
    the WYYH gives "Parting from Hsüeh Sheng-hua on an Autumn Day."
    The Chūgoku Koten Shishū, vol. II, p. 16, points out that Hsüeh
    Hua lived in the eighth century and was an acquaintance of Li
    Po and Tu Fu. This poem was probably to Hsüeh Sheng-hua, to
    whom Wang Po also addressed a parting preface; see Wang Tzu-an
    chi (SPTK), 7.8a-b.

34 For example, T'ai-tsung's "On a Candle," p. 54.

35 WH, 19.

36 For a fuller and rather different treatment of this poem see
    Edward Schafer, "Notes on T'ang Culture III," MS 30 (1972-73),

pp. 108-16.

37 Yü Tzu-shan chi (SPTK), 3.17b.

38 I am grateful to Professor David Knechtges for urging me to
    reconsider the importance of "Long Ago."

Part Three

1 Yi-shan hsien-sheng wen-chi (SPTK), 11.4a.

2 Besides hints in his own works, the first person to claim a
   unique status for Ch'en's work was his friend Lu Ts'ang-yung in
   the preface to Ch'en Tzu-ang's collected works: "The Way had
   perished for some five hundred years, and then there was Master
   Ch'en." Such fu-ku tributes were, however, relatively common
   in prefaces, and do not constitute serious literary historical
   evaluations. The only person who dissented from the majority
   opinion was the late eighth-century poet and calligrapher Yen
   Chen-ch'ing 顏真卿, who thought it overstated. See Yen Lu-
   kung wen-chi (SPTK), 12.1a-b.

3 Ch'en Po-yu wen-chi (SPTK), preface.

4 From Tu-yi chi 獨異記, preserved in T'ang-shih chi-shih
   (SPTK), 8.2a.

5 See Robert Hightower, "Some Characteristics of Parallel Prose,"
   Studies in Chinese Literature, ed. John L. Bishop (Cambridge:
   Harvard, 1966), pp. 118-24.

6 It is impossible to say to what extent examination poems had to
   approximate what we now call "perfect" regulated verses (see
   appendix 2). Clear tonal proprieties did exist, and what later
   became a true tonal "violation" probably struck the ear of the
   examiner of the 680s as an awkwardness, varying in degree with
   the nature of the slip.

7 For example, 04448 and 04449.

8 A good example here might be the difference between the Chien-an
   "Parrot Fu" by Mi Heng, a topical allegory in which the poet
   compares his position with Huang Tsu to the captivity of the
   parrot, and the Western Chin "Wren Fu" by Chang Hua, a general
   allegory in which the wren represents the Taoist value of in-

significance. Attempts to interpret the latter topically are
singularly unconvincing.

9 For this observation I am indebted to Professor Frank Westbrook.

10 Ch'u-tz'u pu-chu (SPTK), 5.2a.

11 Ch'üan San-kuo shih, 5.4b.

12 Preserved in several sources, the most complete being the K'ung-
   tzu chia-yü (SPTK), 8.7a.

13 Ch'en Po-yü wen-chi (SPTK), preface.

14 Ch'en Hang, Shih pi-hsing chien (preface dated 1854; reprinted
   Taipei: Yi-wen, 1963), 3.2b.

15 Cited in ibid., 3.4b. This appears in the Shih-wen-ch'üan-lou
   ts'ung-shu five chüan edition of the Shih-shih, 3.1a-1b. It
   does not appear in the shorter versions, and therefore there
   are questions as to its authenticity.

16 Ch'en Po-yü wen-chi (SPTK), 7.1a-3b.

17 For example, the poetry of Sun Ch'o 孫綽 , Ch'üan Chin-shih,
   5.12a-15a, and of the monk Chih-tun 支遁, Ch'üan Chin shih,
   3.4a-b.

18 Chiang Wen-t'ung wen-chi (SPTK), 4.9b-10a.

19 Shih pi-hsing chien, 3.4a-b.

20 Another example of a poem in a style similar to the Kan yü is
   04443.

21 The term hsien-jen shih-chih comes originally from Liu Hsin's
   劉歆 Shih-fu lüeh 詩賦略 . In the Han, the theme primarily
   refers to political frustration—see Hellmut Wilhelm, "The
   Scholar's Frustration: Notes on a Type of Fu," in J. K. Fairbank,
   ed., Chinese Thought and Institutions (Chicago: University of
   Chicago Press, 1957). Though the political dimension never
   entirely leaves the theme, in many T'ang poets and particularly
   in Ch'en Tzu-ang the "frustration" (shih-chih) becomes a more
   general "disillusionment" with the present world, its impermanence
   and the corruption of its society.

22 The text here has yi-yi 嶷嶷 which is neither an existing compound nor does it rhyme. The compound should perhaps be yi-yi
   嶷嶷 . If we assumed that Ch'en used the mouth radical intentionally, he may have meant ch'i-yi 嘆嶷 , a compound used in

the T'ai-hsüan meaning "to make noise without making any sense."
The meaning would fit here, and Ch'en might have mistaken the
rhyme.   I have taken the level tone yi-yi instead.

23 Irony and parody depend on an acute sense of the propriety in
what is said.   Ch'en's overuse of Buddhist terminology here
seems to lie on the edge of parody, and if it is parody, then
the "doctrine of names" in the last line would refer back
ironically to the preceding abstractions.

24 Shih pi-hsing chien, 3.7a.

25 Li Sao, 1.151.

26 See Kuo-yü, 17, "Ch'u-yü" I.

27 Mu T'ien-tzu chuan (SPTK), 3.1a-b.

28 Shih chi, 38.   This story is clearly related to the Mao interpretation of Shih 65 as a lament for the ruined Chou capital.

Part Four

1 The distinction between "formal" and "informal" occasional poetry
is not hard and fast; however, it represents a genuine stylistic
and often generic distinction.   Social convention demanded a
poem no less when sending a friend of middle rank off to a provincial post than when attending a banquet given by Princess
An-lo, but the difference in rank of the addressee meant a great
difference in the level of diction.

2 Ch'üan T'ang shih-hua, in Li-tai shih-hua, 1.20a.b.   T'ang-shih
chih-shih (SPTK), 9.1b-2a.

3 There are numerous other groupings of writers, most following
the formula, "The X (number word) Y (a descriptive term, such
as "talents: or "friends") of literature."   These groupings are
very problematic: we do not know when they were applied to what
period they refer, nor do we know whether the grouping is literary,
social, or simply because those poets happened to be the best-
known poets of a certain era (as with "The Four Talents of the
Early T'ang".   One of the most interesting poetic groupings
during the last years of Empress Wu's reign is that of the Chu-
ying scholars, treated at length in an unpublished manuscript of

Hellmut Wilhelm. Professor Wilhelm has reconstructed the group
of scholars who compiled the religious encyclopedia San-chiao chu-
ying 三敎珠英 for Empress Wu and has treated them as a poetic
group for their inclusion in the lost anthology, the Chu-ying
hsüeh-shih chi 珠英學士集, compiled in one chüan by Ts'ui Jung.

4 For example, in Fan Kuang 范况, Chung-kuo shih-hsüeh t'ung-lun
   中國詩學通論 (Hong Kong: Shang-wu, 1959), pp. 252-56.

5 Ch'üan San-kuo shih, 2.13b.

6 Ibid., 5.1b.

7 Ch'üan Sung shih, 3.14a.

8 Ibid., 4.26b.

9 Ch'üan Liang shih, 7.8b.

10 Emending 去 for 己.

11 Wen-hsin tiao-lung (SPTK), 7.8a.

12 Ch'üan Han shih, 1.2a.

13 I use the term subgenre to designate the classification by subject matter and occasion and the term genre for the formal, metrical classification.

14 T'ang-shih chi-shih (SPTK), 9.2a-b.

15 The phrase shih-liu 石溜 should mean "stony land," but it is
   clear from the context that Li Chiao is referring to the sound
   of water running over stones.

16 T'ang-shih chi-shih (SPTK), 3.6b.

17 Hsi-ching tsa-chi (SPTK), 4.3a-6a.

18 Ch'üan Chin wen, 33.13a. See Hellmut Wilhelm, "Shih Ch'ung and
   his Chin-ku-yüan," MS 18 (1959), pp. 315-27.

19 Ssu-k'u ch'üan-shu tsung-mu, c.186.11a-13a. The SKCSTM editors
   explain that the collection's absence in early bibliographies
   by saying that banquet collections were preserved privately and
   not listed.

20 T'ang-shih chi-shih (SPTK), 10.24a-b.

21 The poem is so dated in Wang Wei's collected works; however, it
   is possible that he revised it later to leave a good impression
   of his youthful talents.

22 Reprinted in Yu-ts'un ts'ung-shu, 1882.

23 Ibid., preface.

24 These quatrains are preserved in the <u>Wan-shou T'ang-jen chueh-chü</u>; their style is so advanced that I have some doubts as to their authenticity.

25 There is some problem with the attribution of this poem.

26 <u>T'ang-shih chi-shih</u> (SPTK), 11.18a.

27 Ibid., 11.17b-18a.

28 Ibid., 6.12a-b.

29 Ibid., 8.10b.

30 <u>Yüeh-fu shih-chi</u> (SPTK), 29.11b-12a.

31 <u>Ch'eng-chai chi</u> (SPTK), 82.6a-8a.

32 For example, Hsü Wen-yu 許文雨, <u>T'ang-shih chi-chieh</u> 唐詩集解 (Taipei: Cheng-chung, 1954), vol. 2, p. 131.

33 Wei Ch'ing-chih, <u>Shih-jen yü-hsieh</u> (Taipei: Shih-chieh, 1966), p. 59.

34 If we accept the Tu Shen-yen attribution, then we probably should read 照, "shines," rather than the more interesting 轉, "makes coil." 照 is given both in the <u>Wen-yüan ying-hua</u> and in the Ming collection of Tu's poetry, but the <u>San-t'i shih</u> reads 轉 and attributes the poem to Tu Shen-yen.

35 Chin Sheng-t'an, <u>Sheng-t'an hsüan-p'i T'ang ts'ai-tzu shih</u> (Taipei: Cheng-chung, 1956), p. 1.

36 The dedication to Ch'iao Chih-chih is found in the late T'ang anthology <u>Ts'ai-tiao chi</u>, but not in the early eighth-century anthology <u>Sou-yü hsiao-chi</u>.

37 The distinctive fluidity of Shen Ch'üan-ch'i's courtly style appears clearly in the contrast between this poem and the other pieces of the series quoted in <u>WYYH</u>, 176.

38 In the <u>TSCS</u> this poem is attributed to Li Ch'ung-ssu 李崇嗣 who flourished during Empress Wu's reign and who was known by Ch'en Tzu-ang (04423). This quatrain does resemble other quatrains of Li. From its position in the <u>CTS</u> arrangement of Shen's poems, we may presume that the quatrain was also in the main body (rather than the addenda) of Shen Ch'üan-ch'i's <u>Collected Works</u>, which is unfortunately impossible to find now, apart from its inclusion in the <u>CTS</u>.

Part Five

1 This interpretation appears in <u>Shih pi-hsing chien</u>, c.3.26b-27a,
   and has recently been repeated in Daniel Altieri, "The <u>Kan-yü</u> of
   Chang Chiu-ling: Poems of Political Tragedy," <u>Tamkang Review</u>
   4, no. 1 (April 1973), pp. 63-73.

Appendix 2

1 In my observations here I am indebted to Hugh Stimson for his
   numerous discussions with me on the subject of tone patterns and
   for his treatment of the subject in his <u>Fifty-five T'ang Poems</u>
   (New Haven: FEP, 1976).